2010

ASSEMBLY ADDRESS BOOK

&

COMMENDED WORKERS DIRECTORY

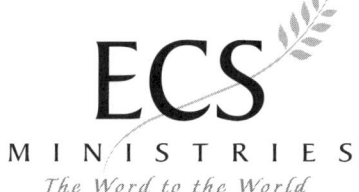

2010 Assembly Address Book and Commended Workers Directory

Published by:
    ECS Ministries
    PO Box 1028
    Dubuque, IA 52004-1028
    (563) 585-2070
    ecsorders@ecsministries.org
    www.ecsministries.org

ISBN 978-1-59387-113-0

Copyright © 2010 ECS Ministries

All rights reserved. No part of this publication may be reproduced or transmitted in any manner, electronic or mechanical, including photocopy, recording, or any information storage and retrieval system including the Internet without written permission from the publisher. Permission is not needed for brief quotations embodied in critical articles and reviews.

Printed in the United States of America

ASSEMBLY ADDRESS BOOK

&

COMMENDED WORKERS DIRECTORY

ASSEMBLY ADDRESS BOOK..5
   Table of Contents..6
   Preface 7
   Organization and Abbreviations 8
   United States..9
   Canada..143
   Other Countries 207

COMMENDED WORKERS DIRECTORY 223
   Table of Contents...224
   Preface 225
   United States..227
   Canada..296
   Index 299

SERVICE ORGANIZATIONS & HOMES....................305
   Service Organizations..307
   Homes..309

UPDATE FORMS 311
   Assembly Update Form 313
   Workers Update Form...315

APPENDIX 317
   Just A Minute...319
   Who is ECS Ministries?...320

2010
ASSEMBLY ADDRESS BOOK

ASSEMBLY ADDRESS BOOK
TABLE OF CONTENTS

UNITED STATES

Alabama 9
Alaska 10
Arizona 12
Arkansas 13
California 13
Colorado 23
Connecticut 25
Delaware 28
District of Columbia 29
Florida 29
Georgia 37
Hawaii 40
Idaho 41
Illinois 41
Indiana 47
Iowa 49
Kansas 55
Kentucky 58
Louisiana 58
Maine 60
Maryland 61
Massachusetts 63
Michigan 65
Minnesota 74
Mississippi 77
Missouri 77
Montana 82
Nebraska 82
Nevada 83
New Hampshire 84
New Jersey 84
New Mexico 90
New York 91
North Carolina 99
North Dakota 104
Ohio 105
Oklahoma 108
Oregon 109
Pennsylvania 111
Rhode Island 119
South Carolina 119
South Dakota 122
Tennessee 122
Texas 124
Utah 129
Vermont 129
Virginia 130
Washington 133
West Virginia 137
Wisconsin 138

CANADA

Alberta 143
British Columbia 146
Manitoba 155
New Brunswick 158
Newfoundland 159
Nova Scotia 161
Ontario 166
Prince Edward Island 196
Quebec 198
Saskatchewan 205

OTHER COUNTRIES

Anguilla 207
Antigua and Barbuda 207
Bahamas 207
Barbados 210
Bermuda 212
Dominica 213
Grenada 214
Jamaica 215
Mexico 217
Puerto Rico 218
Saint Kitts and Nevis 218
Saint Lucia 218
Saint Vincent/Grenadines 218
Trinidad and Tobago 219
Virgin Islands 222

UPDATE FORM 313

ASSEMBLY ADDRESS BOOK
PREFACE

This Assembly Address Book section comprises a list of those assemblies of Christian brethren in various parts of the United States, Canada, and a few other countries who:

1. Have submitted their names, addresses, time and nature of services, and the name of at least one brother as a point of contact for publication herein.

2. Have expressed thereby a desire for Christians to have fellowship with one another.

3. Are believed to be following those principles and practices taught in the Scriptures.

This book is intended for use by Christians who travel or move from place to place to conveniently locate other believers who share like beliefs and practices. We encourage you to carry letters of introduction when visiting other local assemblies, as modeled in the New Testament (Rom. 16:1-2; Acts 18:27-28; Phil. 2:29-30). We also encourage you to contact in advance any assembly you plan to visit.

This book is not to be used as a source of names for solicitation, nor should the owner of a handbook be received because of such ownership. Nor does the book comprise in any sense a list of all Christians in any locality who love, honor, and serve our Lord.

To update your assembly's information in this book, use the "Update Form" provided on page 313. You may also submit your updates online at www.ecsministries.org.

email: ecsorders@ecsministries.org
website: www.ecsministries.org

ORGANIZATION AND ABBREVIATIONS

Each assembly's information is organized as follows:

CITY NAME
  Assembly Name (assembly phone number)
   Street, City, State/Province, ZIP/Postal code
   Assembly website
   Assembly email address
   Assembly meeting times
   note: additional, special notes concerning assembly
   c/o: Contact Person's Name (contact's phone number)
   Contact's Street, City, State/Province, ZIP/Postal code
   contact's email address
   Alt: Alternate contact's name (alt's phone number)
   Alternate's email address

Abbreviations used for assembly meeting times:

B	Breaking of Bread	Mo	Monday
S	Sunday School	Tu	Tuesday
F	Family Bible Hour	We	Wednesday
G	Gospel Meeting	Th	Thursday
M	Ministry/Bible Study	Fr	Friday
Ms	Missionary	Sa	Saturday
L	Ladies Meeting	Su	Sunday
P	Prayer Meeting		
C	Children's	am	morning
Y	Youth	pm	evening

Additional notes:

1. Multiple assemblies may be listed under one city name.

2. We only display information that has been given to us by the assembly. Therefore, many assemblies do not, for example, have an alternate contact person listed.

3. Some assemblies, at their request, are listed under cities other than where they are actually located. The city listed on the assembly's address line (directly under the assembly's name) is always (with some exceptions, see below) the physical location of the assembly.

4. When a PO Box is listed on the assembly's address line, this is the mailing address of the assembly. The physical location then is often listed as a note.

UNITED STATES

ALABAMA

ANNISTON

Anniston Bible Chapel (256-236-0048)
PO Box 103, Anniston, AL, 36201
note: 218 F St

GRAYSVILLE

Westside Believers Chapel (205-674-3501)
1490 1st St SE, Graysville, AL, 35073
Su B 9:30am, M 11:00am; We P 7:00pm
c/o: Craig Criss (205-781-4002)
125 Victoria Lane, Pleasant Grove, AL, 35127
cgcriss@southernco.com
alt: Ken Sanford (205-647-0387)
ksan4sue@bellsouth.net

HUNTSVILLE

Huntsville Bible Chapel (256-881-3882)
Su B 9:30am, M 11:00am
note: Home
c/o: Stephen Funk
13029 Monte Vedra Rd SE, Huntsville, AL, 35803
stephenfunk@comcast.net

IRONDALE

Hope Bible Chapel (205-951-0084)
863 Ivawood Rd, Irondale, AL, 35210
www.HopeBibleChapel.org
Su B 9:30am, F 11:00am; We P 7:00pm
note: use point of contact as church's mailing address
c/o: Alton Sizemore (205-988-9931)
1926 Crestridge Dr, Birmingham, AL, 35244
alton77@charter.net
alt: Buddy Hughes (205-467-2601)
chalktalkbud@alltel.net

LINDEN

Gallion Bible Chapel
Hwy 43, Linden, AL
Su B 10:00am, S/M 11:00am, M 6:00pm; We P 6:00pm
note: about 3 miles north of Linden on Hwy 43
c/o: J.E. Bagley (334-289-3754)
370 Co Rd 35, Gallion, AL, 36742
alt: Walt Weninegar (334-627-3942)
weninegar@frontiernet.net

UNITED STATES — ALABAMA

MILBROOK
Central Bible Chapel (334-285-6524)
3630 Edgewood Rd, Millbrook, AL, 36054
www.CentralBibleChapel.com
central.bible.chapel@juno.com
Su B 9:30am, F/S 11:00am, M 6:00pm; We P 7:00pm
note: mailing address: PO Box 1415, Millbrook, AL, 36054
c/o: Scott Leach (334-365-3374)
825 Upper Kingston Rd, Prattville, AL, 36067
scottleach@bellsouth.net
alt: Joe Burdette (344-283-8479)
joeburdette@mindspring.com

MT BROOK
Bluff Park Bible Church
3001 Hwy 280S, Birmingham, AL, 35243
Su B 10:00am, G 11:00am
note: meets at SE Bible College Rm 123 Ad Bldg
c/o: Edward L Avery (205-663-6090)
1215 Michael Dr, Alabaster, AL, 35007
edavery@juno.com

NEEDHAM
Needham Gospel Center-Bible Chapel (251-843-2034)
2497 Newhope Rd, Needham, AL, 36915
Su B 9:45am, S 10:30am, M 6:30pm; We P 6:30pm
c/o: James Bonner Sr (251-843-5734)
2081 Bonnertown Rd, Needham, AL, 36915
jamsbonr@millry.net

TUSCALOOSA
Westside Bible Chapel
1907 24th St, Northport, AL, 35476
c/o: Herman Pinion Jr
1907 24th St, Northport, AL, 35476

ALASKA

ANCHORAGE
Anchorage Bible Fellowship (907-522-9077)
7348 Elmore Rd, Anchorage, AK, 99507
www.anchoragebiblefellowship.org
abfadmin@mac.com
Su F/C/B 10:30am; We M 7:00pm; Th Y 7:30pm
c/o: Steve DeLisio (907-522-9076)
7348 Abbott Loop Rd, Anchorage, AK, 99507
stevedabf@acsalaska.net
alt: Spencer Steenmeyer (907-522-9078)
steenmeyers@mac.com

UNITED STATES — ALASKA 11

Dimond Blvd Gospel Hall (907-344-8912)
900 W Dimond Blvd, Anchorage, AK, 99515
Su B 10:00am, S/F 11:30am, G 6:00pm; We P/M 7:30pm
c/o: Don Bang (907-258-4804)
10101 Lone Tree Dr, Anchorage, AK, 99507
alt: TJ Thompson (907-248-8807)

FAIRBANKS

Country Bible Chapel (907-457-7400)
317 Old Chena Hotsprings Rd, Fairbanks, AK, 99712
Su B 10:00am, F 11:00am, G 12:00pm; We P 7:00pm
c/o: Guy Herning (907-488-6009)
428 Rhonda Rd, Fairbanks, AK, 99712

Denali Bible Chapel (907-456-5157)
1201 Lathrop St, Fairbanks, AK, 99701
www.DenaliBibleChapel.org
secretary@denalibiblechapel.org
Su S/G 10:30am, B 11:30am
c/o: Jim Wisland (907-456-5157)
1201 Lathrop St, Fairbanks, AK, 99701

The Shelter Bible Church (907-479-0785)
980 Deere St, Fairbanks, AK, 99709
www.shelterbiblechurch.com
ecrabb@ideafamilies.org
Su F/S 10:00am, B 11:30am; We P 7:00pm
note: 10th and Noble
c/o: Ernie Crabb (907-479-0785)
1724 Moose Trail, Fairbanks, AK, 99709
ecrabb@ideafamilies.org
alt: Stephen Bailey (907-474-2886)

PALMER

Valley Bible Fellowship (907-746-0470)
3680 S Skyranch Loop, Palmer, AK, 99645
akbrooks@gci.net
Su B 9:30am, F 11:00am; Th P/M 7:30pm
note: Home
c/o: Jason Brooks (907-746-0470)
3680 S Skyranch Loop, Palmer, AK, 99645
akbrooks@gci.net
alt: Paul Stapley (907-232-6142)

WASILLA

Valley Christian Assembly (907-373-2701)
2701 N Cottonwood Loop, Wasilla, AK, 99654
Su B 10:00am, S 11:30am, G 5:30pm; We P 7:00pm
c/o: John Bang (907-373-2701)
2701 N Cottonwood Loop, Wasilla, AK, 99654
donpbang@cs.com
alt: Forrest Miles (907-376-3449)

ARIZONA

PHOENIX

Gospel Hall (602-253-4932)
1246 E Garfield St, Phoenix, AZ, 85006
Su S 9:30am, B 11:00am, G 7:00pm; Tu P 8:00pm; Th M 8:00pm
c/o: Clarence Van Der Hart (623-872-1007)
8525 W Northern Ave, Glendale, AZ, 85305

Palms Bible Fellowship (602-995-3537)
1906 W Orangewood Ave, Phoenix, AZ, 85021
Su B 9:30am, S/F 11:00am; We P/M 7:00pm
c/o: Don R Salter (602-919-8102; fax: 480-948-9975)
8737 E Berridge Lane, Scottsdale, AZ, 85250
drsalter777@yahoo.com
alt: David Wright (480-917-2771)

Sunnyslope Gospel Hall (602-944-8643)
9027 N 11th St, Phoenix, AZ, 85020
Su B 9:30am, S 11:30am, G 7:00pm; We P/M 7:30pm
c/o: Eric Walberer (623-846-0781)
6202 W Wolf St, Phoenix, AZ, 85033
grandwal@quixnet.net

TEEC NOS POS

Immanuel Navajo Chapel (928-674-3616)
Mailing address: PO Box 2000, Teec Nos Pos, AZ, 86514
immanuelmission@worldnet.attnet
Su F 9:30am, B 11:00am, 12:00m (Navajo); We L/P/M 7:00pm;
c/o: Greg Staley (928-674-3616)
PO Box 2000, Teec Nos Pos, AZ, 86514

TUCSON

Bible Chapel (520-326-4551)
1802 E Grant Rd, Tucson, AZ, 85719
Su B 8:45am, S 9:45am, F 11:00am, P 6:00pm (supper)
note: use point of contact as church's mailing address
c/o: Stephen Rockhold (520-544-9872)
3242 W Calle Fresa, Tucson, AZ, 85741
sdcr3@aol.com

WINSLOW

Immanuel Bible Chapel (928-289-3392)
PO Box 373, Winslow, AZ, 86047
Su B 9:00am, S 10:30am; Th M 7:00pm
note: meets at: 1223 W 3rd St
c/o: Irving Poolheco (928-289-3134)
1012 W Aspinwall, Winslow, AZ, 86047

ARKANSAS

ALPENA

Alpena Gospel Hall
401 Lane St, Alpena, AR, 72611
Su B 10:00am, S 11:20am, G/M 1:15pm; We P 7:00pm
c/o: Fred Stevenson (573-201-1282)
920 Great Oaks Dr., Rolla, MO, 65401
fstev153@embarqmail.com
alt: Willard D Trowbridge (479-665-4189)
wdtemail@gmail.com

EUREKA SPRINGS

Lone Star Bible Chapel (479-253-6609)
3807 Hwy 23 South, Eureka Springs, AR, 72632
Su B 9:00am, S 9:45am, M 10:50am; We P 7:00pm
c/o: Dan Hooton (479-855-4537)
4 Heatherbrooke Ln, Bella Vista, AR, 72715
hoot4@cox.net

LITTLE ROCK

Little Rock Bible Chapel
7 Birchwood Circle, Little Rock, AR, 72211-5701
Su B 9:30am, F 11:00am, P 6:30pm; We M 7:00pm
note: 1601 Reservor Rd, 72227
c/o: John Heller (501-228-2012)
alt: Phil Moffitt (501-223-2538)

CALIFORNIA

ALAMEDA

Alameda Chapel (510-522-5270)
1001 Lincoln Ave, Alameda, CA, 94501
prayer@alamedabiblechapel.org
www.alamedachapel.org
Su B 9:30am, F 11:15am; We P 6:30pm
c/o: John Pillitiere (510-522-5843)
874-A Cedar St, Alameda, CA, 94501
john155@pacbell.net
alt: Warren Elliott (510-865-5334)
warrenhope4@aol.com

ATASCADERO

Atsacadero Gospel Chapel (805-466-0175)
8205 Curbaril, Atascadero, CA, 93422
Su B 8:45am, S 9:45am, G 11:00am, F 6:00pm
note: (Atascadero & Curbaril Ave)
c/o: Ray Johnson (805-461-3650)
PO Box 631, Atascadero, CA, 93423
rayj238@aol.com

BUENA PARK

Buena Park Christian Fellowship (714-521-6341)
8591 Roland St, Buena Park, CA, 90621
www.buenaparkcf.org
Su P 9:00am, B 9:30am, S/M 11:00am; Th P 7:30pm
note: use point of contact as church's mailing address
c/o: John Spence (714-639-4409)
18141 Stratford Circle, Villa Park, CA, 92861
john.spence@att.net
alt: Michael Carter (562-941-6519)
angelacarter@verizon.net

CHICO

Chico Gospel Hall (530-894-1349)
2045 Magnolia Ave, Chico, CA, 95926
www.chicogospelhall.com
info@chicogospelhall.com
Su B 9:30am, M 10:30am, S 11:30am, F 12:00am, G 6:30pm;
We P/M 7:30pm
c/o: Ivan Hoath Jr (530-895-1729)
2053 Magnolia Ave, Chico, CA, 95926
rahoath@juno.com
alt: Dan Strauss (530-894-1051)

CLAREMONT

Claremont Bible Chapel (909-624-7178)
432 W Harrison Ave, Claremont, CA, 91711
www.claremontchapel.org
Su B 9:30am, F 11:00am, M 6:30pm; Tu L 9:15am, Y 6:30pm (Boys Brig.);
We P/M 7:15pm; Th AWANA 6:30pm
c/o: J Harry Elliott (909-621-1064)
457 Grinnell Dr, Claremont, CA, 91711
jhdelliott@aol.com
alt: Rick Markley (909-625-7463)

COLTON

Bible Chapel (909-825-5251)
390 N 9th St, Colton, CA, 92324
Su B 9:45am, S 11:00am

CULVER CITY

Culver City Gospel Hall (310-559-1588)
11138 Venice Blvd, Culver City, CA, 90232
Su B 9:30am, S 11:15am, M 11:45am, G 2:00pm, P 7:30pm
c/o: Neil Rodger (323-663-5905)
4209 Clayton Ave, Los Angeles, CA, 90027

UNITED STATES — CALIFORNIA 15

DAVIS
Grace Valley Christian Center (530-756-5255)
27173 County Road 98, Davis, CA, 95616
www.gracevalley.org
gvcc@gracevalley.org
Su S 9:00am, G 10:00am, B/G 6:00pm; We M 7:00pm
c/o: P.G. Mathew (530-756-5255)
27173 Country Road 98, Davis, CA, 95616
alt: Gerrit Buddingh (916-802-6676)
gjb@gracevalley.org

DOWNEY
An Assembly of Christians (800-311-3817)
11425 Paramount Blvd, Downey, CA, 90241
heathrop@juno.com
Su B 9:30am, F/G 10:30am, S 11:30am; We P/M 7:30pm
note: meets at Thropay Chiropractic Bldg
c/o: Adam D Thropay (562-928-5883)
8115 Dacosta St, Downey, CA, 90240
heathrop@juno.com
alt: Victor Morales (714-523-7143)

EL CAJON
East County Bible Fellowship (619-579-1050)
496 S Third St, El Cajon, CA, 92019
Su B 9:45am, S 11:15am; We P 7:00pm
c/o: Ronald Mears (619-445-1689)
1778 Adrian Ct, Alpine, CA, 91901
brnagyn@cox.net
alt: Donald Butcher (619-659-9455)

FREMONT
Calvary Bible Chapel (510-429-1005)
32701 Falcon Dr, Fremont, CA, 94555
www.fremontcalvary.org
Su B 9:00am, P 10:00am, F 11:15pm
note: use point of contact as church's mailing address
c/o: Matt Clarke (510-483-5464)
1780 Burkhart Ave, San Leandro, CA, 94579-1918
msclark@juno.com

FRESNO
Fresno Gospel Hall (559-266-4161)
2818 E Olive Ave, Fresno, CA, 93701
Su B 9:45am, S 11:30am, G 7:00pm; We P 7:30pm
note: use point of contact as church's mailing address
c/o: Robert Leerhoff (559-291-2918)
6073 E Clinton Ave, Fresno, CA, 93727
rfleerhoff@netzero.com

16 UNITED STATES — CALIFORNIA

FULLERTON

Grace Bible Chapel (714-774-7223)
1119 S Lambert Dr, Fullerton, CA, 92833
gracebiblechapel@juno.com
Su B/Korean 9:00am, S 10:00am, M 11:15am, Romanian 5:00pm
c/o: George Teats Sr (562-803-5030)
10260 Angell St, Downey, CA, 90242

GARDENA

Bethel Gospel Chapel (323-779-2607)
1605 W El Segundo Blvd, Gardena, CA, 90249
Su B 9:00am, S 10:30am, G 11:45am, P/T 7:00pm
c/o: Murvin Tillett (310-715-6380)
18311 S Normandie Ave, Gardina, CA, 90248
pmt2825@aol.com

HAYWARD

Calvary Bible Chapel (510-733-2707)
1074 B St, Hayward, CA, 94541
Su S 9:30am, M 11:00am, B 6:00pm, P/T 7:00pm
c/o: Tom Rodrigues (510-537-8413)
2751 Hansen Rd, Hayward, CA, 94545

Community Bible Chapel (510-732-0290)
26730 Patrick Ave, Hayward, CA, 94544
Su B 9:30am, S 11:00am
note: San Francisco Bay Area
c/o: Timothy Ball (510-481-2902)
19638 Hathaway Ave, Hayward, CA, 94541
timball@juno.com

Home Bible Fellowship (Bethesda Home)
22427 Montgomery St, Hayward, CA, 94541
Su B/S 7:30am; Mo M 6:00pm; We P/M

LAFAYETTE

Sun Valley Bible Chapel (925-934-1378)
1031 Leland Dr, Lafayette, CA, 94549
Su B 9:00am, S 10:15am, F 11:15am; We P 7:00pm
c/o: Harold F Gilmore (925-933-0753)
2229 Tice Valley Blvd, Walnut Creek, CA, 94595
halbevgilmore@aol.com
alt: Rudy Oehm (925-932-6133)

LANCASTER

Antelope Valley Bible Chapel
PO Box 6766, Lancaster, CA, 93539
Su B 3:00pm, F/S 4:30pm; We M 7:15pm (homes)
note: Home Fellowship, call for meeting location
c/o: Brian Sanders (661-946-0645)
44141 Acacia St, Lancaster, CA, 93535
bsanders@antelecom.net
alt: Mike McMillian (661-533-6403)

LOS ANGELES

Avenue 54 Bible Chapel (323-254-2609)
1100 N. Ave 54, Los Angeles, CA, 90042
Su B 9:30am, S/M 11:30am; Tu P 7:30pm; Fr C, Y 7:00pm
c/o: Rodney Hippenhammer (626-351-0060)
3794 Mayfair Dr., Pasadena, CA, 91107-2214
Rodneyhipp@verizon.net
alt: Max Krieger (323-256-1992)
Mmaxnbeth@sbcglobal.net

Sala Evangélica (East Los Angeles Gospel Hall)
4232 E 3rd St, Los Angeles, CA, 90063
Su B 9:30am, M 11:30am, G 7:00pm; Tu P 7:00pm; We BS 7:00pm; Sa Y 7:00pm
note: Spanish
c/o: John P. Thropay (213-819-0070 or 626-256-1378)
120 W. Beverly Blvd, Montebello, CA 90640
jthropay@beverlyoncology.com
alt: Thomas Meneses (626-444-5488)
Ttmeneses@aol.com

Glendale Gospel Chapel/Iglesia Cristiana Evangelica (Spanish) (818-242-6361)
425 W Windsor Rd, Glendale, CA, 91204
Su B 9:30am, S 11:15pm, F/G 11:30am; Tu P 7:45pm
note: use point of contact as church's mailing address
c/o: Edgard Castro (858-451-1524)
12327 Escala Dr, San Diego, CA, 92128
alt: Nicolas Escuadra (818-288-8449)

Iglesia Evangelica (Ave 54) (Spanish) (323-257-6169)
5415 Buchanan St, Los Angeles, CA, 90042
Su B 9:30am, S/M 11:15am; Tu P 7:00pm
c/o: Jesús Robles (323-661-3688)
2820 Knox Ave, Los Angeles, CA, 90039
eekitching@juno.com
alt: Severiano Rico (818-968-9978)
rsrico@yahoo.com

NAPA

Valley Bible Chapel (707-258-8606)
1559 2nd St, Napa, CA, 94559
Su B 9:30am, S 11:00am; We P/M 7:30pm
c/o: Michael Westfall (707-429-8738)
500 Iowa St, Fairfield, CA, 94533
westfall@conl.net

NORCO

Norco Gospel Hall
4151 Sierra Ave, Norco, CA, 92860
tnbaker71@gmail.com
Su B 9:30am, G 11:00am, S/M 12:00pm; We P/M 7:30pm
c/o: Glenn Baker (626-377-6710)
1510 S Sierra Vista, Alhambra, CA, 91801
alt: Tom Baker (626-484-7838)
tnbaker71@gmail.com

OAKLAND

Bethany Gospel Chapel (510-267-3482)
4677 Tompkins Ave, Oakland, CA, 94619
Su B 9:00am, S 10:10am, G 11:00am; Tu M 7:30pm
c/o: Armando Freita (510-276-3482)
16060 Via del Sol, San Lorenzo, CA, 94580

Bethany Gospel Chapel (Romanian)
4677 Tompkins Ave, Oakland, CA, 94619
Su B 9:00am, S 10:10am, P/M 7:00pm
note: meets in chapel basement
c/o: Moses Neagu
2140 W 136th Ave, San Leandro, CA, 94577

PALM SPRINGS

Christians Gathered Together (760-322-7090)
320 W Racquet Club Rd, Palm Springs, CA 92262
Su B 10:00am, S/G 11:30am; We P/M 7:30pm
c/o: Charles Spataro (760-322-7090)
PO Box 1444 (945 Buttonwillow Cr), Palm Springs, CA 92263
cspataro@dc.rr.com

PLEASANTON

Valley Bible Church
7106 Johnson Dr, Pleasanton, CA, 94588

REDONDO BEACH

South Bay Bible Chapel (310-316-3003)
1016 S Prospect Ave, Redondo Beach, CA, 90277
Su B 9:30am, F/S 11:00am, G 6:00pm; We L 10:30am, P 7:00pm;
Fr M 7:30pm (Korean)
c/o: Dick Smith (310-517-9320)
2550 Pacific Coast Hwy #188, Torrance, CA, 90505
dandjsmith@webtv.net
alt: Whan Young Lee (323-931-0020)

RICHMOND

Grace Bible Fellowship (510-215-5724)
2815 Roosevelt Ave, Richmond, CA, 94804
gbfgracenotes@juno.com
Su S 10:00am, F 11:15am, B 6:00pm; Tu P 7:00pm; We Y 7:00pm
c/o: Frederick C Franklin (510-758-4047)
2413 Tomar Court, Pinole, CA, 94564
fnefranklin@juno.com
alt: Charles D Cox (510-724-8831)

RIVERSIDE

Bethel Chapel (909-352-1615)
8045 California Ave, Riverside, CA, 92504
Su B/S, M 6:00pm; Th P/M 7:00pm
c/o: Tim or Jack Bourbonnais (909-689-9620)
8045 California Ave, Riverside, CA, 92504

ROHNERT PARK

Rohnert Park Bible Church (707-584-4509)
5905 Labath Ave, Rohnert Park, CA, 94928
www.rpbiblechurch.org
info@rpbiblechurch.org
Su B 9:30am, F 11:00am; Th L 10:30am, P 7:00pm
c/o: Doug Fuller (707-584-7412)
4408 Graywhaler Lane, Rohnert Park, CA, 94928
alt: Dan Caldwell (707-538-1603)

SACRAMENTO

Bible Chapel (916-922-5940)
1931 Silica Ave, Sacramento, CA, 95815
www.silicabiblechapel.com
silicachapel@yahoo.com
Su P 9:00am, B 9:30am, S 10:50am, M 11:10am
note: mailing address: PO Box 15086, Sacramento, CA 95851

SAN DIEGO

Gospel Hall (619-280-7021)
4646 Twain Ave, San Diego, CA, 92120
Su B 10:00am, G 7:00pm; Th P/M 7:30pm
c/o: William Smith (619-582-2109)
5005 La Dorna St, San Diego, CA, 92115

Laurel Bible Chapel (619-263-4405)
4445 Laurel St, San Diego, CA, 92105
Su B 9:00am, S 10:40am, M 11:25am
c/o: Dan Breuninger (619-280-4075)
4619 Constance Dr, San Diego, CA, 92115

UNITED STATES — CALIFORNIA

Mission Valley Community Chapel (619-286-1336)
6964 Mission Gorge Rd, San Diego, CA, 92120
www.mvcc.us
mvcc7@cox.net
Su B 9:30am, S 10:00am, F 11:00am, G 6:00pm; Tu P(L) 9:30am;
We P 7:30pm; Sa P (Men) 9:00am
c/o: James Mader (619-265-1481)
4926 Old Cliffs Rd, San Diego, CA, 92120
jgmader@cox.net
alt: Ed Dickinson (619-287-7255)
ejdick@cox.net

SAN FRANCISCO

Parkside Gospel Chapel (415-566-8642)
910 Santiago St, San Francisco, CA, 94116
www.parksidegospel.org
Su S 9:15am, F 11:00am, B 12:15pm, L 4:00pm (2nd Su each month);
Tu P/M 7:30pm; Fr Y 7:30pm
note: near 20th Ave
c/o: Jose Illathu (650-251-9038)
allathu@yahoo.com
alt: Abe Kayoumi (415-566-2289)

SAN JOSE

Grace Bible Chapel (408-226-9953)
420 Allegan Circle, San Jose, CA, 95123
www.grace.biblechapel.net
postamaster@biblechapel.net
Su B 9:00am, S 10:00am, M 11:00am
c/o: Jim McCarthy (408-515-1584)
PO 595, Cupertino, CA, 95015
mccarthy@biblechapel.net
alt: Enoch Mylabathula (408-264-3715)
emylabat@att.net

Hillview Bible Chapel (408-446-0996)
1160 S Stelling Rd, Cupertino, CA, 95014
www.hillviewbiblechapel.org
info@hillviewbiblechapel.org
Su B 9:00am, S/P 10:00am, F 11:15am; Mo Y 7:00pm; We C/M 7:00pm;
Fr M 7:30pm
note: mailing address: PO Box 892, Cupertino, CA, 95015
c/o: Steve Caldwell (408-265-7461)
5199 Alan Ave, San Jose, CA, 95124
stcaldwell@comcast.net
alt: Alan Kute (408-253-2315)
agkute@dime.org

SAN LEANDRO
Fairhaven Bible Chapel (510-568-2488)
401 MacArthur Blvd, San Leandro, CA, 94577
www.fbc-sl.org
Su S/G, B 6:00pm; Tu L 10:00am; Sa P 6:00am
c/o: Roger Rayhbuck (510-632-4631)
513 Lewis, San Leandro, CA, 94577
rrayhbuck@fbc-sl.org

SAN RAMON
San Ramon Valley Bible Church (925-743-9540)
1901 San Ramon Valley Blvd, San Ramon, CA, 94583
Su B 10:00am, S 11:30am; We M
c/o: Adel Akl (925-837-8157)
149 San Thomas Way, San Ramon, CA, 94526

SPRING VALLEY
Capilla de Gracia
425 Ramona Ave, San Diego, CA, 91977
Su B 6:00pm; Th G 5:00pm
c/o: David Hall (619-284-0102)
4725 34th St #3, San Diego, CA, 92116

STOCKTON
Stockton Bible Chapel (209-466-1588)
4125 West Lane, Stockton, CA, 95208
www.stocktonbiblechapel.net
info@stocktonbiblechapel.net
Su B 9:00am, S/C 10:00am, F 11:00am; Fr P 7:00pm
note: use point of contact as church's mailing address
c/o: Zrebrie Humphrey (209-466-1588)
P.O Box 8326, Stockton, CA, 95208
zrebrie@stocktonbiblechapel.net
alt: Eugene Briones (209-466-1588)
eugene@stocktonbiblechapel.net

TRACY
Tracy Bible Chapel (209-830-0708)
1755 Lilly Court, Tracy, CA, 95376
lillyct@pacbell.net
Su B 9:00am, S/M 10:15am, F 11:15am; Th P/M 7:00pm
c/o: Terry Willson
lillyct@pacbell.net

UNITED STATES — CALIFORNIA

TRINIDAD

Westhaven Bible Chapel (707-677-0280)
675 Railroad Ave, Trinidad, CA, 95570
www.westhavenbiblechapel.com
westhavenbiblechapel@yahoo.com
Su B 10:00am; We P/M 7:00pm
note: Only Breaking of Bread at 11:00am on first Sunday of the month.
c/o: Eldan Kaukonen (707-442-0374)
2437 Pine St, Eureka, CA, 95501
eljean@suddenlink.net
alt: Gordon Beadle (707-839-8324)

TURLOCK

Turlock Assembly of Believers
3446 N Golden State Blvd, Suite B, Turlock, CA, 95382
Su B 9:45am, F 11:00am, G 12:15pm
note: use point of contact as church's mailing address
c/o: Narendra Singh (209-526-0910)
808 Crater Ave, Modesto, CA, 95351
alt: Shamiran Marshal (209-634-3007)

VISTA

Vista Bible Chapel (760-751-0084)
134 East Dr, Vista, CA, 92083
Su B 9:15am, F 11:00am, We M 7:00pm
c/o: Don Argleben (760-751-0084)
28620 Mountain Lilac Rd, Escondido, CA, 92026

WESTMINSTER

Westminster Bible Chapel (714-897-0667)
7631 13th St, Westminster, CA, 92683
Su B 9:30am, F 10:45am, S 11:45am; Tu L 9:30am, M 7:00pm
c/o: Paul Kersey (714-895-9605)
14051 Olive St, Westminster, CA, 92683
lifewish@juno.com
alt: shawn wicks (714-901-5639)
scw@ix.netcom.com

Iglesia Cristiana (714-897-0667)
7631 13th St, Westminster, CA, 92683
Su S 9:30am, F 10:30am, S 11:15am
c/o: Julio Lopez (714-488-4619)
1061 N. Driftwood Ave, Rialto, CA, 92376
lavozdelosangeles@yahoo.com
alt: Richard Yarrall (562-429-4761)
richwithnanc@gmail.com

COLORADO

ALAMOSA

Calvary Bible Chapel (719-589-2150)
7160 Brush Lane, Alamosa, CO, 81101
chest44@fairpoint.net
Su B 9:45am, G 11:00am; We P 7:00pm
c/o: Chester Jones (719-378-2414)
5231 Barker St, Mosca, CO, 81146
chest44@fairpoint.net
alt: randy brown (719-378-2403)

BOULDER

Boulder Bible Chapel (303-449-4530)
3090 7th St, Boulder, CO, 80304
Su B 9:30am, S 11:00am
c/o: Paul Lambert (303-530-2506)
4445 Glencove Pl, Boulder, CO, 80301

Fairview Bible Chapel (303-449-2110)
368 N. 76th St., Boulder, CO, 80303
Su B 9:00am, F 10:30am; We M/P 7:00pm (homes)
note: mailing address: P.O. Box 270090, Louisville, CO 80027
c/o: Ed Morris (303-682-1669)
938 Pendleton Ave, Longmont, CO, 80501
emorris@noble-minded.org
alt: Scott Valentine (303-666-5727)

COLORADO SPRINGS

Northeast Bible Chapel (719-632-2350)
1722 McArthur Ave, Colorado Springs, CO, 80909
www.northeastbiblechapel.org
nebc99@earthlink.net
Su B 9:00am, other meetings to follow; Tu (Sept-May) L 9:15am, L 6:30pm, Men's M 6:45pm; We C Awana 6:15pm, Y 6:30pm, P 7:00pm
note: Church office open Tu-Fr 8:00am-12:00pm
c/o: Dick Collins (719-636-1535)
1100 S Park St, Woodland Park, CO, 80863
dcolins421@msn.com
alt: Butch Young (719-593-0963)

Southside Bible Chapel (719-475-1695)
1725 South Wahsatch Ave, Colorado Springs, CO, 80905
Su B 9:15am, F 11:00am, M 6:30pm; Tu L 9:30am; Th P/M 7:00pm
c/o: Frank Occhiuzzo (719-576-0070)
4475 Drummond South, Colorado Springs, CO, 80906
frank_kumeko@msn.com
alt: Gee Leong (719-596-5042)
gysl@q.com

UNITED STATES — COLORADO

DENVER
Gospel Hall (303-295-2517)
1631 E Martin Luther King Blvd, Denver, CO, 80205
c/o: James F Reynolds (303-337-3134)
3333 S Wabash Ct, Denver, CO, 80231

GRAND JUNCTION — CLIFTON
Clifton Bible Chapel (970-434-6047)
523 32nd Rd, Grand Junction, CO, 81520
Su B 9:00am, S 10:00am, F 11:00am; We P 7:00pm
c/o: Richard Bishop (970-434-8680)
3192 Kennedy Ave, Grand Junction, CO, 81504
ribishop562@netscape.com
alt: Ken Landry (970-263-4978)

GREELEY
Fellowship Chapel (970-356-0817)
2100 22nd St, Greeley, CO, 80631
Su B 9:30am, F 11:00am; We P 7:00pm
c/o: James Martin (970-454-3500)
415 Cedar Ave, Eaton, CO, 80615
alt: Donald Norbie (970-356-0817)
dlnorbie@juno.com

LAKEWOOD
Southwest Bible Chapel (303-922-1211)
5260 W Florida Ave, Lakewood, CO, 80232
Su B/S, G 6:00pm; We P/M
c/o: Richard I Crews

LIMON
Limon Bible Chapel (719-775-2164)
385 J Ave, Limon, CO, 80828
Su B 9:30am, F 11:00am, Y 6:30pm; Mo C 7:00pm
note: mailing address: PO Box 1208, Limon, CO, 80828
c/o: Jerry Allen (719-775-2164)
460 J Ave, Box 462, Limon, CO, 80828
alt: Rob Larson (719-763-2222)

LITTLETON
Littleton Bible Chapel (303-798-1030)
6023 S Datura St, Littleton, CO, 80120
www.littletonbiblechapel.org
office@littletonbiblechapel.org
Su B 9:30am, S 11:00am
c/o: Kyle Fink (303-798-1030)
6023 S Datura St, Littleton, CO, 80120
kyle@littletonbiblechapel.org

PARKER

Parker Hills Bible Fellowship (303-841-9970)
Parker, CO
Su B 9:30am, S 11:00am; Th P/M 5:30pm
note: meets at Pioneer Elem 10881 Riva Ridge Dr
c/o: Bill James
7137 E Parker Hills Ct, Parker, CO, 80138

RIDGWAY

Ridgway Community Church
PO Box 322, Ridgway, CO, 81432
c/o: John Lamberson
2873 County Rd 23, Ridgway, CO, 81432

SALT CREEK

Salon Biblico (Spanish/English)
1000 Palo Alto, Pueblo, CO, 81006
Su S 10:30am, B 6:00pm, G 7:00pm; We P 7:00pm
c/o: Frank Luna
126 Princeton St, Pueblo, CO, 81005

CONNECTICUT

BRISTOL

Bristol Bible Chapel (850-589-4984)
Bristol, CT, 06010
Su B 9:00am, S 10:45am; We M (homes),
note: meets at Bristol Boys & Girls Club 105 Laurel St
c/o: Brian Sorel (860-589-4984)
185 Greystone Ave, Bristol, CT, 06010

BROOKFIELD

Brookfield Gospel Hall
164 Pocono Rd, Brookfield, CT, 06804
www.gathered.com
Su B 10:00am, G 11:15am, S 12:45pm; Tu P/M 7:45pm
c/o: Jim Batterton Jr (860-672-6157)
235 Kent Rd S, Cornwall Bridge, CT, 06754
jcbjr@gathered.com

BROOKLYN

Community Bible Chapel
PO Box 714, Brooklyn, CT, 06234
c/o: David Bell (203-779-0568)
PO Box 714, Brooklyn, CT, 06234

CHESHIRE

Cheshire Bible Chapel (203-271-0183)
1103 Waterbury Rd, Chesire, CT, 06410
www.chesirebible.org
Su B 9:15am, S/F 11:00am, P 12:15pm, Y at night (home)
note: mailing address: PO Box 1050, Cheshire, CT, 06410
c/o: Phill Belcher (203-271-2375)
1583 S. Main St., Cheshire, CT 06410
phillxian@sbcglobal.net

GROTON

Groton Bible Chapel (860-445-1760)
66 Toll Gate Rd, Groton, CT, 06340
Su S/M, B 6:00pm
c/o: Tim Kulterman
66 Toll Gate Rd, Groton, CT, 06340

Wellspring Bible Fellowship (860-445-0622)
Welles Rd, Old Mystic, CT, 06340
Su B 9:15am, F 10:40am; We P 7:00pm
c/o: John Clifford (860-445-0622)
321 Ring Dr, Groton, CT, 06340
johnpeg2@juno.com
alt: Gary Campbell (860-536-6629)

HAMDEN

West Woods Bible Chapel (203-248-6113)
165 Hillfield Rd, Hamden, CT, 06518
Su B 9:30am, F/S 11:00am; We M/L 7:30pm
c/o: Rich Rogozinski (860-635-3461)
5 Rivercove Dr, Cromwell, CT, 06416
richard_m_rogozinski@dom.com

HARTFORD

Gospel Hall (860-246-6722)
685 Broad St, Hartford, CT, 06106
Su B 10:00am, S 11:45am, P 6:00pm, G 6:45pm; We F 7:45pm
c/o: Richard Sirois (860-563-1043)
105 Hang Dog Lane, Wethersfield, CT, 06109
richardsirois2001@cox.net
alt: Nick Dalfine (866-582-7085)

Prospect Bible Chapel (860-233-3040)
576 Prospect Ave, Hartford, CT, 06105
Su B 9:30am, S/F 11:15am; We P 7:00pm
c/o: Thomas E Woods (860-643-4477)
31 Strickland St, Manchester, CT, 06040
twoods1231@aol.com

MANCHESTER

Gospel Hall (860-646-0373)
415 Center St, Manchester, CT, 06040
Su B 10:00am, S 11:45am, G 7:00pm; We P 7:30pm
c/o: Richard Trombly (860-649-9462)
121 Cushman Dr, Manchester, CT, 06040

Manchester Bible Chapel
375 Hartford Turnpike, Vernon, CT, 06066
Su B 9:30am, F 11:00am
note: meeting at Vernon Teen Center, 375 Hartford Tnpk
c/o: Paul Ballasy (860-875-2132)
19 Settlers Way, Ellington, CT, 06029
prballasy@comcast.net

NEW HAVEN

Westville Bible Chapel (203-397-3417)
201 Alston Ave, New Haven, CT, 06515
Su B 9:15am, S 10:45am; Th M 7:00pm
c/o: Walter T Van Wyck (203-888-7897)
29 Oakwood Dr, Oxford, CT, 06478
annamaps@aol.com

NEWINGTON

Newington Gospel Hall (860-666-4342)
345 E Cedar St (Rt 175), Newington, CT, 06111
Su B 9:45am, S 11:45am, G 7:00pm; Tu P/M 7:30pm
c/o: Matthew J Brescia (860-688-2388)
81 Cobblestone Way, Windsor, CT, 06095
matt@brescias.com

NEWTOWN

Newtown Christian Fellowship
45 Main St, Newtown, CT
www.newtownfellowship.net
Su B 9:30am, F 11:00am; Th P 7:00pm
note: currently meeting at Edmong Town Hall, address above
c/o: Mark Ritter (860-355-4055)
32 Cozier Hill Rd, Sherman, CT, 06784
ritter.m@sbcglobal.net
alt: Richard Farrington (203-888-0159)

NORTH BRANFORD

Branford Bible Chapel (203-488-3586)
212 N Branford Rd, North Branford, CT, 06471
Su B 9:15am, M 11:00am; We P 7:00pm
c/o: Ken Hardisty (203-488-4706)
75 Florence Rd, Branford, CT, 06405
hardct@aol.com

28 UNITED STATES — CONNECTICUT

TERRYVILLE
Terryville Gospel Hall (860-584-1659)
36 N Main St, Terryville, CT, 06786
Su B 10:00am, S 11:45am, G 7:00pm; Tu P/BS 7:30pm
c/o: Stephen Morin (680-583-9904)
16 Prospect St. Ext., Terryville, CT, 06786
semorin55@juno.com
alt: Donald Labbe (860-582-1942)
donaldlabbe@gmail.com

WATERBURY
Waterbury Christian Fellowship (203-756-1743)
West Side Middle School, Chase Pkwy, CT, 06708
www.waterburychristianfellowship.org
Su B 9:15am, F 11:00am, M 7:30pm
note: mailing address: PO Box 3307, Waterbury, CT, 06705
c/o: Paul Forcucci (203-756-1743)
121 Lockhart Ave, Waterbury, CT, 06705
pmforcucci@juno.com
alt: John Monroe (203-272-0106)
jmon7@sbcglobal.net

DELAWARE

DOVER
Dover Bible Chapel (302-697-9632)
6877 Westville Rd, Hartly, DE, 19953
www.bibletruth.net/dedovera
Su B 9:30am, G 11:15am; We P/M 7:15pm
c/o: Norman F Wilkerson Sr (302-492-8024)
2509 Tower Rd, Hartly, DE, 19953
gwilkerson@dol.net
alt: Robert Hawkins (3302-284-0342)

WILMINGTON
Brandywine Bible Chapel (302-478-8859)
2005 Shipley Rd, Wilmington, DE, 19803
www.brandywinechapel.com
Su B 9:30am, F 11:00am, G 6:00pm; We M 7:30pm
c/o: Jim Robinson (302-478-1677)
2306 Berwyn Rd, Wilmington, DE, 19810
jrobin0421@aol.com
alt: Bill Fry (610-455-0160)

DISTRICT OF COLUMBIA

WASHINGTON

Immanuel Bible Assembly (202-269-4329)
3303 10th St NE, Washington, DC, 20017
Su B, M 11:00am, S 12:10pm; We P/M 8:00pm
c/o: Leroy W Burns (202-635-8679)
2019 Franklin St NE, Washington, DC, 20018

Maranatha Gospel Hall (202-291-3081)
4910 13th St NW, Washington, DC, 20011
Su B/M/G, S 12:00pm; Tu P 8:00pm; Th P/M 8:00pm
c/o: Aubrey N Wilson (202-726-3606)
1301 Madison St NW, Washington, DC, 20011

Washington Christian Assembly (202-726-2100)
30 Kennedy St NW, Washington, DC, 20011
Su B, M 10:35am, M 5:30pm, M 12:00pm; We P/M 8:00pm
c/o: Samuel Jeremiah (202-726-2881)
808 Somerset Place NW, Washington, DC, 20011

FLORIDA

ARCHER

Bible Truth Chapel (352-495-3459)
13410 Archer Rd, Gainesville, FL, 32618
bibletruthchapel@windstream.net
Su B 9:30am, S 11:00am; Tu P/M 6:00pm
c/o: Angel Rivas (386-462-1079)
20824 NW 138th Ave, High Springs, FL 32643

BOCA RATON

Boca Raton Bible Chapel (561-391-9319)
3900 NW 3rd Ave, Boca Raton, FL, 33431
Su B 9:30am, S 11:00am, M 6:00pm; Th P/M 7:00pm
note: at Spanish River Blvd
c/o: James Anderson (561-361-6879)
555 NW 4th Ave (#311), Boca Raton, FL, 33432

BROOKSVILLE

Brooksville Bible Chapel (352-799-5556)
21123 Yontz Rd, Brooksville, FL, 34601
www.brooksvillebiblechapel.org
carlbroman@tampabay.rr.com
Su B 9:00am, S 10:30am, F 11:15am; We P 7:00pm
c/o: Carl Broman (352-344-0791)
716 Windy Ave, Inverness, FL, 34452
carlbroman@tampabay.rr.com
alt: Ed Anderson (352-382-4638)

CAPE CORAL
Fellowship Bible Chapel
1406 SE 46th Lane, Cape Coral, FL, 33904
Su B 9:30am, S 11:00am
c/o: Don Jeffers (239-939-0639)
1703 Park Meadows Dr, Fort Myers, FL, 33907

CLEARWATER
Cornerstone Bible Chapel (727-736-6101)
190 Patricia Ave, Dunedin, FL, 34698
www.webchapel.org
cbccorrespondent@earthlink.net
Su B 9:00am, F 10:25am, S 11:15am; We P 7:00pm
c/o: Bill Davis (727-466-0991)
1644 Eden Ct, Clearwater, FL, 33756
billandkarend@earthlink.net
alt: Frank Brzezinski (727-934-4815)

DAVIE
Believers Assembly of South Florida
6565 Stirling Rd, Davie, FL, 33314
c/o: James Poulose
6565 Stirling Rd, Davie, FL, 33314

DELAND
Deland Gospel Hall (386-736-1009)
109 E Rose Hill Ave, Deland, FL, 32724
Su B 10:00am, G 11:30am; We P/M 7:00pm
c/o: Fred W King (386-943-4000)
215 Lake Talmadge Rd, Deland, FL, 32724
fred.king@earthlink.net

FORT LAUDERDALE
Bethel Gospel Chapel (954-764-3372)
1444 NW 15th Ave, Fort Lauderdale, FL, 33311
bethelgc@bellsouth.net
Su B 9:00am, S 10:15am, F 11:30am, M 7:00pm; Th P/M 7:30pm; Fr Y 8:00pm
c/o: Vincent Gordon (954-741-3210)
PO Box 9241, Fort Lauderdale, FL, 33310
alt: Eaton Woodburn (954-484-4636)

Fort Lauderdale Bible Chapel (954-563-6012)
141 NW 38th St, Fort Lauderdale, FL, 33309
Su B 9:00am, S 10:05am, F 11:00am, M 6:00pm; We P/M 7:30pm; Fr Y 6:30pm
c/o: Babu George (561-304-3593)
6156 Willoughby Circle, Lake Worth, FL, 33463
jollybabu@juno.com

Hope Bible Chapel (954-735-1134)
PO Box 100797, Fort Lauderdale, FL, 333107
Su B 9:30am, S 11:00am, M 7:00pm; Th P/M 7:30pm
c/o: Noel Morris (954-739-6346)
4771 NW 18th Ct, Lauderhill, FL, 33313
leo5312@hotmail.com

FORT PIERCE

Gospel Hall (772-465-4700)
3015 Oleander Blvd, Fort Pierce, FL, 34982
Su B 9:30am, G 6:00pm; We P/M 7:30pm
c/o: Dale O Lantis (772-461-6995 or 772-577-0932)

Treasure Coast Bible Assembly (772-336-5115)
2900 Midway Rd, Fort Pierce, FL, 34982
Su B 9:00am, S/M 10:30am, F 11:15am; We M 7:30pm
note: use point of contact as church's mailing address; Expecting to move to permanent location at 4146 Edwards Rd, Fort Pierce, FL, 34982
c/o: Carl Kurtgis (772-336-5115)
6959 NW Hershy Circle, Port Saint Lucie, FL, 34983
efacey999@earthlink.net

FROSTPROOF

Frostproof Bible Chapel (863-635-5414)
185 Marion Pl, Frostproof, FL, 33843
Su B 9:30am, F 11:00am, G 6:00pm; Th P 7:00pm
c/o: Sam Mauger (863-635-3272)
22 Bradford Blvd, Frostproff, FL, 33843
shmaug1@netzero.net

FT. WALTON BEACH/NICEVILLE/VALPARAISO

Emerald Coast Bible Chapel (850-678-5657)
94 S John Sims Pkwy, Valparaiso, FL, 32580
jeffreysj@earthlink.net
Su B 10:00am, F 11:00am; We P 7:00pm
note: mailing address: PO Box 508, Niceville, FL, 32588
c/o: Jimmy D Jeffreys (850-678-5657)
302 Island Ln, Niceville, FL, 32578
jeffreysj@earthlink.net
alt: Richard Stewart (850-897-7645)
rstew26@embarqmail.com

HOLIDAY

Holiday Gospel Assembly (727-945-0466)
1842 Grand Blvd, Holiday, FL, 34690
Su B 9:00am, M 10:00am, G 11:00am; We P/M 7:00pm

HOLLYWOOD

Hollywood Bible Chapel (954-923-8640)
2300 Hollywood Blvd, Hollywood, FL, 33020
Su B 9:15am, F 11:00am, M 6:00pm; We P/M 7:30pm
c/o: J Emory Lowe (954-966-3956)
5300 Madison St, Hollywood, FL, 33021
alt: Dennis Bradley

JACKSONVILLE

Calvary Bible Chapel
300 Johnson, Jacksonville, FL, 32204
Su B 9:00am, S 10:00am, M 11:00am; We M 7:00pm
c/o: Alfred A Mallory (904-388-0038)
5022 Colonial Ave, Jacksonville, FL, 32210

Southside Bible Chapel (904-725-5610)
2701 Dean Rd, Jacksonville, FL, 32216
mflester@yahoo.com
Su B 9:30am, F 11:00am; We P/M 7:00pm
c/o: Michael Lester (904-514-8100)
mflester@yahoo.com
alt: Jerry Powers (904-620-9912)

KEY WEST

Gospel Chapel (305-294-4351)
720 Southard St, Key West, FL, 33040
Su B 9:30am, F 11:00am; We P 7:00pm; Sa L 7:00pm
c/o: Helen Spurlock (305-296-1112)
720 Southard St, Key West, FL, 33040

KEYSTONE HEIGHTS

Park of the Palms Church, Inc. (352-473-6100)
753 Hebron Ave, Keystone Heights, FL 32656
Su B 9:30am, F 11:00am, M 6:00pm; Th P 7:30pm
c/o: Donald Muchmore (352-473-5143)
696 Hebron Ave, Apt A, Keystone Heights, FL 32656
alt: Bruce Whittaker (352-473-4463)
781 Hilltop Dr, Apt B, Keystone Heights, FL 32656

LAKELAND

Ariana Christian Fellowship
1118 O'Doniel Loop North, Lakeland, FL, 33809
c/o: Dr. Byron George
1118 O'Doniel Loop North, Lakeland, FL, 33809

LAND O' LAKES

Land O' Lakes Bible Chapel
5401 Land O' Lakes Blvd, Land O' Lakes, FL, 34639
www.landolakesbiblechapel.org
Su B 9:15am, S 10:15am, F 11:15am; We P/BS 7:00pm
note: use main point of contact address as mailing address
c/o: David Dunlap (daviddunlap@earthlink.net)
3116 Gulfwind Dr., Land O' Lakes, FL, 34639
alt: Mark Ferrera (813-949-7203)
marcinfer@aol.com

MIAMI

Asamblea Evangelica (856-6569)
629 SW 7th St, Miami, FL, 33130
wwwfranescarr@aol.com
Su B 9:30am, S 11:30am, M 7:00pm (Men); Tu P 8:00pm;
Fr M 7:30pm (Ladies)
c/o: Francisco Escarraman (305-856-6569)
613 SW 7th St, Miami, FL, 33130
wwwfranescarr@aol.com

Bible Truth Chapel (305-274-6088)
6300 SW 99th Ave, Miami, FL, 33173
www.bibletruthchapel.com
btc@bibletruthchapel.com
Su B 9:30am, F/S 11:00am, M 6:00pm; We P/M 7:30pm; Fr C 7:30pm, Y 7:45pm
note: meetings – Active sports and evangelism on Tuesdays 7:45pm
c/o: Randy Beers (305-794-7422)
2901 SW 132nd Ave, Miami, FL, 33175
rmbeers4@yahoo.com

Hispano American Church (Sala Evangelica) (305-688-6858)
1165 NW 119th St, Miami, FL, 33168
Su B 9:30am, S 11:00am, G 7:00pm; Th P/M 8:00pm
c/o: Ovilio Diaz (305-688-1891)
821 NW 116th Terr, Miami, FL, 33168

Miami Gospel Chapel (305-688-5330 or 652-)
10900 NW 19th Ave, Miami, FL, 33167
Su B 9:30am, S 11:00am, G 7:00pm; We P/M; Fr Y
c/o: David Corbin (305-688-5330)
10900 NW 19th Ave, Miami, FL, 33167

MONTVERDE

New Testament Believers' Fellowship (407-469-2712)
355 Citrus Tower Blvd., Suite 110, Montverde, FL 34711
Su B 9:30am, F 10:45am; We P 7:00pm
bluedolphin@embarqmail.com
note: use main point of contact address for mail
c/o: Lanny Evans (407-469-2712)
16355 Florence Oak Court, Montverde, FL 34756
bluedolphin@embarqmail.com
alt: Buck Matthews (407-469-2087)

NEW PORT RICHEY

Bible Truth Chapel
6915 Shady Acres, New Port Richey, FL, 34654
Su B 10:00am, G 11:00am
c/o: Charles Falkner
8748 Bass Lake Dr, New Port Richey, FL, 34654
variable@ij.net

NEW SMYRNA BEACH

New Smyrna Bible Chapel (386-423-1936)
101 Hester Ave, New Smyrna Beach, FL, 32168
Su B 9:30am, S/F 11:00am; Th P 7:00pm
c/o: Larry McDonald (386-252-5143)
2306 Old Samsula Rd, Port Orange, FL, 32128
lmacdonald@cfl.rr.com
alt: Leland Snook (386-767-2510)
marlee70@msn.com

NICEVILLE

Forest Lake Bible Church (904-678-5879)
1000 37th St, Niceville, FL, 32578
Su B 9:00am, S 10:10am, M 11:15am; We P 7:30pm

OCALA

Bible Chapel (352-369-5077)
729 NE 2nd St, Ocala, FL, 34470
Su B 9:30am, S 11:00am; We P 6:00pm
c/o: Robert L Saunders (352-732-1188)
2424 SE 12th, Ocala, FL, 34471
b2saun@cs.com

ORLANDO

Asamblea Biblica Cristiana
1900 Hiawassee Rd, Orlando, FL, 32818
Su B 9:30am, S 11:00am, M 6:00pm; We P 7:30pm
note: 1 mi N of Rt 50
c/o: Bill deJager (407-363-9949)
7635 Lake Marsha Dr, Orlando, FL, 32819

Bear Lake Bible Chapel (407-869-0198)
1251 Bear Lake Rd, Apopka, FL, 32703
Su B 9:30am, F 11:00am, M 6:00pm; We P/M 7:00pm
c/o: Philip Guikema (409-822-3650)
5804 Rywood Dr, Orlando, FL, 32810
philguikema@earthlink.net
alt: Robert Harper (407-831-6110)

Hiawassa Bible Chapel (407-295-2551)
1900 N. Hiawassee Rd, Orlando, FL, 32818
Su B 9:30am, S/F 11:00am; We P 7:30pm
note: 1 mi N of Rt 50
c/o: Edwin Scott (352-243-1585)
11915 Overlook Dr, Clermont, FL, 34711
elsorlfl@aol.com
alt: Steve Angy (407-889-0095)
sangy@juno.com

Lake Howell Bible Chapel (407-671-8878)
2315 Lake Howell Lane, Maitland, FL, 32751
www.lakehowellbiblechapel.com
Su B 9:30am, M/S 11:00am, Y 5:00pm, M 6:00pm; Tu L 10:00am;
We P 7:20pm
c/o: Paul B Irvin (407-671-8883)
2896 Old Castle Dr, Winter Park, FL, 32792
pbi.com@juno.com
alt: Mark Sherwood (407-227-0215)

PEMBROKE PINES
Boulevard Bible Chapel (954-987-6290)
6800 Pines Blvd, Pembroke Pines, FL, 33023
www.boulevardbible.org
info@boulevardbible.org
Su B 9:30am, S 11:00am, M 6:00pm; We P/M 7:30pm
note: borders Hollywood
c/o: Aaron Renth (954-447-6850)
1741 NW 88th Ter, Pembroke Pines, FL, 33024
amrenth@bellsouth.net
alt: Malcolm Skelton (954-435-3552)

PORT ST LUCIE
Believers Bible Fellowship (772-878-4591)
1602 SE Ocean Lane, Port St Lucie, FL, 34983
Su B 9:15am, F 11:00am, G 6:30pm; We P/M 7:30pm
note: Port St. Lucie Community Center
c/o: Daniel Latchman (772-878-4591)
1602 SE Ocean Lane, Port St Lucie, FL, 34983
dlatchman@adelphia.net
alt: Neville Murphy (772-343-7305)

SATELLITE BEACH
Bethany Bible Chapel (321-777-2411)
101 SE 1st St, Satellite Beach, FL, 32937
cirvin@cfc.rr.com
Su B 9:30am, F 11:00am, G 6:00pm; Tu P/M 7:00pm;
Th L 9:30am (Sep-May), 9:30am, Y 6:00pm; Sa P 9:30am
c/o: John A Baker (321-773-5058)
8745 S Tropical Trail, Merritt Island, FL, 32952
alt: Clint Irvin (321-779-3375)

ST PETERSBURG
Grace Gospel Chapel (727-327-8740)
2262 5th Avenue North, St Petersburg, FL, 33713
jaspersco@juno.com
Su B 9:30am, F 11:00am, S 11:30am; We P/M 7:00pm
c/o: Jasper Scott (727-812-6836)
3242 San Pedro St, Clearwater, FL, 33759
jaspersco@juno.com
alt: Jim Pizzulli (727-541-5756)
jaykar@tampabay.rr.com

UNITED STATES — FLORIDA

TALLAHASSEE
Emmaus Bible Fellowship (850-893-4349)
3620 Shamrock Rd, Tallahassee, FL, 32309
mbschaper@cs.com
Su B 10:00am, F 11:00am; We P 6:30pm
c/o: Brian Schaper (850-893-4349)
2340 Tuscavilla Rd, Tallahassee, FL, 32312
mbschaper@cs.com

TAMPA
56th Street Gospel Chapel (813-417-1851)
12811 N 56th St, Tampa, FL, 33617
Su S 9:30am, F 11:00am, B 5:00pm; We M 7:45pm; Sa men's brkfst 8:00am
adams@feedwater.com
note: use point of contact as church's mailing address
c/o: Al Adams (813-417-1851)
3902 Corporex Park Dr #650, Tampa, FL, 33619
adams@feedwater.com
alt: Juan Cruz (813-973-87850)
juancruz@rapidsys.com

Carrollwood Bible Chapel (813-961-3320)
15316 Casey Rd, Tampa, FL, 33624
www.biblechapel.com
info@biblechapel.com
Su B 9:30am, S 11:00am, M 6:00pm; We P/M 7:00pm; Fr Y 7:00pm
note: N of Ehrlich 1 mi W of Dale Mabry
c/o: Michael M Gentile (813-962-7771)
17615 Archland Pass Rd, Lutz, FL, 33558
midegentiletampa@gmail.com

Central Bible Chapel (813-837-1969)
12124 N Gunn Hwy, Odessa, FL, 33556
Su B 9:00am, G/F 11:00am; We P 7:00pm
c/o: Mike Hughey (813-837-1969)
5127 Longfellow Ave, Tampa, FL, 33629

North Tampa Gospel Hall (813-932-9530)
12704 Marjory Ave, Tampa, FL, 33612
Su B 10:00am, G 6:00pm, S 12:15pm; We P/M 7:00pm
c/o: Oronzo Dalfino (813-265-2757)
118 E 143rd Ave, Tampa, FL, 33613

WEST PALM BEACH
Grace & Truth Bible Fellowship
Jupiter Christian School, 700 S. Delaware Blvd.
Jupiter, FL 33458
Su B 9:30am, F 11:00am; We M 7:30pm (homes)
note: mailing add: P.O. Box 8734, Jupiter, FL 33468
c/o: Furman Martin (561-746-6995)
mart2541@bellsouth.net

GEORGIA

ALBANY

Albany Gospel Chapel (229-435-3546)
2556 N Slappey Blvd, Albany, GA, 31701
www.albanygospelchapel.com
Su B 9:30am, F 11:00am, M 6:00pm; We P 7:30pm
c/o: Robert L Marshall (229-432-0436)
2811 Capers Lane, Albany, GA, 31721
robertlmarshall@hotmail.com
alt: Carl Gentry (229-439-0559)

ATLANTA

Community Bible Chapel (404-523-6381)
PO Box 18120, Atlanta, GA, 30316
Su B 9:00am, S 10:00am, M 11:30am
note: 1631 Cecilia Dr
c/o: Clifford Ice (404-752-9251)
1723 Fort Valley Dr SW, Atlanta, GA, 30311

North Atlanta Bible Chapel (404-237-2683)
1475 N Druid Hills Rd, Atlanta, GA, 30319
wpulkkin@bellsouth.net
Su B 9:00am, F/S 10:00am, M/Y 11:15am; We P/M 7:00pm
c/o: Cleve Carlin (770-844-6488)
3925 Preston Ct, Suwanee, GA, 30024
thecarlans@bellsouth.net
alt: Wayne Pulkin (770-381-2340)

Southwest Christian Fellowship
645 Grant St, Atlanta, GA, 30312
Su B 10:45am, M 11:15am, S 1:00pm; We P 6:45pm
c/o: Rich Berry (404-681-9632 or 404-758-3810)
645 Grant St, Atlanta, GA, 30312

AUGUSTA

Believers Gospel Chapel (706-793-8906)
3565 Peach Orchard Rd, Augusta, GA, 30906
Su B 9:00am, S 10:00am, F 11:15am; We P 7:00pm
c/o: Edward Myers (706-863-0875)
1110 Fall Creek Lane, Grovetown, GA, 30813

Bethany Bible Chapel (706-733-7127)
401 Millege Rd, Augusta, GA, 30904
Su B 9:00am, S 10:10am, F 11:15am; Tu L 10:00am; We P 7:00pm
c/o: Jules Godin (706-733-5863)
3132 Walton Way, Augusta, GA, 30909

Community Bible Fellowship (706-729-6799)
2813 Regency Blvd., Augusta, GA, 30904
Su B 9:00am, S 10:15am, G 11:30am; Tu men's BS 7:00pm; We P 7:00pm
note: mailing address: P.O. Box 3311 Augusta, GA 30904
c/o: Stephen Fox (706-796-3220)
4120 Pinnacle Way, Hepzibah, GA 30815
stephennif@comcast.net
alt: Larry Jones (706-869-9060)
larryatuniversal@aol.com

Glendale Bible Chapel
2013 Randall Rd, Augusta, GA, 30904
Su B 9:30am, S 11:15am, M 6:00pm; We P 7:00pm
c/o: Lee Lohre (706-722-3931)
PO Box 1704, Augusta, GA, 30903
lelohre@aol.com

AVERA

Gospel Chapel (706-547-6276)
Williams Bridge Rd at Chalker St, Avera, GA, 30803
Su B 9:45am, F 11:00am, G 6:00pm; Th P 7:30pm
note: use point of contact as church's mailing address
c/o: Curtis G Thigpen (706-547-6276)
1074 Sunset Blvd, Avera, GA, 30803

BUFORD

Lake Lanier Bible Chapel (678-482-6616)
Rt. 20 at I-985, Buford, GA, 30518
culloch@bellsouth.net
Su B 9:30am, F 11:00am; We P 7:00pm
note: meeting at Holiday Inn Express; mailing address: PO Box 1687, Flowery Beach, GA, 30542
c/o: Steve Roys (678-316-3931)
7011Pony Lake Rd, Dahlonega, GA, 30533
alt: Ross McCulloch (678-482-6616)
culloch@bellsouth.net

CONYERS

Conyers Bible Chapel (404-427-9593)
1301 Olympic Ct, Conyers, GA, 30012
Su B 9:30am, F 10:30am, S 11:30am; We P/M 7:30pm
c/o: Lubric Johnson (404-427-9593)
1994 Stoneleigh Dr, Stone Mountain, GA, 30087
lubric@comcast.net

DECATUR

Decatur Bible Chapel (770-322-1495)
3355 Snapfinger Rd, Decatur, GA, 30038
Su B 9:00am, S 10:15am, M 11:30am, M 7:00pm; Tu P/M 7:30pm
note: Lithonia
c/o: Frederick R Hart (770-396-5829 or 404-373-4030)
4923 Cambridge Dr, Dunwoody, GA, 30338

UNITED STATES — GEORGIA 39

DORAVILLE
Asamblea Biblica de Norte Atlanta (678-886-1468)
4264 Winters Chapel Rd Suite 100 D, Doraville, GA, 30360
abnanf@hotmail.com
Su B 9:00am, F 10:00am, S 11:00am, G 7:00pm; Tu P 8:00pm; Fr Y 8:00pm;
Sa M 8:00pm
note: Hispanic assembly
c/o: Nestor Flores (678-442-6294)
919 Cavesson Terr, Lawrenceville, GA, 30345
abnanf@hotmail.com
alt: G Adrian Ramos (678-787-8094)

LILBURN
Gwinnett Bible Chapel (770-972-4474)
3819 Five Forks Trickum Rd, Lilburn, GA, 30047
Su B 9:00am, S 10:00am, M 11:00am; We P/M 7:00pm
c/o: S Scott Batterton DDS (770-921-4222)
5109 Browning Way, Lilburn, GA, 30047
ssbatterton@bellsouth.net

LINCOLNTON
Lakeside Bible Chapel (706-359-5403)
2034 Augusta Hwy, Lincolnton, GA, 30817
Su B 9:00am, S 10:15am, F 11:30am; We P 7:30pm
c/o: Steve Hanneman (706-359-5403)
5997 Hwy 220 W, Lincolnton, GA, 30817
simply1237@nu-z.net
alt: Sam Thorpe (706-359-6297)

MACON
Three Oaks Bible Chapel (912-788-4894)
3350 Avondale Mill Rd, Macon, GA, 31216
Su B 9:30am, S 11:00am
c/o: John Moore (912-956-4328)
176 Red Oak Rd, Byron, GA, 31008

MARIETTA
Bible Chapel (770-973-2246)
Powers Ferry Rd 2237 Little John Trail, Marietta, GA, 30067
Su B 9:30am, M 11:00am; We P/M 7:00pm
c/o: RF Haddon (770-427-2677)
157 Normandy Dr SW, Marietta, GA, 30064

MARTINEZ
Martinez Bible Chapel (706-650-2596)
4352 Columbia Rd, Martinez, GA, 30907
markbarinowski@comcast.net
Su B 9:00am, S 10:10am, M 11:15am; We P/C 7:00pm
c/o: Mark C Barinowski (706-541-9085)
2389 Louisville Rd, Appling, GA, 30802
markbarinowski@comcast.net
alt: Glenn Barinowski (803 279 7354)

UNITED STATES — GEORGIA

MIDWAY
Faith Bible Chapel (912-884-3697)
1648 Seabrook Island Drive, Midway, GA, 31320
Su B 9:00am, S 10:00am, F 11:00am; We P 7:00pm
c/o: Thomas Taylor (912-884-5157)
1212 Seabrook Island Drive, Midway, GA, 31320
tj@coastalnow.net
alt: Brooks Williams (912-884-9449)

SAVANNAH
Berean Bible Chapel (912-236-1966)
1413 W 52nd St, Savannah, GA, 31405
Su B 9:00am, S 11:00am, M 12:00pm; We P/M 7:30pm
c/o: Johnny Hands (912-238-3921)
1448 E 40th St, Savannah, GA, 31404

THOMASVILLE
Community Bible Chapel
Su S, B 10:00am; Tu P/M 7:00pm
c/o: Gerald Humbert

VALDOSTA
New Life Bible Church
1244 N Lee St, Valdosta, GA, 31601
Su M, B 10:00am; Tu P/M
c/o: Curtis Jenkins (229-244-9366)
PO Box 2754, 801 Northside Dr, Valdosta, GA, 31604

WAYNESBORO
Burkehaven Chapel (706-554-2822)
498 Park Dr, Waynesboro, GA, 30830
Su B 9:30am, S 11:00am, M 6:00pm; We P/M 7:00pm
note: Corner of Church St

HAWAII

HONOLULU
Waialae Kahala Chapel (737-6611)
1178 21st Ave, Honolulu, HI, 96816
Su B 9:00am, S 10:15am; We P/M 7:30pm
c/o: N Shimoda (839-7020)
3466 Ala Ilima St, Honolulu, HI, 96818

KAHULUI
Community Christian Church (808-871-5416)
101 W. Kamehameha Ave, Kahului, HI, 96732
Su B 1:00pm, F 2:00pm; Th Bible Study 7:00pm
note: mailing address: 246 West Lanai Street, Kahului, HI, 96732
c/o: Roy Fusato (808-871-5416)
246 West Lanai Street, Kahului, HI, 96732
royfusato@hotmail.com
alt: Dr. Ryan Fusato (808-878-7597)
dsdna@msn.com

PEARL CITY
Oceanview Bible Chapel (808-455-7833)
PO Box 653, Pearl City, HI, 96782
Su B 9:00am, F 10:15am; We P 7:00pm; Fr M 7:00pm
c/o: Hideo Yamamoto
98-1430 Kulawai St, Aiea, HI, 96701
alt: Jason Fu (808-384-2716)
jfu@hpu.edu

WAIANAE
Gospel Hall (808-668-2920)
85-794 Farrington Hwy Room D, Waianae, HI, 96792
Su B 10:00am, S 11:20am, G 7:00pm; We P/M 7:00pm
c/o: Keith Vendetta (808-668-2920)
382 Kulawae St, Waianae, HI, 96792
alt: Thomas Vendetta

IDAHO

COEUR D'ALENE
Walnut Avenue Gospel Chapel
corner of Walnut St & 2nd Ave, Coeur D'Alene, ID
Su S 9:55am, F 10:00am, M 6:00pm; We P 7:00pm; 3rd Su of the month B 10:30am
note: mailing address: P.O. Box 1364 Coeur d'Alene, ID 83816
c/o: Donald Unruh (208-664-4620)
alt: Dion Unruh (208-765-5856)

MERIDIAN
Westside Bible Church (208-887-4906)
2040 E Fairview Ave, Boise, ID, 83642
Su B 9:30am, S 11:00am; We P 7:30pm

ILLINOIS

ARLINGTON HEIGHTS
Arlington Countryside Church (847-255-2140)
916 E Hintz Rd, Arlington Heights, IL, 60004
www.acchurch.org
office@acchurch.org
Su M 9:30am, B 10:30am (monthly), G/S 10:30am; Mo L 6:00pm;
Tu L 9:00am, Y 7:00pm; We C/L 7:00pm; Fr M 7:30pm
c/o: Dave Corlew
alt: Jim Young

BELLEVILLE
Villa Hills Gospel Chapel (618-538-7272)
150 Bernard Dr, Belleville, IL, 62223
Su B 9:00am, S 10:00am, M 11:00am; We P 7:00pm
c/o: John Hammon Jr (618-538-5609)
300 Bethesda Dr, Belleville, IL, 62223

CARBONDALE

Neighborhood Bible Fellowship (618-549-7649)
1218 West Freeman, Carbondale, IL, 62901
Su B 9:00am, F 10:00am
note: Call for small group meeting times and locations.
c/o: Glendall & Janet Toney (618-549-2786)
1850 Pleasant Woods Cir, Carbondale, IL, 62902
toneyclan@hotmail.com
alt: Carolyn Tucker (618-529-3733)

Shawnee Bible Chapel
1506 W Walnut St, Carbondale, IL, 62901
c/o: Dr Albert L Caskey (618-549-4226)
1506 W Walnut St, Carbondale, IL, 62901

CHAMPAIGN

Stratford Park Bible Chapel (217-356-5341)
2801 W Kirby Ave, Champaign, IL, 61821
www.stratfordpark.net
spbc@stratfordpark.net
Su B 9:00am, S 10:00am, F 11:00am; We Y 6:30pm
c/o: Ken Raymond (217-954-0601)
907 Maplepark Dr, Champaign, IL, 61821
ken@stratfordpark.net
alt: Jim Dixon (217-359-2555)
lydiadixon@comcast.net

CHICAGO

Chicago West Church (773-777-0797)
5530 N Long, Chicago, IL, 60630
seoulconsult@yahoo.com
Su B 10:00am, M 11:00am; Sa M/P 7:30pm
note: use point of contact as church's mailing address
c/o: John Paik (773-777-0797)
4403 W Lawrence #202, Chicago, IL, 60630
seoulconsult@yahoo.com
alt: Paul Kim (773-895-5786)

Grace & Glory Gospel Chapel
7708 Indiana Ave, Chicago, IL, 60619
Su S/B/G; Th P/M 8:00pm
c/o: Edward Watkins (312-846-9355)
7708 Indiana Ave, Chicago, IL, 60619

Laflin Gospel Chapel
6617 S Laflin St, Chicago, IL, 60636
Su B 9:30am, S 10:30am, M 11:45am
c/o: John F Mostert (708-747-6710)
1900 W 235th St, Steger, IL, 60475

UNITED STATES — ILLINOIS 43

Local Evangelico de Avondale (Spanish)
2814 N Sawyer Ave, Chicago, IL 60618
Su B, S 10:30am, M 11:45am, M 6:00pm; Th 7:00pm
c/o: Jaime Silva (Spanish: 773-486-5017; English: 312-560-9033)
1926 N. Albany Ave, Chicago, IL, 60647
jaimesilva51@hotmail.com

New Life Bible Chapel (815-485-6945)
933 South Riverside Dr, Elmhurst, IL, 60126
abraham_t_john@yahoo.com
Su S 9:00am, B 9:45am, F 11:00am
c/o: Dr. Sajan Mathews (630-771-9909)
262 Clubhouse St, Bolingbrook, IL, 60490
sajan.mathews@moody.edu
alt: Shaji Matthews (630-541-7063)

Northwest Bible Chapel (773-631-7447)
5555 N Lotus, Chicago, IL, 60630
www.northwestbiblechapel.com
Su B 9:30am, F/S 11:00am
c/o: William Carrera (773-775-9330)
6818 Ardmore, Chicago, IL, 60631
wcarrera@gmail.com
alt: Ray Guerrero (773-725-2743)
rguerrero@vertisinc.com

Norwood Gospel Chapel (773-763-0045)
5158 N Nagle Ave, Chicago, IL, 60630
www.norwood gospelchapel.com
norwoodgospel@aol.com
Su B 9:00am, F 11:00am; Tu L 9:30am; We P 7:00pm
c/o: Richard E. Sanders (847-635-9798)
10112 Potter Rd, Des Plaines, IL, 60016-1547
brsanders@aol.com

Portage Park Gospel Chapel (773-736-0171)
5614 W Dakin St, Chicago, IL, 60634
Su B 10:00am, S 11:00am; We P 7:00pm
c/o: Roy Carlson (847-673-4090)
4940 W Estes Ave, Skokie, IL, 60077

Roseland Bible Church (773-785-3634)
233 W 111th St, Chicago, IL, 60628
Su B 9:00am, S 10:00am, F 11:00am; Tu C 6:15pm (Oct-Apr); We P 6:30pm
c/o: James E Albright (773-374-0333)
9773 S Ingleside Ave, Chicago, IL, 60628

South Side Gospel Assembly
863 E 64th St, Chicago, IL, 60637
Su S 10:30am, G 11:15am; We M 6:30pm
c/o: Hamlin A Moseley (312-326-2577)
3440 Cottage Grove Ave #808, Chicago, IL, 60616

Westlawn Gospel Chapel
2115 S St Louis Ave, Chicago, IL, 60623
Su B 9:15am, S 10:00am, M 11:15am, G 7:00pm; We P/M
c/o: LeRoy Yates
555 E 167th St, S Holland, IL, 60473

Woodside Bible Chapel (708-345-6563)
621 N First Ave, Maywood, IL, 60153
Su B 9:30am, F 11:00am; We P/M 7:00pm
note: cnr 1st & Chicago Aves
c/o: Robert F Ramey (630-682-4733)
500 Timber Ridge Dr #302, Carol Stream, IL, 60188
rfr3927@aol.com

DANVILLE
Hillery Bible Chapel (217-443-4418)
110 Chestnut St, Danville, IL, 61832
Su B 9:30am, S/F 11:00am, G/M 6:00pm; We P 7:00pm
c/o: Tim Van Ryn (217-446-8707)
115 Oak St. (Hillery), Danville, IL 61832
timyrna@vanryn.net
alt: Sam Hadley (217-443-0547)
samsieglind@comcast.net

ELGIN
Park Manor Bible Chapel (847-741-7295)
725 W Columbia Ave, Elgin, IL, 60120
Su B 9:00am, F 10:30am, M 5:00pm (every other Su); Tu Y 7:00pm
c/o: William Coyle (630-894-7524 or 847-340-9384)
591 Carlsbad Trail, Roselle, IL, 60172
william.coyle@gmail.com
alt: Steve Modrzejewski (847-742-4024)

EVANSTON
Evanston Gospel Chapel (847-864-5165)
639 Asbury Ave, Evanston, IL, 60202
Su B 9:30am, F/S 11:00am; We P 7:30pm
c/o: Steven P Smith (847-391-5062 or 773-761-1533)

HARVEY
The Learning Center Gospel Chapel
PO Box 1593, Harvey, IL, 60426
Su S 10:00am, B 11:00am; We P 7:00pm
note: meets at 15702 Park Ave
c/o: James Fair (708-957-0853 or 333-5355)
PO Box 1593, Harvey, IL, 60426

HARWOOD HEIGHTS
Romanian Christian Assembly (708-278-5803)
6739 W Montrose Ave, Chicago, IL, 60634
Su S/B 10:00am, G 11:00am, G 6:00pm; Th P 6:30pm
c/o: Floric Boca
alt: Cornel Ciobanu

LANSING

Lansing Gospel Chapel (708-474-1532)
3306 Bernice Rd, Lansing, IL, 60438
pbthomson@juno.com
Su B 9:30am, F/S 11:00am, P/M 6:00pm; Th L 9:30am; Sa M 8:00am (men)
c/o: Peter Thomson (708-946-6631)
965 Keenan Lane, Beecher, IL, 60401
pbthomson@juno.com
alt: EV James (219-924-9091)

LOMBARD

Lombard Gospel Chapel (630-620-4987)
369 N Stewart Ave, Lombard, IL, 60148
www.lombardgospel.org
whatbrowncando@comcast.net
Su B 9:30am, F/S 11:00am, C 6:00pm; We Y 7:00pm
c/o: David C Brown (630-620-9700)
369 N Stewart Ave, Lombard, IL, 60148
whatbrowncando@comcast.net
alt: Tom Hephner (630-629-4011)

MILAN

Oak Ridge Bible Chapel (309-787-7065)
2716 1st St W, Milan, IL, 61264
www.oakridgebiblechapel.com
orbc@oakridgebiblechapel.com
Su B 9:00am, S 10:00am, F 11:00am; We P 6:30pm
note: mailing address: PO Box 644, Milan, IL 61264
c/o: Craig Rolinger (309-755-4337)

MOKENA

New Lenox Gospel Hall (815-485-9064)
13550 West Rt 6, Mokena, IL, 60448
Su B 9:30am, M/S 11:30am, G 7:00pm; We P/M 7:30pm
c/o: Brent Studnicka (815-463-9590)
138 Wallace St, New Lenox, IL 60451-1161
bstudnicka@aol.com
alt: Kerwin Brandt (630-243-8071)

MOLINE

Community Christian Fellowship (309-762-2027)
105 5th Ave, Moline, IL, 61265
Su S 9:00am, M 10:30am, B 6:00pm
c/o: Steve Clark
1702 6th Ave, Moline, IL 61265

46 UNITED STATES — ILLINOIS

OAK LAWN

Oak Lawn Bible Chapel (708-424-4399)
4259 W 107th St, Oak Lawn, IL, 60453
www.oaklawnbiblechapel.org
c_seminara@oaklawnbiblechapel.org
Su B 9:30am, F 11:00am; We P 7:00pm
c/o: Charlie Seminara (815-439-1877)
6102 Smokey Ridge Ct, Plainfield, IL, 60586
c_seminara@oaklawnbiblechapel.org
alt: Phil Nichols (708-258-9707)
7nichols@gmail.com

PALOS HILLS

Palos Hills Christian Assembly (708-974-9791)
10600 S 88th Ave, Palos Hills, IL, 60465
Su B 9:15am, F 11:00am, G 6:00pm; Mo C 7:30pm; We L 9:30am, P 7:30pm;
Fr C 7:30pm
c/o: Bob Stevenson (708-301-8470)
12143 Black Forest Dr, Homer Glen, IL, 60491
b_stevenson8@hotmail.com
alt: Bob Fiebig (708-448-2552)

ROCKFORD

Believers Bible Chapel (815-962-1708)
1925 S Meridian Rd, Rockford, IL, 61102
Su B 9:30am, S 11:00am; We M 6:45pm
c/o: Will Webber (815-964-6462)
2759 Savannah Ln, Rockford, IL, 61102
webbers@fastermac.net

SPRINGFIELD

Grace Bible Chapel (217-585-8514)
3335 Woodhaven Dr, Springfield, IL, 62707
www.bibletruth.net/ilsprina
Su B 9:00am, S 10:20am, G 11:00am, M 7:00pm
c/o: Floyd Pierce (217-544-7419)
915 South 1st St, Springfield, IL, 62704
fpierce@ameritech.net

WARRENVILLE

Warrenville Bible Chapel (630-393-7733)
4s157 Curtis Ave, Warrenville, IL, 60555
www.warrenvillebiblechapel.org
Su B 9:00am, S 10:30am, F 11:30am; Tu Men's M 7:00pm; We P 7:00pm
note: mailing address: PO Box 104, Warrenville, IL, 60555
c/o: Todd Neese (630-393-4665)
tneesel@juno.com
alt: Kevin Schliecher (630-393-9384)
kmschliecher@sbcglobal.net

WAUKEGAN
Local Cristiano
146 S Genesee, Waukegan, IL, 60085
Su B 10:00am, S 10:50am, M 11:50am, G 7:00pm; Tu M 7:00pm; Th M 7:00pm
c/o: Francisco Reyes (847-244-0310)
PO Box 51, Waukegan, IL, 60079

WHEATON
Bethany Chapel (630-653-5285)
404 N President Ave, Wheaton, IL, 60187
www.bethanywheaton.com
bethanychapel@juno.com
Su B 9:00am, F 10:30am; We M 7:00pm
c/o: Brad Stringer (630-260-1812)
1691 Thompson Dr, Wheaton, IL, 60187
string428@aol.com

ZION
North Shore Bible Chapel (847-746-1810)
2800 29th St, Zion, IL, 60099
nsbchapel@netscape.net
Su B 9:30am, F 11:00am; We P 7:00pm
note: use point of contact as church's mailing address
c/o: Heinz Habel (847-244-7549)
16896 W Sibelius Ln, Gurnee, IL, 60031
hlhabel@sbcglobal.com
alt: Allan Leach (262-843-2069)
aleach53168@peoplepc.com

INDIANA

INDIANAPOLIS
Bethany Christian Fellowship (317-844-3689)
1427 Southview Dr, Indianapolis, IN, 46227
Su B 9:15am, S 11:00am; We P 7:00pm
c/o: Steven Stapley (317-887-6339)
6804 Smithfield Blvd, Indianapolis, IN, 46237
stevenstapley@sbcglobal.net
alt: Tim Dunham (317-536-2320)

KNOX
Gospel Meeting House (574-896-2980)
1003 S Prettyman, Knox, IN, 46534
Su B 9:00am, S 10:00am; We M 7:00pm
c/o: Arlin Perry (219-896-2980)
2515 E 800 S, N Judson, IN, 46366

LOGANSPORT

Gospel Chapel
321 Cliff Dr, Logansport, IN, 46947
Su B 10:00am, G 11:00am
c/o: Ralph Garver (574-722-1012)
4307 Jamestown Dr, Logansport, IN, 46947
leegar@lneti.com

MISHAWAKA

Grace Bible Chapel (574-255-6740)
2537 Liberty Dr, Mishawaka, IN, 46544
Su B 9:00am, F 10:30am; We P/M 7:30pm
c/o: David Detrick (269-684-4865)
232 Beeson Rd, Niles, MI, 49120
detrickfamily@juno.com

MUNCIE

Muncie Bible Fellowship
4309 W Riverside Ave, Muncie, IN, 47304
Su B 9:30am, M 6:30pm
c/o: Richard Rawson (765-284-1712 or 744-5559)
4309 W Riverside Ave, Muncie, IN, 47304
alt: David Dixon (765-286-0430)

ORA

Ora Gospel Chapel
Main St, Ora, IN, 46968
Su B 9:15am, S/M 10:00am
note: use point of contact as church's mailing address
c/o: William A Sanders (574-946-4820)
5860 E 900 S, Monterey, IN, 46960

RUSSIAVILLE

Ecclesia Fellowship (765-883-7681)
8166 W 2005, Russiaville, IN, 46979
note: meeting at home, contact for additional information
c/o: David Ihms (765-883-7681)
8166 W 2005, Russiaville, IN, 44979
alt: David Harmon (765-583-2431)

WARSAW

Bethany Fellowship (574-267-6049)
522 W Market St, Warsaw, IN, 46580
Su B 9:00am, S 10:15am, F 11:15am; We Y 7:00pm; 1st Fr L 6:45pm;
Sa P 9:00am
c/o: Irv Lindemuth (574-269-6143)
202 Woodcliff Dr, Warsaw, IN, 46582
irvlindy@cs.com
alt: Aaron Hooks (574-268-9305)
athooks@embarqmail.com

WEST LAFAYETTE
Westside Bible Fellowship (765-583-2431)
4533 US 52 West, West Lafayette, IN, 47906
note: meeting at home
We M 7:15pm
c/o: David Harmon (765-583-2431)
daharm@juno.com

IOWA

AREDALE
Gospel Hall
Su B, S 10:00am, G 8:00pm
c/o: Robert Ayers (515-894-3443)

ATLANTIC
Atlantic Gospel Chapel (712-243-2439)
104 E 13th St, Atlantic, IA, 50022
Su B 9:30am, S 10:45am, M 7:00pm; We P 7:00pm
note: 13th & Elm
c/o: Grant Nelson (712-243-1654)
1405 Redwood Dr, Atlantic, IA, 50022
alt: Stefan Johnson (712-243-1371)

Sunnyside Bible Chapel (243-2744)
1301 Sunnyside Lane, Atlantic, IA, 50022
Su B, S 10:45am, G 7:00pm; We P/M
c/o: Sam Metheny
52652 Mahogany Rd, Walnut, IA, 51577

CEDAR FALLS
Bethany Bible Chapel (319-266-0100)
4507 Rownd St, Cedar Falls, IA, 50613
www.bethanybiblechapel.org
info@bethanybiblechapel.org
Su B 9:00am, S 10:30am, M 6:00pm, P 7:00pm (May-Aug 7:30pm)
c/o: Dennis Anderson (319-988-9859)
3707 Ranchero Rd, Cedar Falls, IA, 50613
andersondr@mchsi.com
alt: David Wilson (319-277-2049),
dwilson@bethanybiblechapel.org

Cedar Falls Gospel Fellowship
W 4th & Washington St, Cedar Falls, IA
Su B 10:00am, S 11:00am, G 6:00pm; We P/M 7:00pm
c/o: Duane Wessels (319-234-9951 or 319-277-8883)
196 Whispering Oaks Lane, Waterloo, IA, 50701

Cedar Falls Gospel Hall (319-277-8011)
1302 Walnut St, Cedar Falls, IA, 50613
Su B 9:30am, S 11:00am, G 7:00pm; We P 7:00pm
note: 13th & Walnut St
c/o: Erwin D Stickfort (319-266-6271)
5027 Sage Rd, Cedar Falls, IA, 50613
alt: Glen Groothuis (319-553-9400)

CEDAR RAPIDS

Cedar Rapids Bible Chapel (319-365-4474)
3412 Oakland Rd NE, Cedar Rapids, IA, 52402
www.crbiblechapel.org
Su B 9:00am, S/F 10:30am; We P 7:00pm
c/o: David Rodgers (319-362-4503)
1208 Harold Dr SE, Cedar Rapids, IA, 52403
alt: Harold Mally (319-377-6728)

CLARKSVILLE

Antioch Gospel Association (641-823-5691)
103 W Rowley, Greene, IA, 50636
Su S/M 9:45am, B 10:30am, G 11:45am; We P 7:00pm
c/o: John P. Wessels (319-267-2909 or 319-269-3493)
25284 Sinclair Ave., Allison, IA 50602
jwfarms@netins.net

COUNCIL BLUFFS

Council Bluffs Bible Chapel (712-323-1919)
810 Avenue E, Council Bluffs, IA, 51501
rlewisr505@juno.net
Su B 9:30am, S 11:00am; We P 6:30pm
c/o: Loyd Andrew (712-322-8514)
208 Pickardy Ln, Council Bluffs, IA, 51501
lgandrew@juno.com
alt: Rich Lewis (402-348-0112)

DAVENPORT

High Point Bible Chapel (563-391-3122)
2600 W 63rd St, Davenport, IA, 52806
www.highpointbiblechapel.org
Su B 9:30am, F 11:00am, M 6:00pm; We P 6:30pm
c/o: Tom Daly (563-391-3795)
4918 Ripley St, Davenport, IA, 52806

DES MOINES

Community Bible Fellowship
2906 Holcomb Ave, Des Moines, IA, 50310
c/o: Ray Lewis (515-277-3201)
2906 Holcomb Ave, Des Moines, IA, 50310

Cornerstone Community Church (515-270-4809)
6207 NW 62nd Ave, Johnston, IA, 50131
www.cornerstonedm.com
info@cornerstonedm.com
Su B 8:30am, S 9:30, F 10:30am; We P 7:00pm
note: meeting at Johnston Middle School
note: mailing address: P.O Box 13185, Des Moines, IA, 50310
c/o: Tom Baird (515-276-1309)
7511 Goodman Dr, Urbandale, IA, 50322
tomyrna57@aol.com
alt: John Ottley (515-331-3567)
john@cornerstonedm.com

Lake Country Bible Chapel
309 Van Dorn St, Polk City, IA, 50226
Su B 9:30am
note: meets in Polk City Community Center
c/o: Tom Messerly (515-254-0891)
4677 Beaver Ave, Des Moines, IA, 50310

DUBUQUE

Arbor Oaks Bible Chapel (563-556-7686)
2843 JF Kennedy Rd, Dubuque, IA, 52002-1081
www.arboroaksbible.org
Su B 9:30am, S/F 11:00am; We M 7:00pm (homes)
c/o: James Dunkerton (563-556-8863)
1865 Horizon Ct, Dubuque, IA, 52001-4033
jdunker343@aol.com

Asbury Community Chapel (563-588-4363)
5025 Saratoga Rd, Dubuque, IA, 52002
www.asburycommunitychapel.org
Su B 9:30am, S/F 11:00am; We P/M 7:00pm
c/o: Jack Fish (563-557-8959 or 563-588-8000 ext 1207)
2570 Asbury Rd, Dubuque, IA, 52001

The Great Adventure Church (563-557-8583)
3430 Dodge St #14, Dubuque, IA, 52003
www.thegreatadventurechurch.org
info@thegreatadventurechurch.org
Su S 9:30am, F 10:30am, B 11:15am
note: meets at Inn Plaza, 3430 Dodge St #14, Dubuque, IA, 52003
c/o: Keith Leverentz (563-557-8583)
11154 High Ridge Drive, Dubuque, IA, 52003

UNITED STATES — IOWA

DUNKERTON

Dunkerton Gospel Hall (319-822-7498)
301 Carroll Blvd, Dunkerton, IA, 50626-9741
www.dunkertongospelhall.com
Su B 9:30am, S 11:00am, G 7:00pm; We P/M 7:30pm
c/o: Harold Stickfort (319-822-4549)
4303 Rice Rd, Dunkerton, IA, 50626-9741
alt: Dennis Stickfort (319-822-7383)
stickhome@dunkerton.net

EDDYVILLE

Parkview Bible Chapel (641-969-4909)
105 4th St, Eddyville, IA, 52553
Su B 9:00am, S 11:00am; We P/M
c/o: Bruce Taylor (641-673-0460)
1547 290th St, Oskaloosa, IA, 52577

GREENFIELD

Greenfield Gospel Chapel (641-743-2601)
401 E Iowa St, Greenfield, IA, 50849
Su B 9:30am, S/F 11:00am; We P 7:30pm
note: mailing address: PO Box 192, Greenfield, IA, 50849
c/o: Gerald W Reed (641-743-2335)
310 SE Linn St, Greenfield, IA, 50849
alt: Phil Cannon (641-743-2945)

HAMPTON

Hampton Gospel Hall (641-456-5133)
Hampton, IA
Su S 10:00am, B 11:00am, G 7:00pm; Th P 7:00pm
note: 3rd St at 5th Ave NE

HITESVILLE

Hitesville Gospel Hall (319-347-2333)
Rural Route, Aplington, IA, 50604
Su S/M 10:00am, B 11:00am, G 7:00pm; We P/BS
note: use main point of contact's address for mailing
c/o: Dr. Larry L Brandt (319-346-1084)
509 Lincoln St -- P.O. Box 683, Parkersburg, IA, 50665
larry.diana@msn.com

LYMAN

Lyman Assembly
68933 Lyman St, Lyman, IA
Su B 9:30am, F 11:00am, C 6:00pm; We P 7:30pm;
Th P 7:30pm (homes in winter)
c/o: William Meyer (712-774-5378)
71033 660th St, Cumberland, IA, 50843
meyerbd@netins.net

MANCHESTER
Gospel Hall (563-927-3887)
1308 N 3rd St, Manchester, IA, 52057
Su S 9:30am, B 11:00am, G 7:30pm; We P 7:30pm
c/o: CF Foster (563-927-2963)
130 Clara, Manchester, IA, 52057

MARION
Marion Gospel Hall
755 Grand Ave, Marion, IA, 52302
Su B 9:30am, S 11:00am, G 7:00pm; We P/M 7:00pm
c/o: Jim Ferris (319-377-1226)
7404 Hampshire Dr NE, Cedar Rapids, IA, 52402

MASON CITY
Christian Assembly
1819 S Coolidge Hwy 19th SW B35, Mason City, IA, 50401
Su G, B 10:30am, M 11:30am; We P
c/o: John Muldoon (641-424-4765)
637 S Washington, Mason City, IA, 50401

Gospel Hall
Su B/G, S 10:00am; We P

NEW HARTFORD
New Hartford Assembly (319-983-2248)
PO Box 187, New Hartford, IA, 50660
Su B 10:00am, F 11:00am, P/M 7:00pm
note: 820 York St
c/o: Edward Behrends (319-983-2248)
PO Box 187, New Hartford, IA, 50660
ebd60smb@peoplepc.com

OSKALOOSA
Hillside Bible Church (641-673-6305)
PO Box 229, Oskaloosa, IA, 52577
liv2tell@kdsi.net
Su S, B 9:00am
note: 2352 Hwy 92E
c/o: Brad Westercamp (641-672-1957)
1411 7th Ave E, Oskaloosa, IA, 523577
liv2tell@kdsi.net
alt: Tom Taylor (641-929-0004)

PELLA
Pella Gospel Chapel (641-628-3479)
510 Union St, Pella, IA, 50219
Su B 9:30am, F 10:45am; We M 7:00pm
c/o: Ray Van Der Hart (641-628-3479)
307 E 2nd, Pella, IA, 50219
alt: James Van Der Hart (641-625-4267)

PLEASANTVILLE

Pleasantville Gospel Chapel
Su F 9:45am, B 11:30am; We M 6:30pm
note: mailing address: 999 McGregor St, Knoxville, IA, 50138
c/o: Jim Best
114 Hwy 5, Swan, IA, 50252
alt: Jarrod Hagenow

REDFIELD

Hilltop Chapel
1413 First Street, Box 416, Redfield, IA 50233
Su B 9:30am, F/S 11:00am; We P 7:00pm
c/o: Jeff Horn (515-523-2864)
2978 130th St., Stuart, IA
thehorns1@juno.com
alt: Eric Barker (515-833-2636)
canoeguys7@juno.com

SIOUX CITY

Sioux City Gospel Hall (712-277-3647)
120 South Leonard St, Sioux City, IA, 51103
george44987@msn.com
Su B 9:45am, M 11:15am, G 7:30pm; We M 7:30pm; Sa C 7:30pm
c/o: Gary A Hayes (712-255-4962)
1625 West 14th St, Sioux City, IA, 51103
george44987@msn.com
alt: Enoch B Hayes (712-277-1176)

Washington Heights Bible Chapel (712-276-3073)
2600 S St Mary's St, Sioux City, IA, 51106
Su B 9:00am, M 10:00am, S 11:00am; We P 7:00pm
c/o: Dan Speichinger (712-276-2445)
2515 S Coral St, Sioux City, IA, 51106

STOUT

Gospel Hall (319-346-1153)
407 3rd St, Stout, IA, 50673
Su S 10:00am, B 11:00am, G 7:00pm; We P/M 7:30pm
c/o: Gary L DeGroote (319-983-2713)
28073 Westbrook St, New Hartford, IA, 50660
gdegroote2@msn.com

STRATFORD

Countryside Bible Chapel (515-838-2549)
3998 Fenton Ave, Stratford, IA, 50249
Su B 9:30am, F 11:00am; We P 7:30pm
www.stratfordcountryside.com
note: use point of contact as church's mailing address
c/o: Mark Westrum (515-838-2502)
3475 Fenton Ave, Stratford, IA, 50249
alt: Doug Anderson (515-838-2491)

WATERLOO
Waterloo Gospel Hall (319-234-2369)
726 Western Ave, Waterloo, IA, 50702-2839
Su B 9:30am, S/M 11:00am, G 7:00pm; We P 7:00pm
note: use point of contact as church's mailing address
c/o: Richard Orr (319-334-3931)
614 Bland Blvd SW, Independence, IA, 50644
rnorr@indyteL.com

WEBSTER CITY
Webster City Bible Chapel (515-832-5419)
1704 Superior Street, Webster City, IA, 50595
dennis@thompsonmonuments.com
Su B 10:00am, M 7:00pm, S 8:30pm
c/o: Denis Thompson (515-832-4814)
1704 Superior Street, Webster City, IA, 50595
dennis@thompsonmonuments.com

WEST UNION
West Union Gospel Hall
E Elm St, West Union, IA, 52135
Su M/S 10:00am, B 11:00am, G 6:30pm; We P/M 7:30pm
c/o: Steve Walvatne (563-578-8505)
18202 V Ave, Hawkeye, IA, 52147
stevewalvatne@hotmail.com

KANSAS

ABILENE
Grace and Truth Gospel Chapel
1227 Deer Rd, Abilene, KS, 67410
www.bibletruth.net/ksabilea
Su S/M, B 10:00am
c/o: Keith Engle (785-479-2239)
1541 Flag Rd, Abilene, KS, 67410

BALDWIN CITY
Coal Creek Gospel Hall (785-979-5012)
1718 N 466 Rd, Baldwin City, KS, 66006
www.bibletruth.net/ksbaldwa
daveolmstead@juno.com
Su B 9:30am, M 10:45am, G/S 11:45am; We C 6:00pm, P/M 7:30pm
note: 1.7 miles N of US 56 on E 1700th Rd. Use main point of contact's address for mail.
c/o: David Olmstead (785-594-6628)
1058 Firetree Ave, Baldwin City, KS, 66006-4172
daveolmstead@juno.com
alt: Dan Stewart (816-461-1714 or 816-694-7326)

Gospel Chapel (785-594-3374)
3rd & Chapel Sts, Baldwin City, KS, 66006
rajones@embarqmail.com
Su B/M 9:45am, S 6:00pm; Th P/M 7:00pm (fellowship supper Th 6:00pm)
note: mailing address: PO Box 45, Baldwin City, KS, 66006
c/o: Dr Ray M Jones (785-594-3374)
PO Box 45, Baldwin City, KS, 66006
rajones@embarqmail.com
alt: Steven Hemphill (785-594-2348)

HUTCHINSON

Hutchinson Gospel Chapel
334 E 6th St, Hutchinson, KS, 67501
www.hutchgospelchapel.com
Su B 8:30am, S 9:30am, F 11:00am
c/o: Duane Schmidt (620-669-0357)
1500 N Baker, Hutchinson, KS, 67501
schmidtd@hutchcc.edu

Mizpah Bible Chapel (620-663-2226)
119 E 6th, Hutchinson, KS, 67501
mizpahbiblechapel@gmail.com
Su B 9:00am, S 10:30am; Th P 7:00pm
note: Home church
c/o: Tony Asberry (620-663-2226)
119 E 6th, Hutchinson, KS, 67501

Northwest Gospel Chapel (620-662-7791)
3804 W 56 Ave, Hutchinson, KS, 67502
Su B 9:00am, S 10:00am, F 11:00am; We L 10:00am, P 7:00pm
note: use point of contact as church's mailing address
c/o: John Denny (620-662-7791)
4508 W 56 Ave, Hutchinson, KS, 67502
jdennykbc@gmail.com
alt: Steve Burson (620-422-3834)

LAWRENCE

Lawrence Bible Chapel (785-841-2607)
505 Monterey Way, Lawrence, KS, 66049
Su P 9:00am, B 9:30am, S 11:00am, F 11:40am; We M 6:00pm
c/o: John R Scollon (785-841-5271)
1127 Randall Rd, Lawrence, KS, 66049
alt: Ron Nadvornik (785-843-7708)

SALINA

Sunset Bible Chapel (785-827-9053)
760 Hancock, Salina, KS, 67401
Su B 9:30am, S 11:00am, P 6:30pm, M 7:30pm
c/o: George Easter (785-827-8900)
638 Highland, Salina, KS, 67401

SHAWNEE

The Bible Chapel of Shawnee (913-248-7877)
12230 W 75th St, Shawnee, KS, 66216
www.the-biblechapel.org
Su B 9:00am, S 10:15am, F 11:20am; Tu C 6:30pm; We P 7:00pm
c/o: Steve Price (913-897-9034)
12103 W 139th Terr, Overland Park, KS, 66221
pricespd@kc.rr.com
alt: N Keith Trevolt (913-299-9607)

TOPEKA

Gospel Chapel (785-273-2100)
5010 SW 20th Terr, Topeka, KS, 66604
Su B 9:00am, S 10:15am, M 11:00am; We P 6:30pm
c/o: Bruce Carey (785-986-6320)
13398 102nd Rd, Hoyt, KS, 66440
careysnks@yahoo.com

WICHITA

Community Bible Chapel (316-744-6252)
4551 N Auburn St, Bel Aire, KS, 67220
Su B 9:00am, S 10:30am, P 7:15pm
c/o: Gary Smith (316-744-3066)

Northside Bible Chapel (316-744-8089)
4510 E 61st St N, Kechi, KS, 67067
Su B 8:45am, S 10:00am, F 11:00am; We P 7:00pm
c/o: Michael D Paddock (316-682-1591)
1400 N Armour, Wichita, Kansas, 67206
mdpaddock1@cox.net
alt: Randy Horn (316-832-9756)
rhorn5@juno.com

Westside Bible Chapel (316-721-3649)
12050 W Central, Wichita, KS 67277
www.westsidebiblechapel.org
arnburkle@att.net
Su B 8:45am, S 10:00am, M 11:00am; We P 7:15pm
note: mailing address: PO Box 93923, Wichita, KS 67277
c/o: Arnold Burkle (316-721-3354)
alt: Eddie Buchanan (316-942-0999)

KENTUCKY

LEXINGTON
Pilgrim Bible Assembly (859-233-9250)
350 Elaine Dr, Lexington, KY 40504
Su B 9:30am, M 11:00am

LOUISVILLE
Louisville Bible Fellowship (502-477-0077)
10496 Bluegrass Pkwy, Louisville, KY 40299
www.louisvillebiblefellowship.org
Su B 9:45am, F 11:00am, S 2:30pm; We P/M 7:00pm
c/o: Jim Sparks (502-538-8892)
1007 Deerwood Dr, Coxs Creek, KY 40013
jb5sparks@aol.com
alt: Mathews Kuravackel (502-526-5459)
Mathewsv@yahoo.com

OWENSBORO
Trinity Bible Church (270-685-4272)
318 Ewing Rd, Owensboro, KY, 42301
Su B 9:30am, P 10:30am, M 11:00am
c/o: David Nale (812-842-2447)
8199 Heather Dr, Newburgh, IN, 47630
joannanale@yahoo.com
alt: Ronnie N O'Bryan (270-658-4272)

RICHMOND
Bluegrass Bible Fellowship (859-625-0096)
2187 Lexington Rd, Suite B1, Richmond, KY, 40475
www.biblefellowship.org
Su B 9:30am, F 11:00am; We 7:30pm
c/o: Jim Harmon (859-626-8509)
1593 Tates Creek Rd, Richmond, KY, 40475
jamesharmon@bellsouth.net
alt: John Frasher (859-754-1269)

LOUISIANA

GRETNA
Household of Faith
712 27th St, New Orleans, LA, 70053
Su B 9:00am, S 10:30am; Fr P 7:30pm
c/o: Booker T Collor (504-348-1639)
2816 Laurie Ln, Marrero, LA, 70072
hgal610@aol.com

HARVEY

Community Bible Chapel (504-367-2847)
2502 8th St, Harvey, LA, 70058
Su B, S 10:45am; We P 7:00pm
c/o: Bernie Additon (504-367-0056)
alt: Gene Luke Novak (504-391-2878)

LAFAYETTE

Lafayette Bible Chapel (337-981-1694)
108 Acadian Dr, Lafayette, LA, 70503
Su B 9:30am, S 10:20am, F 11:15am
note: Butterflies Preschool
c/o: Robert McFatter (337-981-1694)
610 Dutton Dr, Lafayette, LA, 70503
robert.mcfatter@gmail.com
alt: Oran Lambright (337-984-6912)

Southside Bible Chapel (337-989-8928)
4256 W Congress St, Lafayette, LA, 70506
www.southsidebiblechapel.com
wowalker@bellsouth.net
Su B 9:30am, S/F 10:45am; We P 6:30pm
note: mailing address: PO Box 61565, Lafayette, LA, 70596-1565
c/o: William O. Walker (337-232-6577)
103 Robert Dr, Lafayette, LA, 70506
wowalker@bellsouth.net
alt: Alton Guidry (337-235-1313)
alguid@yahoo.com

NEW ORLEANS

Lake Park Chapel (504-394-3087)
201 Schlief Dr, Belle Chasse, LA, 70037
Su B 9:30am, F 10:45am; Tu M 7:00pm; Th P/M 7:00pm
c/o: Ray Cummings (504-393-7083)
103 Dickson Dr, Belle Chasse, LA, 70037
lakeparkchapel@cmaaccess.com

Sala Evangelica (504-394-2267)
201 Schlief Dr, Belle Chasse, LA, 70037
Su B 11:00am, G 12:00pm; We P/M 7:30pm
note: use main point of contact for mailing address
c/o: Julio Sarmiento (504-912-9955)
P.O. Box 3325, Gretna, LA 70054
zjsarmiento@yahoo.com

Sala Evangelica—Las Buenas Nuevas (832-260-6417)
600 N.O. Hammond Hwy, New Orleans, LA 70124
jangel29@cox.net
Su B 2:00pm, F 3:00pm; We P 7:30pm
c/o: Fernando García (832-260-6417)
2338 Barracks St., New Orleans, LA 70119
alt: José Angel Galdamez (504-250-9176)
jangel29@cox.net

SLIDELL

Bible Chapel (985-641-3785)
59334 N Pearl Dr, Slidell, LA 70461
Su B/S, G 3:30pm (nursing home), M 6:00pm; Mo M 7:00pm (homes); We P/M 6:30pm
c/o: Robert R Brown (985-641-4028)
1584 Monaco Dr, Slidell, LA, 70458

MAINE

AUGUSTA

Christians at the Gospel Hall (207-626-2786)
421 Old Belgrade Rd, Augusta, ME, 04330
Su B 10:00am, G 6:00pm; We P/M 6:30pm
c/o: James P Thompson (207-512-2636 or 207-215-7986)
262 Quaker Rd, Sidney, ME, 04330
jptbooks@gmail.com

MADAWASKA

Madawaska Gospel Church (207-728-6252)
125 25th St, Madawaska, ME 04756
Su B 10:00am, S 11:00am, G 7:00pm; We P/M 7:00pm
c/o: Lionel Hebert (207-728-4604)
lionelheb@yahoo.com

MADISON

Madison Gospel Hall (207-696-3102)
554 Main St, Madison, ME, 04950
Su B/S 10:00am, G 11:30am; Th P/M 7:00pm
note: Hwy 148
c/o: Gerald K Paine (207-696-3102)
158 Old Country Rd, Madison, ME, 04950

UNION

Grace Fellowship Bible Chapel (207-785-4905)
197 Payson Rd, Union, ME, 04862
www.gracefellowshipbiblechapel.org
Su B 9:45am, F 11:00am; We P 7:00pm
c/o: Donald Sabins (207-785-4217)
57 Middle Rd, Union, ME, 04862

WESTBROOK

Spring Hill Gospel Hall
225 Spring St, Westbrook, ME, 04092
Su B 9:30am, F 11:15am; We P/M 7:00pm
c/o: Dan Chick (207-449-1492)
95 Maple St, Westbrook, ME, 04092
alt: Barry Stultz (207-247-5238)

MARYLAND

BALTIMORE

Brooklyn Bible Chapel (410-355-5579)
502 Jack St, Baltimore, MD, 21225
www.brooklynbiblechapel.org
Su B 9:30am, S/F 11:00am, C/M 7pm; We P 7:15pm
c/o: Alfred Gray (410-255-9179)
211 Weston Woods Dr, Pasadena, MD, 21122
aasgray@aol.com
alt: Don Brower (410-551-2658)
dojebrower@verizon.net

Forge Road Bible Chapel (410-248-0896)
5040 Forge Rd, Perry Hall, MD, 21128
www.forgeroadbiblechapel.org
Su B 9:15am, S/F 11:00am; We M 7:30pm; Th L 9:30am
c/o: Roger Dunkerton (410-248-0896)
5100 Forge Rd, Perry Hall, MD, 21128
alt: William Dunkerton (443-678-1198)

Glad Tidings Chapel
4801 Garrison Blvd, Baltimore, MD, 21215
Su B 10:30am, S 11:30am; We P/M 7:30pm
c/o: Arthur S Evans (410-566-1242)
1110 Poplar Grove St, Baltimore, MD, 21216

Loch Hill Ekklesia (410-823-2400)
6601 Loch Raven Blvd, Baltimore, MD, 21224
www.ekklesiaoutreach.org
Su S 9:30am, F 10:45am, B 12:30pm; Fr Y; Ladies meeting every 3rd Sa
c/o: Paul Lewis (410-235-0053)
2007 E 32nd St, Baltimore, MD, 21218
pilgml1@verizon.net

CLINTON

Clinton Community Chapel (301-868-2370)
8415 Schultz Rd, Clinton, MD, 20735
Su B/S; We P 6:30pm
c/o: Dale A Pfaff (301-423-8448)
5013 Henderson Rd, Temple Hills, MD, 20748

COLMAR MANOR

Colmar Manor Gospel Chapel (301-774-9215)
3903 Newton St, Colmar Manor, MD, 20722
Su B 9:30am, S 11:00am; We P 7:30pm
c/o: David R Gibson (301-774-9215)
17718 Striley Dr, Ashton, MD, 20861
dave-cathy-gibson@erols.com

UNITED STATES — MARYLAND

CUMBERLAND
Cumberland Gospel Hall Assembly
700 E First St, Cumberland, MD, 21502
Su B 9:30am, S/M 11:15am, G 7:00pm; Th P 7:30pm
c/o: Dick Ganoe (304-738-1116)
PO Box 730, Wiley Ford, WV, 26767

FRAMINGHAM
Igreja Crista Evangelica (508-233-0334)
448 Waverly St, 2nd floor, Framingham, MA, 01702
xpautorepair@verizon.net
Su B 10:00am, S 11:00am, G 7:00pm; Tu F 8:00pm; We P 8:00pm
c/o: Express Auto Repair (508-620-2900)
91 Grant St, Framingham, MA, 01702

LANHAM
Cedar Ridge Community Church
2410 Spencerville Rd, Greenbelt, MD, 20868
Su B 9:00am, B 10:45am
note: Spencerville

LONACONING
Gospel Hall
West Main St, Lonaconing, MD
Su B, S 10:00am, G 7:00pm; Th P/M 7:00pm
c/o: Gary Kirk (301-359-3835)
Rt 1 Box 10, Westernport, MD, 21562

ROCKVILLE
Rockville Bible Fellowship
Rockville, MD
Su B 9:30am, S 11:00am, G 11:40am; We M 7:00pm
note: meets in hotel on Rt 28 (1/4 mi W of I-270 jct)
c/o: George Shakarji (301-417-6744)
821 Diamond Dr, Rockville, MD, 20878
alt: David Anderson (301-279-5418)

SAVAGE
Countryside Fellowship Church (301-490-5737)
8850 Baltimore St, Savage, MD, 20763
Su B 10:30am
c/o: Charles G Coleman (301-352-0717)
12123 Wilmont Turn, Bowie, MD, 20715

SILVER SPRING
New Hampshire Avenue Gospel Chapel (301-622-3733)
12608 New Hampshire Ave, Silver Spring, MD, 20904
Su B 9:15am, S 11:00am, G 6:00pm; Tu P/M 7:45pm
c/o: Clarence Witmer (410-531-5070)
4415 Linthicum Rd, Dayton, MD, 21306
alt: Michael Bryan (301-596-1486)

MASSACHUSETTS

ANDOVER
Andover Bible Chapel (978-475-4733)
266 Lowell St, Andover, MA, 01810
www.andoverbiblechapel.org
Su B 9:15am, F/C 11:00am; We P/M 7:30pm
c/o: Daniel Edwin (978-392-9821)
145 Hayden Rd, Groton, MA, 01450
dedwin2950@aol.com
alt: Rodgers Close (978-922-5191)

ATTLEBORO
Good News Bible Chapel (508-226-2916)
235 West St, Attleboro, MA, 02703
www.gnbc.org
info@gnbc.org
note: use point of contact as church's mailing address
Su B 9:00am, S/F 10:45am; We P 7:00pm
c/o: Steve DuPlessie (508-212-1980)
235 West St, Attleboro, MA, 02703
steve@gnbc.org

BOSTON
Community Gospel Chapel (617-427-4023)
8 Intervale St, Boston, MA, 02119
Su B 9:30am, M 10:30am, G 7:00pm, S 12:00pm; We P/M

BYFIELD
Gospel Hall (508-462-5569)
1 Central St, Byfield, MA, 01922
Su B 10:30am, P 6:30pm, G 7:00pm, S 12:15pm; We P/M 7:30pm
c/o: John H Short (508-465-2207 or 508-465-3254)
145 Main St, Byfield, MA, 01922

CAMBRIDGE
Cambridge Gospel Hall (617-661-6631)
395 Putnam Ave, Cambridge, MA, 02139
Su B 10:30am, G 7:30pm, S/M 12:30pm; We P/M 8:00pm
c/o: John R Webb (617-623-2498)
55 Cameron Ave, Somerville, MA, 02144
alt: Philip Webb (617-625-5357)

DARTMOUTH
Crossroads Bible Chapel (508-997-4632)
334 Cross Rd, Dartmouth, MA, 02747
Su B 9:30am, S 11:30am, G 1:30pm; We M 7:00pm

FRAMINGHAM
Village Bible Chapel
1341 Edgell Rd, Framingham, MA, 01701
Su B 8:30am, S 9:30am, M 10:45am
c/o: Mark Foshager (508-877-7733)
markvbc@ultranet.com

METHUEN
Methuen Gospel Hall (978-794-8679)
51 Meriimack St., Methuen, MA, 01844
methuengospelhall.org
Su B 10:00am, S 11:30am, G 6:30pm; Th P/M 7:30
note: 0.1 miles off Exit 46 - Rt 495
c/o: David Vacca (603-380-0127)
32 Chappy Lane, Salem, NH 03079
dvnet2@myfairpoint.net

LEXINGTON
Countryside Bible Chapel (781-862-7513)
480 Lowell St, Lexington, MA, 02420
www.countrysidebiblechapel.org
info@countrysidebiblechapel.org
Su B 9:00am, S 10:00am, F 11:00am, P 6:30pm; We M 7:30pm
c/o: Jed N Snyder (781-863-8450 or 781-888-1642)
482 Lowell St, Lexington, MA, 02420
jedsnyder@rcn.com

SAUGUS
Walnut Street Gospel Hall (781-233-5570)
213 Walnut St, Saugus, MA, 01906
www.walnutstreetgospelhall.com
Su B 10:00am, G 6:30pm, S 12:00pm; Tu P 7:30pm; Th M 7:30pm
note: just E of Rt 1
c/o: Anthony Grillo (781-334-6363)
46 Grey Lane, Lynnfield, MA, 01940
tonygrillo@netzero.com

SPRINGFIELD
West Springfield Gospel Hall
48 Garden St, West Springfield, MA, 01089
Su B 10:00am, S/M 11:45am, G 7:00pm; We P 7:30pm
c/o: David Hanley (413-224-1049)
216 Canterbury Circle, East Longmeadow, MA, 01028
davidhanley1970@charter.net

SWANSEA
Bethany Gospel Chapel (508-675-0273 or 413-)
65 Lindsey Lane, Swansea, MA, 02777
bgc_office@juno.com
Su B 9:00am, S 10:30am; We P 7:30pm

WATERTOWN

Mount Auburn Gospel Hall (617-924-7696)
226 Mount Auburn St, Watertown, MA, 02472
www.mountauburn.gospelhall.com
Su B 10:00am, M 1:00pm, G 12:30pm; We P 7:45pm
c/o: Joseph Grillo Sr (781-233-8520)
2201 Lewis O Gray Dr, Saugus, MA, 01906
joegrillo@juno.com

WORCESTER

Bethany Gospel Chapel (508-853-6300)
242 Clark St, Worcester, MA, 01606
markea@charter.net
Su B 9:30am, F 11:00am; Tu M 7:30pm
c/o: Mark Andreoli (508-832-7375)
28 Jade Hill Rd, Auburn, MA, 01501
markea@charter.net

Gospel Hall
167 Southwest Ct, Worcester, MA, 01609
Su B 10:30am, G 7:00pm, S 12:00pm; Tu P 7:00pm; Th M 7:00pm
c/o: Timothy Camarra (508-865-2820)
117 Purgatory Rd, Sutton, MA, 01590

MICHIGAN

ALPENA

Alpena Christian Assembly
573 June St, Alpena, MI, 49707
Su B 9:30am, M 11:00am, G 7:00pm; We P/M 7:00pm
c/o: Edward Gapske (517-354-3549)
1438 Wayne Rd, Alpena, MI, 49707

ANN ARBOR

Home Meeting
1027 Ferdon Rd, Ann Arbor, MI, 48104
Su M 10:00am, B 7:00pm; We P 7:00pm
c/o: Van Parunak (734-996-1384 or 996-1767)
1027 Ferdon Rd, Ann Arbor, MI, 48104
van@parunak.com
alt: Dave Nelson (734-429-4331)

BAILEY

Bailey Gospel Chapel (616-834-7959)
845 Peters Rd, Bailey, MI, 49303
Su B 10:00am, S 11:30am
c/o: Bob Bonter (616-834-7200)
940 Peters Rd, Bailey, MI, 49303

UNITED STATES — MICHIGAN

BANGOR

Family Gospel Chapel (616-427-7833)
320 Division St, Bangor, MI, 49013
Su S 10:00am, B 11:00am, M 11:30am; Tu M 6:00pm
c/o: John Fitzgerald (616-427-8941)
320 E Arlington St #13, Bangor, MI, 49013

BATTLE CREEK

Christians Gathered to the Lord Jesus Christ (616-965-9956)
807 E Michigan Ave, Battle Creek, MI, 49014
Su B 9:30am, M 11:00am, G 6:30pm, S 12:00pm; We P/M 7:30pm
c/o: Paul W Mason (616-964-1493)
PO Box 98, Battle Creek, MI, 49016
blessings@surfbest.net

BAY CITY

Gospel Hall
Bay City, MI
Su B 9:30am, S 11:00am, G 7:30pm; We P 7:30pm
note: cnr Dean & Jenny Sts
c/o: Ronald Armstrong

CASS CITY

Hillside Gospel Hall (989-872-5070)
4235 Hurds Corner Rd, Cass City, MI, 48726
pbattel@tisd.k12.mi.us
Su B 10:00am, S 11:15am, G 7:00pm; We P 7:00pm
c/o: Paul Battel (989-872-5070)
4748 Koepfgen Rd, Cass City, MI, 48726
pbattel@tisd.k12.mi.us
alt: Jeff Martin (989-872-5157)

COLDWATER

Coldwater Bible Chapel (517-278-5516)
122 S Jefferson St, Coldwater, MI, 49036
Su B, M 10:30am, S 11:30am

DEARBORN HEIGHTS

Dearborn Chapel (313-277-9152)
4180 Monroe Blvd, Dearborn Heights, MI, 48125
www.dearbornchapel.org
Su B 9:30am, S/F 11:15am, M 6:00pm; Th P 7:00pm
c/o: Robert Bruce (248-488-0467)
27991 Gettysburg St, Farmington Hills, MI, 48133
rbruce@twmi.rr.com
alt: David Donnelly (313-278-4592)

UNITED STATES — MICHIGAN 67

DECKERVILLE
Mills Road Gospel Hall
PO Box 438, Deckerville, MI, 48427
Su B 10:00am, S 11:00am, G 7:30pm; We P 7:30pm
note: 3995 Mills Rd
c/o: Barry C Brinker (810-376-8165)
4800 Shabbona Rd, Deckerville, MI, 48427
brinker@thumb.net

DETROIT
Berean Chapel
8422 Pembroke, Detroit, MI, 48221
Su S 10:00am, M 11:15am, M 7:00pm, B 12:30pm; We P/M 7:45pm
c/o: William Perry (313-366-1507)
8422 Pembroke, Detroit, MI, 48221

Bethany Pembroke Chapel (313-533-6165)
19901 Burt Rd, Detroit, MI, 48219
Su M 10:00am, F 11:00am, B 1:00pm; We P/M/Y 7:00pm
c/o: Michael A Vaughn (313-770-2278)
18314 Parkside, Detroit, MI, 48221
mvaughn01@mailworks.org
alt: Dudley G Williams (313-861-2988)

Curtis Gospel Chapel (313-537-4660)
17753 Lenore, Detroit, MI, 48219
www.curtisgospelchapel.org
Su B 9:30am, S 11:00am, M 6:00pm; We P/M 7:45pm
c/o: Danny Fitzgerald (313-363-8375)
19235 Smock, Northville, MI, 48167
dan@classiccanopy.com

Dunning Park Chapel (303-533-7788)
24800 W Chicago, Redford, MI, 48239
Su B 9:00am, M 10:10am, S 11:15am; We P (homes)
note: at Dixie W of Telegraph
c/o: James E Wallis

Gospel Chapel
16241 Harper, Detroit, MI, 48224
Su S 9:45am, B 11:15am, M 11:45am; Tu P/M 7:00pm
c/o: Arkles Brooks Jr (248-642-6236)
30436 Embassy Dr, Beverly Hills, MI, 48025

Grace Bible Chapel (313-933-9322)
5440 Oakman Blvd, Detroit, MI, 48204
Su G 8:30am, S 9:45am, M 11:15am, B 6:00pm; We P/M 6:30pm
c/o: Ken Hampton (248-354-1443)
28633 E Kalang Cir, Southfield, MI, 48034
john316ken@aol.com

Martin Road Gospel Chapel (313-771-7630)
20505 Martin Rd Box 655, St Clair Shores, MI, 48081
Su S, B 9:15am, M 6:00pm; Tu P/M
c/o: John M Smedes (313-777-7087)
19630 Sunnyside, St Clair Shores, MI, 48080

Metropolitan Community Tabernacle (313-526-8121)
11435 Morang Dr, Detroit, MI, 48224
metrocommtab@sbcglobal.net
Su B 9:30am, F 11:00am; We P 7:00pm
c/o: George Washington (313-526-8121)
11435 Morang Dr, Detroit, MI, 48224
geowwash@yahoo.com

Open Door Gospel Chapel (313-896-2479)
5780 14th St, Detroit, MI, 48208
Su S 9:45am, P 10:45am, M 11:15am, B 12:30pm

EAST LANSING

Carriage Hill Bible Chapel (517-332-4690)
2960 Lake Lansing Rd, East Lansing, MI, 48823
Su B 9:15am, S 10:30am, M 11:30am; We P/M 6:30pm
c/o: Ken Foote (517-336-7444)
325 Wind-n-Wood Dr, Okemos, MI, 48864
kandmfoote@comcast.net
alt: Mark Khol (517-669-1164)

FERNDALE

Ferndale Gospel Hall (248-548-2338)
1720 Kenton Rd, Ferndale, MI, 48220
Su B 9:30am, S 11:15am, G 6:00pm; Th P/M 7:30pm
c/o: Mark Fouts (248-478-0857)
25339 Arden Park Dr, Farmington Hills, MI, 48336
mnmf@juno.com

FLINT

Dextor Street Gospel Chapel (810-742-3264)
3617 Dale Ave, Flint, MI, 48506
Su B 9:15am, F/S 11:00am; We P 7:00pm
c/o: Stuart W Turfus (810-658-7516)
9075 Spring Brook Circle, Davison, MI, 48423
turfuss@aol.com
alt: Patrick Edwards (810-694-3387)

GRAND HAVEN

Gospel Chapel (616-846-1940)
1805 Waverly St, Grand Haven, MI, 49417
Su B 10:00am
c/o: Ken Shady (231-780-4435)
808 Winslow Ct, Muskegon, MI, 49441

GRAND RAPIDS

Asamblea Evangelica (Spanish) (610-247-7969)
635 S Division, Grand Rapids, MI 49503
Su B 9:30am, S 11:00am, Potluck 12:30pm, M 1:30pm; Tu P 7:00pm
c/o: Paul Rogers (616-247-7969)
945 Kendalwood NE, Grand Rapids, MI 49505

Forest Hills Bible Chapel (616-942-5550)
4637 Ada Drive SE, Ada, MI, 49301
www.foresthillsbiblechapel.org
rick@foresthillsbiblechapel.org
Su B 9:00am, F 10:30pm; We P 7:00pm
c/o: Rick Larman (616-956-6120)
4091 Baywood Dr SE, Grand Rapids, MI, 49546
rick@foresthillsbiblechapel.org

Grace & Truth Christian Fellowship
1031 Page NE, Grand Rapids, MI, 49505
Su B 9:30am, M 10:45am; We P/M 7:30pm
note: meets at Creston Christian School
c/o: John Bjorlie (616-364-2767)
3736 Knapp NE, Grand Rapids, MI, 49525
john@bjorlie.net

Northwest Gospel Hall (616-454-2802)
1350 Garfield Ave NW, Grand Rapids, MI, 49504
Su B 9:30am, S 11:15am, G 6:00pm; We M 7:00pm
c/o: Robert Snow (616-785-4096)
5062 Pleasant Creek NE, Comstock Park, MI, 49321
robertsnow@juno.com
alt: Tim Johnson (616-794-4179)

HAZEL PARK

Middle Eastern Bible Fellowship (Arabic)
PO Box 445, Hazel Park, MI, 48030
Su B 1:00pm, M 1:45pm; We M 7:00pm; Fr P/M 7:30pm
c/o: Ata G Mikhael (248-740-9057 or 248-703-6565)
4958 Hubbard Dr, Troy, MI, 48085
atamikhael@earthlink.net

HOLLAND

Gospel Chapel (396-1589)
106 W 26th St, Holland, MI, 49423
Su B/S, M 6:00pm; We P/M 7:00pm
c/o: Pier Wielenga (616-772-4373)
255 N Franklin, Zeeland, MI, 49464

JACKSON
Gospel Hall (517-784-7905)
910 Bennett St, Jackson, MI, 49202
Su B 9:30am, S 11:30am, G 7:00pm; We P/M 7:30pm
c/o: R Douglas Losey (517-787-9169)
3605 Sweetgum Dr, Jackson, MI, 49201
alt: Paul Fouts (517-522-3125)

LAURIUM
Lake Linden Avenue Gospel Hall
Su G, B 10:00am, S 11:15am; We P/M 7:45pm
note: Lake Linden Ave near Florida St
c/o: Charles Savolainen (906-523-4843)
26660 Kuusisto Rd, Lake Linden, MI, 49945

LITTLE LAKE
Little Lake Gospel Chapel (906 346-3066)
M-35, Little Lake, MI, 49833
Su B 9:45am, F 11:00am
c/o: Russell L Westman (906 346-3066)
PO Box 302, Little Lake, MI, 49833

LIVONIA
Stark Road Gospel Hall (734-425-4910)
9280 Stark Rd, Livonia, MI, 48150
www.starkrdgospelhall.com
Su B 9:30am, S/M 11:30am, G 6:00pm; We P/M 7:30pm
note: use point of contact as church's mailing address
c/o: David Vallance (248-446-9346)
21600 Currie Rd, Northville, MI, 48167
davidkv@ameritech.net

MACOMB
Calvary Bible Chapel (586-263-5239)
45690 North Ave, Macomb, MI, 48042
crschroeder@tepse.org
Su B 9:30am, F 11:00am; We P/M 7:00pm
note: meets at Atwood Elem School. AWANA during We P/M
c/o: Michael G Antos (586-992-3822)
14730 Cottonwood Ct, Washington, MI, 48094
alt: Christopher R Schroeder (586-615-6700)

MARNE
Grand Valley Christian (616-677-6175)
12064 Linden Dr, Allendale, MI, 49435
Su B 9:30am, M 11:00am; We P 7:00pm
c/o: Bill Longo (616-892-4389)
Marne, MI, 49435

MESICK

Sherman Gospel Hall (231-885-1738)
102 Sherman St, Mesick, MI, 49668
cspencer@mesickmold.com
Su B 10:00am, S/G 11:30am, M 7:00pm; We P 7:00pm
note: use point of contact as church's mailing address
c/o: Chancy Spencer (231-885-1347)
4773 N 15 Rd, Mesick, MI, 49668
alt: Stuart Thompson (231-885-1402)
stug39@juno.com

MILFORD

Grace Countryside Church
220 Bogie Lake Rd Box 611, Milford, MI
Su B/M
c/o: Thomas G. Lewellen (313-887-3700)
P.O. Box 611, Milford, MI, 48381

MONTAGUE

Friendship Bible Chapel (231-893-0305)
14093 Business US 31, Montague, MI, 49437
www.friendshipbiblechapel.org
john@johnsawin.com
Su B 10:00am, S/F 11:15am; We P/M 7:00pm
note: mailing address: PO Box 124, Montague, MI, 49437
c/o: Ed Burdick (231-893-0305)
6630 Lake Front, Montague, MI, 49437
john@johnsawin.com

OWOSSO

Countryside Gospel Chapel (989-743-3261)
144 N State Rd, Owosso, MI, 48867
Su B 9:30am, F/S 11:00am; We P 7:00pm
c/o: Norman LeCureux (989-723-8376)
215 E Riley Rd, Owosso, MI, 48867
alt: Raymond Fleming (989-743-4095)

PELKIE

Gospel Hall
13550 State Hwy M-38, Pelkie, MI, 49958
Su B 10:00am, S 11:15am; Th G/P
c/o: Samuel M McClung (906-338-2657)
Box 194, Pelkie, MI, 49958

PLYMOUTH

Lake Pointe Bible Chapel (313-420-0515)
42150 Schoolcraft, Plymouth, MI, 48187
Su B 9:00am, S 10:15am, M 11:30am (homes)

UNITED STATES — MICHIGAN

RIVER ROUGE
Bible Assembly (313-841-8022)
329 Beechwood, River Rouge, MI, 48218
Su S 9:45am, B 11:00am, M 11:30am; Tu M 11:00am; We P/M 7:00pm
c/o: Pellam M Love (313-837-7592)
8897 Rosemont, Detroit, MI, 48228

ROCK
Bible Chapel (906-356-6893)
4144 E Maple Rd, Rock, MI, 49880
Su B 10:00am, S 11:00am; Tu M 7:30pm
c/o: Mike Lepisto (906-356-6346)
PO Box 175, Rock, MI, 49880
mlepisto@portup.com

SAGINAW
Madison Street Gospel Hall (989-754-6882)
502 N Porter St, Saginaw, MI 48602
rcd8120@aol.com
Su B 10:00am, S 11:30am, G 6:30pm; We P 7:00pm
c/o: Dr. Robert Dennison (989-652-9553)
360 Groveland Dr., Frankenmuth, MI 48734
rcd8120@aol.com

SAULT STE MARIE
Northland Bible Chapel (705-649-3221)
Sault Ste Marie, MI
Su S 10:00am, M 11:00am, B 6:00pm, M 7:00pm; Th P/M 7:00pm
note: Hwy 17N & 552W
c/o: Stephen Clock (705-649-0687)
RR 2, Goulais River, ON, Canada, P0S 1E0

Sault Ste Marie Assembly (906-235-6241)
801 E Easterday Ave, Sault Ste Marie, MI, 49783
ewallis75@hotmail.com
Su B 9:30am, S 11:00am, G 11:45am; We P 6:30pm
note: use point of contact as church's mailing address
c/o: John Wallis (906-635-5763)
2145 W 5th Ave, Sault Ste Marie, MI, 49783
ewallis75@hotmail.com
alt: Craig Trotter (906-495-7044)
craiganntrotter@centurytel.net

SHERIDAN
Sheridan Bible Chapel
124 N Main St, Sheridan, MI, 48884
Su S/G, B 9:45am; Tu P/M
c/o: Wayne Beard
1693 E Beardsley Rd, Sheridan, MI, 48884

STERLING HEIGHTS

Lakeside Bible Chapel (586-247-5226)
39939 Hayes Rd, Sterling Heights, MI, 48313
www.lbchapel.org
webmaster@lbchapel.org
Su B 9:15am, F 11:00am; We P/M 7:00pm
c/o: David Thurmond (586-247-5226)
39939 Hayes Rd, Sterling Heights, MI, 48313

STURGIS

The Bible Chapel (269-651-3383)
705 E West St, Sturgis, MI 49091
Su B 9:00am, S 10:00am, M 11:00am; We P
c/o: Mark S. Monroe (260-463-2935)
1290 N. 300E, LaGrange, IN 46761
mmpm@isp.com

WARREN

Indian Believers' Gathering
42576 Saddle Ln, Detroit, MI, 48314
note: Sterling Heights, MI
c/o: John M Chacko
42576 Saddle Ln, Sterling Hts, MI, 48314

WILLIAMSTON

Assembly of Christians
3510 Zimmer Rd, Williamston, MI 48895
Su B 10:00am, G/S 12:00pm; We P/M 7:00pm
note: (1/4 mi S of M-43) meets at Zimmer Rd Gospel Hall. Use point of contact as mailing address.
c/o: Richard G. Scherer (517-676-2219)
649 Joan Dr, Mason, MI, 48854
schererrb@yahoo.com

Burkley Road Gospel Hall (517-655-3230)
4021 Burkley Rd, Williamston, MI, 48895
Su B 9:30am, S/G 1:30pm; Tu P/M 6:30pm
note: Burkley Rd & M-43
c/o: Durwood K McCoy (517-655-3230)
130 Germany Rd, Williamston, MI, 48895
dmce_mail@yahoo.com

MINNESOTA

BAUDETTE
Lake Road Chapel (218-634-2873)
734 18th Ave NW, Baudette, MN, 56623
Su B 9:45am, F 11:00am; We P 7:00pm
c/o: Rex Block (218-783-6531)
1420 62nd Ave NW, Williams, MN, 56686
alt: Dan Holen (281-634-1539)

BEMIDJI
Northwoods Gospel Chapel
2520 Great Divide Rd NW, Puposky, MN, 56667
frasers@paulbunyan.net
Su B 9:30am, F 11:00am, S 12:00pm; We P 7:00pm
note: meets in home, 12 miles N of Bemidji. Shared meal usually follows meetings.
c/o: Kent Fraser (218-243-2240)
2520 Great Divide Rd NW, Puposky, MN, 56667
frasers@paulbunyan.net
alt: Jeff Michalicek (218-586-2665)

DULUTH
Duluth Bible Fellowship
313 97th Ave W, Duluth, MN, 55808
Su M/F, B 6:30pm
c/o: Tim Blazevic (218-626-4981)
313 97th Ave W, Duluth, MN, 55808

FRIDLEY
Fridley Gospel Hall (763-780-9151)
5300 6th St NE, Fridley, MN, 55421
jim.brown@usfamily.net
Su B 9:30am, S/M 11:00am, G 11:45am; We P 7:30pm
c/o: Humphrey Duncanson (631-266-3783)
48 Valentine Ave, Huntington, NY, 11743

HINCKLEY
Gospel Hall (320-384-7663)
PO Box 509, Hinckley, MN, 55037
Su B 10:00am, S 11:00am, M 12:00pm; We P 7:30pm
note: 401 Lawler Ave S.
c/o: David Klar (320-245-0559)
609 Hwy 123 W, Sandstone, MN, 55072
djbaklar@pinenet.com

UNITED STATES — MINNESOTA

MINNEAPOLIS

Believers Bible Chapel (763-757-8686)
11024 University Ave NW, Coon Rapids, MN, 55448
www.bbchapel.org
Su B 9:00am, F 11:00am, M 6:00pm; We 7:15pm
c/o: James Upton (651-633-7488)
1639 23rd Ave NW, New Brighton, MN, 55112
jimu@usfamily.net
alt: Chuck Rivers (763-753-8826)

Longfellow Gospel Chapel (612-729-2728)
3012 Longfellow Ave S, Minneapolis, MN, 55407
Su B 9:30am, F 11:00am; We M 7:15pm
c/o: Glen C Ellis (763-572-1379)
4549 5th St NE, Columbia Heights, MN, 55421
glencellis_610@msn.com

Northeast Gospel Chapel (612-781-3541)
2749 Ulysses St NE, Minneapolis, MN, 55418
Su B 9:00am, S 10:25am, G 11:00am, M 6:00pm; We M 7:00pm
c/o: Brad Biddle (651-773-3058)
1847 Kohlman Ave, Maplewood, MN, 55109
bradbiddle@aol.com
alt: Jack Block (763-784-3137)

Plymouth Bible Chapel (763-544-0287)
10605 36th Ave N., Plymouth, MN 55441-2410
Su B 9:00am, S 11:00am, Y 6:30pm; Tu P 7:00pm; We Y 6:30pm
c/o: Ted Gusek (763-535-0195)
3240 Yates Ave N, Crystal, MN 55422

ROCHESTER

Rochester Bible Fellowship
note: This assembly has dissolved, but if you're in the area, I'd love to meet with you.
c/o: Jerome Monsen (507-421-7896)
rdyscribe@juno.com

ROCKFORD

Rockford Bible Church
PO Box 216, Rockford, MN, 55373
Su B 9:00am, M 10:30am, S 6:00pm; We P 6:45pm
note: meets at Riverside Park Comm.Cntr, corner of Main
c/o: Craig Fordahl (612-965-2425)
cafordahl@msn.com
alt: Bill Nibbe (763-658-2007)

ST PAUL

Maryland Bible Chapel (651-776-6393)
606 E Maryland Ave, St Paul, MN, 55130
Su B 9:30am, F 11:00am; We P 7:00pm
c/o: Ted Gliske (651-489-6701)
928 Nebraska Ave W, St Paul, MN, 55117
alt: Bob Upton (651-503-3005)

SUNBURG

Assembly of Christians
211 Isola St, Sunburg, MN, 56289
Su B 10:00am, F 11:15am
note: meetings held in community center
c/o: Ken Arends (320-235-2573)
2176 NE 66th Ave, Willmar, MN, 56201
karends@en-tel.net
alt: David Van Hal (320-366-3541)

VIRGINIA

Virginia Bible Chapel (218-741-4833)
600 South 7th Avenue, Virginia, MN, 55792
Su B 9:30am, S 11:00am; We P 7:00pm
c/o: William Howell (218-865-6241)
5089 Vermillion Trail, Gilbert, MN, 55741
williamh@cpinternet.net
alt: Jerry Brown (218-865-4379)

WABASHA

Hiawatha Bible Chapel (651-565-2977)
907 Hiawatha Dr E, Wabasha, MN, 55981
irv@hbcl.com
wabasha-server.net
Su B 9:20am, S 10:30am, M 7:00pm
c/o: Irving Risch
319 Lawrence Blvd W, Wabasha, MN, 55981
alt: Jerry McMillin (651-565-2238)

WILLMAR

Christians Gathered Together in the Name of the Lord Jesus Christ
Su B 10:00am, M 11:00am, G 7:00pm; We P 7:30pm
note: at East 13th St & Trott
c/o: Ronald C Hagen

WOODBURY

Immanuel Bible Chapel (651-714-8247)
PO Box 25411, Woodbury, MN, 55125
www.immanuelbiblechapel.org
Su B 9:30am, F 11:00am; P 7:00pm
c/o: Bruce Wahlin (651-578-0355)
2977 Leyland Trail, Woodbury, MN, 55125
brucepamela@gmail.com
alt: Kurian Abraham (651-451-2180)
kuriananddaisy@gmail.com

MISSISSIPPI

GREENWOOD

Grace Bible Church (662-453-2936)
801 Sycamore, Greenwood, MS, 38930
Su B 10:30am, M 11:45am; We P/M 7:15pm
c/o: George Whitten (662-455-3286)
310 High St, Greenwood, MS, 38930
gwhitten@netdoor.com

MCCOMB

Maranatha Bible Church (601-684-8665)
530 N Broadway, McComb, MS, 39648
mbcshield@bellsouth.net
Su B, S; M 6:30pm; Th Y 7:00pm; Sa P 7:00am
c/o: Elden Nathan Johnson (601-276-7250)
206 Holly (PO Box 438), Summit, MS, 39666
nracj4@bellsouth.net

MENDENHALL

Mendenhall Bible Church (601-847-3421)
309 Center St, Mendenhall, MS, 39114
Su S 9:30am, M 11:00am, B 6:30pm, M 7:00pm; We P/M 7:00pm
c/o: Artis Fletcher (601-847-3421)
PO Box 368, Mendenhall, MS, 39114

TYLERTOWN

Tylertown Gospel Hall
Oral Church Rd, Tylertown, MS, 39667
Su S 10:00am, B 11:00am, G 6:00pm; We M 7:00pm
c/o: Keith Young (601-268-6802)
1200 Estelle Ave, Hattiesburg, MS, 39402
alt: Ben Lohrbach (228-385-0222)

MISSOURI

AUGUSTA

Augusta Bible Church (314-228-4390)
RR 1 Box 255, Augusta, MO, 63348
Su S, B 9:45am; We M

BROOKFIELD

Brookfield Christian Fellowship (660-258-2255)
409 S State St, Brookfield, MO 64628
Su B 9:00am, S 10:15am, F 11:00am, P 7:00pm; We M 7:30pm
note: P.O. Box 290, Brookfield, MO 64628
c/o: Herb Huck (660-258-5679)
201 Sycamore Dr, Brookfield, MO, 64628

CAPE GIRARDEAU

Cape Bible Chapel (573-334-5948)
2911 Kage Rd, Cape Girardeau, MO, 63701
Su B 8:30am, M 9:15am, S 10:45am; We P/M 7:00pm
c/o: Larry Young (573-243-7007)
1505 Kimbeland Dr, Jackson, MO, 63755

FENTON

Fenton Crossing Bible Chapel (636-326-4769)
855 Gregory Lane, St Louis, MO, 63026
Su B 9:30am, S 11:15am; We Y 7:00pm; Th L/C 6:30pm
c/o: Steven L Leary (636-677-5204 or 314-362-3700)
740 Heatherstone Dr, High Ridge, MO, 63049
learys@dcm.wustl.edu
alt: Kevin Fitzgerald (314-323-7538)

IRONTON

Emmanuel Bible Fellowship (573-546-3731)
Hwy 72 East, Ironton, MO, 63650
Su B 10:00am, F 11:15am; We P 7:00pm
c/o: David Isom (573-546-3731)
PO Box 4, Ironton, MO, 63650

JACKSON

Jackson Gospel Chapel (573-334-5350)
4000 State Hwy Y, Cape Girardeau, MO, 63755
Su B 9:45am, S 11:00am; We P/M 7:00pm (homes)
c/o: Bobby G Clark (573-335-3784)
3536 Quayle Run, Cape Girardeau, MO, 63755

JEFFERSON CITY

Jefferson City Bible Chapel (573-893-3977)
2804 Sue Dr, Jefferson City, MO 65109
www.jcbiblechapel.org
jcbiblechapel@gmail.com
Su B 9:30am, F 11:00am; Mo C&Y 6:30pm; We P 6:15pm; Th L 9:30am
c/o: Jim Allan (573-636-8397)
846 Crestmere Ct., Jefferson City, MO 65109
terallan1@mchsi.com
alt: Charles A. Ridgway (573-291-0377)

KANSAS CITY

Kansas City Gospel Hall (816-924-6346)
4603 E Linwood Blvd, Kansas City, MO, 64128
Su M 9:30am, S 10:20am, B 11:00am, G 7:00pm; We P 7:00pm
c/o: William L Jackson (816-228-3591)
1613 NW Ashland Place, Blue Springs, MO, 64015
alt: Alan Scott (8167391686)
alanesther@earthlink.net

Spruce Hill Bible Chapel (816-763-7167)
11501 E Bannister Rd, Kansas City, MO, 64134
www.sprucehillbiblechapelc.org / biyou@swbell.net
Su B 9:30am, F 11:00am; We P/M 7:00pm
c/o: Pete Youngberg (913-469-6287)
11512 Foster St, Overland Park, KS, 66210
biyou@swbell.net
alt: Kevin Hoesch (816-942-7512)

MARBLE HILL

Bible Chapel (573-238-3513)
Marble Hill, MO, 63764
Su B 9:30am, S 10:45am; We P/M 7:00pm
note: Vine & Poplar
c/o: Ben Burford (573-238-2338)
PO Box 227, Marble Hill, MO, 63764

O'FALLON

Lake Charles Bible Chapel (636-994-5884)
608 Lorene Dr, O'Fallon, MO, 63366
Su B 9:30am, S/F 11:00am; We P 7:00pm
note: use point of contact as church's mailing address
c/o: Tim McNeal (636-583-0727)
4817 St Louis Rock Rd, Villa Ridge, MO, 63089
tmcneal@netscape.com
alt: Les Grimes (636-294-5884)

SEDALIA

Ecclesia Community Bible Church
900 E 9th St, Sedalia, MO, 65301
Su S 9:30am, B 10:30am
c/o: PC Thomas (816-826-9988)
23260 Hwy B, Sedalia, MO, 65301

SPRINGFIELD

Southeast Bible Chapel (417-864-6213)
1051 S Crutcher, Springfield, MO, 65804
www.southeastbiblechapel.com
southeastbiblechapel@yahoo.com
Su B 9:30am, F 11:00am; We P 7:00pm
c/o: Walter Cary (417-882-5279)
3829 W Kingsley, Springfield, MO, 65807
caryrus@juno.com
alt: Ross Ragland (417-883-5990)
rossandlu@juno.com

ST CHARLES

Grace Christian Fellowship
4762 Central School Rd, St Charles, MO, 63304
Su B 10:00am, S 11:30am; Tu M 7:00pm
c/o: Jeffrey Wilson (314-928-7053)
4762 Central School Rd, Saint Charles, MO, 63304

ST LOUIS

Christian Fellowship Community Church
4964 W Florissant Ave, St Louis, MO, 63115
Su S 9:30am, M 11:00am, B 12:30pm; We P/M 7:00pm
c/o: Willie Johnson (314-383-3035 or 383-2402)
4964 W Florissant Ave, Saint Louis, MO, 63115

Emmaus Bible Chapel (314-521-1099)
900 Highmont Dr, St Louis, MO, 63135
www.emmausbiblechapel.org
Su B 9:00am, S 10:00am, F 11:00am; We P 7:00pm
note: Ferguson
c/o: Raymond Baumann (314-837-0543)
7362 Naples Dr, Hazelwood, MO, 63042

Maplewood Bible Chapel (314-647-3208)
7138 Southwest, St Louis, MO, 63143
www.maplewoodbiblechapel.org
Su B 9:00am, F 11:00am; Th M 7:00pm
c/o: Charles W Klein (314-966-5152)
909 N Woodlawn, Kirkwood, MO, 63122
packlein@sbcglobal.net

Saint Louis Gospel Assembly (314-993-9628)
4201 Athlone Ave, St Louis, MO, 63116
Su S 9:30am, B 11:00am, G 12:00pm; We G 7:30pm
c/o: Ralph McCloud (314-383-7969 or 261-4719)
8000 Braddock, University City, MO, 63130

South Side Bible Chapel (314-849-3425)
10255 Musick Rd, St Louis, MO, 63123
www.vcsmo.org
chapel@vcsmo.org
Su B 9:00am, M/S 10:30am; Th C/Y 6:30pm
c/o: Doug Traxler (314-843-8688)
10759 Roxanna Dr, St Louis, MO, 63128
chapel@vcsmo.org

The Church of Our Lord Jesus Christ
7902 Dale Ave, St Louis, MO, 63117
Su S/M, B 1:30pm; Tu M 6:30pm
c/o: Untra Northern
6121 Bermuda Dr, St Louis, MO, 63135

Walnut Park Bible Chapel
5547 Lillian Ave, St Louis, MO, 63120
Su S 10:00am, G 11:00am, M 6:30pm; Th P
c/o: George E Norris (314-524-7234)
1320 Lang Dr, Saint Louis, MO, 63135

West End Gospel Hall
4400 Aldine, St Louis, MO, 63113
Su S 10:00am, B 11:00am, G 8:00pm; Mo M 8:00pm; Tu G 8:00pm; Th P 8:00pm
c/o: Adolphus Hardy Jr (314-382-3955)
4855 Margaretta, St Louis, MO, 63115

UNION

Believers Bible Chapel (636-583-4998)
2032 Hwy 50 W, Union, MO, 63084-2811
www.BelieversBibleChapel.org
bbc@believersbiblechapel.org
Su B 9:30am, M 10:30am, F 11:30am; We P 7:00pm
c/o: Phil Smith (636-583-4998)
1005 Radio Tower Rd, Union, MO, 63084
judysmith1005@affinity4.net
alt: Ken Bowles (636-583-5975)
ken.dl5bk@gmail.com

UNIVERSITY CITY

University City Bible Chapel
1252 North & South Rd, University City, MO, 63130
Su B 9:30am, S 10:30am, M 11:15am, P 7:00pm (Th)
c/o: Ted Jackson (314-895-4439)
tdyj@msn.com

VALLEY PARK

Valley Park Chapel (314-825-2410)
800 Vest, St Louis, MO, 63088
Su B, M 10:45am, B 6:30pm
c/o: Daryl J Lynn
4900 Walnut Grove Dr, Villa Ridge, MO, 63089

WASHINGTON

Bible Truth Christian Fellowship (573-237-3422)
PO Box 2011, Washington, MO, 63090
Su B 9:30am, M 10:35am, S 11:30am; We M 7:00pm
note: 4247 Old Hwy 100
c/o: John Witte (573-237-2972)
105 Mary Hammack, New Haven, MO, 63068

MONTANA

HELENA
Community Bible Fellowship (406-227-5944)
1225 Fern Rd, Helena, MT, 59602
Su B 9:30am, P 10:15am, F 11:00am; We Y 7:00pm
note: N Montana Ave & Fern Rd
c/o: Walt Kerttula (406-227-5944)
2975 Elkview Dr, East Helena, MT, 59635
wmkerttula@netzero.com

PLAINS
Plains Bible Chapel (406-826-3118)
PO Box 942, Plains, MT, 59859
Su S 9:30am, M 11:00am, M 6:00pm, B 12:00pm; Th M 7:00pm
note: 243 Combest Creek Rd
c/o: Joel Banham (406-826-3360)
PO Box 942, Plaines, MT, 59859

STEVENSVILLE
Bible Chapel
510 Buck St, Stevensville, MT, 59870
Su P 9:00am, B 9:45am, S 11:00am
c/o: Jonathan Luibrand (406-777-3784 or 777-5333)
651 Stevi Airport Rd, Stevensville, MT, 59870

NEBRASKA

BURWELL
Gospel Hall (346-5021)
420 Grand Ave, Burwell, NE, 68823
Su S 10:00am, B 11:00am, G 7:30pm; We P 7:30pm
c/o: Laddie Hulinsky (308-346-4194)
RR 1 Box 127, Burwell, NE, 68823

LINCOLN
Hollywood Heights Chapel (402-466-8016)
936 El Avado Ave, Lincoln, NE, 68504
kratzeron@aol.com
Su B 9:30am, F 11:00am; We P 7:00pm
c/o: Ron Kratzer (402-488-7062)
6900 Saylor Circle, Lincoln, NE, 68506
kratzeron@aol.com
alt: Matt Van Essen (402-742-7790)
vanessen@juno.com

OMAHA
Keystone Bible Chapel (402-397-1714)
7840 Maple St, Omaha, NE, 68134
Su B 9:30am, S 11:00am, M 6:00pm; We P 7:30pm
c/o: Chris Downe (402-573-9291)
13440 N 73rd Plaza, Omaha, NE 68122

Northwest Bible Fellowship (402-572-1787)
4905 N 96th St, Omaha, NE, 68134
www.northwestbiblefellowship.org
Su B 9:30am, S/F 11:00am; We P 7:00pm
c/o: Scott Nordstrom (402-573-5432)
11401 Pawnee Rd, Omaha, NE, 68142
dsnordstrom@juno.com
alt: Dale Gleason (402-496-4233)
dalegleason@hotmail.com

Omaha Gospel Hall (402-571-5983)
5622 N 69th St, Omaha, NE, 68104
Su B 9:30am, M 11:15am, G 7:30pm; We P 7:30pm
c/o: Mark Van Der Hart (402-699-0621)
20206 Amelia Ave, Elkhorn, NE, 68022
markvdh@att.net

PALISADE
Bible Chapel
207 S Osborn St, Palisade, NE, 69040
c/o: Ray D Ridlen (308-285-3413)
112 N Parker, Palisade, NE, 69040

NEVADA

LAS VEGAS
Centennial Hills Bible Fellowship (702-645-1132)
7511 Cedargulf Ave, Las Vegas, NV, 89131
greenwd1@cox.net
Su B 9:45am, F 11:00am
note: home meeting
c/o: Ed Greenwood (702-645-1132)
7511 Cedargulf Ave, Las Vegas, NV, 89131
greenwd1@cox.net

SPARKS
Sagebrush Bible Chapel
3290 Lucerne Way, Reno, NV, 89431
Su M (call for times), B 2:00pm
note: Sparks
c/o: Wayne Sommer (775-359-3078)
3290 Lucerne Way, Reno, NV, 89431

NEW HAMPSHIRE

CONCORD
Concord Bible Fellowship (603-228-3344)
25 Rockingham St, Concord, NH, 03301
Su B 9:45am, F 11:00am; We M 7:00pm
c/o: James Blanchard (603-224-4989)
8 Conant Dr, Concord, NH, 03301
alt: Dale Gagnon (603-228-8721)
degagnon@earthlink.net

HILLSBORO
Valley Bible Chapel (603-464-3511)
14 W Main St, Hillsboro, NH, 03244
www.valleybiblechapel.com
chapel@mcttelecom.com
Su B 9:00am, S/F 10:00am; We C/M 6:30pm
c/o: Doug Henderson (603-446-3588)
236 Rice Brook Dr, Stoddard, NH, 03464

LANGDON
Berean Gospel Assembly (603-835-6189)
137 Winch Hill Rd, Langdon, NH, 03602
Su B 9:30am, P 10:40am, F 11:00am; Th M 7:00pm
c/o: Robert Gentile (603-835-6189)
alt: Alan Chidester (603-495-1415)
chidester5@gsinet.net

WALPOLE
Grace Bible Fellowship of Walpole (603-756-3908)
Am Legion #77 Hall, Walpole, NH, 03608
www.gbf4hisglory.com
sanc@sover.net
Su B 9:15am, F 10:45am
c/o: David Waldmann (802-875-3515)
2672 Flamstead Rd, Chester, VT, 05143
dw@vfh.us
alt: Keith Sanctuary (603-756-4837)

NEW JERSEY

BARRINGTON
Barrington Gospel Hall (856-546-6901)
14 Barrington Ave, Barrington, NJ, 08007
www.barringtongospelhall.org
ahigginsmd@msn.com
Su B 10:00am, G 7:00pm, S/M 12:15pm; We P/M 7:30pm
c/o: A.J. Higgins MD (856-547-5730)
803 Station Ave, Haddon Hts, NJ, 08035
ahigginsmd@msn.com
alt: John Amadio (856-547-4990)

UNITED STATES — NEW JERSEY

BAYVILLE
Cedar Creek Community Church (732-269-6204)
370 Nixon Circle, Bayville, NJ, 08721
Su S 9:00am, B 10:00am; We M (homes)
c/o: Ron Fraser
370 Nixon Circle, Bayville, NJ, 08721

BELMAR
Fifth Avenue Chapel (732-681-5430)
Belmar, NJ, 07719
www.fifthavenuechapel.org
Su S, B 9:15am, M 6:00pm; Th P/M 7:15pm
note: 5th Ave & B St
c/o: Peter Bartlett (732-531-1269)
418 Redmond Ave, Oakhurst, NJ, 07755

BERKELEY HEIGHTS
Mountain Ridge Bible Chapel (908-464-2678)
763 Mountain Ave, Berkeley Heights, NJ, 07922
www.mtridge.org
secretary@mtridge.org
Su B 9:15am, F/S 11:00am, M 6:00pm; Tu P/M 7:30pm; We L 8:00pm; Fr Y 7:30pm
c/o: Douglas E. Tremper (908-685-2064)
207 Love Rd, Bridgewater, NJ, 08807
correspondent@mtridge.org
alt: Chapel Secretary

CAMDEN
Pennsauken (Camden) Gospel Hall (856-662-1201)
6530 Caroline Ave, Pennsauken, NJ, 08109
Su B 10:00am, G 6:00pm, S 12:30pm; We P/M 7:30pm
note: At Rt 38 near Browning Rd
c/o: David A Curran (856-429-4443)
326 Windsor Ave, Haddonfield, NJ, 08033
dacurran@aol.com

CHERRY HILL
Community Gospel Chapel
20 Bergen Ave, Voorhees, NJ, 08043
Su B/S, M 6:00pm; We M
c/o: Randall S Robinson (609-566-7494)
2004 Champlain Dr, Voorhees, NJ, 08043

EAST ORANGE
Bethel Gospel Chapel (973-678-9086)
8-10 Grant Ave, East Orange, NJ, 07017
Su B 9:30am, F 11:00am, S 12:30pm, L 6:00pm (3rd); Th P 8:00pm (1st & 2nd), M 8:00pm (3rd & 4th); Fr Y 7:30pm (1st & 3rd)
c/o: Sebert Kelly (973-674-1124)
18 Roosevelt Ave, East Orange, NJ, 07017
alt: Michael Fields (973-253-0098)

UNITED STATES — NEW JERSEY

Brighton Avenue Bible Chapel (973-678-0383)
288 Brighton Ave, East Orange, NJ, 07017
Su B 9:30am, M 11:00am, S 11:15am, G 6:00pm; We P/M 7:30pm
c/o: James Panulla (973-743-5842)

ELIZABETH

Grace Chapel (732-669-9596)
357 Morris Ave, Elizabeth, NJ, 07208
Su B 9:15am, S 10:50am, M 7:30pm (Gatherings in Span.)
c/o: Bill Kother (732-669-9596)
1066 Stone St, Rahway, NJ, 07065
willienancy@comcast.net
alt: Albert Smith (Spanish & English) (732-316-7662)

FANWOOD

Terrill Road Bible Chapel (908-322-4055)
535 Terrill Rd, Fanwood, NJ, 07023
trbc.correspondent@gmail.com
Su B 9:15am, S/F 11:00am, M 6:00pm; We P 7:30pm; Th L 9:15am;
Fr C 7:00pm
c/o: Carl Foresti (908-222-2156)
321 S Plainfield Ave, South Plainfield, NJ, 07080
carl.foresti@gmail.com
alt: Allan Wilks (908-322-1929)
allan@research.att.com

Woodside Chapel (908-889-2375)
5 Morse Ave, Fanwood, NJ, 07023
www.woodsidechapel.org
Su B 9:30am, S 11:00am
c/o: Alan Schetelich (908-580-1279)
8107 Fellowship Rd, Basking Ridge, NJ, 07920

HAMILTON

Hamilton Bible Fellowship (609-585-7946)
Whatley Rd, Hamilton, NJ, 08620
Su B 9:15am, F/S 10:30am; We M 7:00pm
note: use point of contact as church's mailing address
c/o: Thomas Freeman (609-585-1835)
25 Dailey Dr, Hamilton, NJ, 08620
tfreeman3@juno.com
alt: Harry Neil (609-890-0450)

HILLSBOROUGH

South Branch Bible Fellowship
1321 Orchard Dr, Hillsborough, NJ, 08844
www.southbranchbible.org / sbbf@juno.com
Su B 9:00am, G 10:05am, S 11:45am; Th P/M 7:30pm
c/o: Alan Coburn (908-369-7746)
1321 Orchard Dr, Hillsborough, NJ, 08844
sbbf@juno.com
alt: Alan Coburn (908-772-7213)
afcoburn@juno.com

UNITED STATES — NEW JERSEY 87

JERSEY CITY
Grace Gospel Chapel (201-795-2492)
877 Summit Ave, Jersey City, NJ, 07307
Su B/S, M 6:00pm; Tu P/M 8:00pm; Fr M 8:00pm; Sa G (2nd)
c/o: Jonathan Yearwood (908-396-3425)

KEARNY
Kearny Bible Chapel (201-991-2339)
50-52 Quincy Ave, Kearny, NJ, 07032
Su B 9:15am, S 11:00am, G 6:00pm; We M 7:30pm
c/o: Jay Allen (201-991-6957)
41 Madison St, No Arlington, NJ, 07031

KENILWORTH
Kenilworth Gospel Chapel (908-272-6131)
103 S 23rd St, Kenilworth, NJ, 07033
www.kenilworthgospel.org
Su B 9:15am, S/F 11:00am; We P 7:00pm; Fr C/Y 7:00pm
c/o: Donald Dunkerton (908-709-1373)
112 Cranford Ave, Cranford, NJ, 07016
the_dunkertons@yahoo.com

LINWOOD
Linwood Gospel Chapel (609-653-8684)
900 New Road (Rt 9), Linwood, NJ, 08221
www.linwoodgospelchapel.org
Su B 9:30am, F 11:00am; We P 7:30pm
c/o: Robert Bateman (609-927-2406)
639 Sixth St, Somers Point, NJ, 08244
alt: Glenn Wagner (609-399-6516)

LIVINGSTON
Livingston Gospel Hall (973-535-1485)
405 E Mount Pleasant Ave, Livingston, NJ, 07039
Su B 9:30am, S 11:15am, G 12:45pm; Tu P/M 7:45pm
c/o: Allan Valvano (973-377-7839)
31 Townsend Dr, Florham Park, NJ, 07932
allan.valvano@paymedia.net

LONG BRANCH
Long Branch Gospel Hall (732-229-5805)
653 Art St, Long Branch, NJ, 07740
Su B 10:00am, S 11:30am, G 6:00pm; We P/M 7:00pm
note: off Grand Ave uptown
c/o: Paul Grace (732-229-0377)
50 N 5th Ave, Long Branch, NJ, 07740

MAPLEWOOD
Maplewood Bible Chapel (973-761-6430)
127 Burnett Ave, Maplewood, NJ, 07040
Su B 9:00am; Tu P/M 7:45pm; Fr C/Y 7:15pm
note: Burnett & Lexington Ave
c/o: Beresford Ellis (973-761-6430)

MARMORA

Marmora Gospel Chapel (609-390-0066)
22 Lyndhurst Rd, Marmora, NJ, 08223
Su B 9:30am, S 11:00am; Tu P/M 7:30pm
note: off 34th St from Ocean City
c/o: Norman Henry (609-390-3072)
PO Box 708, Marmora, NJ, 08223

MIDDLESEX

Middlesex Chapel (732-968-4179)
100 Fairfield Ave, Middlesex, NJ 08846
www.MiddlesexChapel.com
contact@middlesexchapel.com
Su S/B 9:15am, F 11:00am; Tu M 8:00pm
note: off of Bound Brook Rd
c/o: Martin Gallacher (908-526-2289)
384 Garretson Rd, Bridgewater, NJ, 08807

MIDLAND PARK

The Gospel Hall (201-447-0654)
61 Prospect St, Midland Park, NJ, 07432
www.midlandparkgospelhall.org
midlandparkgospelhall@gmail.com
Su B 10:00am, S 11:45am, G 6:00pm; Th P/M 8:00pm
c/o: Henry T Carmichael (973-427-2072)
100 Rock Rd Apt 92, Hawthorne, NJ, 07506
midlandparkgospelhall@gmail.com

NEWARK

Calvary Bible Chapel
309 Lyons Ave, Newark, NJ, 07112
Su B 9:00am, S 10:15am, M 11:15am; We M 8:00pm

PALISADES PARK

Central Bible Chapel (201-944-6760)
14 W Central Blvd, Palisades Park, NJ, 07650
Su B 9:15am, S 11:00am, G 6:00pm; We P/M 7:45pm
c/o: Stephen Swaim (201-967-2114)
435 Central Park Dr, New Milford, NJ, 07646

PRINCETON

Carter Road Bible Chapel (609-924-4638)
193 Carter Rd, Princeton, NJ, 08540
Su B 9:30am, S 11:00am; We M 7:30pm, Fr C 7.00pm
note: use point of contact as church's mailing address
c/o: Elwood L. Matlack (609-587-9054)
76 Mark Twain Dr, Hamilton, NJ, 08690-2155
ematlack@verizon.net
alt: Ron Marchant (215-364-2632)
ron.marchant@verizon.net

UNITED STATES — NEW JERSEY

RED BANK
Bethel Bible Chapel (732-741-1331)
480 W Front St, Red Bank, NJ, 07701
Su B 9:30am, F 11:00am, M 7:00pm; We P 7:00pm; Th L 9:30am
c/o: Robert Billings (732-758-8463)
167 Manor Dr, Red Bank, NJ, 07701
rebillings@juno.com

RUTHERFORD
Rutherford Bible Chapel (201-933-1225)
PO Box 5, Rutherford, NJ, 07070
www.rchapel.org
rbc161@gmail.com
Su B 9:30am, F/S 11:00am, S 6:00pm; Tu P 8:00pm; Fr Y 7:30pm
note: 161 W Passaic Ave
c/o: Ronald H Rynd (201-939-5296)
40 Ivy Place, Rutherford, NJ, 07070
rhrynd@aol.com
alt: Gerard DeMatteo (201-933-1225)

SILVERTON
Bethany Bible Chapel (732-255-3494)
2341 Church Rd, Toms River, NJ, 08753
Su B 9:15am, S/F 11:00am
note: use point of contact as church's mailing address
c/o: Charles Myers (732-451-9444)
32 Spring Valley Dr, Lakewood, NJ, 08701-7508
alt: Jim Bechtle (702-255-3605)

SOUTH PLAINFIELD
Cedarcroft Bible Chapel (908-756-8244)
1715 Kenyon Ave, South Plainfield, NJ, 07080
www.cedarcroft.org
Su B 9:00am, S 10:30am, F 11:15am, M 6:00pm; Tu M 7:30pm;
We M 7:30pm; Th L 9:30am; Fr L 10:00am, Y (evening)
c/o: Kingsley Baehr (908-757-7598)
1512 Kenyon Ave, South Plainfield, NJ, 07080
kbaehr@verizon.net

TENAFLY
Grace Chapel (201-568-1917)
Tenafly, NJ
Su B 9:30am, S 11:00am, M 6:00pm; We B 9:50am (Korean), M 11:00am,
P 7:45pm, M 8:30pm
note: W Clinton Ave & Tenafly Rd
c/o: Henry Wortche Jr (201-385-6348)
191 Porter Ave, Bergenfield, NJ, 07621

UNION CITY
Bethel Gospel Chapel
3124 Summit Ave, Union City, NJ, 07087
Su B 9:30am, S 11:00am, G 6:00pm; Tu P/M 8:00pm

UNITED STATES — NEW JERSEY

WASHINGTON TOWNSHIP
Valley Bible Chapel (201-664-1432)
56 Pascack Rd, Washington Township, NJ, 07676
www.valleybiblechapel.org
bobhayes@valleybiblechapel.org
Su B 9:45am, F/S 11:00am, Y 5:30pm, M 6:00pm; Tu L 9:30pm;
Th P 7:30pm, M 8:00pm; Fr Y 7:30pm
c/o: Bob Hayes (973-423-2803)
15 Goffle Hill Rd, Hawthorne, NJ, 07506
bobhayes@valleybiblechapel.org
alt: Ken Biswurm (201-652-7257)

WESTHAMPTON
Willingboro Christian Assembly
Willingboro, NJ
Su B 9:00am, S 9:45am, M 11:00am; Tu P/M 7:00pm
note: meets at Burlington Girl Scout Bldg Beverly Rd
c/o: Raymond Hudson
175 Somerset Dr, Willingboro, NJ, 08046

NEW MEXICO

ALBUQUERQUE
Albuquerque Gospel Hall (505-881-0294)
3305 Aztec Rd NE, Albuquerque, NM, 87110
abqgospelhall@aol.com
Su S 9:45am, B 11:00am, G 7:30pm; We P 7:30pm
note: use point of contact as church's mailing address
c/o: Duane Pickett (505-883-0464)
3554 Colorado St NE, Albuquerque, NM, 87110
abqgospelhall@aol.com
alt: Chuck Walker (505-293-1670)
chuckwalker43@aol.com

Garfield Gospel Chapel (505-266-2083)
2406 Garfield SE, Albuquerque, NM, 87106
Su B 9:00am, S 10:30am, M 11:00am; We P/M 7:15pm
c/o: Alan Lennox (505-265-8435)
8005 Kathryn SE, Albuquerque, NM, 87108

BAYARD
Believers' Assembly (505-537-7075)
616 Fahey St, Bayard, NM, 88023
jimrosa@silvercity-nm.com
Su B 9:30am, S 11:30am, M 6:00pm
note: 8 miles east of Silver City
c/o: Jim Rosa (505-537-7075)
616 Fahey St, Bayard, NM, 88023
jimrosa@silvercity-nm.com
alt: Frank Avallone (505-388-4672)

CLOVIS
Clovis Gospel Chapel
1128 S Tennessee, Clovis, NM, 88101
Su B 9:00am, S 10:15am, G 11:00am; We P 7:00pm
c/o: John Metler (505-762-2645)
410 Weatherford St, Clovis, NM, 88101

LAS CRUCES
Bethel Bible Fellowship Inc (505-523-9227)
3890 Stern Dr, Las Cruces, NM, 88001
www.zianet.com/bethelbf
bethelbf@zianet.com
Su B 9:30am, S 11:15am; Tu L 9:30am; We M 6:00am, P 7:00pm
c/o: James Bailey (505-521-3199)
4932 Modoc Trail, Las Cruces, NM, 88011
alt: Sharon Garrison (505-525-1644)

LOS ALAMOS
Los Alamos Christian Fellowship (505-662-4570)
PO Box 1108, Los Alamos, NM, 87544
Su M 10:00am, B 11:00am; We P 7:00pm
note: 2117-B 43rd St
c/o: James H Patterson (505-662-4570)
2117-B 43rd St, Los Alamos, NM, 87544
alt: Jack Jacobson (505-662-5847)

RIO RANCHO
Rio Rancho Bible Chapel (505-896-2915)
1728 Abrazo Rd, Rio Rancho, NM, 87124
rrbc@att.net
Su B 10:00am, G/S 11:15am
note: formerly named Believers Bible Fellowship
c/o: Michael A Campbell (505-896-2915)
2106 Spruce Needle Rd, Rio Rancho, NM, 87124
rrbc@att.net

NEW YORK

ALFRED
Alfred Assembly of Christians
Alfred, NY, 14802
lookup@frontiernet.net
Su B 9:30am, F 11:00am; Fr M 8:00pm
note: Gothic Chapel, corner of Ford & Sayles;
mailing address, PO Box 510, Alfred, NY, 14804
c/o: Thomas Steere (607-276-6380)
343 State Rt 21, Hornell, NY, 14843-9613

BARRYVILLE

Hillside Gospel Chapel (845-557-6710)
326 Van Tuyl Rd, Barryville, NY, 12719
Su B 9:45am, M 11:00am
c/o: John Ackerman (845-386-5308)
235 Drake Rd, Middletown, NY, 10940

BINGHAMTON

Twin Tiers Bible Fellowship
131 Front St, Binghamton, NY, 13905
Su B 9:30am, S 11:00am; We P 7:00pm
note: meets at American Civic Assoc
c/o: Sus Narita (607-772-0756)
5 Riverside Dr #802, Binghamton, NY, 13905
snpstb@attglobal.net

BLASDELL

Blasdell Gospel Chapel (716-826-5110)
88 Arthur Ave, Blasdell, NY, 14219
lehjim@aol.com
Su B 9:30am, S 11:00am, M 7:00pm; Th P 7:30pm
note: 8 mi S exit 56 I-90
c/o: James W Lehmann (716-823-9873)
3975 Delmar Ave, Blasdell, NY, 14219
lehjim@aol.com
alt: Jason Kelly (716-822-0478)

BRONX

Capilla Evangelica del Bronx (Bronx Gospel Chapel) (347-994-0232)
1662 Parker St, Bronx, NY, 10462
Su S 11:15am, G 12:00pm; Tu L 10:30am, P 8:00pm; Th M 8:00pm
note: The above phone number will ring in the houses of all three elders.
c/o: Claudio Viery (718-295-1522)
2414 Creston Ave. Apt. 10, Bronx, NY, 10468
alt: Danilo Perez Jr. (201-694-2813) or Luis Cano Sr. (718-877-0697)
dprpap@hotmail.com or Luis.cano@cebronx.org

Emmaus Bible Chapel (718-655-8577)
1250 East Gun Hill Rd, Bronx, NY, 10469
www.emmausbiblechapel.com
info@emmausbiblechapel.com
Su B 9:00am, M 10:00am, S 11:45am; We P 8:00pm
note: 1250 E Gunhill Rd
c/o: Herbert Locke (718-324-7326)
4090 DeReimer Ave, Bronx, NY, 10466
hlocke@emmausbiblechapel.com
alt: David Foster (718-379-6415)

Indian Brethren Assembly (Malayalam) (718-881-4620)
3241 White Plains Rd, New York, NY, 10467
mattackalms@yahoo.com
Su B 9:00am, S 11:45am, M 12:30pm; Sa L 2:30pm, Y 5:00pm, G 7:00pm
c/o: M.S. Mathew (914-946-0530)
2 Secor Glen Road, Hartsdale, NY, 10530
mattackalms@yahoo.com

BROOKLYN

Asamblea Evangelica Inc (718-384-5250)
219 Lee Ave, Brooklyn, NY, 11206
Su B, S 11:30am, G 7:00pm; Tu P 8:00pm; Fr M 8:00pm
c/o: Rafael A Fraden (718-441-0182)
94-11 129th St, Richmond Hill, NY, 11419

Bethany Chapel (718-469-4333)
204 Fenimore St, Brooklyn, NY, 11225
Su S, B 10:45am, G 7:00pm; We M 8:00pm

Bethany Gospel Chapel (718-922-1234)
521 Thomas S Boyland St, Brooklyn, NY, 11212
Su B 10:30am, M 11:45am; Tu M 8:30pm; Fr P 8:00pm
note: Bethany Christian Grade School at same address

Brooklyn Believers Chapel (718-435-1860)
5801 13th Ave, Brooklyn, NY, 11219
Su S, B 10:00am
c/o: Anthony Sgroi
5801 13th Ave, Brooklyn, NY, 11219

Brooklyn Gospel Chapel
17 E 7th St, Brooklyn, NY, 11228
Su B 10:00am; Tu P/M 8:00pm

Good Tidings Gospel Hall (718-467-5037)
345 Malcolm X Blvd, Brooklyn, NY, 11233
gtidings@integrity.com
Su G 10:00am, B 11:30am, S 1:30pm; Tu M 8:00pm; Fr P 8:00pm
c/o: Patson Agard (718-649-1073)
908 Cleveland St, Brooklyn, NY, 11208
patagard@aol.com

New Life Community Church
8125 Glenwood Road, Brooklyn, NY
Su S 9:45am, B 11:30am; Tu P/M 7:30pm
c/o: New Life (718-444-3765 or 756-8485)
972 E 54th St, Brooklyn, NY, 11234

Spanish Gospel Hall (718-456-2442)
143-45 Evergreen Ave, Brooklyn, NY, 11221
Su B, S 11:30am, G 7:00pm; Tu P 8:00pm; Th M 8:00pm
note: cnr Troutman St
c/o: Henry Sanchez
76-15 58 Rd, Elmhurst, NY, 11373

BUFFALO

Cold Springs Bible Chapel (716-883-8073)
100 Northland Ave, Buffalo, NY, 14208
Su B, S 10:30am; G 11:30am; Tu P/M 7:00pm
c/o: Otis C Tillman (716-883-5327)
PO Box 134, 461 Masten Ave, Buffalo, NY, 14209

CLIFTON PARK

Northway Bible Chapel (518-371-7556)
PO Box 572, Clifton Park, NY, 12065
www.cliftonpark.org/ecommunity/northwaybible
northwaybiblechapel@yahoo.com
Su B 9:30am, F/S 10:45am; We P/M 7:00pm
note: Moe & Par del Rio Roads
c/o: Mike Dore (518-584-9394)
4 Melanie Dr, Saratoga Springs, NY, 12866
dorehouse@juno.com
alt: Dominick Capuano (518-664-7434)

CORONA

Capilla Evangelica (718-592-4204)
110-64 Corona Ave, Corona, NY, 11368
Su B 9:30am, S 11:30am; We M 8:00pm; Fr P 8:00pm
c/o: Miguel Castillo (718-441-7606)
PO Box 680451, Corona, NY, 11368
mymcast@aol.com

Galilee Gospel Chapel (718-335-4436)
102-05 35th Ave, Corona, NY, 11368
Su B 9:00am, S 11:30am, G 11:45am; Fr P 8:30pm
c/o: Geoffrey Daniels (718-429-0289)
102-05 35th Ave, Corona, NY, 11368

EAST AURORA

Gospel Hall (716-655-4071)
cnr Emery & Boies Rds, East Aurora, NY, 14052
Su B 10:30am, G 7:30pm, S 12:00pm; We P/M 7:30pm
c/o: David Boies (716-652-6935)
7357 Boies Rd, West Falls, NY, 14170
alt: Joe Smith (716-537-9302)

ELMONT

India Gospel Assembly (516-775-6846)
439 Meacham Ave, Elmont, NY, 10003
Su B 9:45am, M 11:30am, S 12:30pm; Sa P 7:30pm
c/o: Samuel Varghese (516-833-7796)
141 Schley Ave, Albertson, NY 11507
alt: Abraham George (718-347-4821)

FLUSHING

Hillcrest Gospel Chapel (718-591-8511)
158-48 77th Ave, Flushing, NY, 11366
Su B 9:30am, G 10:30am, S 12:30pm; Fr P 8:00pm
c/o: Victor Gill (718-783-1611)
PO Box 130367, Springfield Gardens, NY, 11413

GLEN HEAD

Gospel Meeting House (516-671-9251)
2 Orchard St, Glen Head, NY, 11545
norm5112@optonline.net
Su B 9:30am, F/S 11:00am; Tu P 7:30pm
c/o: Norman Simpson (516-801-2076)
1 Roosevelt Ave, Glen Head, NY, 11545
norm5112@optonline.net
alt: Cathy Irvin (516-676-7262)

HUNTINGTON

Lawn Street Chapel (631-266-2372)
3 Milton Place, Huntington, NY, 11743
Su B 9:30am, F 11:00am; We P/M 8:00pm
c/o: Thomas Pucheril (614-766-0021)
7512 Bardston Dr, Dublin, OH, 43017
tpucheril@ameritech.net
alt: Leslie Mathew (614-763-0560)

JAMESTOWN

Grace Chapel
379 Buffalo St, Jamestown, NY, 14701
Su B 9:45am, S 11:00am; We P/M 7:00pm
c/o: John K Cole (716-484-1347)
131 Wilson Pl, Jamestown, NY, 14701
jkcheb1012@yahoo.com

LONG ISLAND

Cleft of the Rock Bible Chapel (631-864-3060)
PO Box 404, Commack, NY, 11725
Su B 10:00am, S 11:30am, P 7:00pm, F 7:30pm (homes)
note: cnr Oak Lawn Dr & Veterans Hwy
c/o: Stephen Kelvas (631-289-4230)
3 Blueberry Ln, Patchogue, NY, 11772

Dean Street Chapel (516-379-1333)
23 W Dean St, Freeport, NY, 11520
Su B 9:15am, M 10:15am, F 11:15am, G 6:00pm (spanish); We M 8:00pm
c/o: Joseph Cardillo (516-623-3534)
1047 Lakeside Pl, Baldwin, NY, 11510
bacauto@aol.com

The Bible Church (516-944-8150)
35 Campus Dr, Port Washington, NY, 11050
Su S 9:45am, M 11:00am, B 6:30pm
c/o: Dr John Michael Thomas
35 Campus Dr, Port Washington, NY, 11050
pastorjmt@juno.com

Village Lane Bible Chapel (613-265-8876)
Town Line Rd, Hauppauge, NY, 11788
www.vlbc.org
n2lfj@aol.com
Su B 9:30am, S 11:00am; We P/M 7:30pm
note: Town Line Rd (cnr of Village Lane)
c/o: Michael Luna (631-539-4135)
55 Stone Ave, North Babylon, NY, 11703
n2lfj@aol.com

MANHATTAN

Capilla Evangelica
461 W 166th St, Manhattan, NY, 10032
Su B 9:30am, M 10:30am, S 11:00am, G 12:30pm; Tu P 8:00pm; Th M 8:00pm
note: between Amsterdam & Edgecomb
c/o: Isaac Garcia (212-304-9259)
PO Box 313, Manhattan, NY, 10032

MEDFORD

Igreja Evangelica de Medford (Portugese)
2981 Horseblock Rd, Medford, NY, 11763
Su B 5:30pm, M 6:00pm; Sa M 8:00pm

NEW YORK

Big Apple Chapel (973-837-1041)
520 8th Ave, New York, NY, 10018
www.truthbase.net
jillcobb@yahoo.com
Su B 10:45am, F 11:30am
note: Ripley-Grier Studios, between 36th & 37th, 16th floor; mailing address: 39 Rockledge Rd, Montville, NJ, 07045
c/o: William Cobb (973-837-1041)
40 Mountan View Dr, West Patterson, NJ, 07424
jillcobb@yahoo.com
alt: Vince Hulbert
hulbert5@earthlink.net

Bronx Gospel Hall (718-665-0265)
901 Teller Ave, Bronx, NY, 10451
bgh901@aol.com
Su B 10:00am, G 10:45am, S 12:30pm; Tu P/M, C 5:30pm
note: near 161st St, Open to all the Lord's people
c/o: James McCall (718-994-1318)
1775 Bussing Ave, Bronx, NY, 10466
jimannabel@aol.com

Capilla Evangelica (212-427-7840)
226 E 116th St, New York, NY, 10029
Su S, B 9:15am, M 12:00pm; We P 8:00pm; Fr M 8:00pm

Grace Gospel Chapel (212-281-0642)
102 W 133rd St, New York, NY, 10030
Su B 10:30am, G 11:45am, M 2:15pm; We P&BS 8:00pm; Fr Y 4:30pm
c/o: Livingstone Clarke (718-750-7646)
454 Lenox Rd, Brooklyn, NY, 11203
alt: David James (718-740-1472)

Templo Biblico
503 W 126th St, New York, NY, 10027
Su B/G, M 10:30am, S 11:00am; We M 8:00pm; Fr P/M 8:00pm
note: cnr of Amsterdam Ave

QUEENS

Cambria Heights Gospel Chapel (718-276-5920)
22102 Linden Blvd, Queens, NY, 11411
Su B 9:30am, G 11:00am, S 1:00pm, M 7:00pm; Tu P 8:00pm; Sa Y 7:30pm
c/o: Dr Wade (718-276-5920)
alt: Don Bonner (718-276-5920)

ROCHESTER

Cornerstone Bible Chapel (585-247-5323)
3231 Buffalo Rd, Rochester, NY, 14624
groups.google.com/group/cornerstonebiblechapel/web
lilgamein@frontiernet.net
Su B 9:15am, M/S 11:00am; Tu L 9:30am; We AWANA 6:30, P/M 7:00pm;
Fr Y 7:00pm
c/o: Stuart Milligan (585-426-4313)
2 Phyllis Ln, Rochester, NY, 14624-4704
lilgamin@frontiernet.net
alt: John Cannon (585-426-4101)
jcannon@pol.net

Crossroads Bible Fellowship (585-429-6299)
27 Watchman Ct, Rochester, NY, 14624
www.cbfchurch.org
chuckg@rochester.rr.com
Su M (various), B 9:30am, F 11:00am
c/o: Chuck Gianotti (585-429-5435)
27 Watchman Ct, Rochester, NY, 14624
chuckg@rochester.rr.com

Northgate Bible Chapel (585-865-4621)
240 McGuire Rd, Rochester, NY, 14616
www.northgatebiblechapel.com
jminter@northgatebiblechapel.com
Su B 9:30am, S 10:50am, F 11:30am; We P/M 7:00
c/o: John Minter (585-722-3407)
194 Applewood Dr, Rochester, NY, 14624
jrminter@rochester.rr.com
alt: Jim O'Shea (585-720-0456)
joshea@rochester.rr.com

SCHENECTADY

Bellevue Gospel Chapel (518-377-1186)
2702 Guilderland Ave, Schenectady, NY, 12306
Su B 9:30am, S 11:00am, M 6:30pm; We M 7:00pm
c/o: John E Smith (518-861-6486)
PO Box 496, Altamont, NY, 12009
johnesmith@aol.com
alt: Doug Lewis (518-355-9378)

SEA CLIFF

Sea Cliff Gospel Chapel (516-676-5250)
162 Sea Cliff Ave, Sea Cliff, NY, 11579
www.seacliffchapel.org
davidcollins@seacliffchapel.org
Su Adult S 9:30am, B 10:15am, F 11:00am, S 11:15 am
c/o: James Kroeger (516-671-0098)
26 Philips Rd, Glen Cove, NY, 11542
corner0622@aol.com
alt: David Collins (516-759-2840)
davidcollins@seacliffchapel.org

SYRACUSE

Syracuse Bible Chapel (315-399-5347 or 315-708-3839)
4458 Renee Meadows Dr, Syracuse, NY 13215
Su B 10:00am, F 11:15am; We Bible Study 7:00pm
c/o: Abey Abraham (315-399-5347 or 315-708-3839)
4458 Renee Meadows Dr, Syracuse, NY 13215
abey_a@yahoo.com
alt: Raymond Shetley (423-231-1151)
rlshetley@gmail.com

WEST SENECA

Springbrook Bible Chapel
390 Center Rd, Buffalo, NY, 14224
Su S, B 9:45am; We P; Sa M 8:00am
c/o: Patrick Guerin (716-823-5038)
247 Labelle Ave, Blasdell, NY, 14219

WHITE PLAINS
Shiloh Gospel Chapel (914-946-4626)
27 Juniper Hill Rd, White Plains, NY, 10607
Su B 9:30am, M 11:00am, G 7:00pm, S 12:30pm; Mo P 7:30pm;
We M 7:30pm
c/o: Stanley Fray (914-946-4129)
29 Woodland Pl, White Plains, NY, 10606

White Plains Gospel Chapel (914-949-1146)
436 N Broadway, White Plains, NY, 10603
Su B 9:30am, F 11:00am, S 12:30pm; Tu P 7:30pm
c/o: Attn: Trustee (914-949-1146)
436 N Broadway, White Plains, NY, 10603

YONKERS
Bethany Chapel (914-969-6137)
55 Greenvale Ave, Yonkers, NY, 10703
www.bethanyyonkers.org
Su B 9:30am, S/F 11:00am; Tu P 7:30pm; Fr Y 6:30 (Oct-Apr)
note: mailing address: 676 N Broadway, Yonkers, NY, 10701
c/o: Michael O'Connor (914-968-3004)
676 N Broadway, Yonkers, NY, 10701
mocmoc@uptonline.net
alt: Norm Luetters (914-478-2122)
normrose2@verizon.net

NORTH CAROLINA

ASHEVILLE
Asheville Gospel Chapel (828-298-0328)
350 Old Haw Creek Rd, Asheville, NC, 28805
Su B 9:30am, S/F 11:00am, G 5:30pm; Mo L 8:00pm; Tu L 10:00am;
www.ashevillegospelchapel.com
c/o: Walter R Peck (828-254-5475)
15 Bent Tree Rd, Asheville, NC, 28804
alt: Alan Mojonnier (828-298-3123)

BURLINGTON
Grace Bible Fellowship (336-226-3667)
2228 Moran St, Burlington, NC, 27215
Su B 9:00am, S 10:00am, F 11:00am; We P/M 7:00pm
c/o: Ken Harman (339-578-0777)
1532 Bentwood Dr, Graham, NC, 27253
alt: Ricky Bailey (336-260-6995)

Ireland Street Chapel (336-226-9914)
430 S Ireland St, Burlington, NC, 27215
www.IrelandStreetChapel.org
irelands@irelandstreetchapel.org
Su B 9:30am, S 11:00am, M 6:30pm; We P 7:00pm
c/o: AG Sutton Jr (336-585-0660)
PO Box 549, Burlington, NC, 27215

UNITED STATES — NORTH CAROLINA

CHARLOTTE
Fairbluff Bible Chapel (704-525-3186)
4650 Fairbluff Pl, Charlotte, NC, 28209
Su B 9:15am, F/S 11:00am, M 6:00pm; We P/M 7:00pm
note: Call for summer schedule, youth meetings and Bible study times.
c/o: Bill Longstreet (704-845-2757)
1220 Brightmoor Dr, Matthews, NC, 28105
wdlmel2@carolina.rr.com
alt: Barry Brady (704-365-0632)

DURHAM
Grove Park Chapel (919-596-1152)
805 Sherron Rd, Durham, NC, 27703
www.groveparkchapel.com
Su B 9:00am, S 10:00am, F/C 11:00am, G 5:00 pm; We P 6:30pm; Sa Y 6:00pm
c/o: Dale Brooks (919-596-1152)
805 Sherron Rd, Durham, NC, 27703
gpc@nc.rr.com

Northgate Chapel (919-477-7927)
3207 Duke Homestead Rd, Durham, NC, 27705
www.northgatechapel.org
Su B 9:30am, G/S 11:00am, M 6:30pm; Tu C 6:30pm; We P 7:00pm;
Sa M 8:30am
c/o: Mark W Hartley (919-598-0392)
here2serve@nc.rr.com

FAYETTEVILLE
Fayetteville Bible Chapel (910-488-0986)
414 Country Club Dr, Fayetteville, NC, 28301
biblechapel316@aol.com
Su P 9:00am, B 10:00am, S/G 11:30am; We AWANA/L/M 6:30pm
c/o: Linda Jackson (910-488-0986)
414 Country Club Dr, Fayetteville, NC, 28311
alt: Grant Edwards (910-822-4007)

GOLDSBORO
Goldsboro Gospel Chapel
1806 E Mulberry, Goldsboro, NC, 27530
Su B 9:45am, S 11:00am, M 6:00pm; We P/M 6:30pm
c/o: Dale Harris (919-734-8786)
103 N Lee St, Goldsboro, NC, 27530

GREENSBORO
Shannon Hills Bible Chapel (336-292-4064)
900 W Vandalia Rd, Greensboro, NC, 27406
www.shannonhills-biblechapel.org
Su B 9:30am, F 11:00am, Y 5:15pm, M/C 7:00pm; We P 7:30pm
c/o: Harvey S. Apple (336-674-9269)
6201 Monnett Rd, Julian, NC, 27283
hpapple@bellsouth.net
alt: Mark Shelley (336-674-9584)
mshelley@juno.com

HICKORY

Hickory Gospel Hall (828-324-2118)
253 17th Ave NE, Hickory, NC, 28601
Su B 9:30 am, S/M 11:15 am, G 6:00 pm; We P 7:30 pm
c/o: Tom Turnbull (828-874-6250)
2617 Knob Mountain Dr, Connelly Springs, NC, 28612
tturnbull@charter.net

KERNERSVILLE

Sedge Garden Chapel (336-996-1629)
850 Hastings Hill Road, Kernersville, NC, 27284
Su B 9:30am, S 11:00am, M 6:30pm; We P/M 7:30pm
c/o: Kent R Whicker (336-993-5255)
850 Appaloosa Trail, Kernersville, NC, 27284

MAXTON

Preston Gospel Chapel
1872 Preston Rd, Maxton, NC, 28366
Su S 9:30am, B 10:45am, M 5:00pm; We M 7:30pm; Th P 7:00pm
c/o: Charlie T Locklear (919-521-9059)
1872 Preston Rd, Maxton, NC, 28366

MEBANE

Mebane Gospel Chapel
503 N 9th St, Mebane, NC, 27302
Su B 9:30am, F 11:00am, G/S 6:30pm; We P 7:00pm
c/o: Kenneth F Oakley (336-228-3281)
1206 Ravenwood Dr, Graham, NC, 27253

NEWTON

Conover Gospel Fellowship
2019 N College, Newton, NC, 28658
Su B 10:00am, S 11:15am, G 6:00pm; We P
c/o: Andy Schaper (704-495-7846)
294 NW Road, Hickory, NC, 28601

PEMBROKE

Pembroke Family Fellowship
449 Pinelake Rd, Pembroke, NC, 28372
Su B 9:45am, S 11:00am, M 7:30pm
c/o: Ron Locklear (910-521-2870)
449 Pinelake Rd, Pembroke, NC, 28372

PINEVILLE

Believers Bible Chapel (704-752-1532)
13531 Lancaster Hwy, Pineville, NC, 28134
www.bbccharlotte.com
rex@bbccharlotte.com
Su B 9:30am, F 11:00am, M 6:00pm; Tu P/M 7:00pm
note: Charlotte / Pineville
c/o: Rex Trogdon (704-843-9632)
7200 Winslow Dr, Waxhaw, NC, 28173
rex@bbccharlotte.com

PITTSBORO
Pittsboro Bible Assembly
1825 East St, Pittsboro, NC, 27312
www.pittsborobibleassembly.org
dmm31@nc.rr.com
Su B 9:30am, M 10:45am, M 7:00pm; We P 7:00pm
note: Pittsboro Christian Village (919-542-3151), Gerald Baker
c/o: David M. McCulloch (919-542-6550)
1825 East St, Pittsboro, NC, 27312
dmm31@nc.rr.com

RALEIGH
Faith Bible Fellowship (919-772-6083)
1905 Garner Glen Dr, Raleigh, NC, 27603
www.faith-bible-fellowship.org
Su S 10:00am, G 11:00am, B 6:30pm, M 7:30pm; We P 7:30pm
note: mailing address: c/o William Smith, 8724 Ten Ten Rd, Raleigh, NC, 27603
c/o: Kenneth Branch (919-859-5440)
5120 Milner Dr, Raleigh, NC, 27606
4branches@nc.rr.com
alt: William Smith (919-772-0402)

North Raleigh Chapel (919-787-8561)
5421 Six Forks Rd, Raleigh, NC, 27609
Su B 9:30am, S 11:00am, M 6:00pm; We P/M 7:30pm
c/o: L. D. Collier (919-365-7876)
818 Old Zebulon Rd, Wendell, NC, 27591

North Ridge Bible Chapel (919-847-8661)
7100 Harps Mill Rd, Raleigh, NC, 27615
nrbc@nc.rr.com
http://nrchapel.org
Su B 9:30am, F 11:00am, AWANA 5:45pm, S 6:00pm; We P 7:00pm
c/o: Jeff Oestreich (919-556-1420)
12335 Canolder St, Raleigh, NC, 27614
jeffonc@hotmail.com
alt: Grady Jeffreys (919-872-3240)

RAMSEUR
Ramseur Gospel Chapel (336-824-6045)
5151 Gracewood Rd, Ramseur, NC, 27316
Su B 9:30am, S 10:45am, M 7:30pm
c/o: Michael Moody (336-824-5525)
PO Box 1259, Ramseur, NC, 27316
mcjmoody@yahoo.com

REIDSVILLE
Reidsville Bible Chapel (336-342-5727)
3016 S Park Dr, Reidsville, NC, 27320
Su B 9:30am, S 11:00am; We M 7:30pm
c/o: Stephen Andrews (336-342-2176)
231 Fairfield Rd, Reidsville, NC, 27320
sbacpa@att.net

SANFORD
Sanford Chapel (919-776-2423)
650 Franklin Dr, Sanford, NC, 27330
Su B 9:30am, S 10:25am, F 11:00am; We P/M 7:00pm
c/o: Jim Hancock (919-774-3753)
650N Franklin Dr., Sanford, NC, 27330

SILER CITY
Siler City Chapel
166 S 3rd Ave, Siler City, NC, 27344
Su B 9:45am, S 11:00am, G 7:00pm; We P/M 7:00pm
c/o: Jimmy J Cranford (919-742-3252)
718 John Emerson Rd, Siler City, NC, 27344

WAYNESVILLE
Waynesville Christian Fellowship (828-452-0551)
1115 Dillowood Rd, Waynesville, NC, 28786
Su B 9:30am, F 11:00am
note: opp Lake Junaluska
c/o: Clayton Davis (828-926-1158)
75 Creekside Dr, Maggie Valley, NC, 28751

WENDELL
Wendell Bible Chapel
9 N Main St, Wendell, NC, 27591
Su M, B 10:00am, P 7:00pm; We M 7:00pm
c/o: George Whitman
PO Box 359, Wendell, NC, 27591

WILMINGTON
Wilmington Bible Chapel (910-799-6520)
6004 Fern Ct, Wilmington, NC, 28405
www.wilmingtonbiblechapel.org
Su B 9:30am, M 6:30pm; Tu M 9:30am, Y 7:00pm; We P 7:00pm; Th Y 4:00pm
c/o: Timothy Sorrell (910-791-5977)
4205 Greens Ferry Ct, Wilmington, NC, 28409
tsorrell@viafamily.com
alt: William Hill (910-791-3006)

WINSTON-SALEM

Fair Oaks Gospel Chapel (336-744-5427)
534 Oak Summit Rd, Winston Salem, NC, 27105
hylton@surry.net
Su B 9:45am, F 11:00am; Th P 6:30pm
c/o: Paul Knepp (336-368-1133)
Pilot Mt, NC
alt: Andy Hylton (336-351-3301)

Parkway Chapel (336-785-9222)
2651 Buchanan St, Winston-Salem, NC, 27127
parkwaychapel@juno.com
Su B 9:30am, F 11:00am, M 6:30pm; We P 7:00pm
c/o: James E Beatty (336-377-2550)
6021 Summer Trace Ln, Winston-Salem, NC, 27105
jebeatty@jimbeatty.us

ZEBULON

Union Hope Gospel Chapel
Hwy 97 Rt 1, Zebulon, NC
Su B/S/G; We P
note: 4 mi E of Zebulon
c/o: TW Carter (269-4952)
13230 Social Plain Rd, Middlesex, NC, 27557

NORTH DAKOTA

HARVEY

Harvey Gospel Chapel
208 W 8th St, Harvey, ND, 58341
Su B 9:45am, S 11:00am
c/o: Lewellyn Tewksbury (701-447-2403)
550 Main St W, Mercer, ND, 58559

MINOT

Minot Assembly of Believers
10 3rd St. NE, Minot, ND, 58703
lil.seeds@gmail.com
Su B 9:30am, M 11:00am; We P 7:30pm
note: Bible studies held during week. Monthly fellowship dinner. Google us for map and pictures.
c/o: Caleb Bulow (701-833-5956)
5121 51 Ave SE, Minot, ND, 58701
lil.seeds@gmail.com
alt: Alan Bulow (701-837-9051)

VALLEY CITY
Southwest Bible Chapel (701-845-2792)
826 5th St SW, Valley City, ND, 58072
Su B 9:00am, S 10:00am, F 11:00am; We P 7:30pm
c/o: Willis Wagar (701-845-1399)
3425 Oaks Dr, Valley City, ND, 58072
alt: James VanDyke (701-845-3925)

WEST FARGO
Meadow Ridge Bible Chapel (701-282-4772)
2198 2nd Ave East, West Fargo, ND, 58078
www.meadowridgebiblechapel.org
Su B 9:00am, M 10:15am, S 11:20am, M 6:00pm; We P 7:00pm
c/o: Gary Clark (701-282-2937)
145 Ironwood Dr, Horace, ND, 58047
gdclark@juno.com
alt: Myron Martinson (218-233-9790)

OHIO

BELLBROOK
Believers Assembly (937-848-4644)
3821 Upper Bellbrook Rd, Dayton, OH, 45305
www.bibletruth.net/ohbellba
Su B 9:15am, S 10:45am; We P 7:15pm
c/o: Rod Geiger (937-845-3431)
8815 McNeal Rd, New Carlisle, OH, 45344
regeiger1@juno.com
alt: Dwight McMahan (937-372-7077)

CINCINNATI
Northern Hills Bible Chapel
1155 W Galbraith Road, Cincinnati, OH, 45231
www.northenhillsbiblechapel.org
Su S/M, B 6:30pm; We P
c/o: Phil Miekley (513-729-2803)
994 Hollytree Ln, Cincinnati, OH, 45231
alt: Evan Davis (513-772-0403)

CLEVELAND
Elim Gospel Chapel (216-851-0677)
10522 Amor Ave, Cleveland, OH, 44108
Su S, B 11:00am, M 11:30am; We P/M 7:45pm
c/o: Booker T Miller (216-921-5211)
3297 E 126th St, Cleveland, OH, 44120

Faith Gospel Chapel
Su M 11:00am
note: meets in Eliza Bryant Nursing Home
c/o: Clayton Harris (216-361-2308)
7619 Home Ct, Cleveland, OH, 44103

CLYDE

Clyde Gospel Hall (419-547-0552)
204 Woodland Ave, Clyde, OH, 43410
stevemcmurray6072@earthlink.net
Su B 9:30am, S 11:15am, G 6:00pm; We P/M 7:30pm
c/o: Steve McMurray (419-547-0552)
108 Lynber Ln, Clyde, OH, 43410
stevemcmurray6072@earthlink.net
alt: Kevin Miller (419-547-8645)

COLUMBUS

Columbus Bible Chapel (614-766-0021)
2335 W Case Rd, Dublin, OH, 43235
www.columbusbiblechapel.org
tpucheril@gmail.com
Su B 9:30am, F 11:00am; We P 7:30pm
note: use point of contact as church's mailing address
c/o: Thomas Pucheril (614-766-0021)
7512 Bardston Dr, Dublin, OH, 43017
tpucheril@gmail.com
alt: Leslie Mathew (614-763-0560)
drlesliemathew@gmail.com

No Life Too Small Christian Fellowship (614-301-7392)
Su S 9:30am, M/B 11:00am; We P 6:00pm; Sa C 12:00pm
c/o: Michael Cox (614-301-7392 or 532-0247)

DAYTON

Dayton Bible Chapel (937-279-9573)
4801 North Dixie Dr, Dayton, OH, 45414
www.daytonbiblechapel.org
elders@daytonbiblechapel.org
Su B 9:30am, M 10:45am, S 11:45am; We P 7:30pm; Sa P 7:30am
note: Prayer bkfast for men Sa am, Ladies every other Sa
c/o: Jacob Johns (937-890-0404)
1701 Cawdor Court, Vandalia, OH, 45377
jacobj@pol.net
alt: Walter Belue (937-278-7457)

FAIRLAWN

Akron Gospel Hall (330-867-3818)
2705 Smith Rd, Fairlawn, OH, 44333
Su B 10:00am, S 12:00pm, G 6:00pm; We M 7:30pm
note: use point of contact as church's mailing address
c/o: Ken Webb (330-666-9466)
PO Box 13350, Fairlawn, OH, 44333
kwebb330@aol.com

LORAIN

Grace Gospel Hall (440-244-1410)
3006 Elyria Ave, Lorain, OH, 44055
Su B 9:15am, S 11:15am, G 7:00pm; We P/M 7:00pm
c/o: Randall H Bradford (440-277-5461)
1875 E 34th, Lorain, OH, 44055

Spanish Gospel Hall (440-246-3170)
3002 Elyria Ave, Lorain, OH, 44055
Su B 9:15am, S 11:15am, G 7:00pm; Tu P 7:00pm; Th M 7:00pm
note: Local del Evangelio
c/o: Ramon Rivera Jr (440-277-1349)
2237 E 34th St, Lorain, OH, 44055

MANSFIELD

Assembly of Believers at The Good News Center (419-522-1084)
119 N Park St, Mansfield, OH, 44902
Su B 10:30am, S 11:15am; Th G 7:00pm
c/o: Andrew Vallance (419-775-0051)
1421 Lexington Ave #158, Mansfield, OH, 44907
avallance@juno.com
alt: Roger Sterry (419-756-1985)

Gospel Hall (419-525-3049)
1070 Mansfield-Washington Rd, Mansfield, OH 44903
www.mansfieldgospelhall.com
Su B 9:30am, S 11:15am, G 6:00pm; We P 7:30pm
note: use main point of contact for mailing address
c/o: John P Hoffman (419-884-1990)
1385 Angus Dr, Mansfield, OH, 44903
hoffjohnman@aol.com
alt: Chester Yoder (330-567-9232)
chesyoder@yahoo.com

RICHMOND HEIGHTS

Monticello Gospel Hall (330-963-4104)
4970 Monticello Blvd, Richmond Heights, OH, 44143
Su B 9:30am, M 11:30am, G 12:00pm, G/Y 6:00pm; We P 7:30pm
c/o: Kevin Buck (330-963-4104)
10170 Timothy Ln, Twinsburg, OH, 44087
kevin.buck@deluxe.com
alt: Ronald Berquist (440-473-2268)
ronaldberquist@aol.com

ROSS

Ross Bible Chapel (513-863-3924)
PO Box 563, Ross, OH, 45061
Su B 9:00am, S 10:05am, M 11:00am; We P 7:00pm
note: meets at:2846 Hamilton-Cleves Rd (Hwy 128)
c/o: Steven Walrath (859-525-0309)
48 Achates Dr, Florence, KY, 41042

STEUBENVILLE

Steubenville Gospel Hall (740-282-8827)
Steubenville, OH, 43952
emailus@steubenvillegospelhall.org
Su B 10:00am, G 7:00pm, S 12:00pm; We P/M 7:00pm
note: cnr W Adam & Park Sts
c/o: Richard W Westlake (740-544-5762)
44 Pine Lane, Toronto, OH, 43964
rewestlake@juno.com

TOLEDO

Christian Fellowship of Toledo South (419-866-1332)
6711 Pilliod Rd, Holland, OH, 43528
www.cftoledo.com / cfsecretary@cftoledo.com
Su B 8:45am, F/C 9:30am, S 11:10am; We P 6:45am
c/o: Lou Vasaturo (419-866-1561)
101 Dulton Dr, Toledo, OH, 43615
louvas@bex.net
alt: Terry Priestap (419-866-1332)

UNIONTOWN

Believers Bible Fellowship (330-877-0438)
12160 Hoover Ave NW, Uniontown, OH, 44685
www.believersbiblefellowship.com
john.mizener@gmail.com
Su B 10:00am, F 11:45am; We P/M 7:00pm
c/o: John Mizener (330-877-0438)
12160 Hoover Ave NW, Uniontown, OH, 44685
john.mizener@gmail.com

WESTLAKE

Westlake Bible Fellowship (440-892-1953)
27975 Hilliard Blvd, Cleveland, OH, 44145
Su B 9:30am, S 11:00am, C 5:30pm; We P 7:00pm
c/o: Roger Meng (440-899-1305)
28961 Detroit Rd, Westlake, OH, 44145
handsandnails@bright.net
alt: Todd Eichenauer (440-835-0450)

OKLAHOMA

FORT GIBSON

Fort Gibson Assembly of Believers
128 N 3 Mile Rd, Fort Gibson, OK, 74434
Su B 9:15am, M 11:00am; We P/M 3:30pm
c/o: David S Wilson (918-478-2994)
128 N 3 Mile Rd, Fort Gibson, OK, 74434

GUTHRIE

Guthrie Gospel Chapel
424 E Oklahoma St, Guthrie, OK, 73044
Su B 9:30am, F 11:00am, G 6:30pm; Tu C 7:00pm; We P 7:00pm
note: use alternate contact's address for mailing
c/o: Al Schiete (405-341-6759)
alt: Dan Vreeland (405-282-5599)
1716 E. Roosevelt, Guthrie, OK, 73044

OKLAHOMA CITY

Grace Gospel Chapel (405-632-3348)
3601 S Shields Blvd, Oklahoma City, OK, 73129
Su B 9:00am, M 10:30am, M 11:20am; We P 7:00pm
c/o: Bill Davis (405-386-7591)
14001 Alabama, Newalla, OK, 74857
b4him@mcloudteleco.com
alt: Jim Davis (405-386-6540)
jimokie56@aol.com

TULSA

East Tulsa Bible Chapel (918-234-7244)
1215 S 135th East Ave, Tulsa, OK, 74108
Su B 9:00am, S 10:30am, M 11:30am; Tu C 6:30pm; We P 7:00pm
c/o: Jim Lindamood (918-663-1121)
PO Box 690424, Tulsa, OK, 74169

OREGON

CLACKAMAS

Spring Mountain Bible Church
12152 SE Mather Rd, Portland, OR, 97015
Su B 9:45am, S 11:15am, M 6:00pm (homes), M 7:30pm (homes)
c/o: Greg Matthews (503-698-2864)
12152 SE Mather Rd, Clackamas, OR, 97015

CORVALLIS

Corvallis Gospel Hall (541-752-9035)
410 SE Alexander Ave, Corvallis, OR, 97333
www.corvallisgospelhall.org
Su B 10:00am, S 11:30am, G 7:00pm; We P/M 7:00pm
c/o: Philip Howard (541-757-7829)
1825 NW 14th St, Corvallis, OR, 97330

EUGENE

Willamette Bible Chapel (503-345-0686)
3290 Donald St, Eugene, OR, 97405
Su B/M/S 10:00am; Tu M (homes); We M (homes),
c/o: Paul Gossard (541-345-0844)
1475 W 26th Ave, Eugene, OR, 97405
pca@efn.org

UNITED STATES — OREGON

FOREST GROVE

Forest Grove Gospel Hall
2037 Cedar St, Forest Grove, OR, 97116
Su B 9:45am, G 7:00pm; We P/M 7:30pm
note: use point of contact as church's mailing address
c/o: John Robertson (503-357-3288)
3110 19th Ave #307, Forest Grove, OR, 97116-2656
alt: Mark Robertson (503-357-9118)

GRANTS PASS

Gospel Hall (503-476-3956)
1611 SW G St, Grants Pass, OR, 97526
Su B 10:00am, S 11:45am, G 7:30pm; We P/M 7:30pm
c/o: Donald G Gratias (503-479-4521)
141 Timber Lane, Grants Pass, OR, 97526

GRESHAM

Cascade Community Church (503-661-7084)
18255 SE Clinton St, Gresham, OR, 97030
Su B 9:00am, S 10:00am, M 11:15am, P 7:00pm; Th M 7:30pm
c/o: Bob Sale (503-255-5737)
111 SE Ankeny Circle, Portland, OR, 97233

OREGON CITY

Bible Chapel (503-655-3009)
20611 S Hwy 213, Oregon City, OR, 97045
Su B 8:30am, S 9:30am, M 11:00am
c/o: Phil Howard (503-632-6214)
PO Box 833, Oregon City, OR, 97045

Grace Christian Assembly
15745 S Harley Ave, Oregon City, OR, 97045
Su B 9:00am, F 11:00am
note: We meet in a local grange so there is no way to contact us at the actual grange address. Please feel free to contact Eric Pearson.
c/o: Eric Pearson (503-656-4234 or cell 971-222-7325)
16140 S Thayer Road, Oregon City, OR, 97045
ericmpearson@gmail.com
alt: Jeff Davis (503-557-0175)

PORTLAND

Eastgate Bible Chapel (503-254-8106)
11410 SE Stark, Portland, OR, 97216-3499
egateportland@eschelon.com
Su B 9:30am, S/F 11:00am (children thru 8th grade)
note: mailing address: PO Box 16118, Portland, OR, 97292
c/o: Don Howatt (503-257-7908)
11410 SE Stark, Portland, OR, 97216
don-howatt@comcast.net

Grace Bible Fellowship (503-252-7448)
12420 NE Siskiyou St, Portland, OR, 97230
www.gbf.truepath.com
Su B 9:00am, S 10:00am, F 11:15am; Tu L 11:00am; We P 7:00pm; Th Y 7:00pm
c/o: Gilbert Gleason (503-255-9563)
7272 SE Thorburn, Portland, OR, 97215
gsgleason@integrity.com

Westside Bible Fellowship (503-640-5151)
526 SE 9th Ave, Hillsboro, OR, 97123
www.westside-bible.org
info@westside-bible.org
Su B/S/Y 6:00pm; Tu M 7:30pm (homes); We M 7:30pm (homes); Fr L 9:30am
c/o: Arden Trautman
4742 Fernhill Rd, Forest Grove, OR, 97116
alt: Brad Benson (503-628-2506)

SALEM

Salem Christian Fellowship
768 State St, Salem, OR, 97301
Su S, B 9:45am
c/o: John Tate
4526 Blue Sky Ct SE, Salem, OR, 97301
jstate@home.com

Salem Gospel Hall (503-378-0874)
4583 Swegle Rd NE, Salem, OR, 97301-2013
Su B 10:00am, S 12:00pm, M 12:15pm, G 7:00pm; Th P 7:45
c/o: Gaylord B Lowry (541-967-0575)
536 S Nebergall Loop NE, Albany, OR, 97321-1581
gaylordlowry@aol.com
alt: Verlin Perkins (541-928-2694)
verlinperkins@mac.com

PENNSYLVANIA

ALLENTOWN

Grace Gospel Chapel (610-791-2101)
1642 Ehrets Ln, Allentown, PA, 18103
www.gracegospel.us
Su B 9:15am, S/F 11:00am, M 1:00pm; We M 7:15pm
c/o: Robert Gessner (610-439-8165)
2814 E Texas Blvd, Allentown, PA, 18103
alt: James VanDuzer (610-262-1617)
rutha@vanduzer.us

ARDSLEY

Ardsley Bible Chapel (215-885-9069)
2717 Jenkintown Rd, Ardsley, PA, 19038
Su B 9:00am, F 10:30am, S 11:30am; We P/M 7:30pm
note: Jenkintown Rd and Harrison Ave
c/o: A James Hulshizer (215-887-2838)
225 Buttonwood Way, Glenside, PA, 19038
ajhulshizer@comcast.net
alt: Norman E Roberts (215-836-2409)
alinorm@juno.com

BOILING SPRINGS

Boiling Springs Bible Chapel (717-258-8837)
PO Box 544, Boiling Springs, PA, 17007
Su B 9:15am, S 10:10am, M 11:00am; We P/M 7:15pm
note: 119 Fourth Street
c/o: William Wirl (7172438082)
855 York Rd, Carlside, PA, 17013

BRYN MAWR

Bryn Mawr Gospel Hall (610-525-6539)
8 N Summit Grove Ave, Bryn Mawr, PA, 19010
www.brynmawrgospelhall.org
Su B 10:00am, S 12:00pm, G 7:00pm; We P 7:30pm
c/o: Harold W Stewart (610-825-0384)
403 Revere Rd, Lafayette Hill, PA, 19444
stew403@aol.com
alt: Alan Oliver (610-399-3199)
ado535@juno.com

CHAMBERSBURG

Gospel Chapel
3rd & King Sts, Chambersburg, PA
Su B/S; We P/M 7:00pm
c/o: William Sheaffer
515 Starr Ave, Chambersburg, PA, 17201

DONORA

Donora Gospel Hall
201 Thompson Ave, Donora, PA, 15033
Su B 11:00am; Th P 1:00pm
c/o: Kenneth J McCullough (724-838-1759)
10 Hampshire Dr, Greensburg, PA, 15601-1015

EAST FREEDOM

East Freedom Chapel (814-695-5943)
Mount Pleasant St, East Freedom, PA, 16655
dsh@bedford.net
Su B 9:30am, F 11:00am; We P 7:30pm
c/o: David Harper (814-276-3012)
10194 William Penn Rd, Imler, PA, 16655
dsh@bedford.net
alt: Mike Davis (814-886-5805)

ERIE

Grace Gospel Chapel (814-459-8882)
3218 Tuttle Ave, Erie, PA, 16504
Su B 9:15am, F/S 10:45am; We P 7:00pm
c/o: Jay R Washburn (814-456-2657)
3201 Tuttle Ave, Erie, PA, 16504
jandk4him@verizon.net
alt: David Martin (814-899-9934)

FAYETTEVILLE

Greenwood Hills Assembly (717-352-8934)
7062 Lincoln Way E, Fayetteville, PA, 17222
Su B 9:15am, S 11:00am, M 6:00pm; We P 7:00pm
c/o: R Jeffery Nicklas (717-264-8804)
3384 Interchange Dr, Chambersburg, PA, 17201

GILBERTSVILLE

Grace Gospel Chapel (610-367-5316)
1130 Mega Ln, Gilbertsville, PA, 19525
www.gracegospelchapel.org
krkeyser@hotmail.com
Su B 9:00am, S/F 10:30am, M 6:00pm; We P/M 7:00pm
c/o: Michael Miller (610-369-1307)
708 E 8th St, Boyertown, PA, 19512
alt: Jack Snyder (610-369-5922)

HARRISBURG

Harrisburg Bible Chapel (717-652-8214)
5503 Union Deposit Rd, Harrisburg, PA, 17111
Su B 9:30am, F 11:00am; We P/M 7:00pm
c/o: Robert Walker (717-599-5953)
520 Frog Hollow Rd, Harrisburg, PA, 17112
bobwalker@tycoelectronics.com
alt: Dennis Wagner (717-651-0217)
dennis.wagner1@juno.com

HATBORO

Hatboro Gospel Hall (215-675-2645)
23 W Moreland Ave, Hatboro, PA, 19040
www.hatborogospelhall.org
Su B 9:30am, S/M 11:30am, P 6:30pm, G 7:00pm; We M 7:30pm
c/o: James W Coleman (215-672-6448)
126 Bender Rd, Hatboro, PA, 19040
jimandchris@verizon.net
alt: William P Morrison Jr (215-674-9767)
bmorrisonjr@msn.com

INDIANA

Indiana Gospel Hall (724-349-8799)
501 Locust St, Indiana, PA, 15701
www.indianagospelhall.org
Su B 10:00am, S/M 11:30am, G 6:00pm; We P/M 7:45pm
c/o: J Lindsay Parks (724-349-5778 or 388-2705)
150 Spruce St Evergreen Manor, Indiana, PA, 15701
jlparks@yourinter.net
alt: William H. Calhoun (724-349-3379)

LANSDALE

Montco Bible Fellowship (610-855-0899)
160 E Main St, Lansdale, PA, 19446
Su P/M, B 9:00am, S 10:00am, M 11:00am
c/o: Tony Hart
1625 Latch String Ln, Hatfield, PA, 19440

LANSDOWNE

Collingdale Gosepl Chapel (610-622-5119)
c/o: Robert Hadden (610-909-6073)
112 Drexel Ave, Landsdown, PA, 19050

Lansdowne Bible Chapel (610-622-5119)
133 N Wycombe Ave, Lansdowne, PA, 19050
Su B 9:45am, F/S 11:15am; We P 7:30pm
c/o: Eric Cantwell (610-359-9676)
2986 Highland Ave, Broomall, PA, 19008
ericc@lf-mail.com
alt: Harold A Young Sr (610-494-9142)

LEOLA

Monterey Chapel (717-656-6536)
53 W Eby Rd, Lancaster, PA, 17540
Su B 9:00am, S 10:15am, F 11:15am; We P 7:15pm
c/o: P David Sheaffer (717-392-6810)
1809 Lincoln Hwy E, Lancaster, PA, 17602
alt: George Landis (717-354-5577)

LEWISTOWN

Gospel Chapel
320 W 5th St, Lewistown, PA, 17044
Su B/P/M
c/o: Charles Arentz (717-242-1530)
116 Juniata St, Lewistown, PA, 17044

MALVERN

Malvern Bible Chapel (610-647-4775)
20 Woodland Ave, Malvern, PA, 19355
www.malvernchapel.org
malvernpb@aol.com
Su B 10:00am, S 11:30am; We P/M 7:00pm
c/o: Edgar N Brightbill (610-399-0134)
1407 Thrush Lane, West Chester, PA, 19382

MCKEESPORT

McKeesport Gospel Hall Assembly (412-672-5880)
Mckeesport, PA, 15131
www.mckeesportgospelhall.org
t.clark5@aol.com
Su B 9:45am, S 11:45am, G 1:00pm; We P 7:00pm
note: Prescott & Broadway Streets
c/o: Thomas S Clark (412-724-5283)
2420 Inglewood Dr, White Oak, PA, 15131
tclarkjr5@aol.com
alt: Robert Vinson (412-672-5384)

MCMURRAY

Bethel Bible Church (412-833-4206)
3025 Washington Rd, McMurray, PA, 15317
www.the-bbc.org
rtietz3@verizon.net
Su B 9:30am, F 11:00am
note: meets at Malanos Bldg
c/o: Ronald Tietz (412-833-4206)
5997 Murdock Ave, Bethel Park, PA, 15102
rtietz3@verizon.net
alt: Brian Clelland (412-851-1896)

South Hills Bible Chapel (412-941-8990)
300 Gallery Dr, Mcmurray, PA, 15317
Su S/B 9:15am, B 10:45am (1st Sun), S 10:45am, B 6:30pm (3rd Su)

MURRYSVILLE

Murrysville Bible Chapel (724-733-4083)
4779 Christy Road, Murrysville, PA, 15668
www.murrysvillebiblechapel.org
Su B 9:00am, S 10:15am, F 11:00am; We P 7:30pm
c/o: Terry Ziegler (724-733-5210)
4027 Benden Cir, Murrysville, PA, 15668
correspondent@murrysvillebiblechapel.org

ORELAND

Gospel Chapel – Enfield (215-233-1728)
6 Summit Valley Lane Box 207, Oreland, PA, 19075
GCE.USA@juno.com
Su B 9:45am, S/M 11:00am; We M 7:30pm
note: use point of contact's address as mailing address
c/o: Stuart Dockeray (215-885-4673)
226 Roslyn Ave, Glenside, PA, 19038-3516
alt: Harvey S. Smith (215-672-1922)

OXFORD

Oxford Bible Chapel (610-932-2393)
680 Lancaster Pike, Oxford, PA, 19363
www.oxfordbiblechapel.com
scottkduncan@yahoo.com
Su B 9:30am, F 11:00am, M 1:30pm; Mo C 6:30pm; Tu P 7:30pm
note: Rt 472 at Octoraro Lake
c/o: George D Duncan (610-932-2393)
2004 Kings Row Rd, Oxford, PA, 19363
alt: Kenneth England (410-658-4629)

PHILADELPHIA

Calvary Gospel Chapel (215-477-4848)
4121 W Girard Ave, Philadelphia, PA, 19104
www.eastparkside-mantua.org
jginyard@eastparkside-mantua.org
Su B 9:45am, S 11:00am, G 12:00pm; Th M
c/o: Joseph Ginyard (215-877-1948)
5722 Woodbine Ave, Philadelphia, PA, 19131

Germantown Christian Assembly (215-242-5550)
610 E Mt Pleasant Ave, Philadelphia, PA, 19119
www.gcafamilychurch.org
gcafamily@verizon.net
Su B 8:00am, G 9:10am, S 11:15am; Tu P 7:30pm
c/o: Emmitt Cornelius (241-242-5550)
605 E Mt Pleasant Ave, Philadelphia, PA, 19119

Olney Gospel Hall (215-224-5920)
314 W Chew Ave, Philadelphia, PA, 19120
info@weldonstudio.com
Su B 10:00am, S 11:45am, G 7:00pm; Tu P 7:00pm
note: Occasional Spanish meetings scheduled
note: Mailing address: Roberto Santos, 600 W. 65th Ave, Philadelphia, PA, 19126
note: Landmarks: N on 5th St from Rt 1. Go thru Olney section and right on Chew Ave, to 314 (on right).
c/o: Earl Weldon (215-549-6778)
79 Woodland Rd, Huntingdon, PA, 19006
info@weldonstudio.com
alt: Roberto Santos (215-424-1399)

Roxborough Bible Chapel (215-483-0825)
460 Flamingo St, Philadelphia, PA, 19128
Su B, S 11:15am, P/M 6:00pm
c/o: Paul Roberts (215-836-4516)
8710 Cheltenham Ave, Wyndmoor, PA, 19038

PITTSBURGH

Browns Hill Bible Chapel (412-421-2807)
3349 Beechwood Blvd, Pittsburgh, PA, 15217
www.brownshillbiblechapel.com
Su B 9:30am, F 11:00am; We P 7:00pm
c/o: David Pfeiffer (412-734-5687)
232 McKinley Ave, Pittsburgh, PA, 15202
d_pfeiffer@msn.com
alt: Jon Tietz (412-595-7601)
jptietz@yahoo.com

PLUMSTEADVILLE

Grace Gospel Chapel (215-766-0570)
Rt 611, Plumsteadville, PA
Su B 9:00am, M 10:30am; We P 7:30pm
c/o: Ross Glendinning
5582 Easton Rd, Plumsteadville, PA, 18949

PUNXSUTAWNEY

Elk Run Avenue Chapel
105 Elk Run Ave, Punxsutawney, PA, 15767
Su S 9:45am, B 11:00am, M 7:30pm; We P 7:30pm
note: mailing address: 460 Clawson St, Punxsutawney, PA, 15767
c/o: C Wineberg (814-938-8803)
460 Clawson St, Punxsutawney, PA, 15767
alt: Clifton Wineberg (814-938-7534)

SCRANTON

Calvary Bible Church (570-876-4756)
518 Madison Ave, Jermyn, PA, 18433
Su B 9:00am (1:30pm first Su of), S 10:00am, M 11:00am; We P/M 7:00pm
c/o: Winston Cannon (570-876-2053)
520 Madison Ave, Jermyn, PA, 18433
cannons1@verizon.net

SOUDERTON

North-Ridge Bible Chapel (215-723-8574)
Sellersville, PA
Su S, B 9:15am, M 6:00pm; We P/M 7:15pm
note: Rt 113 & Keystone Dr
c/o: William Wooler (215-538-9472)
2030 Esten Rd, Quakertown, PA, 18951

STROUDSBURG

Maranatha Bible Chapel (570-420-1898)
717 Ave C
Stroudsburg, PA 18360
Su B 10:00am, M 12:00pm
note: Home assembly
c/o: Glenroy H Prince (570-420-1898)
717 Ave C, Stroudsburg, PA 18360
cpaglenroy@aol.com

SUNBURY

New Testament Fellowship (570-286-5916)
136 Fairmount Ave, Sunbury, PA 17801-2437
Su B 9:30am, F/S 11:00am; We P 7:00pm
note: home meeting
c/o: Fred W. Pyers (570-286-5916)
136 Fairmount Ave, Sunbury, PA 17801-2437
alt: Jason Smith (570-797-4106)

Seven Points Chapel (570-286-7900)
1110 Captain Bloom Rd, Sunbury, PA, 17801
Su B 9:15am, S 10:30am, M 6:30pm; We P 7:30pm
c/o: David A Shaffer (570-286-5949)
772 Valley Rd, Sunbury, PA, 17801
alt: Wayne Gemberling (570-286-6267)

WAYNESBORO

Waynesboro Gospel Chapel (717-762-2944)
200 Homewood Ave, Waynesboro, PA, 17268
Su B 9:15am, F 10:30am, M 11:40pm; We P/M 7:00pm
c/o: Bob Deeds (717-762-8711)
303 W North St, Waynesboro, PA, 17268
bdeeds@innernet.net

WAYNESBURG

Waynesburg Bible Chapel (724-852-2611)
800 E Greene St, Waynesburg, PA, 15370
Su B 9:00am, S 11:00am (10 &); We P/M 7:00pm
c/o: Jay C Buckhalter (724-852-2834)
300 Colonial Dr, Waynesburg, PA, 15370

YARDLEY

Believers' Fellowship
64 S Main St, Yardley, PA, 19067
Su B 9:00am, S 11:00am
c/o: Paul Karleen (215-949-3063)
29 Silverspruce Rd, Levittown, PA, 19056

YORK

North York Gospel Chapel (717-779-0082)
2854 Lewisberry Rd, York, PA, 17404
Su S, B 9:15am, M 6:00pm; We P/M 7:15pm
c/o: David J Logan (717-244-1598)
35 Hampton Court, Red Lion, PA, 17356
davidruthann@aol.com

RHODE ISLAND

NEWPORT
Chapel
Newport, RI
note: Newport Naval Base area, see Swansea MA

PAWTUCKET
Christian Brethren of Pawtucket (Portugese) (401-461-8378)
400 Lonsdale Ave, Pawtucket, RI, 02860
Su B 9:00am, G 10:30am, S 12:00pm; We P 7:30pm; Sa M 7:30pm
c/o: Carlos Cerqueira (401-461-8378)
101 Burnside St, Cranston, RI, 02910
cerqueira@cox.net

WARWICK
Buttonwoods Bible Chapel (401-739-8388)
311 Buttonwoods Ave, Warwick, RI, 02886
Su B 9:30am, S 11:00am, M 6:00pm; We P/M 7:30pm
c/o: John Farrell (401-884-5940)
1 Sandro Circle, Warwick, RI, 02886
farrell479@aol.com

Warwick Believers Fellowship
833 Centerville Rd, Warwick, RI, 02886
Su B/M; Tu M (homes),
note: meets at Harold Scott Elem School
c/o: C Russ Carr (401-821-3164)
803 Tollgate Rd, Warwick, RI, 02886

SOUTH CAROLINA

ANDERSON
Concord Community Church (864-225-0133)
729 Concord Rd, Anderson, SC, 29621
ldreeves@aol.com
Su B 9:30am, S 11:00am; We P 7:00pm (homes)
c/o: Larry D Reeves (864-225-0702)
2702 Cedar Ln, Anderson, SC, 29621
ldreeves@aol.com

BEAUFORT
Bible Chapel (843-524-1566)
913 West St, Beaufort, SC, 29901
Su B, S 10:00am, M 12:00pm
c/o: Anthony Vaughn (843-524-7899)
PO Box 1551, Beaufort, SC, 29901

UNITED STATES — SOUTH CAROLINA

CHARLESTON

Grace Tabernacle
125 Romney St, Charleston, SC, 29403
Su S 10:00am, G 11:45am, B 7:00pm; We P
c/o: Ernest Singleton (843-795-4559)
1460 Woodview Lane, Charleston, SC, 29412

COLUMBIA

Bethany Chapel (803-779-0139)
2917 Park St, Columbia, SC, 29201
Su B 9:30am, S 11:00am, M 11:55am; We P 6:30pm
c/o: Mark Sparks (803-407-1903)
109 River Creek Dr, Irmo, SC, 29063
marksparks@bellsouth.net

Woodland Hills Community Church (803-772-1893)
2626 Ashland Rd, Columbia, SC, 29210
www.WoodlandHills-Church.com
secretary@woodlandhills-church.com
Su B 9:00am, S 10:00am, G 11:00am; We P 7:00pm
c/o: Len Wilkerson (803-798-5676)
309 Rapids Ct, Columbia, SC, 29212
len@woodlandhills-church.com
alt: Henry Blackwell (803-691-5286)

CONWAY

Bethany Bible Chapel (843-369-7729)
1668 Four Mile Rd, Conway, SC, 29526
www.bethanybiblechapelconway.org
bethanyb@sccoast.net
Su S 9:30am, F 10:30am, B 6:00pm; Mo C/Y 6:30pm; We P/M 7:00pm
note: mailing address PO Box 1696, Conway, SC 29528
c/o: Larry Deeds (843-369-5665 or 843-450-7414)
PO Box 2066, Conway, SC, 29528
scmountaineer@juno.com
alt: David Rickert (843-248-3488)
drickert@sc.rr.com

FLORENCE

Community Bible Fellowship (843-669-9809)
PO Box 4957, Florence, SC, 29502
Su B 9:00am, S 10:00am, F 11:15am, C 5:30pm; We P 7:00pm
note: at Oakdale & Springdale just off I-95 S of I-20
c/o: John Pritchett (843-665-2852)
847 Thunderbird Dr, Florence, SC, 29501
johnpritchett@sc.rr.com

Florence Bible Chapel (843-669-7193)
1400 Second Loop Rd, Florence, SC, 29505
Su B 9:15am, M 11:00am, B 6:00pm; We P/M 7:00pm
c/o: Robert Floyd (843-662-9776)
914 Cherokee Rd, Florence, SC, 29501
stanebaldwin@compuserve.com

UNITED STATES — SOUTH CAROLINA 121

GREENVILLE
Overbrook Gospel Chapel (864-233-2101)
26 Overbrook Rd, Greenville, SC, 29607
Su S 9:45am, M 11:00am, B 5:30pm, M 6:45pm; We P 7:15pm
note: mailing address: PO Box 31403, Greenville, SC, 29608
c/o: DeWitt Jones (864-232-0529)
120 Wilshire Dr, Greenville, SC, 29609
dewittgjones@bellsouth.net
alt: Ed Goodwin (864-268-7959)

KINGSTREE
Believer's Bible Chapel
2632 Thurgood Marshall Hwy, Kingstree, SC, 29556
Su S, B 10:00am
c/o: Jimmy Stephenson (843-382-2550)
2632 Thurgood Marshall Hwy, Kingstree, SC, 29556

LONGS
Believer's Bible Chapel (843-399-8247)
12151 Hwy 905 N, Longs, SC, 29568
Su B 9:45am, M 11:00am, M 6:00pm; We P/M 7:30pm
c/o: Alvis Alley (910-754-5547)
66 Fairway, Brierwood, NC, 28459
alt: Paul Prince (843-399-8247)

NORTH AUGUSTA
Bible Chapel (803-278-2807)
460 E Martintown Rd, North Augusta, SC, 29841
Su B 9:30am, S/M 11:00am, M 5:30pm (Prison); We M 7:00pm
c/o: ES (Eugene) Sawyer (803-593-4263)
1050 Hammond Drive, North Augusta, SC, 29841
abssawyer@bellsouth.net

NORTH CHARLESTON
Grace Bible Chapel (843-554-5358)
3935 Whipper Barony Ln, North Charleston, SC, 29405
Su S 10:30am, B 7:00pm, G 12:00pm; We P/M 7:00pm
c/o: Robert V Burns Sr (843-559-5961)
2936 Murraywood Rd, Johns Island, SC, 29455
riburns@maxxconnect.net
alt: Daryl W Dowty Sr (843-797-0517)

PENDLETON
Piedmont Christian Fellowship (864-646-7223)
157 Cherry St, Pendleton, SC, 29670
darryljachens@bellsouth.net
Su B 9:30am, P/M 11:00am
note: meets at Pendleton Depot Building
mailing address: 125 Juniper Dr, Pendleton, SC, 29670
c/o: Darryl Jachens (864-646-7223)
125 Juniper Dr, Pendleton, SC, 29670
darryljachens@bellsouth.net
alt: Dennis Dinger (864-654-3155)

UNITED STATES — SOUTH CAROLINA

ST HELENA ISLAND
Grace and Truth Chapel
PO Box 10, St Helena Island, SC, 29920
Su B, S 10:30am, M 6:00pm, M 12:00pm; We P/M 7:00pm
c/o: Benjamin Glover (803-838-2652)
PO Box 10,
137 Oaks Plantation Rd, St Helena Island, SC, 29920

SUMMERVILLE
Summerville Bible Fellowship (843-821-7430)
10428 Dorchester Rd, Summerville, SC, 29485
Su B 9:30am, F 11:00am, M 6:00pm; We P 7:30pm
c/o: Walter H (Skip) Elliott III (843-873-7083)
109 Pine Lane, Summerville, SC, 29485
skipelliott@juno.com
alt: Ted Fry (843-871-5153)

SOUTH DAKOTA

SIOUX FALLS
Sioux Falls Christian Assembly (605-759-5781)
700 N West Ave, Sioux Falls, SD, 57104
www.siouxfallsbible.com
contact@siouxfallsbible.com
Su B 9:00am, F 10:30am, M 6:30pm; We P 7:00pm (homes)
c/o: Larry Sax (605-582-8299)
800 N. West Ave, Sioux Falls, SD, 57104
larssax@alliancecom.net
alt: Mark Huntington (605-338-2565)

TENNESSEE

DRUMMONDS
Bible Chapel
Rt 1 Box 74, Drummonds, TN, 38023
Su S 10:00am, B 11:00am, G 8:00pm; Fr P 8:00pm
c/o: Sidney Smith
1119 Fayne Rd, Brighton, TN, 38011

KNOXVILLE
Foothills Bible Fellowship (865-983-0290)
328 Boyds Creek Rd, Seymour, TN, 37865
www.foothillsbible.org
Su B 9:30am, F 11:00am
note: The closest large city to us is Knoxville, TN
Use point of contact as church's mailing address
c/o: Ben Cox (865-453-0531)
Robert Ridge Rd #1405, Sevierville, TN, 37862
walkinginthelight@charter.net
alt: Kevin Broyles (865-689-6229)
kevinbroyles@earthlink.net

MURFREESBORO

New Heights Chapel (615-890-2004)
2650 St Andrews Dr, Murfreesboro, TN, 37128
www.newheightschapel.com
info@newheightschapel.com
Su B 9:00am, C/G 10:30am, C 5:00-7:00pm (Awana); Tu L 9:30am
note: mailing address: 1601 E Main St, Murfreesboro, TN, 37130
c/o: David Naylor (615-890-2004)
1601 E Main St, Murfreesboro, TN, 37130
david@newheightschapel.com
alt: Dan Decker (615-893-3403)
dan.d@newheightschapel.com

NASHVILLE

Christian Believers Fellowship (615-883-3188)
2209 Whipple Place, Nashville, TN, 37214
Su B 9:45am, S 11:00am; We P/M 7:00pm
c/o: David King (931-364-5515)
4417 Andrew Jackson Pkwy, Hermitage, TN, 37076
dtking@peoplepc.com

Nashville Gospel Chapel (615-352-2195)
7305 Sonya Dr, Nashville, TN, 37209
www.nashvillegospelchapel.org
Su B 9:15am; S 10:20am, M 11:00am, C 5:00pm
c/o: Matthew J Phelan (615-352-1745)
3693 Reed Harris Rd, Lewisburg, TN, 37091
Matt@hortonhaven.org

OOLTEWAH

Chattanooga Bible Chapel (423-645-6103)
4026 Timber Trace Dr, Ooltewah, TN, 37363
davidgmathews@hotmail.com
Su B 10:30am, M 11:30am
note: Chickamauga Station
c/o: George Mathews (423-893-5375)
7310 Standifer Gap Rd Apt 717, Chattanooga, TN, 37421
alt: Sam Kurikesu (423-326-2080)

SUMMERFIELD

Cumberland Bible Chapel
11140 US 41, Monteagle, TN, 37356
Su B 9:00am, S 10:30am; We P/M 7:00pm
note: 3 mi E of Monteagle on Rt 56N

TEXAS

AMARILLO

Amarillo Bible Chapel (806-359-6277)
6402 Palacio Dr, Amarillo, TX, 79109
Su B 9:00am
note: Does not meet on a regular basis.
c/o: Dr Roberto Estevez (806-359-5329)
robertoestevez@cox.net
alt: Alden White (806-622-0406)

CARROLLTON

Believers Assembly (972-466-2354)
2116 Old Denton Rd, Carrollton, TX, 75006
Su B 9:30am, M 11:00am; Sa P/M 7:00pm
note: Indian
c/o: George Kurian (214-254-3457)
2116 Old Denton Rd, Carrollton, TX, 75006

DALLAS

Community Bible Chapel (972-671-3428)
418 E Main St, Richardson, TX, 75081
www.communitybible.org
cbc@communitybible.org
Su B 9:00am, S 10:00am, G 11:00am; We L 9:30am, C/Y 7:00pm, P 7:15pm
c/o: Gary Boatman (972-671-3428)
418 E Main St, Richardson, TX, 75081

Edmonds Lane Bible Chapel (972-353-9779)
1724 S Edmonds Lane, Lewisville, TX, 75067
elbiblechapel@yahoo.com
Su B 9:15am, S 10:45am, F 11:30am, G/M 6:00pm; We P 7:30pm;
Sa C (Pioneer Club)
c/o: George P John (972-242-7725)
1303 Bentley Dr, Carrollton, TX, 75006
gpjohn1303@yahoo.com
alt: Lawton Owen (972-384-6737)

Garland Bible Chapel (972-272-1436)
1420 W Ave B, Garland, TX, 75042
Su B 9:00am, S 10:20am, M 11:10am; We P 7:30pm
c/o: John R Daniels (972-424-9889)
1815 Mimosa Ave, Plano, TX, 75074

DUNCANVILLE

Wheatland Bible Chapel (972-296-6604)
1303 W Wheatland Rd, Duncanville, TX, 75116
Su B 9:00am, S 10:30am, F 11:10am; We P 7:30pm
c/o: Doug Rice (214-339-9629)
3426 E Perryton, Dallas, TX, 75224
alt: John Martin (972-296-4936)

EL PASO

Grace Chapel (915-598-6035)
PO Box 26395, El Paso, TX, 79915
Su B 9:15am, S 10:20am, F 11:00am; We P 7:00pm
note: 7601 Wilcox Dr
c/o: Jim Hunt (915-598-4660)
7717 Springwood Dr, El Paso, TX, 79925
jhunt001@elp.rr.com
alt: Saul Cooper (915-592-9484)

FORT WORTH

Meadowbrook East Bible Chapel (817-451-5181)
1939 Handley Dr, Fort Worth, TX, 76112
Su B 9:20am, S 10:30am, M 11:00am; We P/M 7:00pm
c/o: Dr Keith Livingstone (817-451-6353)
413 Oakmont Lane N, Fort Worth, TX, 76112

GOLDEN

Golden Bible Chapel (903-768-2700)
PO Box 172, Golden, TX
Su B 9:45am, F 11:00am, P 7:00pm
c/o: Grady Dollar (903-768-2700)
PO Box 172, Golden, TX, 75444

HOUSTON

Colonial Hills Bible Chapel (281-931-1120)
14643 Henry Rd, Houston, TX, 77060
mathewthomas@sbcglobal.net
www.colonialhillsbiblechapel.com
Su B 9:30am; We M 7:30pm; Sa P 9:00am
c/o: Mathew M Thomas (281-397-6923)
4219 Northvale Dr, Houston, TX, 77014
mathewthomas@sbcglobal.net
alt: Frank Martin (281-353-0354)

First Colony Bible Chapel (281-265-3411)
3610 Austin Pkwy, Sugar Land, TX, 77479
www.firstcolonybible.org
info@firstcolonybible.org
Su B 9:00am, S 10:00am, M 11:00am;
We L 9:30am, Y 6:45pm, C/L/M/P 7:00pm
c/o: Ronald G Brown (281-261-7223)
4915 Bellmead Dr, Missouri City, TX, 77459
alt: Richard Nohr (281-491-1273)

India Brethren Assembly
14643 ½ Henry Rd, Houston, TX, 77060
Su B 9:30am, S 11:00am
c/o: T John Mathew (281-443-1554)
710 N Sky Dr, Houston, TX, 77073

Manvel Bible Chapel (281-489-7635)
4230 FM 1128, Pearland, TX, 77584
Su B 9:00am, S 10:30am, F 11:20am, P 6:00pm; We P/M 7:30pm
note: 4230 FM 1128, Pearland, TX
c/o: Sherman Weaver (281-331-8697)

Pineview Bible Chapel (713-697-6529)
9742 E Hardy St, Houston, TX, 77093
Su B 9:30am, F 11:00am; We P 7:30pm
c/o: Art Davies (281-480-0704)
1915 Heather Cove Ct, Houston, TX, 77062
adavies@mail.wt.net
alt: Eric Unander (713-697-5159)

Southwest Bible Chapel (281-744-0644)
PO Box 42601, Houston, TX, 77242
c/o: Daniel E Lopez (281-277-1099)
8634 Magnolia Forest Drive, Sugar Land, TX, 77479
danlopez@houston.rr.com

Iglesia Biblica Vida Nueva
13919 Alief Clodine Rd, Houston, TX 77082
c/o: Hugo Garcia

IRVING

Dallas Brethren Assembly (972-253-4621)
1820 W 7th St, Irving, TX, 75060
Su B 9:30am, S 10:30am; Sa M 7:00pm
note: use point of contact as church's mailing address
c/o: K C Mathai (972-253-4621)
1928 Covey Ct, Irving, TX, 75060
alt: John William (972-253-7130)

KARNES CITY

Old Paths Bible Chapel (830-216-4075)
107 East Calvert, Karnes City, TX, 78118
Su B 9:00am, S 10:00am, F 11:15am
c/o: Tom Boynton (830-216-4075)
205 County Rd 403, Floresville, TX, 78114
tboynton@texas.net
alt: Roger Hepworth (830-780-4440)

LONGVIEW

Brookwood Bible Chapel (903-234-0185)
1411 McCann Rd, Longview, TX, 75601
Su B 10:00am, F 11:00am; We P 7:00pm
c/o: Fred Klerekoper (903-759-5974)
9 Alice Circle, Longview, TX, 75605
fredk24@juno.com

LUBBOCK

South Plains Bible Chapel (806-795-0014)
5402 Quaker Ave, Lubbock, TX, 79413
Su B 9:30am, M 11:00am; We P 7:00pm
c/o: Curtis Flory (806-798-3509)
5408 93rd St, Lubbock, TX, 79424
curtf@nts-online.net

MARSHALL

Believers Bible Fellowship
Hwy 43 S, Marshall, TX
c/o: Bob Bryant (214-938-2440)
PO Box 458, Marshall, TX, 75671

MAURICEVILLE

Grace Bible Fellowship
6025 Hwy 12, Vidor, TX, 77662
note: mailing address: PO Box 1298, Mauriceville, TX 77626
Su M 10:00am, M 11:00am, B 6:00pm, M 7:00pm; We P/M 7:00pm;
Th M (homes)

MCKINNEY

McKinney Bible Church (972-548-1976)
501 S Graves, Mckinney, TX, 75069
Su B/S

MESQUITE

Eastfield Bible Chapel
3516 Oates Dr, Mesquite, TX, 75150
Su S 9:45am, M 11:00am, B 6:30pm
c/o: Mike Reeves
2605 Monticello, Mesquite, TX, 75149

NORTH RICHLAND HILLS

North Richland Hills Bible Chapel (817-605-3935)
7700 Hewitt St, North Richland Hills, TX, 76180
www.nrhbiblechapel.com
Su B 9:30am, S/F 11:00am; We P/M 7:00pm
c/o: Bob Newberry (817-980-0840)
1719 L West View Terrace, Arlington, TX, 76103
bob-carole@sbcglobal.net
alt: Rob McLaren (817-992-2980)
cab.driver@charter.net

PARK SIDE

Bethesda Bible Chapel (972-790-5557)
2108 Coral Ct, Irving, TX, 75060
www.bethesdabiblechapel.org
skariahvarghese@yahoo.com
Su S 9:15am, B 10:00am, M 11:30am; We P 7:00pm;
Sa C 6:00pm (Kids Club), L 6:00pm, M 7:00pm
c/o: Skariah Varghese (972-790-5557)
2108 Coral Ct, Irving, TX, 75060
skariahvarghese@yahoo.com

PLANO

Bible Chapel (214-423-5321)
1900 Shiloh Rd Box 152, Plano, TX, 75074
c/o: James E Lewis (214-783-7637)
2108 Scarlet Oak Dr, Richardson, TX, 75081

RICHARDSON

Trinity Fellowship (972-690-9535)
932 S Greenville, Dallas, TX, 75081
Su S 9:00am, B 9:30am, M 11:50am
c/o: Alan R Hull MD (214-692-7645)

ROUND ROCK

Austin Bible Chapel (512-966-4296)
555-D Round Rock W Dr, Ste 100, Round Rock, TX, 78681
fullerfamily@cox-internet.com
http://austinbiblechapel.org
Su B 11:15am, S 12:45pm; We P 7:30pm
c/o: Robin Fuller (512-966-4296)
407 W Esparada Dr, Georgetown, TX, 78628
fullerfamily@cox-internet.com
alt: Billy Tweddell (512-259-5047)

SAN ANTONIO

Cheryl Bible Chapel (210-432-7520)
135 W Cheryl Dr, San Antonio, TX, 78228
www.cherylbiblechapel.com
Su B 9:00am, S 10:00am, F 11:15am; We P 7:00pm
c/o: Kyle Turner (210-681-0293)
8722 Tamarind, San Antonio, TX, 78240
kturner002@yahoo.com
alt: Louis Kreusel (210-349-4563)

Sewanee Gospel Hall
802 Sewanee St, San Antonio, TX, 78210
Su B 11:00am, F 7:00pm; Tu G 7:00pm; Fr P 7:00pm
c/o: Henry T Plummer (210-842-8796)

SOUTH HOUSTON
Iglesia Cristiana Evangelica de South Houston (713-947-2466)
716 Ave I, South Houston, TX, 77587
Su B 9:00am, F 10:25am; We P 7:30pm; Fr Y 8:00pm
c/o: Ruben Bandini (281-481-4495)
716 Ave I, South Houston, TX, 77587
rubenb78@juno.com

SUGAR LAND
Iglesia Cristiana Evangelica Verdad en Amor (281-340-2400)
11000 Dairy Ashford St, Sugar Land, TX, 77478
www.centrofamiliarcristiano.net
Su B 9:30am, S 10:15am, G 11:30am; We P 7:30pm
note: mailing address: PO Box 1828, Sugar Land, TX, 77487
c/o: Daniel Dominguez (281-261-7222)
4115 Jetty Terr, Missouri City, TX, 77459
ddominguez@bdo.com
alt: Daniel Martin (832-435-2125)

WACO
Waco Bible Chapel (254-754-4248)
3300 N 22nd St, Waco, TX, 76708
Su B 9:00am, F 11:00am
c/o: Richard Plowman (254-848-5864)
3101 Pioneer Circle, Waco, TX, 76712
dplowman@hot.rr.com
alt: Jerry King (254-829-2572)

UTAH

OGDEN
Ogden Area Christians
2304 Polk, Ogden, UT, 84041
Su B/M
c/o: Roger Wardell (801-732-1240)
4610 W 4350 S, West Haven, UT, 84075
roger@wardellfamily.com
alt: Mike Greenwood (801-621-3569)

VERMONT

HARDWICK
Gospel Hall (802-472-6110)
PO Box 351, Hardwick, VT, 05843
Su B 10:00am, S 11:30am, G 12:15pm; Th P/M 7:00pm
note: 153 Cherry St
c/o: William D Scott (802-472-6257)
438 Dimick Rd, E Hardwick, VT, 05836

RUTLAND

Bethany Bible Chapel (802-747-7267)
39 Evergreen Ave, Rutland, VT, 05701
robbon2@verizon.net
Su B 9:30am, M 1:00pm
note: use point of contact as church's mailing address
c/o: Robert M Lucas (802-747-7267)
39 Evergreen Ave, Rutland, VT, 05701
robbon2@verizon.net

WHEELOCK

Wheelock Bible Fellowship
444 Cherry Lane, Lyndonville, VT, 05851
Su B 9:30am, F 11:00am; Tu P 6:30pm (homes), M 7:00pm (homes)
note: meets in Town Hall Rt 122
Use point of contact as church's mailing address
c/o: Jim Sanders (802-626-9448)
444 Cherry Lane, Lyndonville, VT, 05851
appleberry_farm@pshift.com
alt: Tim Terhune (802-525-4758)
terhune@afo.net

VIRGINIA

ARLINGTON

Cherrydale Bible Church (703-276-8200)
1905 N Monroe St, Arlington, VA, 22207
www.cherrydalebiblechapel.org
Su B 9:00am, S 10:15am, F 11:30am; We P/M
c/o: Excell Duncan (703-256-0107)
5400 Blacksburg Rd, Springfield, VA, 22151
duncboots@webtv.net
alt: Torrey LaBuff (703-293-9824)

DANVILLE

Danville Bible Chapel (434-822-2882)
214 Parkway Dr, Danville, VA, 24541
Su B 9:30am, F 11:00am; We P/M 7:00pm
c/o: Henry Sasser (434-685-2123)
166 Meadow Brook Cir, Danville, VA, 24541
sasser.hs@sassersigns.com

MARION

Marion Gospel Chapel (276-646-8869)
110 High St, Marion, VA, 24354
dksmith@va.net
Su B 9:45am, F 11:00am, G 6:45pm; We P/M 6:45pm
c/o: David L Smith (276-646-8869)
540 Chestnut Ridge Rd, Marion, VA, 24354
dksmith@va.net

MATOACA
Matoaca Gospel Hall
6204 River Rd, Matoaca, VA, 23803
Su B 9:30am, S 11:00am, G 7:30pm; We P 7:30pm
alt: John Nobles (804-265-5455)
5859 Spring Run Dr, Church Road, VA, 23833

NEWPORT NEWS
Bethany Gospel Chapel (757-596-9682)
40 Ballard Rd, Newport News, VA, 23601
www.bethanygospelchapel.org
believers@bethanygospelchapel.org
Su B 9:30am, F 11:00am, M 6:00pm, C 7:00pm; We P 7:30pm
note: mailing address: PO Box 1847, Newport News, VA, 23601
c/o: Neil Goggin (757-357-4041)
215 Irvin Dr, Smithfield, VA, 23430
kilroygo@verizon.net
alt: Roy Markham (757-596-8433)
rymbbm0519@cox.net

Hampton Roads Community Church (757-273-4380)
28 Harpersville Rd, Newport News, VA, 23601
1gstewart@cox.net
www.hrcchurch.com
note: meets at Poquoson Primary School
c/o: Gary Stewart (757-594-0464)
1gstewart@cox.net

NOKESVILLE
Nokesville Gospel Chapel
12801 Fitzwater Drive, Nokesville, VA 20181
Su B 9:45am, S 10:30am, M 11:05am; We P 7:30pm
Note: mailing address: PO Box 173, Nokesville, VA, 20182
c/o: Robert P. Chambers (703-266-2764)
6877 Ridge Water Court, Centreville, VA, 20121

NORFOLK
Tidewater Gospel Chapel (757-461-0539)
5894 Chambers St, Norfolk, VA, 23502
Su B 9:30am, M 11:30am; We P 7:30pm
c/o: Michael Beverly (757-432-0415)
5894 Chambers St, Norfolk, VA, 23502

RICHMOND
Carlisle Avenue Gospel Chapel (804-222-6020)
2506 Carlisle Ave, Richmond, VA, 23231
Su B/S, G 6:00pm; We P/M 7:00pm
c/o: Tom Brown (804-746-8449)
8065 Rose Hill Dr, Mechanicsville, VA, 23111
alt: Robbie Brown (804-559-4489)

UNITED STATES — VIRGINIA

Grace Gospel Chapel (804-794-4465)
1201 Spirea Rd, Richmond, VA, 23236
www.gracegospelchapel.com
Su B 9:30am, F 11:00am, M 1:15pm; We P/M 7:00pm
c/o: Herman Reams (804-443-4458)
554 E Banbury Rd, Tappahannock, VA 22560
hreams5@gmail.com

ROANOKE
Fleming Chapel (540-563-0298)
134 Maplelawn Ave, Roanoke, VA, 24012
Su B 9:30am, F 11:00am, M 6:00pm; We P 7:00pm
c/o: Wesley Wilson (540-774-9452)
4865 Glen Ivy Ln, #212, Roanoke, VA, 24018
artwes@verizon.net
alt: Andrew Shelor (540-774-4047)
douloichristou@cox.net

SYRIA
Sunnybrook Gospel Chapel (540-547-2727)
20308 Camp Rd, Culpeper, VA, 22743
Su F/S 9:45am, B 11:00am; We P 7:30pm
c/o: McKinley Jenkins (540-547-2727)
20308 Camp Rd, Culpeper, VA, 22701
alt: James Hasse (540-987-8661)

VICTORIA
Northside Gospel Chapel (434-696-1329)
2300 Marshall Ave, Victoria, VA, 23974
Su B 9:45am, F 11:00am, P/M 6:00pm; Tu P 7:00pm
c/o: William H Hardy (434-696-4469)
2617 Nottoway Blvd, Victoria, VA, 23974
alt: Clifford Hood (434-696-4401 or 696-3351)

WAYNESBORO
Waynesboro Bible Chapel (540-652-0204)
591 N Winchester Ave, Waynesboro, VA, 22980
Su B 10:00am, M/F 11:00am
c/o: Todd Knight (540-652-0204)
194 Covenant Place, Shendandoah, VA, 22849
lisaknight66@yahoo.com

WASHINGTON

ARLINGTON
Arlington Gospel Hall (360-435-3797)
323 S Stillaguamish Ave, Arlington, WA, 98223
Su B 9:30am, S 11:30am, G 6:30pm; Mo Y 7:00pm; We P/M 7:00pm
note: use point of contact as church's mailing address
c/o: Tim Klein (360-435-4466)
24224 47th Ave NE, Arlington, WA, 98223
kleinta98223@hotmail.com

BAINBRIDGE ISLAND
Bainbridge Bible Chapel (206-780-0226)
Bainbridge Island, WA
Su B 9:30am, S 11:00am, P 6:30pm; Tu M 6:30am; Th M 7:00pm
note: meets at Ordway Elem School
c/o: Loren Cleven (206-842-1508)
6502 Justin Ct, Bainbridge Island, WA, 98110

BELLINGHAM
Bellingham Bible Chapel
4160 Northwest Dr, Bellingham, WA, 98226
Su B 10:00am, S 11:30am; We P/M 7:00pm
c/o: Steve Banham (360-312-1013)
banhams@verizon.net
alt: John DesChane (360-383-0086)

BREMERTON
Westsound Bible Fellowship
300 Montgomery North, Bremerton, WA
c/o: Tim Morris

CENTRALIA
Bible Chapel (206-736-2483)
209 N Pearl, Centralia, WA, 98531
Su B 9:45am, S 11:00am; We P/M 6:45pm, M 7:30pm
c/o: Richard E Barada (206-736-6466)
512 N Iron, Centralia, WA, 98531

COSMOPOLIS
Gospel Chapel (360-533-5847)
PO Box 524, Cosmopolis, WA, 98537
Su S, B 9:15am, M 6:00pm; We P 7:00pm
note: 1024 3rd St
c/o: Don Norkoski (360-532-2247)
PO Box 483
1009 3rd St, Cosmopolis, WA, 98537

EVERETT
Parkside Bible Chapel (425-259-0272)
2427 Lombard Ave, Everett, WA, 98201
Su B 9:30am, S 11:15am; We M 7:00pm
c/o: Dan Thomson (425-814-4783)
alt: Doug Kazen (425-823-9017)

FEDERAL WAY

Evergreen Bible Chapel (253-927-7999)
34030 21st Ave SW, Federal Way, WA, 98023
www.evergreenbiblechapel.com
info@evergreenbiblechapel.com
Su B 9:30am, F 11:00am, S 11:15am; We P 7:00pm; Th L 10:00am
c/o: Steve Blevin (253-874-0308)
30143 12th Ave SW, Federal Way, WA, 98023
steve@belvins.net
alt: Brahma Nand (253-952-1143)
bnsnand@yahoo.com

KELSO

Christians Gathered to the Name of the Lord Jesus Christ
(360-456-8421)
109 NW 1st, Kelso, WA, 98503
middletn@gte.net
Su G 10:00am, B 11:00am, P 12:00pm; Fr M 7:00pm (Spanish)
note: use point of contact as church's mailing address
c/o: Mike Middleton (360-456-8421)
3502 Ruddell Loop SE, Lacey, WA, 98503

LONGVIEW

Evergreen Terrace Gospel Chapel (360-414-0513)
5052 Pacific Terr, Longview, WA, 98632
Su B 9:30am, F 11:15am; We P/M 7:00pm
c/o: Roy A Eastlick (360-423-2734)
304 Nevada Dr, Longview, WA, 98632

LYNDEN

Lyden Gospel Hall (360-354-2221)
710 E Grover St, Lynden, WA, 98264
Su B 9:30am, G 11:30am; We P 7:30pm
c/o: Brian Fadden (360-988-0756)
605 Arthurs Way, Sumas, WA, 98259

LYNNWOOD

North Lynnwood Bible Chapel (425-742-1344)
15911 Admiralty Way, Lynnwood, WA, 98087
Su B 9:30am, S 10:20am, F 11:30am; We P 7:00pm
c/o: Kevin Roundhill (425-335-7801)
3223 127th Ave NE, Lake Stevens, WA, 98258
ksroundhill@comcast.net
alt: Hyuk-Ki Kwon (425-787-3024)
hysokwon@msn.com

UNITED STATES — WASHINGTON

OKANOGAN
Okanogan Gospel Hall
308 Conconully St, Okanogan, WA, 98840
Su B 10:00am, S/M 11:30am, P/G 6:30pm; We P/M 7:30pm
note: use point of contact as church's mailing address
c/o: Wolter Abbink (509-422-2526)
140 Pleasant Valley Rd, Okanogan, WA, 98840
wabbink@msn.com
alt: Reuben Hale (509-826-5369)

PASCO
Tri-Cities Gospel Hall (509-948-3081)
316 N 11th Ave, Pasco, WA, 99301
Su B 10:00am, S/M 11:30am, G 6:30pm; Mo Y 7:00pm; We P/M 7:00pm
c/o: Bryon Meyers (509-544-0197)
15612 Springfield Dr., Pasco, WA, 99301
bmeyers@whidbey.net
alt: Roy Ficek (509-542-0850)
rsficek@yahoo.com

West Pasco Christians
Pasco, WA, 99301
c/o: Josh Wheatley (509-544-9022)
joshgloria@hotmail.com
alt: RoyFicek (509-542-0850)
rsmijaf@yahoo.com

SEATTLE
Hope Bible Fellowship (206-632-4060)
4000 Whitman Ave N, Seattle, WA, 98103
www.hbfseattle.org
hopebiblefellowship@juno.com
Su B/S 10:00am
c/o: Michael Vederoff (206-892-0052)
5247 19th Ave NE, Seattle, WA, 98105

Northgate Gospel Chapel (206-363-3366)
14330 15th Ave NE, Seattle, WA, 98125
northgatechapel@prodigy.net
Su B 9:30am, F/S 11:00am, M 6:30pm; Mo C 7:00pm; Tu L 9:30am; We P/M 7:45pm
c/o: Brent Holterman (206-364-6078)
PO Box 55666, Shoreline, WA, 98155
holterman@seanet.com
alt: Sumner Osborne Jr (206-364-8039)

Sunrise Fellowship
9207 15th Ave NE, Seattle, WA, 98115
Su S 10:00am, B 11:00am
c/o: Robert Spiro (206-522-3971)
9207 15th Ave NE, Seattle, WA, 98115

UNITED STATES — WASHINGTON

West Woodland Gospel Hall
17826 Hwy 9 SE, Snohomish, WA, 98296
Su B 9:30am, S 11:30am, G 7:00pm; We P/M 7:00pm
note: meeting temporarily at Clearview Center
c/o: Andrew Hale (425-402-8278)
23810 75th Ave SE, Woodinville, WA, 98072
haleco@integrity.com
alt: Dan DeFreece (425-486-1767)

SEATTLE (SOUTH)
Des Moines Gospel Chapel (206-878-2145)
21914 7th Ave S, Des Moines, WA, 98198
www.dmgc.org / info@dmgc.org
Su B/C 9:30am, S/F 11:00am; Tu M/Y 7:00pm; We M/Y 7:00pm;
Th L 10:00am, M 7:00pm
c/o: Mac Sauerlender (206-878-2145)
PO Box 98247, Des Moines, WA, 98198
mac@dmgc.org

SPOKANE
Monroe Park Gospel Chapel
N4123 Monroe, Spokane, WA, 99205
Su B 8:30am, M 9:45am, M 11:15am (Russian); We P/M 7:00pm
c/o: Arlon D Cook (509-467-5027)
5905 W Lonewolf Ave, Spokane, WA, 99208

SUNNYSIDE
Lower Valley Christian Fellowship
16th & Federal Way, Sunnyside, WA
Su B 10:00am, S 11:15am
c/o: John B Flodin (509-837-5084)
3523 Sheller Rd, Sunnyside, WA, 98944
alt: Dr Fred Boboth (509-837-3459)

TACOMA
Tacoma Gospel Hall (253-925-5290)
4064 S A St, Tacoma, WA, 98418
Su B 10:00am, S 11:30am, G 7:00pm; We P/M 7:00pm
c/o: Thomas E Donofrio (360-893-6695)
2100 S 375th St, Federal Way, WA, 98003
dtaldina@comcast.net
alt: Bob Stephens (253-566-4900)

YAKIMA
Tieton Drive Bible Chapel (509-966-6190)
4305 Tieton Dr, Yakima, WA, 98908
Su B 9:00am, S 10:00am, F 11:00am, P 6:00pm (4th Su); We P/M 7:00pm
c/o: Glen Crawford (509-966-6564)
180 W Canyon, Yakima, WA, 98908
alt: Gene Cole (509-678-4878)

WEST VIRGINIA

HINTON
Riverview Chapel (304-466-0769)
16th Ave and Temple St, Hinton, WV, 25951
Su B, S/F, M 6:00pm; Tu L 10:00am (1st Tu of each month, Sept-May);
We P/M 7:00pm
note: use point of contact as church's mailing address
c/o: Brent Jones (304-466-4738)
504 Greenbrier Dr, Hinton, WV, 25951-2624
brentandhope@verizon.net
alt: Frank Jones (304-466-3488)
twinoaks@verizon.net

HUNTINGTON
Huntington Gospel Chapel (304-529-6351)
1236 28th St, Huntington, WV, 25705
Su B 9:30am, S 11:00am, G 7:00pm; We P/M 7:00pm
c/o: Arnold Clary (304-736-1827)
5263 Midway Dr, Huntington, WV, 25705

MULLENS
Welton Bible Chapel (304-294-7458)
Rt 16, Allen Jctn, WV, 25810
Su B 9:30am, F 10:30am, G 6:00pm; We P 7:00pm
note: use point of contact as church's mailing address
c/o: David G Pollock (304-294-4350)
PO Box 7, Mullens, WV, 25882
davidgpollock@yahoo.com
alt: Mr. Douglas Hedrick (304-294-6568)
tensinsorone@yahoo.com

OTSEGO
Otsego Bible Chapel (304-294-8776)
PO Box 114, Mullens, 25882
michaelocook@aol.com
Su B 9:30am, S 10:30am; We M 7:00pm
c/o: Michael O Cook (304-294-8776)
PO Box 114, Mullens, WV, 25882
michaelocook@aol.com
alt: Michael Endreson (304-294-8776)

TERRA ALTA
Hillcrest Chapel
Terra Alta, WV
Su S/G, B 9:00am; Tu P/M 7:00pm
c/o: Larry Sterling (304-789-6271)
Rt 1 Box 199, Terra Alta, WV, 26764

WESTOVER

Crescent Hills Chapel (304-296-7130)
PO Box 2387, Morgantown, 26505
Su B 9:30am, S 11:00am, M 6:00pm; Th P 7:00pm
note: 216 Parkview Dr (Westover)
c/o: Donald Williams (340-296-6040)
2030 Canterbury Dr, Morgantown, WV, 26505
donnywwv@aol.com

WISCONSIN

APPLETON

Fox Valley Bible Chapel
Appleton, WI
Su B 10:00am, S 11:30am, M 6:00pm; Th P 7:00pm
note: meets in Little Chute Civic Center/Library
c/o: Tim Geske (920-766-1325)
917 Desnoyer St, Kaukauna, WI, 54130
tgeske@new.rr.com
alt: Peter Jacques (920-788-0149)

BEETOWN

Beetown Gospel Hall
Beetown, WI, 53802
Su B 10:00am, S/M 10:15am, G 7:30pm; We P 7:30pm
note: 1026 Ridge Ave(Lancaster, WI)
c/o: Marvin R Studnicka (608-723-7156)
1026 Ridge Ave, Lancaster, WI, 53813

BELOIT

Beloit Gospel Hall (608-365-3305)
1129 North St, Beloit, WI, 53511
Su S 9:45am, B 11:00am, G 6:00pm; We P 7:00pm
c/o: Tom Ruff (608-365-5962)
2068 Colony Ct, Beloit, WI, 53511
alt: Tommie Ruff (608-362-5618)

BLACK EARTH

Gospel Hall (608-767-2962)
1316 Center St, Black Earth, WI, 53515
Su B 9:30am, S 11:00am, G 11:45am; We P/M 7:30pm
c/o: Lynn L Larson (608-767-3965)
10247 Schoenemann Rd, Mazomanie, WI, 53560

BLACK RIVER FALLS

Black River Gospel Hall
307 N 8th St, Black River Falls, WI, 54615
Su S 10:30am, B 11:00am, G 7:30pm; We P/M 7:30pm
c/o: Eugene Bruley (715-284-9714)
W 11438 County Hwy P, Black River Falls, WI, 54615

UNITED STATES — WISCONSIN

BLUE RIVER
Gospel Hall
15513 Richwood Estates Lane, Blue River, WI, 53518
Su S 9:45am, B 10:30am, G 8:00pm; Th P/M 8:00pm
c/o: James C Frazier (608-537-2977)
15513 Richwood Estates Lane, Blue River, WI, 53518

BRODHEAD
Gospel Hall
908 1st Ctr Ave, Brodhead, WI, 53520
Su S 10:00am, B 11:00am, G 7:00pm; We P/M 8:00pm
c/o: Chris Kneubuehl (608-897-2385)
4611 Cty Rd T, Brodhead, WI, 53520
alt: Michael Wenger (608-897-8468)

CASCO
Country Bible Church (920-837-2594)
E2179 State Rd 54, Casco, WI, 54205
www.countrybiblechurch.com
Su B 9:00am, M 10:30am; We M 7:00pm
c/o: Mark J Dhuey (920-845-5656)
N5938 Birchwood Cir, Luxemburg, WI, 54217
alt: Robert J. Steiner (920-845-9356)

CHIPPEWA FALLS
River Valley Christian Fellowship
E 1000 Grand Ave, Chippewa Falls, WI, 54729
Su B 9:30am, S 11:00am; We P/M 7:00pm
c/o: Joel Hanson (715-834-7128)
4306 N Shore Dr, Eau Claire, WI, 54703
joelannette@juno.com
alt: Warren Henderson (715-962-3708)

EGG HARBOR
Christians Gathered to the Name of the Lord Jesus Christ
1860 Hwy 42, Egg Harbor, WI, 54209
Su B 10:00am, S 11:30am, G 7:30pm; We P 7:30pm (call for location), M 7:30pm (call for location)
note: Bertschinger Comm Center
c/o: Steve Kalms (920-854-4630)
11278 Old Stage Rd, Sister Bay, WI, 54234

JANESVILLE
Believers in Christ Fellowship (home)
4608 W Brookmeadow Ln, Janesville, WI, 53545
Su B 10:00am, G 11:15am
c/o: Dr David Paul DuPree (608-346-3477)
4608 W Brookmeadow Ln, Janesville, WI, 53545
ddupree959@yahoo.com

UNITED STATES — WISCONSIN

KENOSHA
Grace Bible Chapel (262-654-9631)
3917 59th St, Kenosha, WI, 53144
www.gbc-kenosha.org
Su B 9:00am, F/S 10:30am, G 6:00pm; Tu Y 7:00pm; We L 10:00am, P/M 7:00pm
c/o: Jim Greenwald (262-654-4882)
5807 40th Ave, Kenosha, WI, 53144
gymgreenwald@netzero.com
alt: Ian Taylor (262-697-1383)

KEWAUNEE
Kewaunee Christian Assembly (920-388-2321)
N5524 State Hwy 42, Kewaunee, WI, 54216
terryrpeterson@gmail.com
Su B 4:00pm, F 5:00pm
c/o: Michael S Smits (920-388-2321)
N5524 State Hwy 42, Kewaunee, WI, 54216
alt: Terry R Peterson (920-490-0327)
terryrpeterson@gmail.com

LACROSSE
LaCrosse Gospel Hall (608-783-4390)
1928 George St, Lacrosse, WI, 54603
Su B 9:30am, S 11:00am, G 7:00pm; We P/M 7:30pm
c/o: Cal Erikson (608-790-7724)
1514 Hoffman Pl, Onalaska, WI, 54650
cberikso@hotmail.com
alt: V Paul Aspenson (608-787-0074)
aspensonlumber@hotmail.com

LAKE GENEVA
Lake Geneva Bible Chapel (262-248-8414)
501 South St, Lake Geneva, WI, 53147
Su B 9:30am, S/F 11:00am; Tu L 10:00 am; We P/M 7:00pm
c/o: J. T. Sterk (608-305-0316)
1038 Nantucket Dr, Janesville, WI, 53546
housesterk@hotmail.com

MADISON
Grace Fellowship (608-223-0148)
5201 Turner Ave, Madison, WI, 53716
Su S 9:30am, B 11:00am; We P/M 6:45pm
c/o: David F Brauch (608-846-5023)
6084 Imperial Dr, Waunakee, WI, 53597

MILWAUKEE
Lighthouse Gospel Chapel
3512 W. North Ave, Milwaukee, WI, 52308
Su B, S 9:45am, M 7:00pm (Th)
c/o: James Carrington (414-444-3828)
2636 N 63rd St, Wauwatosa, WI, 53213

Wauwatosa Bible Chapel (414-771-1030)
2200 N 67th St, Milwaukee, WI, 53213
www.wauwatosabiblechapel.org
info@wauwatosabiblechapel.org
Su B 9:00am, F/C/S 10:30am; We P/M 7:00pm; Th L/M 9:30am
c/o: Fred Schwertfeger (262-783-5986)
13020 Oriole Lane, Brookfield, WI, 53045
fschwertfeger@wi.rr.com
alt: Jim Quindt (414-445-1536)

MOUNT STERLING

Christian Assembly (home)
53015 State Hwy 171, Mount Sterling, WI, 54645
Su B 10:00am, M 11:15am; We P 8:00pm
c/o: Gays Mills (608-734-3515)
53015 State Hwy 171, Mount Sterling, WI, 54645

Mount Sterling Gospel Hall
RR 1 Box 219, Mount Sterling, WI, 54626
Su B 10:00am, S/M 11:15am, G 7:30pm; We P/M 7:45pm
c/o: Richard M Dudgeon (608-734-3639)
19663 Stove Rd, Eastman, WI, 54626
rmdudgeon@juno.com

OCONOMOWOC

Oconomowoc Bible Fellowship
PO Box 373, Oconomowoc, WI, 53066
Su B 9:30am, S 10:45am; Tu P 11:00am; Th P/M 7:00pm
note: meets at Country Christian School, 4476 Lakeland Dr, Nashotah, WI, 53058
c/o: Daryl Stephenson (262-244-7226)
234 Henry St, Dousman, WI, 53118
dsteph@wi.rr.com
alt: Mike Brinkman (800-513-3832)

ONTARIO

Gospel Hall
510 Division St, Ontario, WI, 54651
Su S/M 10:00am, B 11:00am, G 8:00pm; We P/M 8:00pm
c/o: Kent Hendrickson (608-489-3519)
E14199 Burr Salem Rd, Ontario, WI, 54651
kbhendrickson@mwt.net

PRAIRIE DU CHIEN

Christian Assembly of Prairie
900 Cliffhaven Dr, Prairie Du Chien, WI, 53821
Su B 10:00am, F 11:00am; We P 8:00pm
c/o: Robert L Borne (608-326-7474)
314 N State St, Prairie Du Chien, WI, 53821

SHEBOYGAN

Zion Christian Assembly
2511 Glenside Cir, Sheboygan, WI, 53081
Su B 9:30am, S 11:00am, G/M 6:30pm
note: meeting in home
c/o: Allen Hanson (920-458-4137 or 452-5014)
2511 Glenside Cir, Sheboygan, WI, 53081
glenside@juno.com

WAUKESHA

Waukesha Gospel Hall
118 W Broadway St, Waukesha, WI, 53186
waukeshagospelhall@earthlink.net
Su B 9:30am, S 11:30am, G 6:30pm; We P/M 7:30pm
c/o: Cory Peppler (262-549-2386)
S45 W22407 Quinn Rd, Waukesha, WI, 53189
cpeppler@earthlink.net
alt: John Orr (262-642-3093)

WAUSAU

Bible Truth Chapel (715-675-2236)
1600 N. First Ave, Wausau, WI, 54401
www.bibletruthchapel.org
Su 9:15am, 6:00pm; We 6:30pm
c/o: Roger W Grebe (715-845-4118)
3016 11th St, Wausau, WI, 54403
alt: John Buch (715-675-6338)

WESTBY

Grace & Truth Bible Chapel (608-634-3671)
103 Willow Lane, Westby, WI, 54667
Su B 9:00am, F 10:45am; We P/M 7:00pm
note: 100 Norseland Ct
c/o: Luke Hartkopf (608-634-4001)
303 W State St, Westby, WI, 54667
alt: Theo Habel (608-787-0323)

CANADA

ALBERTA

BOYLE

Boyle Gospel Chapel (780-689-4124)
Boyle, AB
Su B 10:00am, F 11:00am; Tu P 8:00pm; We L 9:30am; Fr Y 7:30pm
c/o: Ellwood Splane (780-689-2254)
Box 29, Boyle, AB, T0A 0M0
alt: Jim Pettifer (780-689-4124)

CALGARY

Berea Bible Chapel (403-285-0556)
Site 8, Box 8, RR 6, Calgary, AB, T2M 4L5
Su B 10:00am
c/o: Andrew Kettle (403-293-3137)
435 Templeton Rd NE, Calgary, AB, T1Y 4L8
akettle@cadvision.com

Bethany Chapel of Calgary (403-249-8605)
3333 Richardson Way SW, Calgary, AB, T3E 7B6
bethany@bethanychapel.com

Bowood Gospel Chapel (403-288-8393)
6508 Bowood Dr NW, Calgary, AB, T3B 2G8
Su B 9:30am, S 11:00am
c/o: Les Kiffiak (403-247-1853)
3447 Bonita Cres NW, Calgary, AB, T3B 2R9

Good News Bible Chapel (403-619-2816)
739-20th Ave NW, Calgary, AB
www.goodnewsbiblechapel.org
goodnews@goodnewsbiblechapel.org
Su B 10:00am, F/S 11:15am; Mo P 7:30pm
note: mailing address: PO Box 64328, 5512 4th St NW, Calgary, AB, T2K 6J1
c/o: Brent Rawlings (403-730-1677)
145 Sandpiper Circle NW, Calgary, AB, T3K 3R4
rawlings@shaw.ca
alt: John Teigen (403-288-0683)
jjteigen@shaw.ca

Good News Gospel Chapel
PO Box 64328, Calgary, AB, T2K 6J1
Su B 10:00am, S/M 10:45am
note: 5512-2 Street NW (meets in Scandinavian Centre)
c/o: Brent Rawlings (403-730-1677)
gnbcc@shaw.ca

CANADA — ALBERTA

Northside Bible Fellowship
2911 Edmonton Trail NE, Calgary, AB, T2E 3N5
Su B 9:30am, S 11:00am, G 6:00pm; We P 7:00pm
c/o: Andrew Hills (403-230-5344)
461 21st Ave NE, Calgary, AB, T2E 1S7
apcjsn@telus.net

West Hillhurst Gospel Hall (403-289-2688)
2326 7th Ave NW, Calgary, AB, T2N 1A1
gwseale@shaw.ca
Su B 10:00am, G 7:00pm, S 12:15pm; We M 7:30pm
c/o: Jim Robinson (403-280-6016)
64 Martin Grove Way NE, Calgary, AB, T3J 2T1
jimnr@telusplanet.net
alt: Derek Hanna (403-236-4126)

COLEMAN

Coleman Christian Assembly
Coleman, AB, Box 793
c/o: John Russell (403-563-5388)
Box 793, Coleman, AB, T0K 0M0

CROWSNEST

Coleman Christian Assembly (563-5388)
1802 77th St, Crowsnest, AB
Su B/S
c/o: John Russell (563-3827)
Box 783, Coleman, AB, T0K 0W0

EDMONTON

Bethel Gospel Chapel (780-477-3341)
11461 95th St NW, Edmonton, AB, T5G 1L3
Su B 9:30am, F 11:00am, P 12:30pm (1st); Tu & We & Th (in homes);
Fr Y 7:00pm
c/o: Frank Parker (780-479-1330)
11728 - 87 St, Edmonton, AB, T5B 3M7
fparker@interbaun.com
alt: George Idema (780-433-7599)
gidema@interbaun.com

Capilano Christian Assembly (780-469-7801)
9333 50th St NW, Edmonton, AB, T6B 2L5
www.capilano.org
mail@capilano.org
Su B 9:30am, F/S 11:00am; Tu C 7:00pm; Th L 9:15am, L 7:00pm;
Fr Y 7:00pm

Clareview Bible Church
3629 - 145 Ave, Edmonton, AB, T5Y 2S3
Su B 9:00am, S 10:30am, S 11:45am; Fr Y 7:00pm
note: meets at Kirkness School
c/o: Brian Boyle (680-456-7402)
3234 145th Ave NW, Edmonton, AB, T5Y 2E5

Connor's Hill Gospel Hall (780-468-2095)
9302 95th St, Edmonton, AB, T6C 3X2
Su B 10:00am, G 7:00pm, F 12:00pm; Mo C 7:00pm; We P 7:30pm
c/o: Joseph Bowman (780-450-0818)
1325 Knottwood Rd E, Edmonton, AB, T6K 2K5
josephjbowman@gmail.com
alt: Mark Richards (780-416-2024)
jmarkrich@yahoo.ca

Grace Community Church
Edmonton, AB
c/o: Dewit Tekle Isaac (780-420-0032/6170/6969)
11053 110th St, Edmonton, AB, T5H 3E6

Mount Carmel Bible School (780-465-3015)
4725 106th Ave, Edmonton, AB, T6A 1E7
mail@mountcarmel.net
c/o: Wayne Tomalty (780-466-8449)
5915 94B Ave, Edmonton, AB, T6B 0Z5
wayne.tomalty@mountcarmel.net
alt: Jessica Sheppard (780-490-4607)
jessica.sheppard@mountcarmel.net

Westgrove Gospel Chapel (403-455-1161)
10374 147th St, Edmonton, AB, T5N 3C3
Su B 9:30am, S 11:15am, M 6:00pm; Tu P/M 7:30pm
c/o: Tom Thomas (403-487-3790)

ELNORA

Salem Christian Assembly (403-773-2226)
Hwy 590, Elnora, AB, T0M 0Y0
david@salemacres.com
Su B 9:30am, S 11:00am; Tu Y, M 6:00pm
c/o: David Broadhead (403-773-2226)
Hwy 590, Elnora, AB, T0M 0Y0
david@salemacres.ca

GRANDE PRAIRIE

The Gospel Hall
Spring Creek Rd off Hwy 43, Grande Prairie, AB
Su B 10:30am, G 1:15pm, S/M 12:30pm; Tu P/M 7:30pm
c/o: Robert Eyers (780-513-8916)
10201 89th St, Grande Prarie, AB, T8X 1G2
roberteyers49@msn.com
alt: Elton Krenzler (780-539-5686)

PARADISE VALLEY

Gospel Hall
Paradise Valley, AB
Su G, B 11:00am; We P/M 8:00pm
c/o: David Flint (780-745-2560)
Box 35, Paradise Valley, AB, T0B 3R0

CANADA — ALBERTA

RED DEER
Balmoral Bible Chapel (403-347-5450)
RR 2, Red Deer, AB, T4N 5E3
Su B 9:30am, S 11:00am; Tu P/M 7:30pm (homes);
We P/M 7:30pm (homes)
note: E of 30th Ave on 55th Ave
c/o: LE Edwards (403-347-5450)
bbchapel@telusplanet.net

SHERWOOD PARK
Sherwood Park Community Church (780-417-0414)
20101 Sherwood Dr, Sherwood Park, AB, T8A 0Z1
Su M 12:00pm
note: PO Box 57081 EPO
c/o: Ron Kroeker
886 Juniper Ave, Sherwood Park, AB, T8A 2C7

STROME
Strome Community Church
Strome, AB
c/o: Brian McGaffigan (780-376-3638)
Box 147, Strome, AB, T0B 4H0
brianpat@telusplanet.net

WESTLOCK
Westlock Gospel Chapel (780-349-4555)
10227 97th St, Westlock, AB, T7P 2H1
wgchapel@telusplanet.net
Su B 9:30am, S 11:00am; Tu C/Y 4:00pm; We P 7:00am, C/Y 4:00pm;
Fr C/Y 4:00pm
c/o: Tim Gurnett (780-349-6092)
9752 109th St, Westlock, AB, T7P 1P9
alt: Keith Bidne (780-349-7079)

YOUNGSTOWN
Gospel Chapel (403-779-3888)
PO Box 66, Youngstown, AB, T0J 3P0
Su S/M, B 10:00am
c/o: WL Armstrong
Box 169, Youngstown, AB

BRITISH COLUMBIA

100 MILE HOUSE
Horse Lake Christian Fellowship (250-395-1070)
5827 Horse Lake Rd, 100 Mile House, BC, V0K 2E3
info@hlcf.org
Su B 9:00am, M/S 11:00am; Mo Y 6:00pm; Th P 7:30pm; Sa G 7:00pm
c/o: Don Street (250-395-4230)
6511 Mercer Rd, 100 Mile House, BC, V0K 2E3
don.street@shawbiz.ca

ABBOTSFORD

Clearbrook Assembly of Christians (604-853-2323)
#007-2580 Cedar Park Pl, Abbotsford, BC, V2T 2H4
Su B 9:30am, S 11:00am, G 6:30pm; Tu P/M 7:00pm
c/o: Jim Kempster (604-859-5521)
#1-32910 MacLure Rd, Abbotsford, BC, V2S 7V7
jim_kem@bcsympatico.ca

Parkview Gospel Hall (604-859-5637)
2464 Parkview St, Abbotsford, BC, V2T 3K7
www.parkviewgospelhall.com
Su B 10:00am, G 7:30pm, S 12:00pm; We M 7:30pm
c/o: Peter Tolsma (604-859-6290)
alt: John Lightfoot (604-859-6290)

ALDERGROVE

Aldergrove Gospel Chapel
26580 - 29th Ave, Aldergrove, BC, V4W 3B3
Su B 10:00am, F 11:15am; We P 8:00pm
note: use point of contact as church's mailing address
c/o: Mun Hope (604-856-5629)
26572 - 29th Ave Box 41, Aldergrove, BC, V4W 2T7

BOWEN ISLAND

Cates Hill Chapel
Bowen Island, BC
Su B 10:30am
c/o: Larry Adams (604-947-9098)
RR 1, P 24, Bowen Island, BC, V0N 1G0

BURNABY

Parkcrest Bible Chapel (604-299-7913)
6641 Halifax St, Burnaby, BC, V5B 2P9
thescotts@telus.net
www.parkcrest.ca
Su B 9:30am, F 11:00am, P 7:00pm; We L 9:15am, M 7:30pm; Fr C 6:30pm, Y 8:30pm
c/o: Andrew Scott (604-420-7900)
parkcrestyouth@hotmail.com

South Burnaby Gospel Hall (604-986-6114)
6907 Elwell St, Burnaby, BC, V5E 1K3
Su B 9:30am, S/F 11:30am (&E.S.L.), P 6:30pm, G 7:00pm; Tu P 7:30pm
c/o: Ralph C Morton (604-986-6114)
487 Vienna Cres, Burnaby, BC, V7N 3B3

Tenth Avenue Bible Chapel (604-524-5445)
7103 10th Ave, Burnaby, BC, V3N 2R5
Su B, S 11:15am, P 5:45pm, G 6:30pm; We P/M

Westminster Bible Chapel (604-522-9311)
7540 Sixth St, Burnaby, BC, V3N 3M1
www.wbchapel.com
info@wbchapel.com
Su F 10:00am, B 11:30am
c/o: John MacDonald (604-522-9311)
7540 Sixth St, Burnaby, BC, V3N 3M1
john@wbchapel.com

CASTLEDALE

Columbia Valley Bible Fellowship
4908 Arnold Rd, Castledale, BC
Su B 9:30am, S 11:00am; Th P/M 7:00pm
note: Caleb View Farm
c/o: Ralph Kirchhofer (250-348-2059)
Box 20, Harrogate, BC, V0A 1J0

CHILLIWACK

Watson Road Bible Chapel (604-858-7291)
45435 Watson Rd, Chilliwack, BC, V2R 2H5
Su B 9:30am, S 11:00am, M 7:00pm; Tu L 9:45am; We P/M 7:30pm; Fr Y 7:00pm
c/o: Ken Ashton (604-858-9496)
19-45918 Knight Rd, Chilliwack, BC, V2R 3X4

COMOX

Comox Valley Gospel Assembly
1855 Noel Ave, Comox, BC, V9M 2H4
Su B 10:30am, M 11:30am
note: meets in Comox Recreation Centre
c/o: Rowland Mills (250-752-8260)
404 Cottonwood Dr, Qualicum Beach, BC, V9K 1M2
alt: George Gardiner (250-335-0143)

COURTENAY

Elim Gospel Chapel
566 5th St, Courtenay, BC, V9N 1K3
Su B, S 11:30am, M 7:00pm; We M (homes)

DAWSON CREEK

Corner Stone Christian Assembly (250-782-5780)
10221 - 18th St, Dawson Creek, BC, V1G 4C9
gloney@xplornet.com
Su B 10:00am, F 11:30am, M 1:30pm
c/o: George Loney (250-630-2607)
C26 S16 RR#1, Fort St John, BC, V1J 4M6
gloney@xplornet.com
alt: Don Wilson (250-782-8961)
chavuma@shaw.ca

DELTA

Ladner Gospel Assembly (604-946-4224)
4979 - 44A Ave, Delta, BC, V4K 3N7
Su S 10:00am, B 11:15am; We M 7:30pm
c/o: Ray Webber (604-946-9179)
5148 45th Ave, Delta, BC, V4K 1K3
mwebber@dccnet.com
alt: Greg Thompson (604-946-7976)

DUNCAN

Brae Road Gospel Chapel (250-746-5434)
321 Brae Rd, Duncan, BC, V9L 3T9
Su B 9:15am, S 11:00am, M 6:30pm; Th P/M 7:30pm
c/o: Terry Ryan (250-746-5408)
4932 Cowichan Lake Rd, Duncan, BC, V9L 6H3

HARROGATE

Columbia Valley Bible Fellowship (250-348-2059)
4908 Arnold Rd, Harrogate, BC, V0A 1J0
www.calebview.com
gospel@uniserve.com
Su B 9:30am, F/S 11:00am; Mo C 4:00pm; We M 4:00pm; Th M 7:00pm
note: meets at Caleb View Farm
c/o: Ralph Kirchhofer (250-348-2059)
Box 20, Harrogate, BC, V0A 1J0
gospel@uniserve.com

KAMLOOPS

Kamloops Gospel Chapel (604-376-7705)
1365 Tranquille Rd, Kamloops, BC, V2B 3K5
Su B 9:15am, S 11:00am; We P/M 7:15pm
c/o: George Doubroff (250-554-2660)

Westsyde Gospel Hall (250-579-8799)
849 Wawn Rd, Kamloops, BC, V2B 6N3
jfeggers@telus.net
Su B 9:30am, S/M 11:30am, G 7:00pm; Mo C 7:00pm; We P/M 7:00pm
note: use PO Box 2006 Station A
c/o: John Eggers (250-579-8814)
3664 Westsyde Rd, Kamloops, BC, V2B 7H6
jfeggers@telus.net
alt: Ed Stanyer (250-579-8681)
esstanyer@shaw.ca

KELOWNA

Kelowna Bible Chapel (250-762-0222)
1423 Vineland St, Kelowna, BC, V1Y 7R9
Su B 9:30am, S 11:15am; We P/M 7:00pm
c/o: Bruce Aitken (250-765-8156)
900 Rutland Rd N, Kelowna, BC, V1X 3B7
baitken@shaw.ca

LANGLEY

Gospel Hall (604-533-0870)
4775 221st St, Langley, BC, V2Z 1M7
Su B 9:30am, S 11:30am, G 7:00pm; We P/M 7:30pm
c/o: TG Hutchinson (604-556-3450)
32-3354 Horn St, Abbotsford, BC, V2S 7L3

MISSION

West Heights Gospel Chapel
32070 – 7th Ave, Mission, BC
Su B 9:30am, S&F 11:00am, 7:00pm; We P/BS 7:00pm
c/o: Rolan Poirier (604-826-7979 or 604-855-7974)
32699 Cherry Ave, Mission, BC, V2V 2T8

NANAIMO

Wakesiah Gospel Chapel (250-753-4641)
170 Wakesiah Ave, Nanaimo, BC, V9R 3J9
www.wakesiah-chapel.org
brimac1@show.ca
Su B 9:30am, F 11:00am
c/o: Brian McKibbin (250-758-6038)
5990 Blairmore Place, Nanaimo, BC, V9T 6P6
brimac1@show.ca

NORTH

Sutherland Bible Chapel (604-988-8473)
PO Box 86069, 630 E 19th St, Vancouver, BC, V7L 4J5
76512.367@compuserve.com
Su S, B 9:15am, G 7:00pm

NORTH VANCOUVER

Deep Cove Gospel Hall (604-929-3138)
4544 Cove Cliff Rd, North Vancouver, BC, V7G 1H9
Su B 9:30am, S 11:30am, G 7:00pm; We C 7:00pm, P/M 7:30pm
c/o: George Varaljay (604-929-2860)
1955 Easthleigh, North Vancouver, BC, V7G 1W1
varaljay@telus.net
alt: Dave Smith (604-929-2637)
dsmith02@telus.net

Fourth Street Gospel Hall (604-988-2461)
133 E 4th St, North Vancouver, BC, V7L 1H7
Su B 9:30am, S 11:30am, G 7:00pm; Tu P/M 7:30pm
c/o: Allan D McCurrie (604-988-9940)
2939 Colwood Dr, North Vancouver, BC, V7R 2R3
avmccurrie@telus.net

CANADA — BRITISH COLUMBIA 151

PORT ALBERNI

Glenwood Gospel Assembly (250-723-7696)
4450 8th Ave, Port Alberni, BC, V9Y 4S7
Su B 9:30am, F 11:00am, G 7:00pm; We P/M 7:30pm
c/o: Horst Koehle (250-723-7666)
10104 Lakeshore Rd C-2 Site 319, Port Alberni, BC, V9Y 7L7
alt: Brent & Marilyn Laflamme (250-723-7696)
mbkoehle@shaw.ca

Lathom Road Gospel Hall (250-724-0421 or 724-)
PO Box 1148, Port Alberni, BC, V9Y 7L9
Su B 9:30am, S 11:30am, G 7:30pm; We P/M 7:30pm
note: cnr Lathom Rd & Helen Sts
c/o: John E Fairfield (250-248-5085)
222 Potlatch St, Parksville, BC, V9P 1K3
jef69@telus.net

POWELL RIVER

Michigan Heights Gospel Hall
4620 Michigan Ave, Powell River, BC, V8A 2S9
Su G, B 10:00am, S 11:30am; Tu P/M 8:00pm

PRINCE GEORGE

Gospel Chapel
1590 Queensway St, Prince George, BC
Su B/S, G 7:00pm; Th P/M
c/o: Ed Dmicola (250-965-2379)

Kelly Road Gospel Chapel (250-962-6420)
7046 S Kelly Rd, Prince George, BC, V2K 2G9
Su B 9:30am, F 11:00am; We P/M 7:30pm
c/o: P W Shatford (250-563-4876)
332-4377 Hill Ave, Prince George, BC, V2M 7G1
alt: Paul Serup (250-964-0301)

RICHMOND

Bakerview Gospel Chapel (604-274-2124)
8991 Francis Rd, Richmond, BC, V6Y 1A8
Su B 9:00am, S/F 10:30am, P 7:00pm; Tu M 7:30pm; We M 7:30pm; Fr Y 7:00pm
c/o: Carl Dorozio (604-274-7371)
10951 Roseland Gate, Richmond, BC, V7A 2R1
carld@newwestpress.com
alt: Norman Chandler (604-271-1083)
ejeannormr@yahoo.ca

Emmanuel Christian Community Church (604-270-7601)
230-7360 Westminster Hwy, Richmond, BC, V6X 1A1

West Richmond Gospel Hall (604-277-1441)
5651 Francis Rd, Richmond, BC
Su B/G, S 11:30am; We P/M
c/o: TSA (Ashley) Milne (604-270-4702)
10591 Granville Ave, Richmond, BC, V6Y 1R5

SAANICHTON

Saanichton Bible Fellowship (250-652-6311)
2159 Mt Newton Cross Rd, Saanichton, BC, V8M 1T8
www.mysbf.org / office@mysbf.org
Su B 9:00am, F/S 10:00am; We L 9:00am; Fr Y 7:00pm
c/o: Travis Stewart
tstewart@mysbf.org
alt: Annabelle Turek (250-652-4582)
aturek@mysbf.org

SALMON ARM

Little Mountain Bible Chapel (250-803-0161)
PO Box 343, 3481 10th Ave SE, Salmon Arm, BC, V1E 4N5
Su B 9:30am, S 11:00am; We P 7:00pm
c/o: Ken Spohr (250-832-2652)
20 16th St NE, Salmon Arm, BC, V1E 1N5
kenspohr@hotmail.com

SURREY

Fleetwood Gospel Hall (604-597-2255)
8725 - 158th St, Surrey, BC, V4N 1G9
Su B 9:30am, S 11:30am, G 7:00pm; We P/M 7:30pm
c/o: Simon DeGroot (604-585-4744)
15665 - 93rd Ave, Surrey, BC, V4N 3B2
alt: J Poulsen (604-888-6391)
poulsen@canada.com

Newton Christian Assembly (604-501-1515)
23-8528 123rd St, Surrey, BC, V3W 3V6
Su B 10:00am, S 6:00pm; We P/M
c/o: Gary Bonderud (604-590-5039)
13355 65A Ave, Surrey, BC, V3W 8T2

North Surrey Gospel Chapel (604-588-9122)
13044 96th Ave, Surrey, BC, V3V 1Y3
www.gospelchapel.ca
Su B 9:30am, S 11:05am, G 7:00pm, M 7:30pm
c/o: Allister Shedden (604-596-8534)
5966 Parkside Place, Surrey, BC, V3X 2B6
ashedd@shaw.ca
alt: John Schoberg (604-581-6614)

TERRACE

Terrace Gospel Hall (250-635-8504)
4802 Scott Ave, Terrace, BC, V8G 2B4
Su B 10:00am, S/M 11:30am, G 12:30pm; We P/M 7:00pm
c/o: William A McCullough (250-635-6627)
693 Kalum Lake Dr, Terrace, BC, V8G 0C2
alt: Victor Pedro (250-635-3874)

CANADA — BRITISH COLUMBIA 153

VANCOUVER

Carleton Gospel Hall (604-435-7221)
3395 E 45th Ave, Vancouver, BC
Su B, S 11:30am, G 7:00pm; We P/M
c/o: SR Logue (604-435-8331)
604-6240 McKay Ave, Burnaby, BC, V5H 4L8

Fairview Gospel Hall (604-733-8822)
1666 W 10th Ave, Vancouver, BC, V6J 2A1
Su B 10:00am, G 7:30pm, S 12:00pm; Tu P 8:00pm; Th M 8:00pm
c/o: David Bagnall (604-321-6300)
2436 E 51st Ave, Vancouver, BC, V5S 1P6

Granville Chapel (604-263-4121)
5901 Granville St, Vancouver, BC, V6M 3C9
www.granvillechapel.com
office@granvillechapel.com
Su F 11:00am (please call or visit webiste for other meeting times)
c/o: Andy Perrett (604-263-4121 ext. 23)
andyperrett@granvillechapel.com
alt: Joe White (604-263-4121 ext. 24)
joewhite@granvillechapel.com

Heather Bible Chapel (604-327-8212)
777 W 68th Ave, Vancouver, BC, V6P 2T8
Su B 9:30am, S 11:00am, G 6:30pm; We P/M 7:30pm
c/o: Mrs Peggy Norris (327-8212)

Knight Road Gospel Chapel (604-879-5911)
4195 Knight Rd, Vancouver, BC, V5N 3M1
Su B 9:30am, S/G 11:00am; We P/M 7:00pm
c/o: Hari Rao (604-327-2744)
1541 E 35th Ave, Vancouver, BC, V5P 1B2

Marineview Chapel (604-261-1444 or 266-)
4000 W 41st Ave, Vancouver, BC, V6N 3G2
mpcjb@bigfoot.com

Sixteenth Avenue Gospel Chapel (604-733-0915)
2756 W 16th Ave, Vancouver, BC, V6K 3C4
www.rainbowltd.ca/chapel.htm
Su B 9:30am, S/G 11:15am; Tu M 7:30pm
c/o: Harold Summers (604-738-8943)
2907 W 27th Ave, Vancouver, BC, V6L 1W4
alt: Harold Budd (604-266-9485)

South Main Gospel Hall (604-324-8118)
7601 Main St, Vancouver, BC
Su B 9:30am, S 11:30am, G 7:30pm; Tu P/M 7:30pm
note: 60th Ave
c/o: Om Chand (604-321-3331)
285 E 51st Ave, Vancouver, BC, V5X 1C4

University Chapel (604-222-0800)
5375 University Blvd, Vancouver, BC, V6T 1K3
Su M 10:00am

Victoria Drive Gospel Hall (604-879-1617)
4659 Victoria Dr, Vancouver, BC, V5N 4N7
www.vdgh.ca
Su B 9:30am, S 11:45am, G 7:30pm; Th P/M 7:30pm
c/o: Philip Broadhead (604-468-4979)
#115-678 Citadel Dr, Port Coquitlam, BC, V3C 6M7
pbroadhead@telus.net

VERNON

Vernon Gospel Chapel (250-545-3022)
4106 Pleasant Valley Rd, Vernon, BC, V1T 4M2
Su B 9:30am, S 11:00am, G 7:00pm; We P/M 7:30pm
c/o: Chuck Baker (250-547-4788)
428 Scenic Dr, Coldstream, BC, V1B 2W9

VICTORIA

Lambrick Park Church (250-477-9721)
1780 Feltham Rd, Victoria, BC, V8N 2A5
Su S/M 9:00am, M 11:00am, B 6:30pm; Tu M 6:30pm (homes); We M 6:30pm (homes); Th M 6:30pm (homes); Fr Y 7:00pm
c/o: Tom Cowan (250-721-2469)
tcowan@islandnet.com

Oak Bay Gospel Assembly (250-598-3114)
1900 Oak Bay Ave, Victoria, BC, V8R 1C7
walla@shaw.ca
Su B 9:30am, G/S 11:30am; We P/M 7:30pm; Th L/Y 7:00pm
c/o: Ed Wallace (250-477-7256)
1853 Chimo Pl, Victoria, BC, V8N 4Y1
walla@shaw.ca
alt: John Allen (250-384-8879)
j_allen@shaw.ca

Westview Gospel Chapel (250-479-1233 or 250-656-2491)
313 Brunswick Pl, Victoria, BC, V8Z 1V5
pandptown@shaw.ca
Su B 9:30am, F/G/S 11:15am, M 6:30pm; Tu P 7:30pm; Th L 9:30am; Fr Y 7:00pm
c/o: Phil Townshend (250-656-3491)
5 – 2070 Amelia Ave, Sidney, BC, V8L 4X6
pandptown@shaw.ca
alt: Larry Page (250-479-6277)
lrpage1@telus.net

WEST

Hollyburn Christian Fellowship (604-922-3522)
1403 Duchess Ave, Vancouver, BC, V7T 1H7
Su B/G, M 11:15am, M 7:00pm; Tu P/M 8:00pm
c/o: Alan Morton (604-926-3732)
alt: Derek Muller (604-922-1726)

WESTBANK

Highway Gospel Hall (250-768-3923)
2549 Hebert Rd, Westbank, BC, V4T 2J6
Su B 9:30am, S 11:30am, G 7:30pm; We P/M 7:30pm
c/o: Glenn A Griffin (250-768-3343)
3344 Elliott Rd, Westbank, BC, V4T 1P2
griffarm@telus.net

Westbank Bible Chapel (250-768-2444)
2412 Apollo Rd, Westbank, BC, V4T 1P6
jsstutters@shaw.ca
Su B 9:30am, F 11:15am; Tu P/M 7:00pm; Th L 9:30pm; Fr Y 7:00pm
note: Co-sponsors of Morning Star Bible Camp
c/o: John Stutters (250-768-4651)
#72 - 2550 Louie Dr, Westbank, BC, V4T 2M6
jsstutters@shaw.ca
alt: Roy Howard (250-767-3499)

WHITE ROCK

Hilltop Gospel Chapel
15110 Thrift Ave, White Rock, BC, V4B 2K7
Su B 9:30am, S 11:00am, M 6:30pm; Mo C 6:30pm; Th P/M
c/o: Neil Lines (604-946-6282)
6061 Crescent Dr, Delta, BC, V4K 2G1

MANITOBA

AUSTIN

Gospel Hall
Austin, MB
Su B 10:00am, S 11:30am, G 7:00pm; We P/M 7:30pm
note: Bishop St & Government Rd
c/o: Lyle Knox (204-637-2115)
Box 151, Austin, MB, R0H 0C0

BINSCARTH

Gospel Hall
Binscarth, MB
Su B 10:00am, S 11:30am; Tu P
c/o: Harvey Ronald (204-532-2251)
Box 309, Binscarth, MB, R0J 0G0

CANADA — MANITOBA

BRANDON

Gospel Hall (204-728-7849)
1412 22nd St, Brandon, MB, R7B 2S8
Su B 9:30am, S 11:30am, G 7:00pm; Tu P/M 7:30pm
c/o: Alan G Ritchie (204-727-4971)

LOCKPORT

Ashfield Gospel Hall (204-757-4727)
(Sept-May) Su B 10:00am, S 11:45am, G 1:00pm; We P/M 7:30pm
(June-Aug) Su B 10:00am, G 11:15am; We P/M 7:30pm
note: directions: 1/4 mi E of Hwy 59 & 44, 12 mi north of Winnipeg
note: use point of contact as church's mailing address
c/o: Burke Dittberner (204-757-4727)
Box 15 Grp 364 RR 3, Winnipeg, MB, R3C 2E7

OAKVILLE

Fortier Gospel Chapel
Box 277, Oakville, MB, R0H 0Y0
Su B, S 11:15am, G 7:00pm

PORTAGE LA PRAIRIE

Crescent Heights Chapel (204-239-6774)
1745 Saskatchewan Ave W, Portage La Prairie, MB, R1N 0R5
Su B 9:30am, S 11:00am; Tu P/M 7:30pm
c/o: D Garth Ronald (204-239-6484 or 239-1004)
6 Saskatchewan Ave W, Portage La Prairie, MB, R1N 0L9
dgronald@mb.sympatico.ca

Portage Gospel Hall (204-857-7218)
102 1st St NW, Portage La Prairie, MB, R1N 3J9
Su B 9:30am, S 11:30am, G 7:00pm; Tu M 8:00pm (Nov-April 7:30pm); Th P 8:00pm (Nov-April 7:30pm)
c/o: David Vanstone (204-857-8435)
Box 1231, Portage La Prairie, MB, R1N 3J9
vanstones@gmail.com

ROSEISLE

Gospel Hall (204-828-3484)
Roseisle, MB
Su B 10:00am, S 11:20am, P 6:30pm, G 7:00pm; We P/M 8:00pm
c/o: Peter H Dyck (204-828-3509)
Box 46, Roseisle, MB, R0G 1V0

SELKIRK

Selkirk Gospel Chapel (204-482-4717)
211 Eaton Ave, Selkirk, MB, R1A 0W7
Su B 9:30am, S 11:00am; We P/M 7:30pm
c/o: Ed Struch (204-482-6081)
517 Vaughan Ave, Selkirk, MB, R1A 0T2

CANADA – MANITOBA

WINKLER
  Garden Valley Christian Fellowship (204-362-6044)
  Main St, Red River College, Winkler, MB, R6M 1M3
  www.john4fourteen.com
  john4fourteen@gmail.com
  Su B 10:00am, S/F 11:00am, G 7:00pm; We P 7:30pm
  note: use point of contact as church's mailing address
  c/o: Kevin Minnett (204-362-6044)
  102 Mountain St, Morden, MB, R6M 1H3
  canadiakev@gmail.com

WINNIPEG
  Believers Bible Chapel (204-256-1701)
  600 Shaftesbury Blvd, Winnipeg, MB, R3P 0M4
  www.believersbiblechapel.ca
  hzimmermann@shaw.ca
  Su B 9:30am, S/F 11:00am; We P 7:30pm (homes),
  note: use point of contact as church's mailing address
  note: meets at the Canadian Mennonite University
  c/o: Helmut Zimmermann (204-256-1701)
  78 Pine Bluff Rd, Winnipeg, MB, R2J 2N5
  hzimmermann@shaw.ca
  alt: Oscar Lucash (204-237-5247)
  drlucash@mts.net

  Grace Chapel (204-253-0190)
  19 Berrydale Ave, Winnipeg, MB, R2M 1M1
  Su B 9:45am, S 11:30am, M 6:30pm; Tu P/M 8:00pm
  c/o: Mathew Maniate (204-269-0900)
  45 Meadow Ridge Dr, Winnipeg, MB, R3T 5N5

  Maples Community Church (204-694-0713)
  1640 Leila Ave, West Kildonan, MB, R2P 0S5
  maplescc@mb.imag.net
  Su S 9:30am, G 11:00am, B 6:30pm; We M 7:00pm
  c/o: Dave Christmas
  rooftreesii@mts.net
  alt: Rick Krystik (204-339-9154)

  Oxford Bible Church
  621 Oxford St, Winnipeg, MB, R3M 3J3
  Su B 9:30am, S 11:00am, G 6:30pm; We P/M 7:30pm
  c/o: Ernie Schmidt (204-453-6689)
  117-35 Valhalla Dr, Winnipeg, MB, R2G 0G5
  schmidte@mts.net
  alt: Glenn Hayes (204-488-8393)

  St James Gospel Chapel (204-888-1535)
  337 Inglewood St, Winnipeg, MB, R3J 1X1
  Su B 9:30am, S 11:15am, M 6:30pm; We P/M 6:30pm
  c/o: David Jarvis (204-832-1707)
  35 Down's Ave, Winnipeg, MB, R2Y 0A5

West End Gospel Hall (204-783-6679)
492 Victor St, Winnipeg, MB, R3G 1R2
Su B 10:00am, S 12:30pm, M 12:45pm, G 7:00pm; Tu M 7:30pm
c/o: Wayne Friesen (204-889-0126)
49 Normandy Dr, Winnipeg, MB, R2Y 1J1
wgmlk@mts.net

NEW BRUNSWICK

E ST JOHN
Courtenay Avenue Gospel Hall (506-657-7450)
61 Courtenay Ave, Saint John, NB, E2J 1M6
Su B/S, G 7:00pm; We P/M
c/o: Stephen Budd (506-847-4303)
5 Charity Lane, Quispamsis, NB, E2G 1L7

FREDERICTON
McAdam Avenue Gospel Hall (506-472-1125)
109 McAdam Ave, Fredericton, NB, E3A 1G6
Su B 9:30am, S 11:30am, G 7:00pm; We P/M 7:30pm
c/o: Robert M Griffin (506-472-5512)
1192 Rt 105, Douglas, NB, E3A 7K1
rdlgriff@nb.sympatico.ca
alt: Bob Stairs (506-363-3927)
bwstairs@nbnet.nb.ca

McLeod Hill Assembly of Christians (506-459-4896)
171 McLeod Hill Rd, Fredericton, NB, E3A 6H5
www.mcleodhill.com
Su B 9:30am, S/G 11:00am, M 6:00pm; Mo C 6:30pm; We P/M 7:30pm;
Th Y 7:00pm
c/o: Ernie Adsett (506-363-3896)
127 Rocky Rd, Keswick Ridge, NB, E6L 1V1
ernie@adsett.com
alt: Steve Tranquilla (506-452-7817)

MONCTON
Mountain Road Gospel Hall (506-382-3165)
195 Mountain Rd, Moncton, NB, E1C 2L2
info@monctongospelhall.com
http://monctongospelhall.com
Su B 9:30am, S 11:30am, G 7:00pm; We P/M 7:30pm
c/o: William Swan (506-859-0090)
45 Ashworth Dr, Moncton, NB, E1A 6J8
wswan@rogers.com
alt: A Eastwood (506-386-3310)

ST BASILE
Chretiens Reunis (French)
37 Smith Rd, Green River, NB, E7C 2J6
Su B 10:00am, S 11:30am, G 7:00pm; We P/M 8:00pm
c/o: Gilles Roy (506-263-5507)
156 Principale, Green River, NB, E0L 1E0

NEWFOUNDLAND

BONAVISTA BAY
Templeman Gospel Hall
Wesleyville, NF
c/o: Elmore Stokes
Deadman's Bay, NF

FOGO ISLAND
Gospel Hall (709-266-2433)
Mercer Memorial Dr, Fogo, NF
Su B 9:30am, S 11:00am, G 7:30pm; We P/M 8:00pm
c/o: Harry Torraville (709-266-2428)
PO Box 143, South Side Fogo, NF, A0G 2B0

SQUARE ISLANDS
Gospel Hall
Charlottetown, NF
Su B 11:00am, S 2:30pm, G 7:00pm; We M 8:00pm
c/o: Lewis Powell (709-949-0226)
PO Box 26, Charlottetown, NF, A0K 5Y0

BONNE BAY
Gospel Hall
Main St, Rocky Harbour, NF
Su B 10:00am, M 3:00pm (3rd Su), G 7:00pm; Th P/M 8:00pm
c/o: Peter H Mathews (709-458-2461)
Box 95, Norris Pt, NF, A0K 3V0
peter.mathews@nf.sympatico.ca

BUCHANS
Gospel Hall
Buchans, NF, A0H 1G0
c/o: Melvin Penny (672-4431)

BURNT POINT
Burnt Point Gospel Hall
Burnt Point, NF
Su B 10:30am, G 7:30pm; We M 8:00pm; Sa M 8:00pm
c/o: Andrew Pottle
Box 33, Old Perlican T.B., NF, A0A 3G0

CARBONEAR
Gospel Hall
Musgrave St, Carbonear, NF
Su B 10:30am, G 7:00pm; Tu P/M 7:30pm
c/o: Ernest Powell (709-596-2344)
16 Bunker Hill, Carbonear, NF, A1Y 1B9
ernest@nf.sympatico.ca

CORNER BROOK
Country Road Gospel Hall (709-632-5992)
168 Countriy Rd, Corner Brook, NF
Su B 9:45am, S 11:30am, G 7:00pm, M 12:00pm; We P/M 7:30pm
c/o: Gordon J Hollett (709-632-5905)
29 Glenhaven Blvd, Corner Brook, NF, A2H 4P7

FLOWERS COVE
Gospel Hall
Flowers Cove, NF, A0K 2N0
c/o: Augustus Norman

FORTEAU
English Point Gospel Hall
Forteau, NF
Su B 10:30am
c/o: Bert Belben (709-931-2651)
PO Box 40, Forteau, LB, A0K 2P0

FORTUNE BAY
Gospel Hall (709-851-6161)
Seal Cove, NF
Su B 10:30am, G 7:00pm, S 12:30pm; We P/M 8:00pm
c/o: Douglas A Loveless (709-851-5371)
Box 46, Seal Cove, NF, A0H 2G0

L'ANSE AU-LOUP
Gospel Hall (709-927-5204)
L'anse Au Loup, NF
Su B 10:30am, S 2:00pm, P 6:30pm, G 7:30pm; Th P/M 7:30pm
c/o: Francis Barney (709-927-5696)
Box 32, L'anse Au-Loup, LB, A0K 3L0

MAIN POINT
Gospel Hall (709-676-2910)
Gander Bay, NF
Su G 7:30am, B 10:30am, S 2:30pm; Tu P/M 7:30pm; Th P/M 7:30pm
c/o: Alvin Blake (676-2885)
Main Point, NF, A0G 3G0

PARSONS POND
Parsons Pond Gospel Hall
Main St, Parsons Pond, NF, A0K 3Z0
Su M (last Su in month), B 10:00am, G 7:00pm; We P/M 8:00pm
c/o: Harley W Payne (709-243-2261)
PO Box 142, Parsons Pond, NF, A0K 3Z0

RED BAY
Gospel Hall
Red Bay, NF
c/o: Ewert Bridle
Red Bay, NF, LB A0K 4K0

SANDRINGHAM
Gospel Hall (709-677-3123)
Eastport, NF
Su B 9:30am, S 11:00am, G 7:30pm; Th P/M 7:30pm
c/o: Alexander M Feltham (709-533-2873)
Box 178, Glovertown S, NF, A0G 2M0

ST JOHN'S
Faith Bible Chapel (709-726-8242)
43 Kenmount Rd, St John's, NL, A1B 1W1
faithbiblechapel@nf.aibn.com
Su B 9:45am, F 11:00am, S 11:20am, G 7:00pm; Tu P/M 7:30pm;
Fr Y 6:45pm; Sa Y 7:30pm
c/o: Stephen Bryant (709-738-3080)
6 Dorset St, St John's, NL, A1B 1W1
faithbiblechapel@nf.aibn.com
alt: Don Rideout (709-754-1968)

TRINITY BAY
Gospel Hall (709-582-2060)
New Harbour, NF
c/o: James W Foss (709-582-3195)
Box 64, Trinity Bay, NF, A0B 2P0

WAREHAM-CENTREVILLE
Gospel Hall
Wareham Centreville, NF
Su G, B 10:00am, S 11:30am, P 8:00pm
c/o: Mark Button
Wareham, NF, A0G 4P0

NOVA SCOTIA

AMHERST
Gospel Hall (902-667-1776)
20 Elmwood Dr, Amherst, NS, B4H 3Y1
Su B 9:30am, S 11:30am, G 7:00pm; We P/M 7:00pm; Fr C 7:00pm
c/o: Charles Hurley (902-667-7996)
RR 3, Brookdale, NS, B4H 3Y1

ANNAPOLIS COUNTY
Gospel Hall
Clementsvale, NS
Su B 10:30am, S 1:30pm, G 7:30pm; We P 8:00pm; Sa M 8:00pm
c/o: Lionel Cress (902-467-3115)
RR 1, Clementsvale, NS, B0S 1G0

AVONPORT

Gospel Hall (902-542-9701)
Avonport, NS
Su B 10:00am, S 11:45am, G 7:00pm, P 7:15pm
c/o: Hugh Kelly (902-542-7374)

BADDECK

Gospel Hall
Baddeck, NS
Su G, B 10:00am, S 11:30am; Tu P/M 8:00pm
c/o: Lloyd MacRitchie (902-295-2348)
PO Box 205, Baddeck, NS, B0E 1B0

BEAR RIVER

Greenland Bible Chapel (902-467-3353)
RR#1 Greenland Rd, Bear River, NS, B0S 1B0
Su B 10:00am, S 11:15am, G 6:00pm (every other wk)
c/o: Jamie Peck (902-467-3353)
RR 1, Bear River, NS, B0S 1B0
alt: Homer Peck (902-467-3295)

CAMBRIDGE

Cambridge Gospel Hall
Su B 11:00am, G 6:00pm; We P/M 7:30pm
note: Walton, Hunts Co
c/o: Timothy H Lake (902-633-2247)

CAPE BRETON

Blues Mills Gospel Hall
34 Mountain Rd, Blues Mills, NS, B0E 2Y0
Su B 10:00am, S 11:45am, G 7:00pm; We P/M 7:30pm
c/o: Blues Mills Gospel Hall

Westside Bible Chapel
6 Coxheath Rd, Sydney, NS, B1R 1R3
Su B/S/P/M, G 7:00pm
c/o: Doug Phillips (902-562-5869)
34 Keefe Ave, Coxheath, NS, B1R 1R3

CAPE NORTH

Cape North Gospel Hall (902-383-2610)
Cape North, NS
Su B 10:00am, S 11:30am, G 7:00pm; Sa P 7:00pm
c/o: Gordon Swan (902-383-2986)
57 Mtn View Rd, Dingwall, NS, B0C 1G0
gordraswan@hotmail.com
alt: Oliver MacKinnon (902-383-2558)

CANADA — NOVA SCOTIA

CUMBERLAND CTY

Pugwash Junction Gospel Hall (902-257-2205)
Pugwash Junction, NS, B0K 1M0
Su B 10:00am, S 12:00am, G 7:00pm; Tu P 7:30pm
c/o: HE Elliott (902-257-2236)
13340 Hwy 6, Wallace, NS, B0K 1Y0
wiretrap@ns.sympatico.ca

DARTMOUTH

Bethany Gospel Chapel (902-462-8815)
14 Bruce St, Dartmouth, NS, B2W 4Y3
www.chebucto.ns.ca/~ac572/Profile.html
ac572@chebucto.ns.ca
Su B 9:15am, S/F 11:00am, G 6:00pm; We P 7:15pm
note: use point of contact as church's mailing address
c/o: Fred S Gordon (902-488-4456)
89 Bellroyal Ct, Dartmouth, NS, B2V 2B4
fredgordon@eastlink.ca
alt: Walter Jackson (902-434-5838)
walter.jackson@ns.sympatico.ca

Northbrook Bible Chapel (902-463-2603)
225 Victoria Rd, Dartmouth, NS, B3A 1W5
Su B 9:30am, S 11:00am, M 6:00pm; Th P 7:00pm
c/o: Don Salmans (902-462-2759)
393 Astral Dr, Dartmouth, NS, B2V 2J1
don.salmans@sympatico.ps.ca

DEBERT

Gospel Hall
Main St, Debert, NS
Su B 10:00am, G 7:30pm; Tu P 7:30pm
c/o: Robert Swan (902-893-1486)
29 Burris Dr, Truro, NS, B2N 5B2

FALL RIVER

Fall River Community Bible Chapel (902-860-2662)

GUYS COUNTY

Gospel Hall
Port Bickerton, NS
Su B, S 10:00am, G 7:00pm; We P/M 7:00pm
c/o: Vaughan Boutilier (902-364-2241)
Box 44, Bickerton West, Guysboro County, NS, B0J 1A0

HALIFAX

Colby Drive Bible Chapel (902-435-5967)
131 Colby Dr, Dartmouth, NS, B2V 1Y2
www.colbychapel.com
mstuart@ns.sympatico.ca
Su B 9:30am, F/S 11:00am, Y 4:00pm; We M/M 7:30pm; Th M 7:30pm; Fr C 6:30pm, Y 7:30pm
c/o: Malcolm Stuart (902-462-5785)
43 Stratford Drive, Dartmouth, NS, B2V 2M7
alt: Chris Watts (902-435-4765)
chris.watts@dal.ca

Gospel Hall (902-454-4237)
2756 Swaine St, Halifax, NS, B3L 3R5
Su B 9:30am, S 11:15am, G 7:00pm; We P/M 7:30pm
c/o: Arthur Harnish (902-857-9265)
RR 1, Hubbards (Lun Co), NS, B0J 1T0

Grace Chapel (902-445-2711)
20 Lansdowne Dr, Halifax, NS, B3M 4B3
gracechapel@ns.sympatico.ca
Su B 9:30am, S 11:00am, M 6:30pm

LOWER ARGYLE

Argyle Christian Assembly (902-762-3183)
Lower Argyle, NS, B0W 1W0
nicke@ns.sympatico.ca
Su B 10:00am, G 7:00pm, M 7:30pm
c/o: Philip Nickerson (902-762-3183)
RR 1, Glenwood, NS, B0W 1W0
nicke@ns.sympatico.ca

NEW GLASGOW

Gospel Hall (902-752-0454)
454 S Frederick St, New Glasgow, NS, B2H 9Z9
Su B 10:00am, S 11:30am, G 7:00pm; We P/M
c/o: Bill Watson (902-752-8006)
416 Beech St, New Glasgow, NS, B2H 1A4

NINEVEH

Gospel Hall
Nineveh, NS
Su G, B 10:30am, S 12:00pm; We P 8:00pm
c/o: Robert J Kaulback (902-543-5530)
19 Medway St, Bridgewater, NS, B4V 1J8

OXFORD

Gospel Hall (902-447-2449)
Waverley St, Oxford, NS
Su B 9:45am, G 7:30pm; Th P/M
c/o: Clifford Budd (902-686-3819)
RR 1, Collingwood, NS, B0M 1E0

PLEASANT LAKE
Living Waters Christian Fellowship (902-648-2676)
318 Mood Rd, Yarmouth, NS
Su B 10:00am, S 11:30am, M 6:00pm
note: 1 km N off Hwy 103
c/o: Ashton Spinney (902-643-2490)
RR 1, Glenwood, NS, B0W 1W0

PORT HOWE
Port Howe Gospel Hall
7682 Hwy 6, Port Howe, NS, B0K 1L0
Su B 10:30am, G 7:00pm; We P 7:30pm
note: Cumberland County
c/o: Lawrence Patterson (902-243-2764)
PO Box 247, Pugwash, NS, B0K 1L0
patte@ns.sympatico.ca

STRATHCONA
River Hebert Gospel Hall (902-251-2467)
River Hebert East, Strathcona, NS
Su B 10:00am, G 7:00pm; Tu P/M 7:00pm; Fr Y 7:00pm
c/o: Claude McAloney
PO Box 94, Joggins, NS, B0L 1A0
alt: Cecil V Morton (902-667-6151)
cecilmorton@eastlink.ca

SYDNEY MINES
Gospel Hall
269 Yorke St, Sydney Mines, NS, B1V 3L5
Su B 9:30am, S 11:15am, G 7:00pm; We P/M 7:30pm
c/o: Norman A MacQueen (902-736-9690)
7 Victoria Dr, Sydney Mines, NS, B1V 3B4
normanmacqueen@ns.sympatico.ca

TATAMAGOUCHE
Gospel Hall (902-657-3366)
136 Blair St, Tatamagouche, NS
Su B/G, S 11:30am; We P/M 8:00pm
c/o: Gordon Swan (902-657-3440)
RR 2, Tatamagouche, NS, B0K 1V0

TRURO
Young Street Gospel Hall
51 Young St, Truro, NS, B2N 3W6
Su B 10:00am, G 7:30pm, S 12:00pm; Tu M 7:30pm
c/o: Donald A. Hatt (902-895-3400)
RR 2, 273 Brookside Branch Rd, Truro, NS, B2N 5B1
alt: Ross Swan (902-662-3723)

WEAVER'S SETTLEMENT
Gospel Hall
Rt 340, Weaver's Settlement, NS
Su B 10:30am, S 1:00pm, G 7:30pm; Tu P 7:30pm
note: 4 mi W of Weymouth
c/o: Anthony Amero (902-837-5232)
RR 2, Box 22B, Rt 340, Weymouth, NS, B0W 3T0

WEST SYDNEY
Sydney Gospel Hall
West Sydney, NS
Su B/S, G 7:00pm; Th P/M 7:45pm
note: cnr Whitney Ave & Terrace
c/o: David Williams (902-794-2922)
PO Box 115, North Sydney, NS, B2A 3M1

YARMOUTH COUNTY
Hubbards Point Gospel Hall
#633 Hwy 308, Hubbard's Point, NS
Su B 10:00am, S 11:45am, G 7:00pm; Th P/M 7:30pm
c/o: Terry Moulaison (902-648-3087)
Box 181 RR 1, Ste Ann du Ruisseau, NS, B0W 2X0
tcmoulaison@klis.com
alt: Roland Landry (902-648-2712)

ONTARIO

AGINCOURT
Bridlegrove Bible Chapel (416-497-7667)
2575 Pharmacy Ave, Toronto, ON, M1W 2K2
Su B 9:30am, S 11:00am, M 6:30pm; We P/M 7:45pm; Th C 6:30pm; Fr Y 7:30pm
c/o: Neville Eccleston (416-497-9191)

AJAX
Rossland Ridge Bible Chapel (905-619-3331)
1 Stevensgate Dr, Ajax, ON, L1T 0G1
www.rosslandridge.ca
kirk@rosslandridge.ca
Su B 9:30am, F/S 11:15am; Mo C 6:30pm; Tu L 9:15am; We P 7:30pm; Fr Y 7:00pm
note: use point of contact as church's mailing address
c/o: Kirk Dupre (905-723-1278)
39 Meadow Cres, Whitby, ON, L1N 3J2
kand.d@rogers.com

ALMA

Alma Bible Church (519-638-3886)
Alma, ON, N0B 1A0
kenic@sympatico.ca
Su B 9:30am, F/S 11:00am; Tu L 9:30am; We M 7:30pm; Sa Y
c/o: Ken Nicoll (519-846-0511)
54 Mathieson St, Elora, Ontario, N0B 1S0
alt: Glen Brubacker (638-376-6579)

ANGUS

Pinewoods Gospel Chapel (705-424-1294)
52 Brian Ave, Angus, ON, L0M 1B3
Su B/S, M 7:00pm; We M 7:00pm

ARKONA

Elim Bible Chapel (519-828-3076)
PO Box 127, 566 5th St, Arkona, ON, N0M 1B0
www.elimbiblechapel.com
lateepleman@hotmail.com
Th P/M 8:00pm
c/o: David J Daley (519-828-3288)
ddaleysr@golden.net

ARNSTEIN

Gospel Hall
10762 Hwy 522, Arnstein, ON, P0H 1A0
Su B 9:45am, S 11:45am, G 7:00pm; We P/M 7:30pm
c/o: Don Brunne (705-757-2030)
Box 70, Arnstein, ON, P0H 1A0

ATWOOD

Cornerstone Bible Fellowship
Atwood, ON
c/o: Maynard Bauman (519-356-2282)
info@lencodairy.on.ca

BANCROFT

Bible Chapel (613-332-2480)
PO Box 866, Bancroft, ON
Su S/G, B 9:15am; We P/M; Fr Y/P 8:00pm
note: Hastings St N
c/o: Peter Degeer (613-332-1670)
RR 1, Bancroft, ON, K0L 1C0
dunganon@mercury.kosone.com

Lakeview Gospel Hall
Bancroft, ON
Su B 9:30am, S 11:15am, G 7:00pm; We P/M 7:00pm
c/o: Mark Freymond (613-332-4317)
RR 1, Bancroft, ON, K0L 1C0

168 CANADA — ONTARIO

The Bridge Community Church
Bancroft, ON
c/o: Jim Mitchell (613-332-3696, 332-5554 or 332-5666)
RR 2, Bancroft, ON, K0L 1C0
mitjim@halhinet.on.ca

BARRIE

Northside Bible Chapel (705-726-1842)
8 Gunn St, Barrie, ON, L4M 2H3
www.northsidebiblechapel.com
Su B 9:30am, F/S 11:00am, M 6:30pm; Th P 7:30pm
c/o: Jim Comte (705-726-1187)
186 Hanmer St W, Barrie, ON, L4N 7J9
alt: Ken Wallace (705-835-6830)
kcwallace@sympatico.ca

Parkside Drive Gospel Hall
19 Parkside Dr, Barrie, ON, L4N 1W7
Su B 10:00am, S 11:30am, P/M 6:30pm, G 7:00pm; Th P/M 7:30pm
c/o: Elmer Jasperson (705-733-0026)
148 Patterson Rd, Barrie, ON, L4N 3W4

BELLEVILLE

Quinte Bible Chapel (613-962-3885)
188 Victoria Ave, Belleville, ON, K8N 2B8
Su G/S 10:30am, B 11:30am
c/o: Ross Harrington (613-966-4902)
80 Gilbert St, Belleville, ON, K8P 3H2

BOLTON

Gospel Hall
72 King St W, Bolton, ON, L0P 1A0
Su B 10:30am, G 7:00pm, S 12:00pm; We P/M 8:00pm

BOULTER

Boulter Gospel Chapel
241 Havergal Rd, Boulter, ON, K0L 1G0
Su B 9:30am, F/S 11:00am; Tu C 7:00pm
c/o: Don Reise (613-332-2214)
RR 4, Bancroft, ON, K0L 1C0
alt: Elwin Kaine (613-332-1377)

BRANTFORD

Bethel Park Bible Chapel (519-759-7362)
252 N Park St, Brantford, ON, N3R 4L1
Su B/S, M 6:30pm; Tu P/M
c/o: Sterling McElrea (519-753-1685)

Brant Community Church
Brantford, ON
c/o: Andy Flatt (519-756-3993)
26 Garden Ave, Brantford, ON, N3T 5M1
andy_flatt@hotmail.com

BRUCE MINES
Bible Centre
Bruce Mines, ON
Su B 9:45am, S 11:00am, G 7:00pm (homes); Th P
c/o: Alan Miller (705-785-3335)
Box 222, Bruce Mines, ON, P0R 1C0
alan.miller@sympatico.ca

BURGESSVILLE
Burgessville Gospel Hall (519-424-9135)
610 Main St N, Burgessville, ON, N0J 1C0
Su B 10:00am, F/S 11:30am, G 7:00pm; Tu P/M 7:30pm
c/o: Luke Winkels (519-424-2796)
7 Church St W, Burgessville, ON, N05 1C0
lukeandgerda@execulink.com

BURLINGTON
Forestview Bible Church
Burlington, ON
fvchurch@idirect.com
c/o: Mike Stone (905-335-6744)
PO Box 93130, 1450 Headon Rd, Burlington, ON, L7M 4A3

Shoreacres Bible Chapel (905-637-3668)
370 Shoreacres Rd, Burlington, ON, L7L 2H5
Su B 9:15am, S 11:00am, M 6:30pm; Tu C 6:30pm; We P 7:15pm
c/o: John Clode (905-332-0160)
3216 Wade Ct, Burlington, ON, L7M 2W4
jmclode@sympatico.ca

CAMBRIDGE
Cambridge Community Church (519-624-8411)
73 Pollock Ave, Cambridge, ON, N1R 2B4
www.cambridgecommunity.ca
info@cambridgecommunity.ca
Su B, M 10:00am
c/o: Rob Heintz

Cambridge Gospel Hall
31 South St, Cambridge, ON, N1R 2N6
Su B 11:00am, G 7:30pm, S 12:30pm; We P 8:00pm
c/o: Jim Reeve (905-659-1781)
RR 3 1550 Hwy 97, Puslinch, ON, N0B 2J0
jreeve001@sympatico.ca
alt: Phillip Watson (519-740-1470)
finalrest@bellnet.ca

Valens Gospel Hall
RR 6, Valens, ON, N1R 5S7
Su B 10:30am, G 7:00pm, S 12:00pm; We P 8:00pm
c/o: Ted Lapsley (519-621-9727)
RR 2, Puslinch, ON, N0B 2J0
lapsley@look.com

CAMPBELLFORD
Bible Chapel
RR 2, Springbrook, ON, K0L 1L0
We P/M 8:00pm
c/o: Paul Reid (705-653-5529)
RR 4, Marmora, ON, K0K 2M0

CHAPLEAU
Community Bible Chapel
Box 877, Chapleau, ON, P0M 1K0
Su B 9:30am, M 11:00am
c/o: Al Tremblay (705-864-0470)
Box 76, Chapleau, ON, P0M 1K0
ajtrembl@onlink.net

CHARLTON
Gospel Hall
Charlton, ON
Su B 10:00am, S 11:45am, G 8:00pm; Tu P 8:00pm
c/o: Harvey R Pratt (705-544-7758)
RR 1, Charlton Station, ON, P0J 1B0

CHATHAM
Chatham Bible Fellowship (home) (519-351-6025)
17 Regency Dr, Chatham, ON, N7L 4E4

Chatham Gospel Hall (519-352-7063)
235 Joseph St, Chatham, ON, N7L 3H2
www.chathamgospelhall.com
info@chathamgospelhall.com
Su B 9:45am, S 11:45am, Bible Reading/M 12:00pm; G 7:00pm;
We P/Bible Reading 7:30pm
c/o: David Robertson (519-352-7533)
315 Baldoon Rd, Chatham, ON, N7L 1E5
daverob@sympatico.ca

CHELMSFORD
Espanola Bible Fellowship
Chelmsford, ON
c/o: Kurt Ruby
745 Joanette Rd, Chelmsford, ON, P0M 1L0

CLINTON
Joseph Street Gospel Hall (519-482-8687)
PO Box 329, Clinton, ON, N0M 1L0
Su B 10:00am, S 11:30am, G 7:30pm; We P/M 8:00pm
c/o: Keith Bachert (519-526-7135)
PO Box 329, Clinton, ON, N0M 1L0
kjbachert@sympatico.ca

CLYDE
Clyde Gospel Hall
See Cambridge Gospel Hall in Cambridge, ON, Clyde, ON

COCHRANE

Cochrane Gospel Chapel
212 15th Ave, Box 1266, Cochrane, ON, P0L 1C0
Su S/B, G 7:00pm
note: cnr 5th St
c/o: Real Gendron (705-272-5173)

COLLINGWOOD

Gospel Hall (705-444-5188)
420 Ste Marie St, Collingwood, ON, L9Y 3K9
Su B 9:30am, S 11:30am; We P 8:00pm
c/o: William Shaw (705-446-2737)
217 Batteaux Rd RR 2, Collingwood, ON, L9Y 3Z1

COURTICE

Pine Ridge Bible Chapel (905-434-6426)
397 Townline Rd N, Courtice, ON, L1E 2J4
Su B 9:15am, S/F 11:00am, G 6:30pm; We L 9:30am, M/P 7:30pm
c/o: Terry Devitt (905-623-4282)
6 Quinn Dr, Bowmanville, ON, L1C 3T1
tjs.devitt@sympatico.ca
alt: George McCann (905-623-2223)
Geoann@sympatico.ca

DESERONTO

Deseronto Gospel Hall (613-354-6240)
96 St George St, Deseronto, ON, K0K 1X0
Su B 9:45am, S 11:15am, G 7:00pm; We P/M 7:30pm
note: use point of contact as church's mailing address
c/o: Allen D Madigan (613-354-6240)
Box 448, Deseronto, ON, K0K 1X0

DOWLING

Larchwood Bible Chapel
16 3rd Ave, Dowling, ON
Su S, B 9:00am, G 7:00pm; We P/M
note: on Hwy 144
c/o: Arnold Spears
PO Box 24, Dowling, ON, P0M 1R0

EARLTON

Gospel Hall
3 mi W, Earlton, ON
Su B 10:30am, G 8:00pm, S 12:00pm; We P/M 8:00pm
c/o: Philip Potter (705-563-2942)
Box 182, Earlton, ON, P0J 1E0

EDEN GROVE

Eden Grove Gospel Hall
Eden Grove, ON
Su B 10:30am, S 11:45am, G 7:30pm; We P 8:00pm
c/o: John W Boddy (519-366-2302)
RR 4, Walkerton, ON, N0G 2V0

ELK LAKE

Elk Lake Bible Chapel
Elk Lake, ON
Su B 10:00am, S 11:00am; We P/M 8:00pm
c/o: Ron Hartford (705-678-2177)
P0J 1G0

ELLIOT LAKE

Elliot Lake Bible Chapel (705-461-7555)
20 Lisbon, Elliot Lake, ON, P5A 3N9
Su B 10:00am, F 11:00am; We P/M 7:00pm
note: use point of contact as church's mailing address
c/o: Douglas E Price (705-848-8660)
3 Athens Rd, Elliot Lake, ON, P5A 2W3
deprice@personainternet.com

ELMIRA

Woodside Bible Fellowship (519-669-1296)
200 Barnswallow Dr, Elmira, ON, N3B 3K2
woodside@wbf.on.ca
Su S 9:15am, B 9:45am, S 11:00am, M 6:00pm

ELMVALE

Elmvale Community Church
12 Queen E, Elmvale, ON, L0L 1P0
c/o: John Cross (705-322-1539)
jhtcross@simcoe.net

Waverly Gospel Hall (705-322-9682)
17017 Hwy 27, Waverly, ON, L0L 1P0
Su B 9:30am, F 11:00am; Th P 7:30pm
c/o: Don Chapman (705-835-5314)
6414 Line 3N RR 1, Midland, ON, L4R 4K3
alt: Roger Langley (705-534-3323)

EMBRO

Embro Gospel Hall (519-475-4197)
115 Commissioner St E, Embro, ON
Su B 11:00am, S/G 12:15pm; We P/M 7:30pm
note: use point of contact as church's mailing address
c/o: Joe W Daniel (519-423-6722)
RR 5 404422 Union Rd, Ingersoll, ON, N5C 3J8
alt: (519-457-2515)

ENGLEHART

Gospel Hall (705-544-2404)
Box 902, Englehart, ON, P0J 1H0
Su B 10:00am, S 11:30am, G 7:00pm; Th P/M
note: cnr 5th St & 6th Ave
c/o: Mervyn Marshall (705-544-7591)
23 10th Ave, Englehart, ON, P0J 1H0

CANADA – ONTARIO 173

ETHEL

Cornerstone Bible Fellowship (519-887-6123)
85 Main St, Ethel, ON
Su B 9:45am, S 11:00am; Tu P/M 7:30pm
c/o: Andrew Versteeg (519-335-6321)
Box 151, Fordwich, ON, N0G 1V0
ajversteeg@gate-way.net

EXETER

Exeter Bible Fellowship (519-235-3501)
187 Huron St W, Exeter, ON, N0M 1S2
Su B 9:30am, F 11:00am; Th P/M 7:30pm
c/o: Bob Heywood (519-235-0874)
RR 3, Exeter, ON, N0M 1S5

FOREST

Forest Bible Chapel (519-786-2600)
33 Main St N, Forest, ON, N0N 1J0
Su B 9:30am , F 11:00am, F 6:30pm (Summer); Th P 7:00pm
c/o: Alex McIntosh (519-786-5038)
6036 Townend Line; Box 126, Forest, ON, N0N 1J0
alt: Richard Hoornweg (519-786-2070)
hoornweg@xcelco.on.ca

Lake Shore Gospel Hall
8908 Fuller Rd, Forest, ON, N0N 1J0
Su B 10:00am, S 11:15am, G 7:00pm; We P 7:30pm
c/o: Russell Fuller (519-786-6229)
8638 Vance Dr, RR#5, Forest, ON, N0N 1J0
fullru@xcelco.on.ca

GALT

Westside Bible Chapel (519-621-1710)
143 Glenmorris, Cambridge, ON, N1S 2Z4
Su B, S 11:15am, M 7:00pm; We P/M
c/o: Antonio Medeiros (519-622-5268)
30 Albert St, Cambridge, ON, N1R 3M6

GEORGETOWN

Halton Hills Bible Chapel (905-873-1005)
Georgetown District Seniors Centre, 318 Guelph St. Unit #9, Georgetown, ON, L7G 4B5
www.haltonhillsbiblechapel.com
info@haltonhillsbiblechapel.com
Su B 10:00am, M 11:20am, lunch 12:10pm, M 1:15pm; We P 7:30pm
note: meets in a rented facility
c/o: Hanniel Ghezzi (905-877-9066)
9742 Trafalgar Rd, Georgetown, ON, L7G 4S5
hannielghezzi@hotmail.com
alt: Galen Roberts (905-877-3591)
galenroberts@hotmail.com

174 CANADA — ONTARIO

GLOUCESTER
Pine Grove Bible Church (613-745-4664)
2144 E Acres Rd, Ottawa, ON, K1J 9A5
Su B/S

GOLDEN LAKE
Deacon Gospel Chapel
408 Chapel Rd, Golden Lake, ON, K0J 1X0
c/o: Reginald Briscoe (613-757-2806)
14308B Hwy 60 RR 1, Golden Lake, ON, K0J 1X0

GOODWOOD
Goodwood Gospel Hall (905-852-4874)
304 Hwy #47, Goodwood, ON, L0C 1A0
www.Goodwood.GospelHall.com
Todd.Snooks@sympatico.ca
Su B 9:30am, S/M 11:00am, P 6:40pm, G 7:00pm; Th P/M 7:00pm
note: send mail to main point of contact's address
c/o: Todd Snooks (905-852-4874)
10 Byam Place, Uxbridge, ON, L9P 1A8
Todd.Snooks@sympatico.ca
alt: Bob Diebel (905-852-5241)
rdiebel@sympatico.ca

GORE BAY
Gore Bay Gospel Hall
Gore Bay, ON
Su B 10:00am, S 11:45am, G 7:30pm; Th P/M 8:00pm
c/o: Frank McAndry (705-377-4970)
Gen Del, Providence Bay, ON, P0P 1T0

GORRIE
Gorrie Bible Fellowship (519-335-3500)
Gen Del, Gorrie, ON, N0G 1X0
Su B/S/P
c/o: Claude Martin (519-335-6276)
RR 1, Fordwich, ON, N0G 1V0

GOULAIS RIVER
Northland Bible Chapel (705-649-3221)
RR 2, Goulais River, ON, P0S 1E0
Su S 10:00am, M 11:00am, B 6:00pm, M 7:00pm; Mo C 6:00pm (Sept-May); Th P/M 7:00pm; Fr Y 7:00pm
note: cnr Hwy 17N & 552W
c/o: Stephen Clock (705-649-0687)
RR 2, Goulais River, ON, P0S 1E0

GRAND BEND
Grand Bend Gospel Hall
Box 605, Grand Bend, ON, N0M 1T0
Su B 10:00am, S 11:45am, G 7:00pm; We P/M 8:00pm
c/o: Don Gratton (519-238-2820)
Box 605, Grand Bend, ON, N0M 1T0
dagrattn@hay.net

GRANTON

Community Bible Church
Granton, ON
c/o: Doug Loveday (519-225-2580)
RR 3, Lucan, ON, N0M 2J0

GUELPH

Arkell Road Bible Chapel (519-836-4593)
RR 2, 39 Arkell Rd, Guelph, ON, N1H 6H8
Su B 9:30am, S 11:00am, M 6:30pm; Tu P/M 7:30pm
c/o: Arkell Road Bible Chapel

Grace Community Church (519-837-1457)
7427 Marden Road, RR 5, Guelph, ON, N1H 6J2
www.gracecommunity.ca
info@gracecommunity.ca
Su B 9:15am, F 11:00am
c/o: John Fairchild (519-837-1457)
7427 Marden Road, RR 5, GUELPH, ON, N1H 6J2
jfairchild@gracecommunity.ca
alt: Joyce Baker
info@gracecommunity.ca

Guelph Bible Chapel (519-822-7290)
216 Silvercreek Pkwy S, Guelph, ON, N1H 3S7
www.guelphbiblechapel.ca
pj-gbc@rogers.com
Su B 9:30am, F 11:00am, M 7:00pm; Tu P 7:00pm; Fr Y 7:00pm

Lakeside Bible Church
Guelph, ON
lbc@lakesidechurch.on.ca
c/o: David Ralph (519-836-8141)
PO Box 24042, Guelph, ON, N1E 6V8

Yorkshire Street Gospel Hall (519-836-7162)
4 Yorkshire St, Guelph, ON, N1H 5A5
Su B 10:00am, G 7:00pm, S 12:00pm; We P/M
c/o: Frank Rehmann (519-824-0584)

HAMILTON

Bethany Gospel Chapel (905-544-4326)
155 Gage Ave N, Hamilton, ON, L8L 7A3
Su B/S, M 6:30pm; We P/M 8:00pm
c/o: Don Ruddle (905-547-0064)
42 Hilda Ave, Hamilton, ON, L8M 3E6
alt: Robert I Cooper (Miss. Corr) (905-529-0785)

Kensington Avenue Gospel Hall
Hamilton, ON
Su B 10:30am, G 7:00pm, S 12:00pm; Tu M 7:45pm
note: Kensington Ave & Cannon St
c/o: Paul Glenney
99 Blanmora Dr, Stoney Creek, ON, L8G 4A9
p.glenney@sympatico.ca

Stone Ridge Bible Chapel (905-383-3067)
1457 Upper Sherman Ave, Hamilton, ON, L8W 1C4
Su B 9:30am, S 11:00am, M 6:00pm
c/o: Roy Greene (905-383-9687)
127 Welbourn Dr, Hamilton, ON, L9A 3N5
helroygreene@sympatico.ca

West Fifth Bible Chapel (905-383-5095)
440 West Fifth St, Hamilton, ON, L9C 3P6
Su B 9:30am, S 11:15am, G 6:30pm; We M 7:30pm
c/o: Paul Grant (905-574-8323)
56 Karen Cres, Hamilton, ON, L9C 5M6
standfast@mountaincable.net

HEARST

L'Assemblee Chretienne de Hearst (705-362-8386)
PO Box 2680, 1721 Hwy 11 W, Hearst, ON
Su B 9:30am, S 11:00am, M 7:15pm; We P/M 7:15pm
c/o: Omer Pepin (705-372-1079 or 372-1134)
PO Box 2124, 48 St Laurent, Hearst, ON, P0L 1N0

HEIDELBERG

Heidelberg Bible Fellowship (519-699-5418)
2720 Kressler Rd, Heidelberg, ON, N0B 1Y0
www.hbfweb.org
info@hbfweb.org
Su B 9:30am, F 11:00am, M 7:00pm; We M 7:15pm
c/o: Randy Hoffman (519-699-4311)
2933 Kressler Rd, St Clements, ON, N0B 2MO
randyhoffman@sympatico.ca
alt: Kevin Shantz (519-503-1822)
kevin@shantz.org

HUNTSVILLE

Huntsville Gospel Hall (705-789-3767)
20 Main St W, Huntsville, ON, P1H 1K9
Su B 10:00am, S/M 12:00pm, G 7:00pm; Tu P/M 7:30pm
note: use point of contact as church's mailing address
c/o: David Traves (705-789-8420)
10 A West Rd, Huntsville, ON, P1H 1K9
dhtraves@sympatico.ca
alt: Vernon Cottrill (705-789-5230)

ILLDERTON

Community Bible Church
100 Meadowcreek Dr, Illderton, ON, N0M 2A0
c/o: Scott Dakin (519-666-3049)
sedakin@netcom.ca

IROQUOIS FALLS

Iroquois Falls Bible Chapel (705-232-5544)
1065 Victoria Rd, Iroquois Falls, ON
Su B/S; Th P/M 7:00pm; Fr Y 7:00pm
c/o: Steven Millson (705-232-4702)
Box 909, Iroquois Falls, ON, P0K 1E0

KANATA

Bridlewood Bible Chapel (613-591-8514)
465 Eagleson Rd, Kanata, ON, K2M 1H3
www.bridlewoodbiblechapel.ca
Su B 9:30am, F/S 11:10am, M 6:30pm; We P 7:00pm
c/o: Chris Kruszelnicki
2 Trotting Way, Kanata, ON, K2M 1B2
ckruszelnicki@gmail.com

KAPUSKASING

Kapuskasing Gospel Hall (705-335-2005)
154 Mill St, Kapuskasing, ON, P5N 2V9
Su B 10:00am, S 11:45am, G 7:00pm; Th P/M 7:00pm
c/o: Gerald LaBelle
glabelle@nt.net

KINGSTON

Union Street Gospel Chapel (613-545-0909)
195 Union St, Kingston, ON, K7L 2P5
Su B 9:30am, S 11:00am, M 6:30pm; We M 7:00pm
c/o: William Graham (613-547-4387)
megbill@kgs.net

KIRKFIELD

Victoria Road Gospel Hall
1108 Fenel Rd RR 3, Kirkfield, ON, K0M 2B0
Su B 10:30am, G 7:00pm, S 12:00pm; We P 7:00pm
c/o: Kenneth F Stone (705-374-4688)
187 Sandhills Rd, RR 3, Woodville, ON, K0M 2T0
kenstone@sympatico.ca

KIRKLAND LAKE

Kirkland Gospel Hall
38 Porteous Ave, Kirkland Lake, ON
Su B 10:00am, S 11:30am, G 7:00pm; We P/M 7:00pm
c/o: Douglas Yade (705-567-5951)
29 Hillcrest Dr, Kirkland Lake, ON, P2N 3N6

Kirkland Lake Bible Chapel (705-567-5554)
PO Box 1349, Kirkland Lake, ON, P2N 3P2
Su B 9:30am, S 11:00am; We P 7:00pm
note: cnr of Premier & Prospect
c/o: Doug Robinson (705-642-9153)
Swastika, ON, P0K 1T0

KITCHENER
Gospel Hall
184 Madison Ave S, Kitchener, ON, N2G 3M8
Su B 10:00am, G 7:00pm, S 12:00pm; Tu M 8:00pm
c/o: Phil McKinley (519-570-1976)
73 Bent Willow Dr, Kitchener, ON, N2N 2L1

Highview Community Church (519-745-4211)
295 Highview Dr, Kitchener, ON, N2N 2K7
highview@aiming.net
Su B/M 10:30am; We M 8:00pm; Th M 8:00pm
c/o: D Pirrie (519-658-4170)
509 River Rd, Cambridge, ON, N3C 2B8

L'AMABLE
L'Amable Bible Chapel (613-332-4958)
PO Box 55, L'amable, ON, K0L 2L0
Su B 9:15am, S 11:00am, M 7:00pm; Tu C/M 7:00pm
c/o: Durl Lott (613-332-2154)
200 Coe Island Lake Rd, Bancroft, ON, K0L 1C0

[handwritten: SGNT TO G60.T. OCT. 21, 2010.]

LAKEFIELD
Lakefield Gospel Chapel (705-652-6689)
140 Water St, Lakefield, ON, K0L 2H0
Su B 9:30am, S 11:00am, M 6:30pm; We P/M 7:30pm
c/o: Donald K Steele (705-750-0351)
931 Armour Rd Unit 112, Peterborough, Ontario, K9H 7H1
dsteele@nexicom.net
alt: David Orbell (705-652-8142)

LINDSAY
Lindsay Gospel Hall (705-324-9002)
5 Howard Ave, Lindsay, ON, K9V 2W1
Su G, B 10:30am; Th P/M 8:00pm
c/o: Craig Foreshew (705-374-4407)
RR 3, Woodville, ON, K0M 2T0

LISTOWEL
Bible Chapel
545 Blake St E, Listowel, ON
Su B 9:30am, S 11:00am, M 7:30pm; We P/M 8:00pm
c/o: Mervin Martin (519-291-1379)
RR 3, Listowel, ON, N4W 3G8

LONDON

Byron Community Chapel
London, ON
c/o: John Mackie (519-473-3210)
336 Glenrose Dr, London, ON, N6K 2A8
jmackie@byroncc.on.ca

Faith Bible Chapel (519-433-2356)
439 Moore St, London, ON, N6C 2C1
faithbiblechapel.lweb.net
lesdoey@sympatico.ca
Su B 9:30am, F/S 11:00am, M 6:30pm; We P/M 7:00pm
c/o: Les Doey (519-768-2356)
104 Sexton St. Box 583, West Lorne, ON, N0L 2P0
lesdoey9@sympatico.ca
alt: Ab Birch (519-637-8906)
birch.kinfolk@sympatico.ca

Highbury Avenue Gospel Hall (519-451-8233)
1196 Highbury Ave, London, ON, N5Y1A7
Su B 9:30am, S 11:30am, G 6:30pm; Tu P 8:00pm; Th M 8:00pm
c/o: Philip P Lampkin (519-472-8747)
1742 Attawandaron Rd, London, ON, N6G 3N1
felipe524@execulink.com

North Park Community Church
London, ON
c/o: Terry Sanderson (519-457-1400)
1510 Fanshawe Park Rd E, London, ON, N5X 4A3
terry@northpark.on.ca

Southdale Bible Chapel (519-686-0111)
1214 Southdale Rd E, London, ON, N6E 1B4
Su M, S 9:45am, B 6:30pm; We P/M
c/o: Douglas Idema (519-657-5461)
14 Cottonwood Cres, London, ON, N6G 2Y8

LUCAN

Community Bible Church
RR 3, Lucan, ON
Su M 9:15am, M 11:00am
c/o: D Loveday (519-225-2580)
RR 3, Lucan, ON, N0M 2J0

MABERLY

Gospel Hall (613-268-2001)
RR 1, Maberly, ON, K0H 2B0
Su B 9:30am, S 11:15am, G 7:00pm; We P/M 7:30pm
note: 15 mi W of Perth 1/2 mi N of Hwy 7
c/o: Gordon McLeod (613-268-2616)
RR 1, Maberly, ON, K0H 2B0

MARKHAM

✓ **Markham Bible Chapel** (905-294-7369) SGNT OCT. 22, 2010
50 Cairns Dr, Markham, ON, L3P 6G9
www.markhambiblechapel.org
Su B 9:30am, F 11:15am, M 6:00pm; We P/M 7:30pm
c/o: <u>Ron Gee</u> (905-640-9646)
61 Katherine Cres, Stouffville, ON, L4A 1K4
rdgee@sympatico.ca

MASSEY

Bible Chapel
316 Castle St, Massey, ON
Su B/S, P 7:00pm; We M (homes); Th M (homes)
c/o: Mike Kelly (705-865-2581)
Cutler Lake Rd RR 2, Massey, ON, P0P 1P0

MATHESON

Gospel Chapel
705-273-3022, Matheson, ON
Su B/S, G 7:00pm; Tu P/M 7:00pm
c/o: John McLaughlin (705-273-2940)
294 2nd St, Box 54, Matheson, ON, P0K 1N0

MAYNOOTH

Bible Chapel (613-338-2090)
RR 1, Graphite, ON, K0L 2S0
Su S, B 9:45am, G 7:00pm; We P/M; Sa Y
c/o: Kevin Wadsworth

MIDLAND

Midland Gospel Hall (705-526-8023)
248 Midland Ave, Midland, ON, L4R 4P4
Su B 9:30am, G 7:00pm, M 12:00pm; We P/M 7:30pm
c/o: Paul Barbour (705-526-3516)
328 John St, Midland, ON, L4R 2J5
barbour@fsumail.net

MILTON

Milton Gospel Hall (905-878-0765)
306 Ontario St N, Milton, ON, L9T 2T9
Su B 10:00am, F/S 11:45am, G 7:00pm; We P 7:30pm
c/o: David M Regis (905-878-3873)
483 Valleyview Cres, Milton, ON, L9T 3L3
daveregis@sympatico.ca
alt: W Hildebrandt (905-844-1238)
whildebrandt@sympatico.net

MISSISSAUGA

Applewood Heights Gospel Hall (905-316-1922)
4030 Tomken Rd, Mississauga, ON, L4W 1J5
Su B 9:45am, S/F 12:00am, G 6:30pm; Th M/P 7:30pm
c/o: Dr. Paul Robinson (416-255-4993)
323 Lake Promenade, Toronto, ON, M8W 1A6
drback@interlog.com
alt: Sterling Payne (905-270-3817)

Erindale Bible Chapel (905-277-4618)
1400 Dundas Cres, Mississauga, ON, L5C 1E7
Su B/S, M 6:30pm
c/o: Peter McKnight
pmcknight@sympatico.ca

Grace Gospel Chapel (905-790-9362)
167 Queen St. South, Unit 8, Mississauga, ON, L5M 1L2
www.gracegospelchapel.ca
ianroberts2007@yahoo.com   SGNT OCT. 20, 2010.
Su B 9:15am, G/M/S 10:30am; Tu P & Bible Study 6:30pm
note: meetings held at Village English School
note: mailing address: 411 - 4 Kings Cross Rd, Brampton, ON, L6T 3X8
c/o: Ian Roberts (905-790-9362)
411 - 4 Kings Cross Rd, Brampton, ON, L6T 3X8
ianroberts2007@yahoo.com
alt: Churchill Wilson (905-828-7230)
wilson7230@rogers.com

NEW LISKEARD

Bethel Gospel Chapel (705-647-6200)
Sheperdson Rd at McCamus, New Liskeard, ON, P0J 1P0
Su B 9:30am, S/G 11:00am, F/M 1:00pm; We P 7:00pm; Th C 6:30pm
note: mailing address: Box 705, New Liskeard, ON, P0J 1P0
c/o: R Bearomore (705-647-6543)
551 Broadwood Ave, Box 443, New Liskeard, ON, P0J 1P0
alt: Peter Kerr (705-544-7707)

NEWBURY

Newbury Gospel Hall
370 Walnut Dr RR 3, Newbury, ON
Su B 10:00am, G 7:00pm, S 12:00pm; Th P/M 7:45pm
c/o: David J Cooper (519-674-3073)
82 Goodall Ave, Box 1218, Ridgetown, ON, N0P 2C0
dcooperd@mnsi.net

NEWMARKET

Gospel Hall (905-853-1430)
736 Davis Dr, Newmarket, ON, L3Y 2R4
Su B 9:30am, S 11:30am, G 6:30pm; Tu P/M 8:00pm
c/o: Timothy B Scheeer (905-898-4369)
222 Lloyd Ave, Newmarket, ON, L3Y 5M3
tescheer@excite.com

River Drive Bible Chapel (905-836-1798)
PO Box 13004, Bradford, ON, L3Z 2Y5
Su B/S, M 6:30pm; We P/M
note: 20246 Bathurst St, Hwy 11 & Queensville Rd
c/o: Leon Wease (905-830-0037)
wease5@sympatico.ca
alt: R. Minard (905-895-0524)

NIAGARA FALLS

Oakwood Gospel Hall
Adams & Hawkins St, Niagara Falls, ON
Su B 9:30am, S 11:30am, G 7:00pm; We P/M 7:30pm
note: 1 blk N of McLeod Rd exit E from Queen E Hwy
c/o: William Smith (905-354-8272)
7467 Merritt Ave, Niagra Falls, ON, L2G 5C3

NORTH BAY

Bethel Gospel Chapel (705-474-4920)
1710 O'Brien St, North Bay, ON, P1B 8L8
www.bethelgospelchapel.com
Su B 9:30am, F/S 11:15am; Tu L 10:00am, C 6:30pm; We P 7:00pm;
Fr Y 6:30pm
note: point of contact is church's mailing address
c/o: Harold Fiss (705-474-6747)
263 Greenhill Ave, North Bay, ON, P1B 8L8
hmfiss@sympatico.ca
alt: Donald Bushey (705-474-4627)
busheyd@onlink.net

Nipissing Junction Gospel Hall (705-474-3384)
1340 Lakeshore Dr, North Bay, ON, P1B 8Z4
su b 9:30am, s 11:30am, g 7:00pm; we p 7:00pm
note: use point of contact as church's mailing address
c/o: Clarence R Black (705-497-1284)
63 Massey Dr, North Bay, Ontario, P1A 3Y3
bjbcrb@ontera.net
alt: Fred S Culin (705-495-3557)

OAKVILLE

Hopedale Bible Chapel (905-827-8327)
342 Sherin Dr, Oakville, ON, L6L 4J3
Su B 9:30am, S/G 11:00am, M 6:30pm; We P 7:30pm
c/o: Alex Hayworth (905-637-3239)
Burlington, ON

OIL SPRINGS

Gospel Hall
Victoria St, Oil Springs, ON
Su B 10:00am, S 11:30am, G 7:30pm; Th P 7:30pm
c/o: Arthur Whitton (519-882-1686)
RR 3, Oil Springs, ON, N0N 1P0

CANADA — ONTARIO

ORANGEVILLE

Hackley Valley Bible (519-942-8200)
PO Box 64, Orangeville, ON, L9W 2Z5

ORILLIA

Dominion Gospel Hall (705-325-8113)
30 Andrew St S, Orillia, ON
Su B 9:30am, C/M 11:30am, G 7:00pm; Tu P/M 7:30pm
note: use point of contact as church's mailing address
c/o: Andrew Adams (705-326-9698)
#11-441 Barrie Rd, Orillia, ON, L3V 6T9
adamsa@rogers.com

Hillside Bible Chapel (705-326-9572)
PO Box 67, Orillia, ON, L3V 6H9
Su B/S, G 7:00pm; We P/M; Th L
note: Hwy 12 W & Fairgrounds Rd
c/o: Robert Farquharson (705-325-9907)

Orillia Community Church (705-329-2139)
4337 Burnside Line Unit 7, Orillia, ON, L3V 6H4
occ@encode.com

Simcoside Lifepointe Church (705-325-4144)
113 Simcoe St, Orillia, ON, L3V 1G8
Su B 10:00am, F 11:00am, M 6:30pm; Tu M 7:00pm; We L 9:30am
c/o: Donald L Mackie (705-325-5030)
393 Victoria Cres, Orillia, ON, L3V 6H1
lodmaci@infinity.net
alt: Chuck Doubrough (705-327-8966)
chuck@doubrough.ca

OSGOODE

Osgoode Bible Chapel (613-826-3347)
Old George St, Osgoode, ON, K0A 2W0
keknuth@magma.ca
Su B 9:30am, S 11:00am, G 6:30pm; We M 7:00pm
c/o: Karl Knuth (613-821-1353)
Box 9, Osgoode, ON, K0A 2W0
keknuth@magma.ca

OSHAWA

Albert Street Gospel Hall (905-433-1644)
150 Albert St, Oshawa, ON, L1H 4R2
Su B 10:00am, G 7:00pm, S 12:00pm; Tu P/M 7:30pm
c/o: Kenneth Nicholson (905-579-7540)
753 Central Park Blvd N, Oshawa, ON, L1G 6B2

OTTAWA

Rideauview Bible Chapel (613-225-8452)
1249 Prince of Wales Dr, Ottawa, ON, K2C 1N1
Su B, S 11:15am, M 6:30pm; Tu P/M
c/o: Brian Foreman (613-521-6585)

River Road Gospel Hall (613-748-0269)
1087 N River Rd, Ottawa, ON, K1K 3W1
Su B 10:00am, G 7:30pm, S 12:00pm; Tu P/M 7:30pm
c/o: Kenneth E Prince (613-733-3738)
1246 Kitchener Ave, Ottawa, ON, K1V 6W5

River Road Gospel Hall
Ottawa, ON
c/o: Mervyn Cottrill (613-225-4708)
207 Winthrow Ave, Ottawa, ON, K2G 2J8

OWEN SOUND

Gospel Hall (519-376-6040)
912 9th Ave E, Owen Sound, ON, N4K 3E7
Su B 11:00am, G 7:00pm, S 12:30pm; Th P/M 8:00pm
c/o: Donald T Curry (519-371-9564)
RR 3, Owen Sound, ON, N4K 5N5

PARKHILL

Grace Bible Chapel (519-294-0211)
227 Main St, Box 148, Parkhill, ON, N0M 2K0
gracechapel@ns.sympatico.ca
Su B/S, M 7:00pm; Tu P; Fr Y 7:00pm

PARRY SOUND

Gospel Hall
13 River St, Parry Sound, ON, P2A 2T7
Su B 9:30am, S 11:00am, G 7:00pm; We P 7:00pm
c/o: Thomas F Hulcoop (705-746-5919)
9 Edward St, Parry Sound, ON, P2A 2W5

PEMBROKE

Pembroke Bible Chapel (613-735-1149)
Pembroke, ON
Su B 9:30am, S 11:00am; We P/M 7:00pm
note: cnr of B-Line & Hwy 148
c/o: Allan Lockley (613-687-6296)
29 Earl St, Petawawa, ON, K8H 3M4

PETERBOROUGH

Auburn Bible Chapel (705-742-1032)
911 Armour Road, Peterborough, ON, K9H 2A7
auburnbiblechapel.com
auburn@nexicom.net
Su B 10:15am

Braidwood Bible Chapel (705-743-8609)
306 Braidwood Ave, Peterborough, ON, K9J 1V6
Su B 9:30am, S 11:00am, M 6:30pm; Tu C 6:45pm; We P/M 7:00pm;
Th L (monthly); Fr Y 7:00pm
c/o: Reg Curtis (705-944-5608)
18 Pine Tree Cres, RR 1, Fraserville, ON
curtisr@ptbo.igs.net

Edmison Heights Bible Chapel (705-743-6467)
939 Hilliard St, Peterborough, ON, K9H 5R9
klbc@peterboro.net
Su B 9:30am, S 11:00am, M 6:00pm; Tu C 6:30pm; We M 9:30am,
M 7:00pm; Fr Y 7:00pm
c/o: Norm Budge (705-742-6339)
831 Rishor Cres, Peterborough, ON, K9H 5E1

Park Street Gospel Hall (705-741-5571)
592 Park St N, Peterborough, ON, K9H 4S2
Su B 9:30am, S 11:15am, G 7:00pm; We P/M 7:30pm
c/o: Arthur R Morrison (705-760-9242)
700 Trailview Dr, Peterborough, ON, K9V 8P2

Westmount Bible Chapel (705-742-9661)
1150 Clonsilla Ave, Peterborough, ON, K9J 5Y7
Su B/G/F/S 10:30am; We P 7:00pm; Th L 9:00am; Fr Y 7:00pm
c/o: Rudy Solomon (705-748-3530)
376 Summerhill Dr, Peterborough, ON, K9H 5L9
solomonr@sympatico.ca
alt: David Aldom
the.aldoms@sympatico.ca

PICTON

Picton Gospel Hall (613-476-5617)
3 McFarland Dr, Picton, ON, K0K 2T0
Su B 9:30am, S 11:15am, G 7:00pm; Th P 7:30pm
c/o: Art Knight (613-476-6718)
20 Barker St Box 9, Picton, ON, K0K 2T0

PORCUPINE

Bible Fellowship Assembly (705-235-3532)
207 Lawrence St, Porcupine, ON
Su B 9:30am, F/S/G 11:00am; Tu L 9:30am, C 6:30 pm; Fr Y 7:00pm;
several home Bible studies and prayer meetings
note: mailing address: PO Box 6120, South Porcupine, ON, P0N 1K0
c/o: Philip E Donaldson (705-235-5179)
PO Box 569, Porcupine, ON, P0N 1C0
phildonaldson@persona.ca
alt: Dr. David Hook (705-267-4991)
drdghook@ontera.net

PORT COLBORNE

Portal Village Bible Chapel (905-835-5656)
309 Elgin St, Port Colborne, ON, L3K 6A2
Su B 9:30am, F/S 11:00am, G 6:30pm; Tu P/M 7:30pm; We C 6:30pm;
Sa Y 7:00pm
c/o: Harold MacDougall (905-834-0646)
309 Elgin St, Port Colborne, ON, L3K 6A2
hrm@everyday.on.ca
alt: David Shatford (905-892-1535)
shatford@vaxxine.com

PORT HOPE
Port Hope Gospel Hall
182 Cavan St, Port Hope, ON, L1A 3C2
Su B 9:30am, S/G 11:00am; Th P/M 7:00pm
c/o: Doug Booth (905-349-2701)
250 Finley Rd, RR 5, CoBourg, ON, K9A 4J8
dbooth@eagle.ca

PORT SYDNEY
Deer Lake Gospel Hall
654 Deer Lake Rd, Port Sydney, ON, P0B 1L0
Su B 10:00am, S 11:40am, G 7:00pm; We P/M 7:30pm
c/o: Benjamin VanNoppen (705-385-0268)
812 Deer Lake Rd, RR2, Port Sydney, ON, P0B 1L0
ben.vannoppen@sympatico.ca
alt: Benjamin Huggins (705-385-2081)

RICHARDS LANDING
Island Bible Chapel (705-246-2673)
1360 Littleton St, Richards Landing, St. Joseph Island, ON, P0R 1J0
Su P 9:30am, B 10:00am, F 11:15am
c/o: Dean Love (705-246-1628)
RR #1, Richards Landing, ON, P0R 1J0
deanernestlove@vianet.ca
alt: Dean Love (705-246-0004)
mo_tulloch@yahoo.com

RICHMOND HILL
Richvale Bible Chapel (905-889-7073)
24 Oak Ave, Richmond Hill, ON, L4C 6R7
www.richvale.ca
info@richvale.ca
Su B 9:30am, F/S 11:00am; Th L 9:30am
c/o: Conrad Adams (905-895-8373)
207 Alexander Rd, Newmarket, ON, L3Y 5P2

RIDGEVILLE
Ridgeville Bible Chapel (905-892-3347)
418 Canboro Rd, P.O. Box 48, Ridgeville, ON, L0S 1M0
Su B 9:30am, S 11:00am, M 6:00pm; We P/M 7:15pm
c/o: Albert Nickel (905-732-7164)

SAINT MARY'S
St. Marys Gospel Hall
632 Jones St E, Saint Mary's, ON
Su B 10:30am, S 12:00pm, G 7:30pm; We P/M 7:30pm
note: use point of contact as church's mailing address
c/o: Glen Woodside (519-284-3509)
24167 Fairview Rd, RR 3, Thorndale, ON, N0M 2P0
thewoodsides@cyg.net
alt: John Hackett (519-229-6183)
jrhackett@hotmail.com

SAINT THOMAS

Gospel Hall (519-631-1940)
1 Sunset Dr Hwy 4, Saint Thomas, ON, N5P 3T2
Su B 9:45am, G 7:00pm, S 12:00pm; Th P/M 7:30pm
c/o: Lyle McCandless (519-637-1602)
45 Pol Ct, Saint Thomas, ON, N5R 5P9
wade.steers@sympatico.ca

SARNIA

Devine Street Gospel Chapel (519-337-7161)
714 Devine St, Sarnia, ON, N7T 1X2
Su B 9:30am, F 11:00am; Tu P/M 7:30pm
c/o: Robert Watson (519-542-5156)
1044 Fairlane Ave, Sarnia, ON, N7S 3J8
alt: Ralph Grace (519-862-1272)

Gospel Hall
102 College Ave S, Sarnia, ON
Su B 9:30am, S 3:00pm, G 7:00pm; Tu P 8:00pm; Th M 8:00pm
c/o: Shadrach Kember Sr (519-337-7476)
1726 Confederation St, Sarnia, ON, N7T 7H3

SAULT STE MARIE

Believers Bible Chapel (705-254-5249)
423 Henry St, Sault Ste Marie, ON, P6C 2W7
Su B 9:30am, F 11:00am, M 6:00pm; We P 6:30pm
c/o: Joe Reese (705-946-0289)
199 4th Line E, Sault Ste Marie, Ontario, P6A 5K8
joeandann@gmail.com
~~joereese@shaw.ca~~
alt: Gary Mattila (705-759-0077)

Bethel Bible Chapel (705-254-2191)
407 McNabb St, Sault Ste Marie, ON, P6B 1Z2

Riverside Bible Chapel
155 Hugill St, Sault Ste Marie, ON
Su B/S
c/o: J Douglas Rankin (705-759-3414)
71 Park St, Sault Ste Marie, ON, P6A 5G7

Sault Ste Marie Gospel Hall (705-949-1101)
475 Wellington St E, Sault Ste Marie, ON, P6A 2M2
dcwest@sympatico.ca
Su B 9:30am, F/S 11:15am, M 7:00pm; Tu P 7:30pm
c/o: David West (705-945-9245)
483 River Rd, Sault Ste Marie, ON, P6A 5K9
dcwest@shaw.ca
alt: Robert Clark (705-949-4523)
robann_clark@sympatico.ca

SEVERN BRIDGE

Severn Bridge Christian Assembly
Southwood Rd, Severn Bridge, ON
Su B 9:45am, F 11:15am; We P/M 7:30pm
c/o: Larry Babineau (705-687-2226)
1121 Muskoka Beach Rd, Gravenhurst, ON, P1P 1R1

SHELBURNE

Bethel Bible Chapel (519-925-3910)
419 Main St E, Shelburne, ON, L0N 1S4
Su B/F/C; We M 6:30pm; Th P/M 7:30pm
c/o: RGR Lewis (519-925-2180)
1-108 2nd Ave W, Shelburne, ON, L0N 1S1

SIMCOE

Simcoe Gospel Chapel (519-426-7131)
4152 Hwy #3 East, Simcoe, ON, N3Y 4K8
simcoegospel@kwic.com
Su S 9:30am, M 10:30am
note: mailing address: Box 25, Simcoe, ON, N3Y 4K8
c/o: Thomas Sero
alt: Marty Brown

ST CATHARINES

Brockview Bible Chapel (905-684-7161)
326 Pelham Rd, St Catharines, ON, L2S 1Y3
Su B 9:00am, F/S 11:00am, M 6:30pm; Th P/M 7:30pm
c/o: Brian Gunning (905-627-7073)
7 Wood-dale Dr, St Catharines, ON, L2T 1Y9
bgunning@sympatico.ca

Scottlea Gospel Chapel (905-646-0761)
500 Scott St, St Catharines, ON, L2M 3X2
www.scottleagc.org
scottleagc@yahoo.com
Su B 9:15am, F 11:00am, M 6:00pm; Tu C 9:30am, P/M 7:30pm; We C 6:15pm; Fr Y 7:00pm
c/o: Desmon McCurry (905-708-1109)
1103-250 Lake St, St Catharines, ON, L2R 5Z4
dmccurry@cogeco.ca

STIRLING

Grace Bible Chapel (613-395-5022)
Edward St, Stirling, ON, K0K 3E0
Su S/M, B 9:45am; We P/M; Fr Y
c/o: Paul C Tyrer (613-398-6980)
Box 502, Stirling, ON, K0K 2C0

STRAFFORDVILLE
Straffordville Gospel Hall
53 Plank Rd, Straffordville, ON, N0J 1Y0
Su B 10:00am, M 11:30am, G 7:00pm; Tu P 7:30pm
c/o: Jake Friesen (519-773-3890)
50709 Talbot Ln, RR 1, Aylmek, ON, N5H 2R1

STRONGVILLE
Strongville Gospel Hall
1583 Strongville Rd, RR 1, Strongville, ON
Tu P/M 7:00pm
c/o: Doug Black (705-721-7658)
92 Doran Rd Box 111, Midhurst, ON, L0L 1X0
leather@heritan.com

SUDBURY
Alder Street Gospel Hall (705-674-6083)
215 Alder St, Sudbury, ON, P3C 4J3
Su B 10:00am, S 11:45am, G 7:00pm; We P/M 7:30pm
c/o: Walter Foreshew (705-855-3996)
3306 Hwy 144 W, Chelmsford, ON, P0M 1L0
wv4shew@sympatico.ca

Sudbury Bible Fellowship (705-560-3889)
1661 Lansing Ave, Sudbury, ON, P3A 4S9
Su B 9:30am, F/S 11:15am, M 6:30pm; We P/M 7:00pm
c/o: James Martin (705-560-5646)
1761 Rutherglen Cr, Sudbury, ON, P3A 2K4
james@thesword.ca

SUNDRIDGE
Chapman Valley Gospel Hall (705-384-5280)
9 Miller Rd. (Hwy #124 & Miller Rd), Municipality of Magnetawan, ON, P0A 1Z0
Su B 9:45am, S/F 11:30am, G 7:00pm; We P/F 7:30pm
note: use main point of contact for mailing address
c/o: Russell Longhurst (705-387-4393)
28 River Rd. RR #2, Sundridge, ON, P0A 1Z0
russdianne@yahoo.com

South River Christian Assembly
Sundridge, ON
c/o: Harold O'Brien (705-384-5447)
Box 441, Sundridge, ON, P0A 1Z0
mattsue@onlink.net

TAVISTOCK
Tavistock Bible Chapel (519-655-2413)
corner of William & Oxford Sts, Tavistock, ON, N0B 2R0
Su B 9:30am, F 11:00am, M 7:00pm; Th P/M 7:00pm
note: use point of contact as church's mailing address
c/o: Jim Cormack (519-284-0203)
20 Ontario St S, PO Box 1141, St Marys, ON, N4X 1B7

THESSALON
Bible Chapel
Thessalon, ON
Su B/S, G 8:00pm; We P/M 8:00pm; Fr Y 8:00pm
note: Algoma Ave

THORNHILL
Langstaff Gospel Hall (905-881-1645)
1350 Langstaff Rd, Toronto, ON
Su B 10:00am, G 7:00pm, S 12:00pm; We P/M 7:45pm
c/o: Harry Clingen (905-889-1556)
1300 Langstaff Rd, Thornhill, ON, L4J 8P8

THOROLD
Thorold South Gospel Chapel (905-227-0310)
319 Davis St, Thorold, ON, L2B 1G2
www.tsgc.ca
rjmcintee@sympatico.ca
Su B 9:30am, S/F 11:00am, M 6:00pm; We P/M 7:00pm; Th C 6:30pm
c/o: Ross McIntee (905-684-6772)
195 Woodside Dr, St Catharines, ON, L2T 1X8
rjmcintee@juno.com

THUNDER BAY
Farrand Street Bible Chapel (807-344-9038)
246 Farrand St, Thunder Bay, ON, P7A 3J4
Su B 9:30am, S 11:00am; We M 7:00pm
c/o: Dr Arnot Hawkins (807-345-2664)
123 Cottonwood Cres, Thunder Bay, ON, P7A 3L8
ahawkins1@shaw.ca

Gosepl Hall
101 Pine St, Thunder Bay, ON, P7A 5X4
Su B 10:30am, S 12:30pm, G 7:00pm; Tu P&M 7:30pm
c/o: George Stieh (807-344-5315)
129 McKibbon St, Thunder Bay, ON, P7A 4B4
gestieh@tbaytel.net

Westmount Gospel Chapel (807-475-4025)
101 W Brock Street, Thunder Bay, ON, P7E 4H9
Su B/S/F 10:30am
note: use point of contact as church's mailing address
c/o: David Smith (807-622-6671)
2633 Ridgeway St, Thunder Bay, ON, P7E 5K4
desdsmith@show.ca
alt: James Minor (807-622-1204)
emptynest16@lycos.com

TILLSONBURG
Tillsonburg Bible Chapel (519-842-7410)
63 Queen St, Tillsonburg, ON, N4G 3H1
Su B/S, G 7:00pm; Th P

TIMMINS

Timmins Gospel Hall (705-267-3163)
1550 MacLean Dr, Timmins, ON, P4N 7C3
Su B 10:00am, S 11:45am, G 7:00pm; We P 7:00pm
note: use point of contact as church's mailing address
c/o: Wayne Aldred (705-235-9420)
Box 6077, S Porcupine, ON, P0N 1K0
wgaldred@ontera.net
alt: Tom Skwarok (705-264-1087)
epitron@ntl.sympatico.ca

Grace Bible Chapel (705-267-5541)
1037 McLean Dr, Timmins, ON, P4N 8E8
Su B 9:15am, S 11:00am, M 6:30pm; We P/M 7:30pm
note: PO Box 2351
c/o: Ralph Carr (705-268-5071)
92 Hemlock St, Timmins, ON, P4N 6S5

TORONTO

Bendale Bible Chapel (416-431-1220)
330 Bellamy Rd N, Toronto, ON, N1H 1E8
Su B/S, M 6:00pm; We M (homes)

Broadview Avenue Gospel Hall (416-463-0425)
194 Broadview Ave, Toronto, ON, M4M 2G5
Su B 10:00am, G 7:00pm, S 12:00pm; Tu P/M 7:45pm
donald.jennings@sympatico.ca
note: use point of contact as church's mailing address
c/o: D.K. Jennings (416-757-7019)
53 Karnwood Dr, Scarborough, ON, M1L 2Z7
donald.jennings@sympatico.ca

Danforth Gospel Hall
2237 Danforth Ave, Toronto, ON, M4C 1K4
Su B, M 11:30am, G 7:00pm, T 8:00pm
c/o: Vince Latchman

Eglinton Avenue Gospel Hall (481-6373)
503 Eglinton Ave E, Toronto, ON, M4P 1N4
Su B 10:00am, G 7:00pm, S 12:00pm; Tu P/M 8:00pm

Fairbanks Gospel Hall
Toronto, ON
Su B 10:00am, S 3:00pm, G 7:00pm; Sa P/M 8:00pm
note: Ennerdale & Dynevor Rd
c/o: John Pompeo (633-6370)
32 Bengal Court, Downsview, ON, M3L 1X9

Greenwood Gospel Chapel (416-465-8347)
949 Greenwood, Toronto, ON, M4J 4C5
Su B 9:30am, S 11:15am, M 6:30pm; Tu P 7:30pm
c/o: Robert RG Theakston (416-463-1144)
11 Mountjoy Ave, Toronto, ON, M4J 1J4
bob.theakston@interbiz.ca

Hilltop Chapel (416-249-1411)
243 LaRose Ave, Toronto, ON, M9P 1G6 SGM OCT. 20, 2010.
hilltopchapel62@gmail.com
Su B 10:00am, F 11:10am; Tue P/M 8:00pm
c/o: Hugh Rodger (416-247-8482)

Leaside Bible Chapel (416-422-3135)
826 Eglinton Ave E, Toronto, ON, M4G 2L1
Su B 9:30am, S 11:00am; Tu P 7:30pm
c/o: Ian J Ferguson (416-920-9568)
1 Clarendon Ave #103, Toronto, ON, M4V 1H8

Rexdale Gospel Hall (416-742-5990)
72 Bergamot Ave at Islington Ave, Toronto (Etobicoke), ON, M9W 1V9
www.rexdalegospel.org
Su B 9:30am, S/G 11:10am, M 7:00pm; We P/M 8:00pm
note: use point of contact as church's mailing address
c/o: Roy Lutley (905-791-8971)
22 Hanover Rd Suite 301, Brampton, ON, L6S 5K7

Sanctuary
Toronto, ON
c/o: Greg Paul (416-922-0628)
25 Charles St E, Toronto, ON, M4Y 1R9
redrain@interlog.com

Unionville Gospel Hall (905-477-3501)
24 2nd St, Toronto, ON, L3R 2C3
Su B 9:30am, S 11:30am, G 6:30pm; We M 8:00pm
c/o: Stanley Darnell (905-294-1432)
28 Christman Court, Markham, ON, L3P 3C8
darnell.stan@sympatico.ca
alt: William Stainton (905-471-4408)

Victoria Park Gospel Hall (416-285-1611)
1266 Victoria Park Ave, Toronto, ON, M4B 2L1
www.victoriapark.gospelhall.com
Su B 10:00am, S/F 12:00pm, G 6:30pm; We P/F 7:00pm
note: at Furnival Road
note: for mailing address of Gospel Hall, use address of contact below
c/o: Keith Potter (416-497-8478)
8 Allangrove Cres, Toronto, ON, M1W 1S5

West Hill Gospel Hall (416-281-0616)
159 Morningside Ave, Scarborough, ON, M1E 3C8
Su B 9:30am, S/G 11:30am, G/M 6:30pm; We P 8:00pm
c/o: Douglas Joyce (416-724-9777)
20 Dean Park Rd, Suite 210, Toronto, ON, M1B 3G9

TRENTON
Lorne Avenue Bible Chapel
Trenton, ON
Su S, B 9:00am, M 7:00pm; We M 8:00pm
note: Lorne Ave & Wilkins St

UTTERSON
Port Sydney Bible Chapel
370 South Mary Lake Rd, Utterson, ON, P0B 1L0
c/o: Cliff Peat
20 Clarke Cres RR 1, Port Sydney, P0B 1L0
cliff@creative.on.ca

WALLACEBURG
Wallaceburg Gospel Hall (519-627-7637)
121 Gillard St, Wallaceburg, ON, N8A 1N1
Su B 10:00am, S 11:45am; We P/M 7:00pm
c/o: Charles Workman (519-627-8743)
1027 James St, Wallaceburg, ON, N8A 2P9
charlesworkman@bellnet.ca
alt: Robert Tulloch (519-627-5882)

WALLENSTEIN
Wallenstein Bible Chapel (519-669-2319)
4522 Herrgott Rd, Wallenstein, ON, N0B 2S0
www.wallensteinbiblechapel.org
Su B 9:30am, S 11:00am, M 7:00pm
note: P/M – call for information. Times & locations vary.
c/o: Paul Hoffman (519-699-5468)
PO Box 51, Wallenstein, ON, N0B 2S0
paulhoffman@alumni.uwaterloo.ca
alt: Ron Seabrooke (519-698-0068)

WATERLOO
Bethel Chapel (519-886-3110)
16 Laurel St, Waterloo, ON, N2J 2H2
Su B 9:30am, S 11:00am, M 7:00pm; We P/M 7:30pm
c/o: Dennis Purcell (519-622-3927)
24 Enfield Dr, Cambridge, ON, N1P 1A5
dypurcell@rogers.com

New Hope Community Church (519-746-8891)
265 Westvale Dr, Waterloo, ON, N2T 1Z2
newhope@newhope.on.ca
Su B 10:00am
note: meets in Westvale Elementary School
c/o: Steve Tulloch (519-746-8891)

WAUBAUSHENE

Waubaushene Gospel Hall (705-538-1063)
219 Pine St, Waubaushene, ON, L0K 2C0
Su B 9:30am, F/S 11:25am, G 6:30pm; Tu P 7:30pm
c/o: Ed Heels (705-534-3698)
PO Box 29, WAUBAUSHENE, ON, L0K 2C0
edheels@bigfoot.com

WELLAND

Welland Gospel Hall (905-732-2021)
405 Lyons Creek Rd, Welland, ON
Su B 9:45am, S/F 11:30am, G 7:00pm; We P 7:30pm
note: use point of contact as church's mailing address
c/o: Joseph Kucman (905-735-3283)
44 Vanier Dr, Welland, ON, L3B 1A2
jkucman@sympatico.ca

WEST GUILFORD

Gospel Chapel
West Guilford, ON
Su B 9:30am, S 11:00am, M 6:30pm; We P/M 7:30pm
c/o: Neil Moore (705-754-3775)
Box 68, West Guilford, ON, K0M 2S0

WESTON

Westmount Gospel Chapel (416-241-2120)
59 Kingdom St, Toronto, ON, M9P 1W4
Su B 9:30am, F/S 11:00am, M 6:30pm; Mo P 7:00pm; We P/M 8:00pm
c/o: Reinhart Wieland (416-767-7276)
34 Montye Ave, Toronto, ON, M65 2G9
reinhart.wieland@primus.ca
alt: Paul Lamont (416-245-4519)
wingsofthemorning@hotmail.com

WILLOWDALE

Don Valley Bible Chapel (416-491-6421)
25 Axsmith Cres, Toronto, ON, M2J 3K2
www.dvbc.com
info@dvbc.com
Su B 9:15am, F/S 11:00am
c/o: Paul Chow (905-479-6800)
45 Randall Avenue, Markham, ON, L3S 1H9
paulchow@sympatico.ca
alt: Dave Sparrow (416-332-9705)
david@dvbc.com

Lansing Gospel Hall (416-225-2442)
41 Elmhurst Ave, Toronto, ON, M2N 1R3
www.lansinggospelhall.com
Su B 9:45am, G 6:30pm; Tu P/M 7:45pm
c/o: Joseph Paul (905-731-0167)
7071 Bayview Ave Ste 306, Thornhill, ON, L3T 7Y8
joepaul@rogers.com

WINCHESTER

Bethany Chapel (613-774-3352)
557 Main St, Winchester, ON, K0C 2K0
Su B 10:00am, F/S 11:00am, M 6:30pm; Tu P 7:30pm
c/o: Malcolm Clark (613-821-2879)
alt: Stephen MacDonald (613-984-2722)

WINDSOR

Berean Bible Chapel (519-250-1766)
2280 Foster Ave, Windsor, ON, N8W 5C9
Su B 9:30am, S 11:00am, G 7:00pm; We M 7:30pm
note: at Walker Rd
c/o: Victor S Salmons (519-969-0805)
3070 Radisson Ave, Windsor, ON, N9E 1Y5

Windsor Gospel Hall (519-966-0365)
644 Partington Ave, Windsor, ON, N9B 2N7
Su B 10:00am, S/M 12:00pm, G 6:00pm; Tu P/M 7:30pm
note: use point of contact as church's mailing address
c/o: Raymond T Fairley (519-966-0365)
3575 Rockwell Ave, Windsor, ON, N9E 2B1
rfairley@sympatico.ca
Alt: Robert Wylie (519-969-6347)

Middle Eastern Bible Fellowship (Arabic) (519-945-9342)
3385 Forest Glade Dr, Windsor, ON, N8R 2E1
Mo P/M 7:30pm; Sa M 7:30pm
c/o: Philippe Yaacoub
6219 Thornberry, Windsor, ON, N8T 3A5

Oakwood Bible Chapel (519-969-5730)
2514 Cabana Rd W, Windsor, ON, N9G 1E5
Su B/S, G 6:00pm; Tu P/M
c/o: Bruce Cameron (519-969-1744)
3446 Charlevoix, Windsor, ON, N9E 3R1

Turner Road Chapel (252-7812)
2100 Turner Rd, Windsor, ON, N8W 3K3
Su B/S, L 10:00am, G/Y/B 7:00pm; We P/M; Th Y/G 6:30pm

WINGHAM

Wingham Bible Chapel (519-357-1511)
177 Boland St, Wingham, ON, N06 2W0
www.winghambiblechapel.ca
church@wightman.ca
Su B 9:30am, S 11:00am; We P/M 7:30pm
c/o: Harry Reid (519-528-2661)
RR 5, Lucknow, ON, N0G 2H0
braeburn@scsinternet.com

PRINCE EDWARD ISLAND

ST PETER'S

Upton Gospel Chapel
RR 3, Dundas, PE
Su S/G, B 10:00am; Th M
c/o: Henry B MacDougell (961-2936)
St Peters Bay, PE, C0A 2A0

CHARLOTTETOWN

Charlottetown Bible Chapel (902-894-5121)
35 Lincolnwood Dr, Charlottetown, PE, C1A 6H4
www.charlottetownbiblechapel.org
Su B 9:15am, S 11:00am, G 7:00pm; We P/M 7:30pm
c/o: Don Crozier (902-892-5047)
61 Cedar Ave, Charlottetown, PE, C1A 6K5
doncrozier@pei.aibn.com

Faith Bible Chapel
Charlottetown, PE
c/o: David Reid (902-894-5369 or 566-9730)
2 Crestwood Dr, Charlottetown, PE, C1A 3H3
david.b.reid@pei.sympatico.ca

Gospel Hall (902-892-0724)
143 Upper Prince St, Charlottetown, PE
Su B 10:00am, G 7:00pm; Tu P/M 7:30pm
c/o: Douglas G MacLeod (902-892-6805)
20 Ferndale Dr, Sherwood, PE, C1A 5J3

CRAPAUD

Gospel Hall (902-658-2343)
304 Old Post Rd, Crapaud, PE, C0A 1J0
Su B 10:00am, S 11:45am, G 7:00pm; We P 7:00pm
c/o: Grant L Thomas (902-437-2510)
21757 Trans-Canada Hwy, RR 2 North Tryon, Albany, PE, C0B 1A0
grant.thomas@pei.sympatico.ca

FREETOWN

Gospel Hall
Freetown, PE
Su B 10:00am, G 7:30pm; Th P 7:30pm
c/o: Ira Kember (902-436-4647)
Linkletter Rd RR 2, Summerside, PE, C1N 4J8

MONTAGUE

Montague Bible Fellowship (902-962-2270)
PO Box 507 Sackville St, Montague, PE
Su B/G, S 10:45am; Tu P/M 8:00pm
c/o: Ed Van Donkersgoed (902-838-4048)

CANADA — PRINCE EDWARD ISLAND

Emmanuel Bible Chapel
Montague, PE
Su B/S, M 7:00pm; Tu M
note: Queens Rd
c/o: Robert MacGregor (902-838-3403)
PO Box 674, RR 5, Montague, PE, C0A 1R0

ROSEBANK

Rosebank Gospel Hall
Rosebank, PE
Su B 10:00am, G 7:30pm; Fr P 8:00pm
c/o: James Thomas (902-859-1576)
PO Box 335, 451 Main St, O'Leary, PE, C0B 1V0

SPRINGFIELD

Springfield West Gospel Hall
Springfield, PE
Su B 10:30am, G 7:30pm; Tu P 8:00pm
c/o: Albert MacKenzie (902-859-2171)
Springfield West RR 1, O'Leary, PE, C0B 1V0

SUMMERSIDE

Bible Chapel (902-436-5534)
540 Granville St, Summerside, PE, C1N 4P6
Su B 9:30am, S 11:00am, G 7:00pm; We P/M 7:00pm; Fr C 6:30pm
note: PO Box 127
c/o: Spurgeon Robbins (902-436-7335)
770 Westchester St, Summerside, PE, C1N 4V6

Calvary Bible Church
Summerside, PE
c/o: Brian MacIsaac
RR 2 Stn Main, Summerside, PE, C1N 4J8
ulnooe@canada.com

QUEBEC

AYER'S CLIFF
Ayer's Cliff Gospel Chapel (819-838-4954)
873 Clough St, Ayer's Cliff, QC, J0B 1C0
alecvz@aei.ca
Su B 9:30am, F 11:00am; Tu P/M 7:30pm
c/o: Edwin Down (819-838-4959)
957 Sanborn St, Ayer's Cliff, QC, J0B 1C0
alt: Alec Van Zuiden (819-838-4812)
alecvz@aei.ca

BAIE COMEAU
Assemblee Chretienne Evangelique De Baie Comeau
(418-589-4936)
691 Jalbert, Baie Comeau, QC, G4Z 2G9
jn316.free.fr
marc.dallaire@bc.cgocable.ca
Su B/M 9:30am; We P 7:30pm
c/o: Louise Dugas
C.P. 131, Baie Comeau, QC, G4Z 2G9
alt: Michel Ferland (418-589-4936)
michferland@hotmail.com

BELOEIL
Groupe Biblique du Richelieu (450-467-9966)
www.lfv.qc.ca
fsl@videotron.ca
Tu P/B 7:30pm (B on 1st Tu of the month)
note: meetings in homes; use point of contact for mailing address
c/o: Fernand Saint-Louis (450-467-9966)
567 Iberville, Beloeil, QC, J3G 2N7
fsl@videotron.ca

CABANO
Assemblee Chretienne
Cabano, QC
c/o: J-M Michaud (418-854-3807)
CP 1229, Cabano, QC, C0L 1E0

CHIBOUGAMAU
Eglise Evangelique de Chibougamau
101 rue Jaculet, Chibougamau, QC, G8P 2K5
c/o: Robert Gagne (418-748-3963)
129 Obalski, Chibougamau, QC, G8P 2E8

CHICOUTIMI
L'Eglise Evangelique de Chicoutimi (418-549-4637)
265 Malraux, CP 1202, Chicoutimi, QC, G7H 5G7
Su B; Tu P/M 8:00pm
c/o: Jean-Marc Petit (418-673-7175)
691 Gravel, St-Honore, QC, G0V 1L0

COOKSHIRE
Assemblee Chretienne de Cookshire
125 rue Principale, Cookshire, QC
Su B/S; We P
c/o: Levi Gendron (819-875-5166)
723 Rte 210 RR 3, Cookshire, QC, J0B 1M0

DRUMMONDVILLE
Assemblee Chretienne
2020 Boul Mercure, Drummondville, QC
Su B/G, S 10:50am; We P
c/o: Normand Gosselin (819-472-4441)
1018 1ere Allee, St-Nicephore, QC, J2A 1N3

FARNHAM
Assemblee Chretienne de Farnham
1901 rue Principale Est, Farnham, QC, J2N 1N5
c/o: Alain Levesque (450-293-4650)
1901 rue Principale Est, Farnham, QC, J2N 1N5

GIRARDVILLE
Assemblee Chretienne de Girardville
1081 rang Notre Dame, Girardville, QC
c/o: Regis Neron (418-276-8468)
1081 rang Notre Dame, Girardville, QC, G0W 1R0

GRANBY
Assemblee Chretienne de Granby
324 ouest Denison Ave, Granby, QC
Su B/S/G; We P/M 8:00pm
c/o: Claude Vachon (450-378-6539)
155 Boul Fortin #4, Granby, QC, J2G 3Z8

GRAND-MÈRE
Assemblee Chretienne de Grand-Mère (819-538-9549)
1751 18th Ave, Grand-Mère, QC
Su B 9:30am, S 11:00am; Th P/M 7:30pm
c/o: Rene Corriveau (819-535-3240)
1160 Chemin Hèroux, St-Boniface, QC, G0X 2L0

HULL
Groupe Biblique de l'Outaouais
Hull, QC
c/o: Jack Harvie (613-445-3205)
C. P. 79187, Hull, QC, J8Y 6V2

JONQUIERE
Assemblee Chretienne de Jonquiere
(418-542-5092 or 418-695-0355)
1985 rue Price, CP 2244, Jonquiere, QC, G7X 7X7
Su B, S 10:45am, G 7:00pm; We P/M
c/o: Lucien Fortin (418-542-0752)
CP 2244, Jonquiere, QC, G7X 7X7

LA BAIE

Assemblee Chretienne de la Baie (418-544-5798)
1652 St-Marc, La Baie, QC
Su B 9:30am, S 11:00am, G 7:00pm, M 7:30pm
note: meets at Atelier Des Arts
c/o: Denis Simard
CP 52, La Baie, QC, G7B 3P9

LA TUQUE

Assemblee Chretienne de La Tuque
2902 Boul Ducharme, La Tuque, QC
c/o: Real Pilon (819-523-4692)
359 St-Augustin, La Tuque, QC, G9X 2Y1

Le Centre chretien evangelique LaTuque
540 rue Saint-Antoine, La Tuque, QC
c/o: Norman Gagne (819-523-6930)
380 rue Tessier, La Tuque, QC, G9X 3E5

LEBEL-SUR-QUEVILLON

Assemblee Chretienne de Quevillon
Lebel Sur Quevillon, QC
note: meetings in homes
c/o: Serge Labrie (819-755-4083)
57 des Melezes, CP 1232, Lebel-sur-Quevillon, Ungava, QC, J0Y 1X0

LONGUEUIL

Groupe Biblique de la Rive-Sud
530 Rue Saint-Jean, Longueuil, QC, J4H 2YH
Su B 10:00am; We P/M 8:00pm
c/o: Noel Aubut (524-671-9196)
1623 des Pins, Ville Lemoyne, QC, J4P 3K8

MONTMAGNY

Assemblee Chretienne de Montmagny (418-248-1867)
419 boul Tache est, Montmagny, QC, G5V 1E4
Su B 10:00am, M 10:45am
c/o: Rene Lavoie (418-248-1867)
291 rue St-Ignace, Montmagny, QC, G5V 1S4
renelav@globetrotter.net

MONTRÉAL

Assemblee Chretienne du Centre-Sud de Montréal
(450-722-3304 or 888-322-4253)
5205 rue St-Zotique EST (Salle Guillemette), Montréal, QC, H1T 1N6
Su B 9:30am, S 10:45am; We P/M
c/o: Yvon Audet (450-477-1264)
1092 Avenue de Normandie, Mascouche, QC, J7L 1Y8

Rosemount Bible Church (514-728-5911)
6000 13th Ave, Montréal, QC, H1X 2Y5
www.rbc.qc.ca
Su B 9:15am, F/S 10:45am; Fr Y 7:00pm
c/o: Dr D Dawson (514-341-5748)
230 Surrey Dr, Town of Mount Royal, QC, H3P 1B4
daveandpatdawson@videotron.ca

NEW CARLISLE
New Carlisle Bible Chapel
New Carlisle, QC
Su B/S, G 7:00pm
c/o: Jarvis S Flowers
40 Green St Box 25, New Carlisle, QC, G0C 1Z0

NEW RICHMOND
Bethel Bible Chapel (418-392-6798)
116 Veteran St Box 848, New Richmond, QC, G0C 2B0
Su B/S/G
c/o: D Dugas

PIERREFONDS
Westview Bible Church (514-626-5460)
16789 Pierrefonds Blvd, Montreal, QC, H9H 4T3
www.westviewbiblechurch.ca
office@westviewbiblechurch.ca
Su S/F 10:30am; Fr Y 7:00pm
c/o: Steve MacDonald

PINCOURT
Grace Gospel Hall
50 Rieme Ave, Pincourt, QC, J7V 5K7
Su B 9:30am, S/M 11:00am, G 7:00pm; We P 7:45pm
note: 50 Fifth (5e) Ave, Pincourt, QC, J7V 5K7
c/o: Stephen Johnston (514-630-1168)
Box 40533; 2963 St Charles Blvd, Kirkland, QC, H9H SG8
stephenj@canada.com
alt: Gilles Bouchard (514-453-1496)
gilles@clubimprimerie.com

POINTE CLAIRE
Bethel Chapel (514-697-2344)
105 Dieppe Ave, Montreal, QC, H9R 1X5
Su B/S; We P/M 8:00pm
c/o: Real Frenette
101 Montrose, Montreal, QC, H9R 2S6

QUEBEC
Assemblee Evangelique de Sainte-Foy (418-839-9780)
3033 de Dompierre, Sainte Foy, QC, G1X 3W4
Su B/S/G; We P/M
c/o: JP Gosselin
2750 ch Sainte-Foy, Quebec, QC, G1V 1V6
sobib@qc.aira.com

L'Assemblee Chretienne Bonne Nouvelle
215 rue Caron, Quebec, QC, G1K 5V6
Su B/M
c/o: Sylvain St-Jean (418-653-1791)
215 rue Caron, Quebec, QC, G1K 5V6

RIVIERE-DU-LOUP
Assemblee Chretienne De Riviere-Du-Loup (418-862-7283)
17 Rue Anseville, Riviere Du Loup, QC, G5R 4H8
Su B 10:00am, S/F 11:00am; We P/M 7:30pm
note: all meetings in French

ROLLET
Assemblee Chretienne
744 Principele, C.P. 154, Rollet, QC, J0Z 3J0
Su B 9:30am, S/F 11:00am
c/o: Gaston Jolin (819-493-6411)
1155, rue des Peupliers, Rollet, QC, J0Z 3J0
gastonjolin@hotmail.com

SAINT-HYACINTHE
Eglise Bethanie (514-774-6996)
3925 Bel-Air, Saint Hyacinthe, QC, J2S 7N8
Su B 10:00am, S 11:00am; We P/M 7:30pm
c/o: Nil Labrecque (450-375-7195)
3925 Bel-Air, St-Hyacinthe, QC, J2S 7N8

SAINT-LAURENT
Arabic Gospel Church (514-334-8000)
1720 Decarie, Saint Laurent, QC, H4L 3N3
silas@itcompass.com
Su B 6:00pm, S/G 7:00pm; Fr Y 5:00pm, M 7:00pm
c/o: Dr Silas Rahhal (514-335-1989)
313 Bleignier St, Saint-Laurent, QC, H4N 1B1
silas@itcompass.com
alt: Mr. Ayman Surial (450-969-9024)
asurial@yahoo.com

SAINTE-ANNE-DE-SOREL
Assemblee Chretienne de Sorel (450-746-0409)
294 de la Rive, Sainte Anne De Sorel, QC, J3P 1K4
assembleechretienne@bellnet.ca
Su B 9:30am, G 11:00am; Tu P 7:30pm
c/o: Jean-Pierre Cloutier (450-746-0084)
9 Des Sables, Sorel-Tracy, QC, J3P 5E7
assembleechretienne@bellnet.ca
alt: Rejean Allard (450-792-0100)
triboallard@videotron.ca

SAINTE-JEAN-CHRYSOSTOME
Assemblee Evangelique de la Rive Sud (418-839-0250)
1029 de la Prairie ouest, Sainte-Jean-Chrysostome, QC, G6Z 2Z4
ffrechette@sympatico.ca
Su B 9:30am, S/F 11:00am; We P/M 7:30pm
c/o: Francois Frechette, (418-839-3311)
909 Marronniers, Sainte-Jean-Chrysostome, QC, G6Z 2Y9
ffrechette@sympatico.ca

STINTE-JEAN, RICHELIEU
Assemblee Chretienne Evangelique
380 St-Michel, St Jean, Richelieu, QC
note: meets at St John's High School
c/o: Marcel Monette (450-346-3530)
CP 638, Saint-Jean sur Richelieu, QC, J3B 6Z8

SHAWINIGAN
Assemblee Chretienne de Shawinigan
1763 69 rue CP 73, Shawinigan, QC, G9N 6T8
Su B 9:30am, S 10:45am; We P/M 7:30pm
c/o: Gaetan Bellemare (819-539-5190)
1763-69c rue, Shawinigan, QC, G9N 6T8

SHERBROOKE
Assemblee Chretienne
715 rue Desormeaux, Sherbrooke, QC
Su B/G, S 10:00am; We P/M
c/o: Denis Grenier (849-823-2110)
890 Laviolette, Sherbrooke, QC, J1G 2V1

Assemblee Chretienne Source de Vie
267 rue de Montréal, Sherbrooke, QC
Su B 9:30am, S 10:30am; We P 7:30pm
c/o: J Houle (819-835-0016)
CP 93, Sherbrooke, QC, J1M 1Z3

Grace Chapel (819-569-3490)
267 Montreal St, Sherbrooke, QC, J1H 1E4
Su B 9:30am, S/G 11:00am, M 2:00pm
c/o: Douglas Beattie (819-889-2963)
1134 Rte 210, Sawyerville, QC, J0B 3A0
jwr@abacom.com
alt: Richard Strout (819-569-8012)

Huntingville Community Church (819-822-2627)
1399 Campbell St, Sherbrooke, QC, J1M 0C1
hcc@videotron.ca
Su B 9:00am, S 10:00am, F 11:00am; We P/Y 7:00pm
c/o: Kim Davis (819-434-2627)
1399 Campbell St, Sherbrooke, QC, J1M 0C1
hcc@videotron.ca

STANSTEAD

L'Assemblee Chretienne
9 Hackett St, Stanstead, QC, J0B 3E0
walterscott@sympatico.ca
Su B 9:30am, F 11:00am; Tu M 7:00pm
note: English
c/o: Walter Scott (819-838-4260)
1001 Round Bay Rd, Ayers Cliff, QC, J0B 1C0
walterscott@sympatico.ca

STE-ANNE-DES-MONTS

Assemblee Chretienne
447 Premiere ouest, Ste Anne Des Monts, QC, G0E 2G0
c/o: Rene Lepage (418-763-2054)

STE-MARIE-DE-BEAUCE

Assemblee Chretienne Evangelique
525 Route Saint-Elzear, Ste Marie De Beauce, QC
c/o: Lawrence Fortin (418-387-5970)
465 Ch St-Etienne Sud, Ste-Marie-De-Beauce, QC, G6E 3A7

TERREBONNE

L'Assemblee Chretienne Lamater (514-471-8888)
60 Boul Archambault, Terrebonne, QC, J6W 4R6
Su B, S 10:45am; We P
c/o: Gerald Kraemer (450-964-3242)
4490 d'Argyle, Terrebonne, QC, J6X 1K2

THETFORD MINES

Assemblee Chretienne (418-335-2876)
725 rue Simoneau, Thetford Mines, QC, G6G 1V3
Su B 9:30am, G 7:30pm; We M 7:30pm
c/o: Norman Bilodeau (418-335-6539)
1050 7e Ave, Thetford Mines, QC, G6G 2G7

TROIS-RIVIÈRES

Assemblee Chretienne
3310 Boul Saint-Jean, Trois-Rivières, QC
c/o: Michel Tremblay (819-377-1387)
831 ch des Petites-Terres, Trois-Rivières, QC G9B 7G5

Assemblee Chretienne de Cap-de-la-Madeleine
225 Lupien, Cap De La Madeleine, QC
Su B/S/G; We P/M 8:00pm
c/o: Michel Pedneault (819-375-9510)
67 Rue Guay, Trois-Rivières, QC, G9A 3B4

WESTMOUNT
Bethel Gospel Chapel (514-935-9793)
4250 de Maissoneuve, Westmount, QC, H3Z 1K6
www.bethelgospelchapel.net
Su B 10:00am, F 11:30am, G 6:00pm; Mo P 7:30pm; We M 7:30pm; Fr Y 7:00pm
c/o: Carl Worrell (450-671-2545)
8135 Santiago, Brossard, QC, J4X 1J5

West End Christian Fellowship (514-933-1956)
386 Lansdowne Ave, Montreal, QC, H3Z 2L4
Su B 10:00am, S 11:15am; We P/M
c/o: Eric Rumsby
erumsby@videotron.ca

SASKATCHEWAN

ARBORFIELD
Gospel Hall
Box 426, Arborfield, SK, S0E 0A0
Su B 10:30am, G 7:30pm, S 12:45pm; We P/M 7:30pm
c/o: Wallace Miller (306-769-8628)
Box 422, Arborfield, SK, S0E 0A0

GLEN EWEN
Glen Ewen Gospel Hall (306-925-4805)
Box 128, Glen Ewen, SK, S0C 1C0
Su B 10:00am, F/S 1:00pm, G 7:30pm; We P/M 7:45pm
c/o: Sidney Griffin (306-925-2248)
Box 308, Carnduff, SK, S0C 0S0
sgriffin@sasktel.net

MAIDSTONE
Gospel Hall
Maidstone, SK
Su B 10:00am, S 11:30am; Tu P/M 7:30pm
note: 4th Ave & Main St
c/o: Harry K McLaren (306-893-4614)
Box 481, Maidstone, SK, S0M 1M0

MERVIN
Mervin Gospel Hall
133 Railway St S, Mervin, SK
Su B 10:30am, S 12:00pm; We P 8:00pm
c/o: Lennard D Heath (306-845-2627)
Box 274, Turtleford, SK, S0M 2Y0

MOOSE JAW

Stadacona Gospel Chapel (306-692-1700)
68 Stadacona St W, Moose Jaw, SK, S6H 1Z1
Su B 9:30am, S/F 11:15am; Th L 10:00am, L 2:00pm; Th M 7:00pm
c/o: John McCubbing (306-692-9372)
101 - 55 Wood Lily Dr, Moose Jaw, SK, S6J 1H1
j.mccubbing@sasktel.net

REGINA

Bethany Gospel Chapel (306-522-6441, 543-73)
1850 Parker Ave, Regina, SK, S4S 4S2
llott@cableregina.com
Su B 9:30am, S 11:00am, P/M 6:00pm
c/o: Edwin H Seed (305-545-4276)
1208 Horace St, Regina, SK, S4T 5L4
eseed@accesscomm.ca

SASKATOON

Fairhaven Bible Chapel (306-384-1919)
3503 Fairlight Dr, Saskatoon, SK, S7M 4L6
cmhumphries@hotmail.com
Su B 9:45am, F/S 11:15am; Tu C 7:00pm; Th P 7:30pm (homes)
c/o: Charles Humphries (306-373-1756)
107 Middleton Cres, Saskatoon, SK, S7J 2W5
cmhumphries@hotmail.com

Lawson Heights Gospel Hall (306-249-5044)
131 LaRonge Rd, Saskatoon, SK, S7K 5T3
Su B 9:30am, S 11:15am, G 7:00pm; We P 7:30pm
c/o: Murray Buckingham (306-477-9117)
518 Denham Way, Saskatoon, SK, S7R 1E7
buckinghamms@sasktel.net
alt: Chad Coziahr (306-382-7346)
chadcoziahr@sasktel.net

TAYLORSIDE

Gospel Hall (306-752-3810)
Taylorside, SK
Su B 10:30am, G 7:30pm, S 12:30pm; Tu P/M 7:30pm
note: 3 mi S & 4 mi W of Beatty
c/o: John C Parker (306-752-4079)
Box 2666, Melfort, SK, S0E 1A0

OTHER COUNTRIES

ANGUILLA

ANGUILLA
Bethany Gospel Hall
Stony Ground Rd
c/o: William Ashby

ANTIGUA AND BARBUDA

ALL SAINTS
Ebenezer Gospel Hall
Su G, B 11:00am, S 2:00pm; Tu M 8:00pm; Th M 8:00pm
c/o: Edward Theodore (809-461-1937)
Wireless Rd, St John's

ST JOHN'S
Bethel Gospel Hall
St Johnston's Village
Su G, B 11:00am, S 4:30pm; Tu M 8:00pm; Th M 8:00pm
c/o: Dalmar Edwards (809-461-1445)
PO Box 372, Wireless Rd

Shiloh Gospel Hall
Nevis St
Su B, S 4:30pm, G/M 7:00pm
c/o: Laurent A Gilkes (809-461-0779)
PO Box 1827, Flagg Staff

BAHAMAS

ABACO
Bethany Gospel Chapel
PO Box AB-20456, Marsh Harbour, Abaco
Su G, S 9:45am, B 12:15pm; Th M
c/o: Livingston Williams

International Gospel Mission (242-367-3784)
PO Box AB-20074, Marsh Harbour
c/o: Robinson E. Weatherford (242-367-3784)

Man-O-War Cay Gospel Chapel
General Delivery, Man O War Cay, Abaco
Su B 10:00am, S 11:15am, G 6:30pm; Th M

Marsh Harbour Gospel Chapel (242-367-2204)
PO Box AB-20426, Marsh Harbour, Abaco
Su S, B 12:15am, G 7:00pm; We M
c/o: David Cartwright (242-367-2204)

New Life Bible Church
General Delivery, Man O War Cay, Abaco
Su G, S 9:45am, B 7:00pm; We M
c/o: Scott Weatherford

New Plymouth Gospel Chapel
General Delivery, Green Turtle Cay, Abaco
Su B 10:00am, M 11:30am, G 7:00pm; Tu M
c/o: Floyd Lowe

Seaside Gospel Chapel (242-365-5007)
General Delivery, Great Guana Cay, Abaco
Su M, S 10:00am, G 7:00pm, B 12:00pm
c/o: Sylvon Bethel

Strong Tower Community Church (242-367-5089)
PO Box 20958, Murphy Town, Abaco
c/o: Stephen Knowles

NORTH ANDROS

Nicholls Town Gospel Chapel
General Delivery, Nicholls Town, North Andros
c/o: Fred Russell Jr

Renewal Bible Church
General Delivery, Nicholls Town, North Andros

CAT ISLAND

Old Bight Gospel Chapel (242-342-4103)
Old Bight Mission Home, Old Bight, Cat Island

ELEUTHERA

Bible Gospel Chapel (242-332-2172)
PO Box EL-11, Governor's Harbour, Eleuthera
c/o: Francis Carey or Cyril Griffin

Current Gospel Chapel
General Delivery, The Current, Eleuthera
c/o: Derek Eldon

Ebenezer Gospel Chapel
PO Box EL-25058, Tarpum Bay, Eleuthera
c/o: David Morley

Palmetto Point Gospel Chapel (242-332-1093)
PO Box EL-25094, Palmetto Point, Eleuthera
c/o: Grarth Thompson

Spanish Wells Gospel Chapel
PO Box EL-28407, St. Georges Cay, Spanish Wells, Eleuthera
c/o: Roddie Pinder

GRAND BAHAMA

Elim Gospel Assembly (242-352-8670)
PO Box F-42477, Freeport, Grand Bahama
c/o: Theophilus Major (242-352-8670)

Freeport Gospel Chapel (242-373-5600 or 242-373-2655)
PO Box F-40226, Freeport, Grand Bahama
c/o: Hartley Thompson

LONG ISLAND

Burnt Ground Gospel Chapel (242-338-7010)
General Delivery, Burnt Ground, Long Island
c/o: Alphonso Shearer

Cartwright's Gospel Chapel (242-337-0029)
General Delivery, Deadman's Cay, Long Island
c/o: Everett Cartwright (242-337-0029)

Seymour's Gospel Chapel
PO Box 163, Seymour's, Long Island
c/o: Reuben Gibson

Simm's Gospel Chapel
General Delivery, Simm's, Long Island
c/o: Norman Carroll or Locksley Knowles

NASSAU, NEW PROVIDENCE

Abundant Life Bible Church (242-393-8134)
PO Box SS-6579, Abundant Life Rd, Nassau, New Providence
www.albcm.org
info@albcm.org
Su G, S 9:45am, B 6:00pm, G 7:00pm; We M 8:00pm
c/o: Ed Allen

Believers Gospel Chapel (242-324-3500)
Prince Charles Dr and Trinidad Ave
PO Box EE-17383, Nassau, New Providence
believersfamily@hotmail.com
c/o: Barton Duncanson or Roderick Rolle

Blue Hill Gospel Chapel (242-341-4598)
PO Box CR-54226, Baillou Hill Rd, Nassau, New Providence
Su B 11:00am, S 5:00pm, G 7:00pm; Th M
c/o: Perry Wallace

Central Gospel Chapel (242-325-2921)
PO Box N-4059, Dowdeswell and Christie St, Nassau, New Providence
Su B, S 9:45am, G 7:00pm; We M 8:00pm

Christ Community Church (242-361-8782 or 242-361-2848)
PO Box CR-56504, Bellot Rd off Faith Ave, Nassau, New Providence
cccbahamas@coralwave.com
c/o: Deanza Cunningham

East Street Gospel Chapel (242-322-3874)
#83 East St N, Nassau, N-8632
esgchapel@gmail.com
Su S 9:45am, G 11:00am, B 6:00pm; We P 7:00pm, Y 6:30pm
c/o: Thomas Roberts (242-322-3874)
#83 East St N, Nassau, N-8632
troberts@coralwave.com
alt: Al McCartney

Emmanuel Gospel Chapel (242-361-2072)
PO Box GT-2525, Emmanuel Dr, Malcolm's Allotment, Nassau, New Providence
emmanuelgc@batelnet.bs
Su B, S 10:00am, G 7:00pm; We M 8:00pm
c/o: Joshua Sands Sr.

Englerston Gospel Chapel (242-325-2364)
PO Box EE-15285, Cordeaux Ave West, Nassau, New Providence
c/o: Ricardo E. Turner

Grace Community Church (242-393-7223 or 242-393-8120)
19 Grace Ave, Palmetto Village
PO Box SS-5267, Nassau, New Providence
www.gracebahamas.com
info@gracebahamas.com
Su S 9:30am, G 11:00am, B 6:00pm; We M
c/o: Lyal Bethel

Lifeline Ministries
PO Box SB52403, Nassau, New Providence
c/o: Joshua Sands Jr

Shirley Heights Gospel Chapel (242-325-8001 or 242-325-8698)
PO Box N-3484, Mt. Royal Ave, Nassau, New Providence
Su B 9:30am, S 11:00am, M 6:00pm; We M 7:30pm

NORTH ANDROS
Renewal Bible Chapel
General Delivery, Nicholls Town, North Andros

BARBADOS

BRIDGETOWN
Ebenezer Gospel Hall
Crumpton St
Su B 11:00am, G 7:00pm; Th M 7:00pm
c/o: Munroe Franklin (432-0811)
Clarkes Rd #1, Derricks, , St James

CHRIST CHURCH
Dayrells Road Assembly
Dayrells Road
Su B 11:00am, G 7:00pm; We M 7:15pm
c/o: Alfred Aince (420-3757 or 426-4650)
Kendal Hill B

Stream Road Gospel Hall
St Lawrence
Su G, B 11:00am; Tu M 7:15pm
c/o: Reginald G Boxill (428-4349)
Lodge Rd

ST ANDREW
Belleplaine Gospel Hall
Belleplaine

ST GEORGE
Ellerton Gospel Hall
Ellerton

ST JAMES
Glad Tidings Gospel Hall
Fitts Village, St James
c/o: Sidney Benskin
Fitts Village, St James

ST JOHN
Cherry Grove Gospel Hall
Cherry Grove, St John
Su S 8:30am, G 9:30am, B 6:00pm; Tu M 7:30pm
c/o: Lionel Weekes (246-433-2312)
Henleys Land, St John
joyfulministry@sunbeach.net

ST JOSEPH
Airy Hill Gospel Hall
Airy Hill, St Joseph
Su B 11:00am, S 4:00pm, G 7:00pm; Mo P 7:30pm; We M 7:30pm
c/o: Cecil Gill (246-433-8239)
Braggs Hill, St Joseph

Melvins Hill Gospel Hall
Melvins Hill

ST JOSEPH BATHSHEBA
St Elizabeth's Gospel Hall
St Elizabeth Village, St Joseph Bathsheba
Su B 11:00am, S 3:00pm, G 7:00pm

ST MICHAEL
Fairfield Gospel Hall
Carrington Village near Tweedside Rd, St Michael
c/o: Franklin O Browne (424-2681)
Rock Dundo Hts, , St Michael

OTHER COUNTRIES — BARBADOS

ST PETER
 Grace Gospel Hall
  Speights Town
  c/o: Edmund Rowe
  Round-the-Town

ST PHILIP
 Kirtons Gospel Hall
  Kirtons

BERMUDA

COBB'S HILL
 Cobb's Hill Gospel Chapel (441-236-9413)
  70 Cobb's Hill Road, Warwick, WK BX
  Su B 9:00am, S 10:00am, M 11:15am; We P 8:00pm; Fr Y 8:00pm
  c/o: Edward Richardson (441-236-6070)
  14 White Sands Rd, Paget, PG 06
  ejrich@ibl.bm

CRAWL
 Hamilton Parish Gospel Hall (441-293-0035)
  167 North Shore Rd, Hamilton Parish, CR01
  Su S 9:30am, M 11:00am, B 6:00pm; We M 7:30pm (Oct-Apr),
  M 8:00pm (Apr-Oct)
  c/o: Dean Furbert
  18 Claytown, Baileys Bay, , Hamilton Parish, CR03
  dfurbert@ibl.bm

DEVONSHIRE
 North Shore Gospel Chapel
  Glebe Rd
  Su S/B/G
  c/o: Chesterfield Morris (809-292-3842)
  Glebe Rd, Devonshire W

HAMILTON
 Shiloh Gospel Chapel
  Church St
  Su S/M/G, B 12:00pm
  c/o: William Francis
  17 Cottage Hill Rd W, Whistling Winds, 3

HARRINGTON SOUND
 Gospel Hall
  Harrington Sound Rd, Smith's Parish
  Su M, S 9:45am, B 12:00pm
  c/o: Franklin Zuill

PAGET WEST
Paget Gospel Chapel
Middle Rd
Su B 9:15am, S 11:00am, G 7:00pm; We M 8:00pm
c/o: John Ward (236-9453)
25 Bostock Hill W, Box 123, Ebenezer, PG02

SOMERSET
Mangrove Bay Gospel Hall
Sound View Rd, Mangrove Bay
c/o: Dr Bertram Ross
4-0910

White Hill Gospel Chapel (441-234-0496)
1 Georges Bay Rd, Sandys, SB-02
Su B 9:00am, S 10:00am, M 11:15am, G 7:00pm; We M 8:00pm
c/o: Norbert Seymour (441-234-0073)
Pitchfork Lane, Sandys, MA05

SOUTHAMPTON
Calvary Gospel Chapel
18 Middle Rd
calvarygospel@ibl.bm
Su S 9:30am, G 11:00am, B 6:00pm, M 7:00pm
c/o: D Troy Hassell (441-234-3250)
PO Box SN150, SNBX

ST GEORGE'S
Gospel Chapel (809-297-1635)
#30 Mullet Bay Road, GE02
Su B/S/G; Tu M 8:00pm
c/o: MacDonald Tucker (809-297-1350)
#10 Broken Hill Lane, Smith's Parish, H.S. 02

DOMINICA

COCHRANE
Cochrane Gospel Hall
c/o: Francis Oscar

COULIBISTRIE
Gospel Hall
c/o: Louis Wintel (phone 66483)

LAUDAT
Laudat Gospel Hall
c/o: Merill Matthew (phone 84974)

PETITE SAVANNE
Petite Savanne Gospel Hall
c/o: Bernard Darroux (phone 63570)

ROSEAU
Roseau Gospel Hall
17 Victoria St
Su G, B 10:00am; Tu M; Th M
c/o: Clifford Nicholas (phone 91126)
17th Street, Canefield

SALISBURY
Gospel Hall
c/o: Cedrick Gardier (phone 96384)

GRENADA

CARRIACOU
Grand Bay Gospel Hall (473-443-7911)
Grand Bay Carriacou
Su B 10:00am, S 11:15am, G 7:00pm; We M/F 7:00pm
c/o: Leborn John
c/o Harbour Light, Mt Pleasant, , Carriacou

ST ANDREW'S
Crochu Gospel Hall
Su B 9:00am, S 3:00pm, G 7:00pm; We M 7:15pm
c/o: Goel Peters (440-1779)
Modern Photo Studio, , St George's

La Digue Gospel Hall
Su B 9:00am, S 3:00pm, G 7:00pm; We M 7:00pm
c/o: Philip James (809-442-6357)
La Digue PO
alt: Finbar Hopkins (809-442-8013)

ST DAVID'S
Corinth Gospel Hall
Corinth
Su B 9:00am, S 11:00am, G 7:00pm; Tu M 7:00pm; Th M 7:00pm
c/o: Ralph Neckles (809-444-6231 or 440-5857)
Perdmontemps PO

Laura Gospel Hall (809-443-2933)
N Thomas, Perdmontemps PO
Su B 10:00am, S 3:00pm, G 7:00pm; Tu M

ST GEORGE'S
Calivigny Gospel Hall (443-5316)
E Gladston Rouse, Woburn PO
Su B 11:00am, S 4:00pm, G 7:00pm; We M

Tyrell Street Gospel Hall
Tyrell St
Su B 10:00am, S 3:00pm, G 7:00pm; We M
c/o: James Peters (809-440-2692)

JAMAICA

CLARENDON
Shiloh Gospel Hall
3 Gordon St, May Pen
Su B 10:00am, S 4:00pm, G 7:15pm; Mo M 7:15pm; Th M 7:15pm

HANOVER
Canaan Gospel Hall
Johnson Town, Lucea PO
Su G, B 10:00am, S 4:00pm; We M

KINGSTON
Assembly Hall
188 Orange St
Su S 9:00am, B 10:30am, G 7:15pm; We M 7:00pm
c/o: Leo Smith

Bethany Gospel Hall
9A Hagley Park Rd, Box 239, Kingston 10
Su G, B 9:00am, S 4:00pm; Mo M; We M
c/o: L.E.A. Chambers (809-926-5041 or 924-7250)

Elim Assembly (876-925-2838)
7 1/2 Shortwood Rd, Kingston 8
Su B 8:30am, S 9:40am, G 11:00am; We M 7:30pm
c/o: George Markland (876-925-2610)
20 Tunbridge Dr, Kingston 19

Galilee Gospel Hall
2A Dunoon Rd, Kingston 2
Su S 8:45am, B 10:30am, G 7:15pm; We M
c/o: George Webster

Gospel Hall
cnr Granby & James Sts

Maranatha Gospel Hall
7 Deanery Rd, Kingston 3
Su G, B 9:00am, S 3:30pm; Mo M; We M
c/o: A Madden

Olivet Gospel Hall
43B Waltham Park Rd, Kingston 11
Su B 9:00am, S 3:30pm, G 7:15pm; We M 7:15pm; Th M 7:15pm
c/o: Victor McGibbon

Swallowfield Chapel (936-7163)
5 Swallowfield Rd, Kingston 5
Su S 9:00am, M 10:30am, B 5:30pm; Th M
c/o: Cecil Ho

MANCHESTER

Christiana Gospel Chapel
Main St Christiana
Su B 9:00am, S 10:00am, M 11:00am, G 7:00pm; Tu M 7:00pm; We M 7:00pm

PORTLAND

Bethesda Gospel Hall
1 Smatt Rd, Port Antonio
Su B 9:00am, S 4:00pm, G 7:00pm; Th M 7:00pm
c/o: A Burton

Gideon Gospel Chapel
PO Box 15, Buff Bay, Kildare
Su G, B 9:00am, S 3:30pm; Th M
c/o: Noel Aiken

ST ANN

Bethlehem Gospel Hall
10 King St, St Ann's Bay
Su S 9:00am, B 10:30am, G 7:00pm; We M 7:00pm
c/o: Gerald McKenzie

ST ANN (ST ANN'S BAY)

Ocho Rios Gospel Chapel
61 Main St
Su S/G, B 1:00pm; We M
c/o: Joseph Prendegast

ST CATHERINE

Byndloss Gospel Hall
Linstead
c/o: Harold Thomas

Linstead Gospel Hall (876-985-9894)
22 Hopeview Ave, Linstead
Su B 9:00am, M 10:30am, B 12:00pm; Th M 7:00pm
c/o: Earl Clunis (876-985-9640)

Treadways Gospel Hall
Treadways
Su B 11:00am, G 7:00pm, S 12:30pm; We M 7:00pm
c/o: Will Edwards (876-985-2216)
Box 10, Linstead

ST ELIZABETH

Emmaus Gospel Chapel
Balaclava
Su M, S 9:00am, B 6:00pm; Th M

Grace Gospel Chapel
School St, Black River
Su S 9:00am, B 10:00am, S 4:00pm, G 7:00pm; We M
c/o: Valney Little

ST MARY

Annotto Bay Gospel Hall
Annotto Bay
Su S, B 9:00am, G 7:15pm; We M 7:15pm

Central Gospel Hall
Clonmel
Su B, S 9:15am, G 7:15pm; We M 7:15pm

Guys Hill Gospel Chapel
Guys Hill
Su B, S 11:15am, G 7:15pm; We M 7:15pm
c/o: Hezekiah Martin

Highgate Gospel Hall
Box 37 Highgate PO, Highgate
Su S/B/G; Tu M
c/o: Lloyd Purser

The Gospel Chapel
Stennet St, Port Maria
Su B/G, S 9:00am

TRELAWNEY

Bethel Gospel Hall
Jackson Town PO, Jackson Town
Su G, B 11:30am, S 4:30pm, M 12:30pm
c/o: Gerald Bailey

MEXICO

For information about assemblies in Mexico, contact:

Organization:
   Hermanos Congregados en el Nombre del Señor Jesús A.R.

Contact Name:
   Manuel Ochoa Sotelo

Address:
   José Morán # 245
   Col. Daniel Garza
   Del. Miguel Hidalgo
   México, D.F. C.P. 11830

Phone: (55) 55 16 29 34   Fax: (55) 55 16 29 34

Email: hermanoscongregados@prodigy.net.mx

PUERTO RICO

MAYAGÜEZ
Templo del Evangelio (787-280-5102)
181 Santiago R. Palmer Esq. Oriente, Mayagüez, PR, 00680
Su B 9:15am; Tu P 7:30pm; Fr M 8:00pm
note: sixty years of serving the Lord in Mayagüez.
Mailing address: P.O. Box 396, Isabela, PR, 00662-0396
c/o: Guillermo Adrian (787-280-5102)
P.O. Box 396, Isabela, PR, 00662-0396

SANTURCE
Local Evangelico
Monte Flores Ave Eduardo, Conde 2088, Santurce (met. San Juan)
Su G, B 9:00am, S 10:30am

SAINT KITTS AND NEVIS

BROWN HILL
Brown Hill Chapel (469-3608)

CHARLESTOWN
Emmaus Chapel (469-5386)
Main St
Su G, B 10:30am, S 2:00pm

GINGERLAND
Zion Chapel (469-2015)

SAINT LUCIA

CASTRIES
Gospel Hall
33 Victoria St
Su B 9:00am, S 10:30am, G 7:00pm; Th M

SOUFRIERE
Gospel Hall
Bay St
Su B/S/G; Th M

SAINT VINCENT AND THE GRENADINES

BEQUIA ISLAND
Lower Derrick Gospel Hall

GEORGETOWN
Rehoboeth Gospel Hall
Su B 11:00am, S 2:00pm, G 7:00pm

UNION ISLAND
Ashton Gospel Hall
Su S 9:00am, B 10:00am, G 7:15pm
c/o: Leroy Thomas

TRINIDAD AND TOBAGO

AVOCAT
Avocat Gospel Hall
Harris Village, Avocat, South Oropouche, Trinidad
c/o: David Francis (868-677-5381)
Harris Village, Avocat, South Oropouche, Trinidad

BELLE VUE
Olivet Gospel Hall
11 Belle Vue Terr via Long Circular Rd, Belle Vue, St James, Trinidad
c/o: Alva Corbin (868-622-7169)
11 Belle Vue Terr, Belle Vue, St James, Trinidad

CANAAN
Bethesda Gospel Hall
Bon Accord, Canaan, Tobago, Tobago

CARNBEE
Carnbee Gospel Hall
133 Carnbee Main Rd, Carnbee, Tobago, Tobago
c/o: Anthony Roberts (868-639-8065)
21 Clarke Trace, Mt Pleasant, Tobago, Tobago

CHARLOTTEVILLE
Gospel Hall
Spring St
Su G, B 10:30am
c/o: Cartwright Carrington (639-4408)
N Baird, Bel Air

CHASE VILLAGE
Orangefield Gospel Hall
Orangefield Rd, Chase Village, Carapichaima, Trinidad
c/o: John Campbell (868-636-1902)
West Boundary St, California, Couva, Trinidad

CUMANA
Anglais Gospel Hall
1/2 MM Anglais Rd, Cumana, Toco, Trinidad
c/o: Edmond Thom (868-670-0649)
Anglais Rd, Cumana, Toco, Trinidad

GONZALES
Bethany Gospel Hall
Parrylands Rd, Gonzales, Guapo, Trinidad
c/o: John Frederick (868-648-9294)
Bassa Hall, La Brea, Trinidad

JERNINGHAM JUNCTION
Jerningham Junction Gospel Hall
Foster Rd, Jerningham Junction, Cunupia, Trinidad
c/o: Hugh Aberdeen (868-663-3692)
Foster Rd, Jerningham Junction, Cunupia, Trinidad

LA HORQUETTA
Christian Brethren Ministries
Cor. Plumbago Ave & Paradise Ln, La Horquetta, Arima, Trinidad
c/o: Clayton Thomas (868-623-4609 or 662-9189)
6 Church St, Success Village, Laventille, Trinidad

LE COTEAUX
Hill Top Gospel Hall
Arnos Vale Rd, Le Coteaux, Tobago
c/o: Alford Paul (868-660-0338)
Le Coteaux, Tobago, Tobago

LODGE PLACE
Bethesda Gospel Hall
5 Lodge Place, Port Of Spain
Su B, S 3:00pm, G 7:00pm; Tu M 7:00pm
c/o: Bernard W Stephen (624-3583)
56 Norfolk St, Belmont Trinidad North

MAHAICA
Mahaica Gospel Hall
61 Canaan Rd, Mahaica, Point Fortin, Trinidad
c/o: Paul Millet (868-648-0217)
20 Beach Rd, Cap De Ville, Point Fortin, Trinidad

MAJUBA
La Brea Gospel Hall
Gospel Hall Rd, Majuba, La Brea, Trinidad
c/o: Lloyd George (868-648-7212)
234 Point D'or St, La Brea, Trinidad

MON REPOS
Emmanuel Gospel Hall
24 Kelshall St, Mon Repos, San Fernando, Trinidad
c/o: Desmond Brown (868-657-8567)
2 David Pitt St, Les Efforts East, San Fernando, Trinidad

MORNE DIABLE
Divine Glory Christian Brethren Assembly
191 Quarry Rd, Morne Diable, Via Penal, Trinidad
c/o: Lawrence Haggard (868-647-2827)
21 Grant Trace, Morne Diable, Via Penal, Trinidad

SCARBOROUGH
Glen Road Gospel Hall
Glen Rd, Scarborough, Tobago
c/o: Augustus Awah (868-639-2517)
PO Box 284, Scarborough, Tobago, Tobago

SPEYSIDE
Speyside Gospel Hall
53 Top Hill St, Speyside, Tobago
c/o: David Roberts (868-660-4654)
7A Top Hill St, Speyside, Tobago, Tobago

ST CATHERINE
Hampton Green Gospel Hall
Spanish Town St, Catherine
Su G, B 9:00am, S 10:30am; We M
c/o: Allan Smith
PO Box 118

SUCCESS VILLAGE
Maranatha Gospel Hall
6 Church St, Success Village, Laventille, Trinidad
c/o: Lennie George (444-8133)
Gouyave PO

TUNAPUNA
Assembly Hall
64 Tunapuna Rd, Tunapuna, Trinidad
c/o: Evans Holder (868-662-7248)
2 Brathwaite Trace via St. Vincent St, Tunapuna, , Trinidad

WHITELAND
Whiteland Gospel Hall
113 Mayo Rd, Whiteland, Williamsville, Trinidad
c/o: Ramnath Gunness (868-656-1267)
13 Alley St, Whiteland, Williamsville Post Office, Trinidad

WOODBROOK
Ebenezer Gospel Hall
98 Roberts St, Woodbrook, Port of Spain, Trinidad
c/o: Neville Baird (868-638-1880)
184 Eastern Main Rd, Petit Bourg, San Juan, Trinidad

VIRGIN ISLANDS

ST CROIX

Emmanuel Gospel Chapel
56 Eliza Retreat, Christiansted
Su G, B 10:00am, S 11:15am; We M
c/o: Crecy Scotland (340-778-6515)
PO Box 3434, Christiansted, 00820

ST THOMAS

Grace Gospel Chapel
Su G, B 9:00am, S 11:30am; Th M
c/o: Adolphus Mills (809-775-1726)
Box 7094, 00801

2010

COMMENDED WORKERS DIRECTORY

COMMENDED WORKERS DIRECTORY
TABLE OF CONTENTS

United States

Alabama	227
Alaska	227
Arizona	228
Arkansas	229
California	229
Colorado	234
Connecticut	237
District of Columbia	238
Florida	238
Georgia	243
Hawaii	245
Idaho	246
Illinois	246
Indiana	252
Iowa	252
Kansas	257
Kentucky	258
Louisiana	259
Maine	259
Maryland	260
Massachusetts	261
Michigan	261
Minnesota	266
Missouri	266
Montana	269
New Hampshire	270
New Jersey	270
New Mexico	272
New York	272
North Carolina	274
Oregon	278
Pennsylvania	279
Rhode Island	283
South Carolina	284
South Dakota	286
Tennessee	286
Texas	287
Virginia	291
Washington	292
West Virginia	294
Wisconsin	294

Canada

British Columbia	296
Ontario	297
Quebec	298

Workers Index 299

Update Form 315

COMMENDED WORKERS DIRECTORY
PREFACE

In 2009 Assembly Care Ministries took over responsibility for maintaining a list of Christians commended to the Lord's work by New Testament assemblies across North America. As this is our first year working with the directory, our focus has been on familiarizing ourselves with the overall task, updating its contents and putting the directory into an online version. This is a work in progress, and we are already looking toward changes for the next directory including the addition of commended workers from Canada.

We Need to Hear From You: Please contact Assembly Care (ACM) with suggestions, comments, and corrections. If we can do something to make the directory more useful please inform us by phone (850-391-2411), email (info@assemblycare.org), or on the web (www.assemblycare.org).

To update Commended Worker information in this book, use the "Update Form" provided on page 315. You may also submit your updates online at www.assemblycare.org.

The purpose of this directory is to provide assemblies with up to date contact information for Christian workers commended to the Lord (Acts 13:1-4) by North American assemblies.

COMMENDED WORKERS DIRECTORY

ALABAMA

Orrett and Marva Bailey
1200 Kirby Terrace, Anniston, AL 36207
Cell: 256-454-2151   **Fax:** 256-237-1960
Email: orrettb@hotmail.com
Commendation: Anniston Bible Chapel, AL, 2006
Ministry: Leadership Development, Pastoral Care

Hellen Sheridan
913 Mountain Branch Drive, Vestauia Hills, AL 35226
Phone: 205-979-6186
Commendation: Kalmia Hill Chapel, SC, 1965
Ministry: Visitation, Women's Ministry Senior Worker (65+)
Other Info: Senior Worker (65+)

John and Barbara Tillery
104 Guilford Ln, Prattville, AL 36066
Phone: 719-640-7428   **Cell:** 719-640-7430
Email: Tillery04@msn.com
Commendation: Centralia Bible Chapel, WA, 2004
Ministry: Military Chaplain

ALASKA

Spencer and Carol Steenmeyer
3213 Woodland Park Dr, Anchorage, AK 99517-2110
Phone: 907-248-1022   **Cell:** 907-240-8248
Fax: 907-522-9079
Email: abfadmin@mac.com
Commendation: Anchorage Bible Fellowship, AK, 1982
Ministry: Pastoral Care, Teaching

Thomas and Marjorie Thompson
2800 Pribilof St, Anchorage, AK 99517-1425
Phone: 907-248-8807
Commendation: Dimond Blvd Gospel Hall, AK, 1960; Maranatha Gospel Hall, Ireland, 1954
Ministry: Evangelism, Preaching
Other Info: Senior Worker (65+)

ARIZONA

John and Ruth Bloom
Immanuel Mission PO Box 2000, Teec Nos Pos, AZ 86514-2000
Phone: 917-254-4023
Email: bloomjr@gmail.com
Commendation: Hutchinson Bible Hall, KS, 1975
Ministry: Ministry Administration, Teaching—School

Anne Denny
Immanuel Mission PO Box 2000, Teec Nos Pos, AZ 86514-2000
Phone: 928-674-3616
Email: dennyanne@gmail.com
Commendation: Westside Bible Chapel, KS, 1990
Ministry: Teaching—School, Women's Ministry

Georgia Hunter
37880 S. Escocia Lane, Tucson, AZ 85739
Phone: 520-825-3282
Email: georgia_hunter@sil.org
Commendation: Hope Bible Fellowship, WA, 1968
Ministry: Women's Ministry, Writing and Publishing
Other Info: Senior Worker (65+)

Rebecca Knopf
Immanuel Mission PO Box 2000, Teec Nos Pos, AZ 86514-2000
Email: knopfbecky@hotmail.com
Commendation: Dearborn Chapel, MI, 1989
Ministry: Discipleship, Teaching—School

John and Stacey Lynch
7301 North 17th Ave, Phoenix, AZ 85021-7929
Phone: 602-995-4873   **Fax:** (602-242-0416
Email: Lynch12345@cox.net
Commendation: Open Door Fellowship, AZ, 1988
Ministry: Pastoral Care, Preaching
Other Info: Senior Worker (65+)

Bruce and Janet McNicol
9031 N. Arroya Vista Drive, Phoenix, AZ 85028
Fax: 602-249-0611
Email: bruce@truefaced.com
Commendation: Spring Mountain Bible Church, OR, 1977; Open Door Fellowship, AZ, 1996
Ministry: Leadership Development, Pastoral Care

Melissa Meinzinger
P.O. Box 2000, Teec Nos Pos, AZ 86514
Email: meizinger.77@gmail.com
Commendation: Dearborn Chapel, 2006
Ministry: Teaching—School

Raymond Morris
6650 W Butler Dr Apt 21, Glendale, AZ 85302-4315
Phone: 623-930-5625
Email: rm10phx@msn.com
Commendation: Middlesex Chapel, NJ, 1961
Ministry: Senior's Ministry, Visitation
Other Info: Senior Worker (65+)

Gregory and Kathy Staley
PO Box 2000, Teec Nos Pos, AZ 86514-2000
Commendation: Immanuel Navajo Chapel, AZ, 1973
Ministry: Elder, Teaching

Randy Thompson
6509 S. Rossevelt St, Tempe, AZ 85283
Phone: 480-730-0855   **Cell:** 480-730-0855
Email: Randy@randythompson.org
Commendation: Open Door Fellowship, AZ
Ministry: Pastoral Care

Stuart and Jacqueline Wilson
7570 E Speedway Blvd., Unit #211, Tucson, AZ 85710-8815
Phone: 520-742-1711   **Fax:** 520-742-1711
Email: scjwilson@aol.com
Commendation: West Guilford Gospel Chapel, ON, 1953
Ministry: Pastoral Care, Teaching
Other Info: Senior Worker (65+)

ARKANSAS

John and Mary Faulkner
217 CR 1522, Eureka Springs, AR 72632
Phone: 479-253-9183
Commendation: Southside Bible Chapel, LA 1981
Ministry: Pastoral Care, Teaching
Other Info: Senior Worker (65+)

CALIFORNIA

June Aston
1815 A Wildbrook Ct, Concord, CA 94521-1465
Ministry: Children's Ministry
Other Info: Senior Worker (65+)

Shirley Beggs
21092 Cranbridge Drive, Lake Forest, CA 92630
Phone: 949-855-1849
Email: CliffordBeggs@gmail.com
Commendation: Bethany Gospel Chapel, CA, 1978
Ministry: Prayer Ministry Senior
Other Info: Senior Worker (65+), Widow

John and Catherine Bourbonnais
PO Box 1989, Wrightwood, CA 92397
Phone: 760-249-3699   **Fax:** 760-249-4447
Email: papajohn@verdugopines.org
Commendation: Bethel Chapel, CA, 2000
Ministry: Camp Ministry, Pastoral Care

Robert and Jeanne Bruton
Mission Peak Bible Church 4571 Evelena Ct, Fremont, CA 94536
Phone: 510-793-5912
Email: pastorbob@missionpeakbiblechurch.org
Commendation: Mission Peak Bible Church, CA, 1980
Ministry: Counseling, Pastoral Care
Other Info: Senior Worker (65+)

Gerrit Buddingh
2935 Avila Bay Place, Davis, CA 95616
Phone: 530-756-4145   **Fax:** 530-756-4822
Email: gjb@gracevalley.org
Commendation: Grace Valley Christian Center, CA, 2005
Ministry: Elder, Pastoral Care

Steve Caldwell
5199 Alan Ave, San Jose, CA 95124
Phone: 408 265-7461   **Cell:** 408 250-2107
Email: stcaldwell@comcast.net
Commendation: Hillview Bible Chapel, Cupertino, CA
Ministry: Adult Ministry, Counseling, Discipleship, Elder, Evangelism, Family Ministry, Leadership Development, Ministry Administration, Pastoral Care, Shepherding, Preaching, Teaching, Visitation, Youth Ministry

Edward Dickinson
San Diego Hebrew Mission 2100 Greenfield Rd, El Cajon, CA 92019
Phone: 619-287-7255   **Fax:** 619-501-1940
Email: SPHMEJD@cox.net
Commendation: Mission Valley Community Chapel, CA, 1983
Ministry: Domestic Missions, Evangelism

Pedro and Lucy Dillon
10353 Imperial Ave, Cupertino, CA 95014-5948
Phone: 408-253-9096   **Fax:** 408-446-4455
Email: dillon@dime.org
Commendation: Hillview Bible Chapel, CA, 1973
Ministry: Elder, Literature
Other Info: Senior Worker (65+)

Paul and Betty Freeman
6762 Rycroft Dr, Riverside, CA 92506
Phone: 951-780-8819
Email: paulandbetty@att.net
Commendation: Grace Bible Chapel, CA, 1994
Ministry: Preaching, Prison Work

Earle and Julie Fries
1301 Leisure Lane No 5, Walnut Creek, CA 94595
Phone: 925-926-0307
Email: earlefries@comcast.net
Commendation: Valley Bible Church, CA, 1998
Ministry: Adult Ministry, Teaching
Other Info: Senior Worker (65+)

Jack and Irene Heseltine
Sierra Pines Mobile Pk #19 Wendy Cr, Grass Valley, CA 95945
Phone: 530-273-7694
Commendation: Sacramento Bible Chapel, CA, 1968; Grace Bible Chapel, 1968; Rogue Valley Bible Chapel, OR
Ministry: Camp Ministry, Preaching
Other Info: Senior Worker (65+)

Robert and Norma Irvine
The Meadows 4000 Pierce St No 137, Riverside, CA 92503
Phone: 909-359-7052   **Fax:** 909-787-0486
Email: Norob2@juno.com
Commendation: Bethel Chapel, CA, 1991
Ministry: Pastoral Care, Senior's Ministry
Other Info: Senior Worker (65+)

Ruth Kyle
14500 Fruitvale, Apt 2161, Saratoga, CA 95070
Phone: 831-335-2873
Email: ruth_kyle@comcast.com
Ministry: Counseling, Writing and Publishing
Other Info: Senior Worker (65+)

Glenn and Marjorie Layton
496 Whidbey St, Morro Bay, CA 93442-2964
Phone: 805-772-2414
Commendation: Atascadero Gospel Chapel, CA, 1971
Ministry: Pastoral Care, Visitation
Other Info: Senior Worker (65+)

Malcolm and Jo Lee
923 View Dr, Richmond, CA 94803-1247
Phone: 510-222-1688 **Fax:** 510-222-1688
Email: famolee@sbcglobal.net
Commendation: Grace Chapel, CA, 1975
Ministry: Pastoral Care, Preaching
Other Info: Senior Worker (65+)

Julio and Leticia Lopez
1061 N Driftwood Avenue, Rialto, CA 92376
Phone: 909-421-4841 **Cell:** 714-488-4619
Fax: 909-421-4841
Email: lavozdelosangeles@yahoo.com
Commendation: Iglesia Cristiana De Westminster, 2005
Ministry: Elder, Radio Ministry

James and Jean Mader
4926 Old Cliffs Rd, San Diego, CA 92120-1147
Phone: 619-265-1481 **Cell:** 619-274-7070 **Fax:** 619-501-1940
Email: jgmader@adnc.com
Commendation: Mission Valley Community Chapel, CA, 1952
Ministry: Elder, Pastoral Care
Other Info: Senior Worker (65+)

G.V. and Mariamma Mathai
18902 Godinho Ave, Cerritos, CA 90703-6065
Phone: 562-924-5169 **Fax:** 562-484-0889
Email: gvmathai@gmail.com
Commendation: Grace Bible Chapel, CA, 1985
Ministry: Elder, Evangelism, Foreign Missions
Other Info: Senior Worker (65+)

P.G. and Elizabeth Mathew
Grace Valley Christian Center, 27173 County Rd 98, Davis, CA 95616-9742
Fax: 530-756-4822
Email: gvcc@gracevalley.org
Commendation: Grace Valley Christian Center, CA, 1974
Ministry: Foreign Missions, Pastoral Care
Other Info: Senior Worker (65+)

Richard and Mary Matthews
c/o Dan and Carol Worgull, 7933 Cranford Lane, Dublin, CA 84568
Phone: 925-829-9151 **Cell:** 510-366-5758
Email: Dick.mary44@yahoo.com
Commendation: Ottumwa, IA, 1949; Ladera, Inglewood, CA, 1965
Ministry: Counseling, Discipleship
Other Info: Senior Worker (65+)

Jim and Jean McCarthy
PO Box 595, Cupertino, CA 95015
Phone: 408-515-1584
Email: mccarthy@biblechapel.net
Commendation: Hillview Bible Chapel, CA, 1983
Ministry: Church Planting, Teaching

Irene Papineau
7255 Navajo Rd Unit C290, San Diego, CA 92119
Phone: 619-741-1119   **Cell:** 619-933-2860
Email: GIpapineau@cox.net   **Fax:**
Commendation: Mission Valley Community Chapel, CA, 1986
Ministry: Ministry Administration, Teaching
Other Info: Senior Worker (65+)

Gregory Perry
2918 Avila Bay Place, Davis, CA 95616
Phone: 530-759-9796   **Fax:** 530-756-4822
Email: gvcc@gracevalley.org
Commendation: Grace Valley Christian Center, CA, 2007
Ministry: Evangelism, Youth Ministry

Clifford Peterson
12151 Dale St, Apt. C-321, Stanton, CA 90680
Phone: 714-971-6721
Email: Cpeterson14@socal.rr.com
Commendation: Laurel Bible Chapel, CA, 1986
Ministry: Adult Ministry
Other Info: Senior Worker (65+)

Todd and Lisa Rettberg
2218 Tulip Ave., Upland, CA 91784
Phone: 909-931-9770   **Fax:** 909-946-7802
Email: ptsvcc@msn.com
Commendation: Sierra Vista Community Church, CA, 2000
Ministry: Pastoral Care, Preaching

Hugo and Kathleen Santucci
6 Harold Dr, Moraga, CA 94556-1506
Phone: 925-376-1486
Email: hsantucci@bigplanet.com
Commendation: Sun Valley Bible Chapel, CA, 2000
Ministry: Elder, Pastoral Care
Other Info: Senior Worker (65+)

Shawn Wicks
15911 Quartz St., Westminster, CA 92683
Phone: 714-901-5639 **Cell:** 714-742-7887
Email: buru@verizon.net
Commendation: Westminster Bible Chapel, 2002
Ministry: Adult Ministry, Camp Ministry, Counseling, Discipleship, Elder, Pastoral Care, Shepherding, Preaching, Teaching

Erich and Diane Wieger
19824 Forest Ave, Castro Valley, CA 94546
Phone: 510-698-6214 **Cell:** 510-926-1428
Email: ewieger@gmail.com
Commendation: Fairhaven Bible Chapel, San Leandro, 1987 & 2009
Ministry: Discipleship, Preaching, Teaching

Richard and Nancye Yarrall
3455 N Bellflower Blvd, Long Beach, CA 90808-2630
Phone: 562-429-4761 **Cell:** 562-708-6340
Fax: 562-429-4761
Email: lem5@juno.com
Commendation: Avenue 54 Bible Chapel, CA, 1991; Westminster Bible Chapel, 1991
Ministry: Church Planting, Radio Ministry
Other Info: Senior Worker (65+)

COLORADO

Don and Dorothy Anderson
2218 South St, Canon City, CO 81212
Phone: 719-275-3284
Commendation: Calvary Bible Chapel, CO, 1983
Ministry: Counseling, Evangelism
Other Info: Senior Worker (65+)

David and Martha Dunkerton
5920 Topview Court, Colorado Springs, CO 80918
Phone: 719-282-0791
Email: dave@dunkerton.com
Commendation: Community Bible Church, NY, 1973; Park Manor Bible Chapel, IL, 1973
Ministry: Adult Ministry
Other Info: Senior Worker (65+)

Dan and Teri Faulkner
5567 Painted Rocks Rd, Woodland Park, CO 80863-9602
Phone: 719-528-8111 **Fax:** 719-594-6690
Email: dtkfaulkner@juno.com
Commendation: Harvest Bible Fellowship, CO, 1994
Ministry: Camp Ministry, Pastoral Care

Kyle and Allyson Fink
1557 W. Fair Avenue, Littleton, CO 80120
Phone: 303-783-4611
Email: Kyle@littletonbiblechapel.org
Commendation: Littleton Bible Chapel, CO, 2007
Ministry: Elder, Ministry Administration

Craig and Beryl Glass
15728 Paiute Circle, Monument, CO 80132
Phone: 719-229-8258 **Cell:** 719-229-8258
Email: cmglass@adelphia.net
Ministry: Leadership Development, Men's Ministry

Kevin and Zoe Grimes
446 Florence Rd, Grand Junction, CO 81504-8626
Phone: 970-243-3684 **Cell:** 970-201-2495
Fax: 970-434-1461
Email: KevinZoeG@aol.com
Commendation: Clifton Bible Chapel, CO, 1984; Waynesburg Bible Chapel, 1984
Ministry: Foreign Missions, Ministry Administration

Curtis and Mavis Holmes
3665 Newport St, Denver, CO 80207-1507
Phone: 303-388-9030 **Cell:** 720-849-6917
Fax: 303-388-9030
Email: Curtisholmes.1@juno.com
Commendation: Metropolitan Community Tabernacle, MI, 1964
Ministry: Pastoral Care, Prison Work
Other Info: Senior Worker (65+)

James and Janet McCormick
2119 Mariposa, Boulder, CO 80302
Phone: 303-442-6502
Email: jimmcor@myaffinity4.com
Commendation: Boulder Bible Chapel, CO, 2000
Ministry: Domestic Missions, Senior's Ministry Senior Worker (65+)
Other Info: Senior Worker (65+)

Lois Nelson
2928 Illinois Ave, Colorado Springs, CO 80907-6437
Phone: 719-473-3845
Commendation: Westside Christians, CO, 1983
Ministry: Counseling, Women's Ministry
Other Info: Senior Worker (65+)

COMMENDED WORKERS — COLORADO

Donald and Marie Norbie
621 23rd St. Apt 3, Greeley, CO 80631
Phone: 970-356-0817
Email: dlnorbie@juno.com
Commendation: Bethany Chapel, IL, 1949
Ministry: Camp Ministry, Prison Work, Teaching
Other Info: Senior Worker (65+)

Elaine Sapp
1101 E Carolina Ave #1, Fruita, CO 81521
Phone: 970-858-0160
Commendation: Northeast Bible Chapel, 1995
Ministry: Discipleship, Administration, Senior's Ministry
Other Info: Senior Worker (65+)

Greg and Debra Stier
Dare to Share PO Box 745323, Arvada, CO 80005
Phone: 303-425-1606
Commendation: Grace Evangelical Church, CO, 1989
Ministry: Evangelism, Preaching
Other Info: Senior Worker (65+)

Alexander and Marilyn Strauch
1446 W Fair Ave, Littleton, CO 80120-2642
Phone: 303-794-3410   **Fax:** 303-798-9271
Email: alex@lewisandroth.org
Commendation: Littleton Bible Chapel, CO, 1980
Ministry: Elder, Preaching

Letizia Trulli
1880 S. Cascade Ave, Colorado Springs, CO 80905
Phone: 719-633-3886   **Fax:** 719-632-7100
Commendation: Southside Bible Chapel, CO, 1969
Ministry: Children's Ministry, Family Ministry
Other Info: Senior Worker (65+)

Grace Watson
777 Saturn Drive 200, Colorado Springs, CO 80905-7827
Phone: 719-634-4588
Email: gracewats@mailbug.com
Commendation: Southside Bible Chapel, CO, 1950
Ministry: Teaching, Women's Ministry
Other Info: Senior Worker (65+)

Jim and Louise Wright
3115 Dent Ave, Colorado Springs, CO 80904-1248
Phone: 719-471-1295
Email: JimWright33@wmconnect.com
Commendation: Southside Bible Chapel, CO, 1991; Northeast Bible Chapel, CO, 1995
Ministry: Music Ministry, Pastoral Care Senior Worker (65+)
Other Info: Senior Worker (65+)

CONNECTICUT

Lloyd and Heidi Bayreuther
151 Pennsylvania Ave, Niantic, CT 6357
Phone: 860-739-0219
Email: lloyd@grotonbiblechapel.org
Ministry: Caring Ministry

Gary and Kristi Campbell
512 Shewville Rd, Ledyard, CT 6339
Commendation: Groton Bible Chapel, 2006
Ministry: Youth Ministry

Mark and Judy Johnson
243 Whalehead Rd, Gales Ferry, CT 6335
Phone: 860-464-1557   **Cell:** 860-694-4034
Email: mark.r.johnson1@us.army.mil
Commendation: Groton Bible Chapel, CT, 2008
Ministry: Counseling, Military Chaplain

Carrie Matzdorff
24 Spicer Avenue, Groton, CT 6340
Phone: 860-449-8207
Email: Carrie@grotonbiblechapel.org
Commendation: Groton Bible Chapel, CT, 2007
Ministry: Children's Ministry

Tim and Vicki McClelland
290 Johnson St, Naugatuck, CT 6770
Phone: 203-723-0210   **Cell:** 203-598-5054
Email: tjmcc19@sbcglobal.net
Commendation: Cheshire Bible Chapel, CT, 2000
Ministry: Elder, Teaching—School

Bob and Joanne McCoy
96 Farmstead Ave, Mystic, CT 06355-2106
Phone: 860-536-2156
Email: Bob@grotonbiblechapel.org
Commendation: Groton Bible Chapel, CT, 1983
Ministry: Pastoral Care, Teaching

John and Ruth Spender
112 Doolittle Dr, Bethany, CT 06524-3156
Phone: 203-393-0078
Email: jonalansp@juno.com
Commendation: West Woods Bible Chapel, CT 1974
Ministry: Church Planting, Teaching
Other Info: Senior Worker (65+)

Frank and Audrey Vitale
22 Stoney Hill Drive, Mystic, CT 6355
Phone: 860-536-4427
Email: frank@gotonbiblechapel.org
Commendation: Groton Bible Chapel, CT, 2004
Ministry: Ministry Administration, Music Ministry

David and Elsie Ward
36 Watrous Ave, Mystic, CT 06355-1026
Phone: 860-536-3170   **Fax:** 860-445-4386
Email: DEW06355@aol.com
Commendation: Groton Bible Chapel, CT, 1948; Bethany Chapel, NY, 1949
Ministry: Discipleship, Preaching
Other Info: Senior Worker (65+)

DISTRICT OF COLUMBIA

Samuel and Maud Jeremiah
808 Somerset Pl NW, Washington, DC 20011-1133
Phone: 202-726-2881   **Fax:** 202-726-2881
Commendation: Washington Christian Assembly, DC, 1981
Ministry: Pastoral Care, Preaching
Other Info: Senior Worker (65+)

Josephine Wilson
1301 Madison St NW, Washington, DC 20011-3521
Phone: 202-726-3606   **Cell:** 202-489-8457
Fax: 301-860-3144
Email: jwilson@bowiestate.edu
Commendation: Maranatha Gospel Hall, DC, 1975
Ministry: Church Planting, Teaching
Other Info: Senior Worker (65+)

FLORIDA

Kenneth and Sonja Additon
PO Box 17173, Tampa, FL 33682
Phone: 813-964-0970
Email: chapadditon@yahoo.com
Commendation: Community Bible Chapel, LA; 1987; Central Bible Chapel, FL, 1993
Ministry: Chaplain, Pastoral Care

Elmer and Alice Anderson
699 D Park Drive, Keystone Heights, FL 32656
Phone: 352-473-5365
Commendation: Shannon Hills Chapel, NC, 1976; Park of the Palms Church, FL
Ministry: Camp Ministry
Other Info: Senior Worker (65+)

Betty Lou Beers
5049 Sherry Lane, New Port Richey, FL 34653
Phone: 727-844-3300
Commendation: Bible Truth Chapel, Fl 1998
Ministry: Women's Ministry
Other Info: Senior Worker (65+), Widow

Dave and Nancy Bosworth
1761 NW 109th Ave, Pembroke Pines, FL 33026
Phone: 954-435-5312   **Cell:** 954-830-5907
Email: dbosworth@boulevardbible.org
Commendation: Boulevard Bible Chapel, Pembroke Pines, FL, 2007
Ministry: Discipleship, Elder, Teaching, Visitation

David and Kristen Burson
5516 Garden Grove Circle, Winter Park, FL 32792
Phone: 407-673-2393   **Fax:** 407-673-2393
Email: david_burson@htm.org
Commendation: Lake Howell Bible Chapel, FL, 2003
Ministry: Foreign Missions

David and Ann Calderwood
512 Liberia Court, Sanford, FL 32771
Phone: 407-321-4321
Email: dave_calderwood@ntm.org
Commendation: Hiawassa Bible Chapel, FL, 1980
Ministry: Foreign Missions, Preaching
Other Info: Senior Worker (65+)

J.C. Coble
c/o Park of the Palms 706 Palm Circle, Keystone Heights, FL 32656
Commendation: Hiawassa Bible Chapel, FL, 1989
Ministry: Camp Ministry
Other Info: Senior Worker (65+), Widow(er), Physically Retired

Gerald and Esther Dallimore
c/o Park of the Palms, 231 Maranatha Rd #65, Keystone Heights, FL 32656
Phone: 352-473-8311
Email: Gdalli@Juno.com
Commendation: Brighton Avenue Bible Chapel, NJ, 1980; Grace Gospel Chapel, FL, 1985
Ministry: Elder, Evangelism

Tom and Melissa Dowell
Park of the Palms, Inc. 706 Palm Circle, Keystone Heights, FL 32656
Phone: 352-235-2127   **Fax:** 352-333-6835
Email: Tdowell@parkofthepalms.org
Ministry: Preaching, Senior's Ministry

David and Faith Dunlap
3116 Gulfwind Drive, Land O'Lakes, FL 34639
Phone: 813-996-1053
Email: daviddunlap@earthlink.net
Commendation: Grace Gospel Chapel, PA, 1990; Bethel Bible Chapel, 1983
Ministry: Preaching, Writing and Publishing

Francisco and Maria Escarraman
629 Southwest 7th St, Miami, FL 33130
Phone: 305-856-6569   **Cell:** 786-395-4189
Email: Escarramanf@Bellsouth.net
Commendation: Assemblea Evangelica, NY, 1982
Ministry: Adult Ministry, Pastoral Care

Ruth Gawley
PO Box 862, Keystone Heights, FL 32656-0862
Phone: 352-473-2407
Commendation: Park of the Palms Church, FL
Ministry: Adult Ministry

Joseph and Connie Giordano
13215 Greenview Ct, Hudson, FL 34669
Phone: 727-856-4196   **Cell:** 727-267-0048
Email: jgiordano24@aol.com
Commendation: Grace Gospel Chapel, NJ, 1949; Bethany Chapel, NY, 1949
Ministry: Pastoral Care, Preaching

Phil and Edna Guikema
5804 Rywood Dr, Orlando, FL 32810
Phone: 407-563-3931   **Cell:** 321-287-8663
Email: PhilGuikema@earthlink.net
Commendation: Hiawassa Bible Chapel, FL, 1975; Bear Lake Bible Chapel, FL
Ministry: Preaching, Youth Ministry

COMMENDED WORKERS – FLORIDA

Helmut and Shirley Haltrich
201 Newport Ln, Deerfield Bearch, FL 33442
Phone: 954-298-3460 **Cell:** 954-298-3385
Email: richstop42@hotmail.com
Commendation: Rosemount Bible Church, QC, 2005
Ministry: Evangelism, Foreign Missions

Robert and Jeanette Harper
229 Cherrywood Dr, Maitland, FL 32751-3410
Phone: 407-831-6110
Email: rwharper@juno.com
Commendation: Park Manor Bible Chapel, IL, 1960
Ministry: Preaching, Prison Work

Joseph and Uldine Jeremiah
824 Scenic View Circle, Minneola, FL 34715
Phone: 352-227-9471 **Cell:** 301-538-3906
Commendation: Colmar Manor Gospel Chapel, MD, 1986
Ministry: Evangelism, Teaching

Hesketh and Dawn Johnson
2844 NW 42nd Avenue, Coconut Creek, FL 33066
Phone: 954-978-9013
Commendation: Grace Gospel Chapel, PA, 1953
Ministry: Adult Ministry, Literature Distribution

David and Linda Marcy
10209 Serotina Ct, Orlando, FL 32832
Phone: 407-273-0517 **Fax:** 407-852-3601
Email: DLMARCY1@earthlink.net
Commendation: Arlington Countryside Church, IL, 1981
Ministry: Literature Distribution, Translation

J. Dave and Audrey Moffatt
Project Turning-Point, Inc. PO Box 156, Edgewater, FL 32132
Phone: 386-428-5973 **Cell:** 386-566-6388
Fax: 386-428-8134
Commendation: New Smyrna Bible Chapel, FL
Ministry: Prison Work, Youth Ministry

Hal and Mary Moore
322 Scenic Drive, Cocoa, FL 32926
Phone: 321-639-8659
Email: Halmary1@earthlink.net
Commendation: Groton Bible Chapel, CT 1979
Ministry: Adult Ministry, Pastoral Care

COMMENDED WORKERS — FLORIDA

David and Nancy Pavey
645 Coquina Court, Fort Myers, FL 33908
Phone: 239-243 0703   **Cell:** 239-297-7431
Email: davidjpavey@mac.com
Commendation: Valley Church of Moraga, CA; 1968; Pinebrook Church, IL, 1989
Ministry: Foreign Missions
Other Info: Senior Worker (65+)

Larry and Wanda Price
32742 Windy Oak St., Sorrento, FL 32776
Phone: 352-735-2729
Commendation: Southside Bible Chapel, FL, 1982; Hiawassa Bible Chapel, 2000
Ministry: Preaching, Teaching

Enrique "Henry" and Lisa Sardiña
113 Clairbourne Ave, Satellite Beach, FL 32937
Phone: 321-773-5058   **Cell:** 636-346-7174 / 305-803-2290
Email: forgiven2bholy@aol.com / theroosterqueen@aol.com
Commendation: Bible Truth Christian Fellowship, Washington, MO, 1993; Bethany Bible Chapel, Satellite Beach, FL, 2008

Edwin and Phyllis Scott
11915 Overlook Dr, Clermont, FL 34711
Phone: 352-243-4585
Email: elsorlfl@aol.com
Commendation: Hiawassa Bible Chapel, Fl 1990
Ministry: Pastoral Care, Preaching

Steve and Kitty Slusser
7375 Sunnyside Dr, Leesburg, FL 34748
Phone: 352-728-5822   **Cell:** 352-874-6820
Fax: 352-728-8694
Email: steve@slusserlife.com
Commendation: North 56th St Chapel, FL, 2001
Ministry: Camp Ministry, Preaching

Myrue and Patricia Spivey
436 Easton Forest Circle SE, Palm Bay, FL 32907-2423
Phone: 321-725-1792
Email: preacher4Christ@juno.com
Commendation: Berean Bible Church, MD, 1982; Grace Bible Santuary, FL, 1986; Southern Gospel Mission Assoc, 1989
Ministry: Leadership Development, Pastoral Care

William and Mary Stevenson
8521 Parrots Landing, Tampa, FL 33647
Phone: 813-558-9831   **Cell:** 813-334-9577
Email: Billystevenson58@msn.com
Commendation: Warrenville Bible Chapel, IL, 1990
Ministry: Evangelism, Preaching

Franklin and Patricia Taylor
14434 Seafarer Dr, Jacksonville, FL 32224-1811
Phone: 904-223-3243   **Fax:** 904-223-8486
Email: seafarerharbor@yahoo.com
Commendation: Riverview Chapel, WV, 1977
Ministry: Pastoral Care

Ralph and Lucy Van Demark
7373 Sunnyside Dr, Leesburg, FL 34748
Phone: 352-728-1392   **Cell:** 352-406-8995
Fax: 352-728-8694
Email: Rvandemark1@cfl.rr.com
Commendation: Hiawassa Bible Chapel, FL, 2002
Ministry: Camp Ministry

Moy Walters
1620 Mayflower Rd., Ft. Pierce, FL 34950
Phone: 772-466-6165
Commendation: Treasure Coast Bible Assembly, Fl
Ministry: Family Ministry, Senior's Ministry

Ray Zander
1107 Duncan Circle #104, Palm Beach Gardens, FL 33418
Phone: 561-626-1475
Commendation: Bryn Mawr Gospel Hall, PA, 1953; Carlisle Avenue Gospel Chapel, VA, 2000
Ministry: Evangelism, Preaching

GEORGIA

Michael and Anne-Marie Attwood
Po Box 511, Washington, GA 30673-0511
Phone: 706-678-3180   **Cell:** 706-340-5997
Email: watchingservant@gmail.com
Commendation: Grace Gospel Chapel, Saint Petersburg, 1990; Lakeside Bible Chapel, Lincolnton, Georgia, 2008
Ministry: Preaching, Teaching

Timothy and Lorie DeJong
6722 Green Plantation Rd, Harlem, GA 30814-5003
Phone: 706-556-1767   **Cell:** 619-864-2904
Email: tim.dejong@juno.com
Commendation: Believers Gospel Chapel, 2003/2009
Ministry: Domestic Missions, Evangelism, Foreign Missions, Teaching

Nestor and Magda Flores
919 Cavesson Terrace, Lawrenceville, GA 30045
Phone: 770-807-0502   **Cell:** 678-886-1468
Email: ABNANF@hotmail.com
Commendation: Asamblea Biblica De N Atlanta, GA, 1990
Ministry: Pastoral Care, Prison Work

Michael Flowers
PO Box 370603, Decatur, GA 30037-0603
Phone: 770-987-1858
Commendation: Decatur Bible Chapel, Lithonia, Georgia
Ministry: Church Planting, Preaching

Fred and Mattie Gladstone
PO Box 712, Darien, GA 31305-0712
Phone: 912-437-4687
Commendation: Northwest Bible Chapel, IL, 1957
Ministry: Camp Ministry, Correspondence Ministry
Other Info: Senior Worker (65+), Physically Retired

Ken and Pat Gross
2328 Laurel Lane, Augusta, GA 30904-3138
Phone: 706-738-5697   **Cell:** 706-799-5697
Fax: 706-738-5697
Email: KGross@GSP.net
Commendation: Believers Gospel Chapel, GA, 1999
Ministry: Evangelism, Law Enforcement Chaplain

Sue Hollingsworth
3412 Wentworth Pl, Augusta, GA 30906-5051
Phone: 706-798-1234
Commendation: Believers Gospel Chapel, GA, 1985; Bethany Chapel, GA, 1952
Ministry: Adult Ministry

Cliff and Lee Ice
1723 Fort Valley Dr SW, Atlanta, GA 30311
Phone: 404-209-0145   **Cell:** 404-886-7385
Fax: 404522-9222
Email: Spenc70356@hotmail.com
Commendation: Community Bible Chapel, GA, 1990
Ministry: Counseling, Pastoral Care

Curtis and Katherine Jenkins
PO Box 2754, Valdosta, GA 31604-2754
Phone: 229-244-9366   **Cell:** 229-563-1350
Commendation: Community Bible Chapel, GA, 1987; New Life Bible Church, GA
Ministry: Church Planting, Evangelism

Le Roy and Virginia Lohre
PO Box 1704 235 Broad St, Augusta, GA 30901-1515
Phone: 706-722-3931   **Fax:** 706-722-3806
Email: LELOHRE@aol.com
Commendation: The Bible Chapel, GA, 1973
Ministry: Preaching, Teaching

Austin and Dee Meadows
7011-A Pony Lake Rd, Dahlonega, GA 30533
Phone: 770-287-9861   **Cell:** (678-316-9536
Fax: 770-287-9861
Email: austinmeadows@juno.com
Commendation: North Atlanta Bible Chapel, GA, 2005
Ministry: Camp Ministry, Preaching

Doris Miller
4011 Roswell Rd Apt B3 Rosehill Apartments, Atlanta, GA 30342-4127
Phone: 404-233-3149
Commendation: North Atlanta Bible Chapel, GA
Ministry: Adult Ministry

Steve and Teresa Roys
7011 Pony Lake Rd, Dahlonega, GA 30533
Phone: 678-316-7309   **Cell:** 678-316-7309
Fax: 770-536-4787
Email: camphopega@arilion.com
Commendation: Lake Lanier Bible Chapel
Ministry: Camp Ministry

Robert and Carol Scheid
4513 Legend Hollow Lane, Powder Springs, GA 30127
Phone: 770-222-9568
Email: scheid@bellsouth.net
Commendation: Community Bible Church, NY, 1972
Ministry: Prison Work, Teaching

HAWAII

Dennis and Grace Medeiros
PO Box 1265, Pearl City, HI 96782-8265
Phone: 808-456-6581
Commendation: Fleming Chapel, VA, 1995
Ministry: Preaching, Teaching

IDAHO

Eldred and Shirley Bagley
2127 W State Street, Boise, ID 83702
Phone: 208-344-4876 **Cell:** 208-571-6813
Commendation: Springdale Bible Chapel, OR, 1990
Ministry: Discipleship, Evangelism

John and Nancy Hook
2007 W. Silver Creek Dr., Nampa, ID 83686
Phone: 208-442-6547 **Cell:** 909-965-6289
Fax: 208-498-0801
Email: jhook@maf.org
Ministry: Evangelism, Missionary Aviation

Dion Unruh
2415 N. 9th St, Coeurd'Alene, ID 83814
Phone: 208-765-5856
Commendation: Walnut Ave. Gospel CHapel, ID, 2004
Ministry: Music Ministry, Preaching

Donald Unruh
PO Box 1364, Coeur D'Alene, ID 83816-1364
Phone: 208-664-4620
Commendation: Walnut Ave. Gospel Chapel, ID, 1991
Ministry: Family Ministry, Pastoral Care

Dave and Jean Wunsch
12695 Rockledge Lane, Nampa, ID 83686
Phone: 208-461-2228
Email: JWunsch@maf.org
Commendation: Forest Hills Bible Chapel, MI, 1976
Ministry: Adult Ministry

ILLINOIS

Abner and Rosie Bauman
121 Mandel Ln, Prospect Heights, IL 60070-1745
Phone: 847-827-3017 **Fax:** 847-255-7986
Ministry: Foreign Missions, Pastoral Care

Rich and Zo Becker
7029 Nathan Lane, Carpentersville, IL 60110
Phone: 847-428-4108 **Fax:** 847-429-0800
Commendation: Wauwatosa Bible Chapel, WI, 1972
Ministry: Ministry Administration, Preaching

Kenneth and Patty Botton
450 North Crooked Lake Ln, Lindenhurst, IL 60046
Phone: 847-265-9195 **Cell:** 847-204-8676
Fax: 847-265-8925
Email: kbotton@aol.com
Commendation: Bethany Chapel, IL 1997
Ministry: Chaplain, Ministry Administration, Preaching

David and Ann Brown
225 N. Martha St., Lombard, IL 60148
Phone: 630-620-4987 **Cell:** 630-709-7354
Email: whatbrowncando@comcast.net
Commendation: Lombard Gospel Chapel, IL, 2005
Ministry: Pastoral Care, Preaching

James and Anita Callahan
1859 North Oak Park Ave, Chicago, IL 60707
Phone: 773-237-9385 **Cell:** 630-674-5220
Email: james.p.callahan@comcast.net
Commendation: Bethany Chapel, IL
Ministry: Pastoral Care, Teaching

George and Rosemary Carrera
3605 N Drake, Chicago, IL 60618
Phone: 773-583-8245 **Cell:** 773-454-3762
Commendation: Northwest Bible Chapel, IL 1999
Ministry: Pastoral Care, Visitation

Donald and Naomi Cole
120 Windsor Park Drive A119, Carol Stream, IL 60188
Phone: 630-982-1966 **Fax:** 630-351-4576
Email: mbipastor@aol.com
Commendation: Central Gospel Hall, ON, 1945; Central Gospel Hall, MI, 1947; Moody Bible Institute, IL, 1971
Ministry: Preaching, Radio Ministry

Dave and Karen Corlew
916 E Hintz Rd, Arlington Heights, IL 60004
Phone: 847-749-1103 **Cell:** 847-529-6284
Fax: 847-255-7986
Email: Dave@acchurch.org
Commendation: Arlington Countryside Church, IL, 2005
Ministry: Pastoral Care, Preaching

Craig and Anne Dyer
1585 Laburnum, Hoffman Estates, IL 60195
Phone: 847-202-8685 **Fax:** 847-519-0024
Email: Info@BrightHope.org
Commendation: Arlington Countryside Church, IL, 1991
Ministry: Ministry Administration, Preaching

COMMENDED WORKERS — ILLINOIS

Kevin and Eloise Dyer
810 Willow Hills Ln, Prospect Heights, IL 60070-2581
Phone: 847-259-3808 **Fax:** 847-259-3809
Email: kevinandeloise@brighthope.org
Commendation: Grace and Truth Gospel Chapel, KS 1959
Ministry: Foreign Missions, Preaching

Mark and Sue Dyer
2060 Stonington Avenue, Suite 101, Hoffman Estates, IL 60169
Phone: 847-398-4552
Email: interestministries@hotmail.com
Commendation: Neighborhood Bible Fellowship, IL
Ministry: Foreign Missions, Urban Ministry

James and Brozine Fair
18852 Center, Homewood, IL 60430-4105
Phone: 708-957-0853
Email: bfair@cps.K12.il.us
Commendation: Learning Center Gospel Chapel, IL
Ministry: Hospital Chaplain, Teaching

Dann and Nancy Farquhar
806 W Highland Ave, Elgin, IL 60123
Phone: 847-931-5018 **Cell:** 847-652-6003
Fax: 847-429-0800
Email: Farquhar@iteams.org
Commendation: Denali Bible Chapel, AK, 1987
Ministry: Ministry Administration

Mark and Deb Foshager
411 West River Road, Elgin, IL 60123
Phone: 847-531-8050 **Cell:** 847-420-3627
Fax: 847-429-0800
Email: mark.foshager@iteams.org
Commendation: Crossroads Community Church, MA, 1995
Ministry: Domestic Missions, Foreign Missions

Robert and Alice Fryling
6220 Stable Road, Woodridge, IL 60517-1212
Phone: (630-435-5625 **Fax:** (630-734-4201
Email: BFRYLING@ivpress.com
Commendation: Mascher Street Gospel Hall, PA, 1969
Ministry: Leadership Development, Writing and Publishing

Mariano and Pearl Gonzalez
PO Box 371, Lombard, IL 60148-0371
Email: Josuecaleb@audiolit.net **Fax:** (630-495-9671
Commendation: Oconomovoc Bible Fellowship, WI, 2001; Local Cristiano, IL, 2001
Ministry: Radio Ministry, Writing and Publishing

Charlie and Lorna Hollensed
541 Hill Avenue, Glen Ellyn, IL 60137
Phone: 630-469-0079   **Cell:** 630-202-2787
Email: whollensed@gmail.com
Commendation: Warrenville Bible Chapel, IL 2007
Ministry: Medical Missions, Ministry Administration

Joel and Melanie Honegger
24223 W Rose Ave, Lake Zurich, IL 60047
Phone: 847-438-3063
Email: Jeeeem@juno.com
Commendation: Arlington Countryside Church, IL, 2000; Alpine Chapel, IL, 2004
Ministry: Adult Ministry, Leadership Development

Walter and Olive Liefeld
436 N. Crooked Lake Ln, Lindenhurst, IL 60046
Phone: 847-265-8760   **Fax:** 847-265-8760
Email: liefeld@sbcglobal.net
Commendation: Sea Cliff Gospel Chapel, NY, 1959
Ministry: Teaching, Writing and Publishing
Other Info: Physically Retired

Bud and Shirley Morris
800 East Eight Street, Delavan, IL 61734
Phone: 309-244-7471
Email: surebud@sbcglobal.net
Commendation: Grace Bible Chapel, IL, 2007
Ministry: Preaching, Teaching

Robert Ramey
500 Timber Ridge Dr No 302, Carol Stream, IL 60188-2882
Phone: (630-682-4733
Email: RFR3927@aol.com
Commendation: Woodside Bible Chapel, IL, 1994
Ministry: Pastoral Care, Preaching

Ken and Tascha Raymond
907 Maplepark Dr, Champaign, IL 61821
Phone: 217-954-0601
Email: ken@stratfordpark.net
Commendation: Stratford Park Bible Chapel, IL, 1994
Ministry: Elder, Ministry Administration, Pastoral Care, Preaching, Teaching

Craig and Nancy Rolinger
1800 7th Street Unit 11A, East Moline, IL 61244
Phone: 309-755-4337   **Cell:** 309-781-7604
Email: rolinger@rolinger.org
Commendation: Oak Ridge Bible Chapel, IL, 1986
Ministry: Camp Ministry, Preaching

Derrick and Eileen Rollerson
3413 Butterfield Rd, Bellwood, IL 60104-1452
Phone: 708-547-1471 **Cell:** 708-785-6135
Fax: 708-547-6353
Email: DSRoller@aol.com
Commendation: Westlawn Gospel Chapel, IL, 1980
Ministry: Elder, Pastoral Care

Harry Roundtree
1023 N Monitor Ave, Chicago, IL 60651-2568
Phone: 773-921-8452
Commendation: Village Church of Oak Park, IL
Ministry: Family Ministry, Prison Work

Laura Routley
1800 7th St., Unit 2F, East Moline, IL 61244-2229
Phone: 309-755-4611
Email: lauraroutley@sbcglobal.net
Commendation: High Point Bible Chapel, IA, 1965
Ministry: Senior's Ministry

Richard and Betty Sanders
10112 Potter Rd, Des Plaines, IL 60016-1547
Phone: 847-635-8578 **Cell:** 847-707-7201
Fax: 847-635-8578
Email: BRSanders@aol.com
Commendation: Norwood Gospel Chapel, IL, 1987
Ministry: Elder, Pastoral Care

Mark and Jennifer Soderquist
2121 S St. Louis, Chicago, IL 60623-3122
Phone: 773-522-1320 **Fax:** 773-522-7847
Email: Mark.Soderquist@iteams.org
Commendation: Bethany Chapel, IL, 1981
Ministry: Ethnic Ministry, Urban Ministry

James and Betty Stahr
327 W Prairie Ave, Wheaton, IL 60187-3408
Phone: 630-665-3757
Commendation: Woodside Bible Chapel, NJ, 1954
Ministry: Preaching, Writing and Publishing

Forrest and Estelle Stampley
327 Home Ave Apt 2S, Oak Park, IL 60302
Phone: 708-785-6192
Email: forrest418@juno.com
Commendation: Westlawn Gospel Chapel, IL, 1993
Ministry: Children's Ministry, Elder

Steven and Felecia Thompson
10046 S St Lawrence, Chicago, IL 60628-2230
Phone: 773-387-6183
Commendation: Laflin Street Gospel Chapel, IL, 1978; Oak Lawn Bible Chapel, IL, 1998
Ministry: After-Care/Follow-up, Prison Work

Jeff Tichelar
4620 W 128th St, Alsip, IL 60658-2705
Phone: 708-597-4450
Email: jeffagzus@hotmail.com
Commendation: Riverdale Fellowship, 2005; Woodside Bible Chapel, IL, 2007
Ministry: Evangelism, Preaching

Glendall and Janet Toney
1850 Pleasant Woods Circle, Carbondale, IL 62902
Phone: 618-549-2786
Commendation: Cape Bible Chapel, MO, 1979
Ministry: Discipleship, Preaching

Bob and Debbie Whattoff
806 Wesley, Savoy, IL 61874-9555
Phone: 217-352-5233   **Cell:** 217-766-6883
Email: whattoff@insightbb.com
Commendation: Grace Bible Chapel, IL, 1997; Stratford Park Bible Chapel, IL, 1985
Ministry: Elder, Evangelism

Harry and Jean Williams
114 Windsor Park Drive B208, Carol Stream, IL 60188
Phone: 630-690-2420
Commendation: Palm Bible Chapel, FL, 1968
Ministry: Pastoral Care, Visitation

Leroy and Beverly Yates
555 E 167th St, South Holland, IL 60473-2911
Phone: 708-333-2762   **Cell:** 312-485-2762
Fax: 708-333-2840
Email: Bevleroy@wideopenwest.com
Commendation: Westlawn Gospel Chapel, IL, 1978
Ministry: Counseling, Pastoral Care

Anil and Christina Yesudas
6044 N. Fairfield Avenue, Chicago, IL 60659-3918
Phone: 773-973-3526   **Cell:** 773-580-6510
Email: anil.yesudas@yahoo.com
Commendation: Woodside Bible Chapel, IL, 2004
Ministry: Evangelism, Homeless Ministry, Orphanage or Homeless Shelter Outreach

INDIANA

Warren and Florence Dunham
6241 Belfry Way, Indianapolis, IN 46237
Phone: 317 641 5714 **Cell:** 317 828 7393
Email: wdunham1@juno.com
Commendation: Norwood Gospel Chapel
Ministry: Adult Ministry, Ethnic Ministry
Other Info: Senior Worker (65+)

Ben Scripture
3214 S. SR 25, Warsaw, IN 46580
Phone: 574-491-3214 **Fax:** 574-491-3214
Commendation: Bethany Bible Chapel, IN, 2001
Ministry: Conference Ministry, Elder

IOWA

David and Lorraine Allison
2427 Spruce Wood Dr, Dubuque, IA 52002-2308
Phone: 563-583-8001 **Fax:** 563-585-1661
Commendation: Bethany Chapel, Rhodesia, 1977
Ministry: Ministry Administration, Senior's Ministry

Duane and Alice Brown
613 Poplar St, Atlantic, IA 50022
Phone: 712-243-5047
Email: debrown@metc.net
Commendation: Sunnyside Bible Chapel, IA, 2005; Atlantic Gospel Chapel, 1983
Ministry: Adult Ministry, Children's Ministry

Lillian Catron
1816 Glenwood Ct, Dubuque, IA 52002-2648
Phone: 563-557-8605
Commendation: Village Lane Bible Chapel, NY, 1960
Ministry: Children's Ministry, Teaching—School

Bruce and Geneva Collins
3828 Memory Lane, Waterloo, IA 50701-9351
Phone: 319-296-9871 **Cell:** 319-230-9140
Email: collinsbd@hotmail.com
Commendation: Bethany Bible Chapel, IA 2002
Ministry: Camp Ministry, Radio Ministry

Kenneth and Carol Daughters
11123 Hidden Springs Court, Dubuque, IA 52003-9659
Phone: 563-557-9513 **Fax:** 563-588-1216
Email: kdaughters@emmaus.edu
Commendation: Grace Bible Chapel, CA, 1983
Ministry: Elder, Ministry Administration

COMMENDED WORKERS — IOWA

James and Carolyn Dunkerton
1865 Horizon Court, Dubuque, IA 52001-4033
Phone: 563-556-8863 **Cell:** 563-663-4604
Fax: 563-588-1216
Email: JDunker343@aol.com
Commendation: Forge Road Bible Chapel, MD, 1984; The Gospel Chapel, TN, 1984
Ministry: Elder, Pastoral Care

George and Gail Farber
710 Burbank Ave, Waterloo, IA 50702
Phone: 319-232-4168
Email: georgefarber@mcleodusa.net
Commendation: Bethany Bible Chapel, IA, 1980
Ministry: Camp Ministry, Teaching

Jay and Dorothy Fippinger
2814 NW North Creek Circle, Ankeny, IA 50023
Phone: 515-964-3787
Email: JayTD_Fippinger@sil.org
Commendation: Northeast Gospel Chapel, MN 1981
Ministry: Ethnic Ministry, Translation

Jack and Nancy Fish
Emmaus Bible College, 2570 Asbury Rd, Dubuque, IA 52001-3044
Phone: 563-557-8959 **Fax:** 563-588-1216
Email: JFish@emmaus.edu
Commendation: Woodside Chapel, NJ, 1969
Ministry: Pastoral Care, Teaching

Charles and Darlene Fizer
5785 Sun Valley Dr, Asbury, IA 52002-2465
Phone: 563-588-3494 **Cell:** 563-580-0329
Email: cFizer@hotmail.com
Commendation: Welton Bible Chapel, WV; Riverview Bible Chapel, WV; Otsego Bible Chapel, Updated 2001
Ministry: Pastoral Care, Preaching
Other Info: Senior Worker (65+)

Kenneth and Helena Fleming
3140 St. Anne Drive, Dubuque, IA 52001-3949
Phone: 563-557-1977 **Fax:** 563-588-1216
Email: kflem3140@aol.com
Commendation: Hope Bible Fellowship, WA, 1950
Ministry: Teaching, Teaching—School

David Glock
11306 Lakeview Dr, Dubuque, IA 52003-9211
Phone: 563-582-5969   **Cell:** 563-590-5416
Fax: 563-588-1216
Email: dglock@emmaus.edu
Commendation: Asbury Community Chapel, IA, 1990
Ministry: Conference Ministry, Teaching—School
Other Info:

David and Rose Hammond
8212 Lakeshore Dr, Dexter, IA 50070-7520
Phone: 515-523-2357
Email: Hammond9@Juno.com
Commendation: Hilltop Chapel, IA, 1985
Ministry: Evangelism, Preaching

Mary Ann Harper
340 Mississippi View Dr, Dubuque, IA 52003-7816
Phone: 563-557-9399
Commendation: Sturgis Bible Chapel, MI
Ministry: Women's Ministry

Joel and Amy Hernandez
893 W Locust St, Dubuque, IA 52001
Cell: 563-580-5474
Email: joelandamy@gmail.com
Commendation: Community Bible Chapel, 2007
Ministry: Teacher—Training

Stefan and Linda Johnson
11175 Hidden Springs Ct, Dubuque, IA 52003
Phone: 563-556-5623
Email: sjohnson@emmaus.edu
Commendation: Atlantic Gospel Chapel, IA, 1993
Ministry: Preaching, Youth Ministry

Philip and Betty Leverentz
11154 High Ridge Drive, Dubuque, IA 52003
Phone: 563-557-8583   **Cell:** 563-590-4202
Email: p.leverentz@mchsi.com
Commendation: Northeast Gospel Chapel, 2008;
Longfellow Gospel Chapel, MN, 1984
Ministry: Elder, Teaching—School

David and Linda MacLeod
1851 Asbury Rd, Dubuque, IA 52001-4114
Phone: 563-557-1934   **Fax:** 563-588-1216
Email: DavMacLeod@aol.com
Commendation: Little Bible Chapel, CO, 1978
Ministry: Preaching, Teaching—School

Arthur and Lois Manning
4995 Northrange Ct, Dubuque, IA 52002
Phone: 563-582-9337
Email: amanning@emmaus.edu
Commendation: Long Lake Community Church, MN 2004
Ministry: Camp Ministry, Teaching—School

Benjamin and Jenna Mathew
977 Mt. Loretta Ave, Dubuque, IA 52003
Phone: 563-564-9132   **Fax:** 563-588-1216
Email: bmathew@emmaus.edu
Commendation: West Fifth Bible Chapel, ON, 2004
Ministry: Preaching, Teaching—School

Eric and Jean McCullough
4934 Bluebell Road, Cedar Falls, IA 50613
Phone: 319-266-0333
Email: emcc@cfu.net
Commendation: Stout Gospel Hall, IA, 1957; Cedar Falls Gospel Hall, IA
Ministry: Conference Ministry, Preaching

Bill and Carol Moore
127 East Oneil Drive, Ames, IA 50010
Phone: 515-232-1167   **Cell:** 515-520-9609
Email: wjmclm127@yahoo.com
Commendation: Countryside Bible Chapel, 2002
Ministry: Pastoral Care, Teaching

John and Kathleen Ottley
9114 Oakridge Place, Johnston, IA 50131
Phone: 515-331-3567   **Cell:** 515-720-5189
Fax: 515-276-3558
Email: jkottley@gmail.com
Commendation: McKinney Bible Church, TX, 1982; Cornerstone Community Church, IA, 1998; Servants Church, IL, 1995
Ministry: Pastoral Care, Preaching

Roger and Sarah Poling
1615 Born, Dubuque, IA 52001
Phone: 563-556-4810   **Cell:** 563-663-1598
Fax: 563-588-1216
Email: spoling@emmaus.edu
Commendation: Warrenvile Bible Chapel, IL, 2000
Ministry: Children's Ministry, Teaching—School

Robert and Ami Randazzo
100 Hickory Glen, Grimes, IA 50111
Email: abishai22@msn.com
Commendation: Cornerstone Community Church, IA, 2003
Ministry: Elder, Pastoral Care

Jeff and Jeanette Riley
5132 Park Pl, Asbury, IA 52002
Phone: 563-588-1169 **Cell:** 563-580-8004
Email: jriley@emmaus.edu
Commendation: Des Moines Gospel Chapel, 2008
Ministry: Youth Ministry

Steven and Julie Sanchez
953 Wilson St., Dubuque, IA 52001
Phone: 563-584-1700 Office: 563-588-8000
Email: ssanchez@emmaus.edu
Commendation: Community Bible Chapel, 2005
Ministry: Teaching, Teaching—School

Steve and Cheryl Seeman
825 W. 11th St, Dubuque, IA 52001
Phone: 563-582-1346
Email: sseeman@emmaus.edu
Commendation: Des Moines Gospel Chapel, WA, 2006
Ministry: Adult Ministry

Daniel and Martha Smith
3127 Arbor Oaks Dr, Dubuque, IA 52001-1518
Phone: 563-588-3455 **Fax:** 563-588-1216
Email: dsmith@emmaus.edu
Commendation: Mapplewood Bible Chapel, MO, 1959
Ministry: Preaching, Teaching—School

Dann and Linda Speichinger
2515 S Coral Ave, Sioux City, IA 51106-3327
Phone: 712-276-2445
Commendation: Washington Heights Chapel, IA, 1973
Ministry: Pastoral Care, Teaching

Mark and Tonya Stevenson
1770 Chaney Road, Dubuque, IA 52001
Phone: 563-582-7820 **Cell:** 563-580-3095
Fax: 563-588-1216
Email: mstevensonemmaus.edu
Commendation: Evanston Gospel Chapel, IL, 2000
Ministry: Preaching, Teaching—School

Milo and Gladys Vande Krol
1510 Pinnicle Place, Waterloo, IA 50701
Phone: 319-234-4464 **Cell:** 319-240-2140
Email: milovk@forbin.net
Commendation: Hillside Bible Chapel, IA, 1990; Bethany Bible Chapel, IA
Ministry: Adult Ministry, Preaching

Wayne and Angela VandeKrol
1411 7th Ave East., Oskaloosa, IA 52577
Cell: 515-473-8289
Email: VandeKrolandbonds@yahoo.com
Commendation: Grove Park Chapel, NC May, 2008
Ministry: Chaplain

Steven and Wendy Witter
3436 Glencove Ln, Dubuque, IA 52002
Phone: 563-556-3157   **Cell:** 563-599-2008
Fax: 563-588-1216
Email: switter@emmaus.edu
Commendation: Chambersburg Gospel Chapel, PA, 1995; Boiling Springs Bible Chapel, PA, 1995
Ministry: Ministry Administration, Preaching

Mark and Laura Woodhouse
14053 Constance Court, Dubuque, IA 52001
Phone: 563-584-2937   **Fax:** 563-588-1216
Email: mwoodhouse@emmaus.edu
Commendation: Keystone Bible Chapel, NE, 2000
Ministry: Preaching, Teaching—School

KANSAS

Scott and Lynn DeGroff
2510 SW 35th Terrace, Topeka, KS 66611
Phone: 785-271-5617
Commendation: Topeka Gospel Chapel, KS, 2005
Ministry: Preaching, Teaching

John Denny
Kansas Bible Camp, 4508 W. 56th Street, Hutchinson, KS 67502
Phone: 620-662-7791
Email: kbc@ksbiblecamp.org
Commendation: Hutchinson Bible Chapel, KS
Ministry: Camp Ministry, Elder

Andrew and Michelle Hawkinson
4508 West 56th Ave, Hutchinson, KS 67502
Phone: (620-664-6496
Email: ahawkinson@ksbiblecamp.org
Commendation: Hutchinson Gospel Chapel; Northwest Gospel Chapel, KS, 2004
Ministry: Camp Ministry, Music Ministry

Fred and Patty Heeren
13842 S. Sycamore Street, Olathe, KS 66062
Phone: 913-390-5754   **Cell:** 913-787-1375
Fax: 913-768-9037
Email: fred@day-star.org
Commendation: Arlington Countryside Church, IL, 1996
Ministry: Evangelism, Literature Distribution

Robert and Sharon Lindsted
5450 E 45th N, Wichita, KS 67220-1722
Phone: 316-744-2450   **Fax:** 316-744-2450
Commendation: Community Bible Chapel, KS, 2006
Ministry: Foreign Missions, Teaching—School

Dale and Linda Schrag
4508 West 56 Avenue, Hutchinson, KS 67502
Phone: 620-665-3682   **Cell:** 620-665-3682
Email: daleandlinda@gmail.com
Commendation: Hutchinson Gospel Chapel, 1992
Ministry: Camp Ministry

Georgiana Truax
9142 W. 102 Terr, Overland Park, KS 66212
Phone: 913-908-4770
Commendation: Bethany Chapel, SC, 1983
Ministry: Prayer Ministry, Visitation
Other Info: Senior Worker (65+)

KENTUCKY

Michael and Nicole Johnson
1433 Bastogne Ave, Apt A, Fort Campbell, KY 42223
Phone: 931-338-1344
Email: michael.j.johnson13@us.army.mil
Commendation: Trinity Fellowship Church, TX, 2008
Ministry: Military Chaplain

Vena Preston
165 Toronto Rd., Lexington, KY 40515
Phone: 859-335-5090   **Cell:** 859-361-6777
Email: prestonvena@yahoo.com
Commendation: Manvel Bible Chapel, 1982
Other Info: Widow of Commended Worker, Senior Worker (65+),

LOUISIANA

Robert and JoAnne Brown
1584 Monaco Dr, Slidell, LA 70458-2947
Phone: 985-641-4028 **Cell:** 985-502-8760
Fax: 985-649-1960
Email: jesusistheway@juno.com
Commendation: Slidell Bible Chapel, LA, 1985; Grace Gospel Chapel, PA, 2002; Lake Park Chapel, LA, 1985
Ministry: Evangelism, Preaching

Ray and Peetsie Cummings
103 Dickson Dr, Belle Chasse, LA 70037-2439
Phone: 504-393-7083 **Cell:** 504-239-7068
Fax: 504-394-3085
Email: lakeparkchapel@cmaaccess.com
Commendation: Lake Park Chapel, LA, 1995
Ministry: Counseling, Preaching

Alfred and Glen Marie Young
PO Box 630, Covington, LA 70434-0630
Phone: 985-892-7375 **Fax:** 985-893-5882
Commendation: Faith Bible Church, Covington, LA, 2001
Ministry: Evangelism, Pastoral Care

MAINE

Mark and Sara Cowperthwaite
12 Emery Avenue, Thomaston, ME 4861
Phone: 207-542-8916
Email: cowperthwaitefamily@gmail.com
Commendation: Grace Fellowship Bible Chapel of Union, Maine, 2008
Ministry: Discipleship, Evangelism

Justin and Jocelin Humes
37 Stirling Road, Warren, ME 4864
Cell: 207-691-2850
Email: jhumesfamily@hotmail.com
Commendation: Grace Fellowship Bible Chapel, Union, Maine, 2008
Ministry: Evangelism, Preaching

MARYLAND

Charles and Lydia Cade
3903 Newton St, Colmar Manor, MD 20722-2132
Phone: 301-864-0340   **Cell:** 202-359-9392
Fax: 301-864-0340
Email: chas_lydia_cade@hotmail.com
Commendation: Colmar Manor Gospel Chapel, MD, 1990
Ministry: Children's Ministry, Evangelism

J. Michael and Margo Clark
4915 Crain Hwy, White Plains, MD 20695-2849
Phone: 301-627-1433   **Cell:** 301-509-9391
Fax: 301-934-2427
Email: Mike.clark@southpotomac.org
Commendation: South Potomac Church, MD, 2002
Ministry: Elder, Ministry Administration

Sheela Dandekar
14713 Prince John Ct, Burtonsville, MD 20866
Email: sheela@dandekar.com
Commendation: New Hampshire Ave Gospel Chapel,
Ministry: Counseling, Evangelism
Other Info: Senior Worker (65+), Widow(er)

Barbara Davidson
22632 Davidson Ln, Lexington Park, MD 20653-0007
Phone: 301-862-3755
Commendation: SAYSF Bible Church, MD, 1991
Other: Widow of Commended Worker

Arthur and Vivian Garnes
7710 Fontaine St, Potomac, MD 20854-3303
Phone: 301-299-8254
Commendation: Grace Gospel Chapel, NY, 1978
Ministry: Elder, Pastoral Care

Kerensa Huffman
4915 Crain Hwy, White Plains, MD 20695
Phone: 240-349-2212   **Cell:** 301-542-2346
Fax: 301-934-2427
Email: kerensa.huffman@southpotomac.org
Commendation: South Potomac Church, MD
Ministry: Evangelism, Youth Ministry

Oliver and Tish Leigh John-Baptiste
21903 Ivy Leaf Drive, Boyds, MD 20841
Cell: 301-461-2418
Email: obtljohnbaptiste@yahoo.com
Commendation: Rockville Bible Fellowship, 2009
Ministry: Church Planting, Evangelism

Gertrude Lewis
2007 32nd St, Baltimore, MD 21218-3108
Phone: 410-235-0053   **Cell:** 443-570-4970
Fax: 410-261-5509
Email: pjlgml1@verizon.net
Commendation: Berean Bible Chapel, MD, 1972; Christian Fellowship Bible Church, MD, 1991; Loch Hill, MD, 2003

John Watson
4915 Crain Hwy, White Plains, MD 20695
Phone: 301-233-9992   **Fax:** 301-934-2427
Commendation: South Potoma Church, MD
Ministry: Teaching, Youth Ministry

MASSACHUSETTS

Steve DuPlessie
235 West Street, Attleboro, MA 2703
Phone: 508-212-1980   **Cell:** 508-212-1980
Fax: 508-699-7897
Email: steve@gnbc.org
Commendation: Good News Bible Chapel, 2005
Ministry: Adult Ministry, Pastoral Care, Preaching, Teaching, Visitation

Jack Fish
482 Lowell St, Lexington, MA 02420
Phone: 781-862-7513   **Cell:** 781-835-7520
Fax: 781-862-4483
Email: jack@countrysidebiblechapel.org
Website: www.countrysidebiblechapel.org
Commendation: Countryside Bible Chapel, MA, 2009

MICHIGAN

John and Ann Bjorlie
3736 Knapp NE, Grand Rapids, MI 49525
Phone: 616-364-2767   **Cell:** 616-706-7558
Fax: 616-314-2767
Email: john@bjorlie.net
Commendation: Grace & Truth Christian Fellowship, MI
Ministry: Preaching, Writing and Publishing

Kathleen Boudet
PO Box 395, Armada, MI 48005
Cell: 706-513-5895
Email: KPBoudet@Tepse.org
Commendation: Believers Gospel Chapel, August, GA, 2008
Ministry: Evangelism, Ministry Administration

Edward and Peggy Burdick
6630 Lake Front, Montague, MI 49437-9308
Phone: 231-893-0305
Commendation: Friendship Bible Chapel, MI, 1989; Dunning Park, MI, 1980
Ministry: Adult Ministry, Counseling

Bruce and Susan Calderwood
25835 Forest View, Southfield, MI 48033-2813
Phone: 248-357-4892 **Fax:** 313-831-2299
Email: calderwoodbruce@hotmail.com
Commendation: Dunning Park Bible Chapel, MI, 1979
Ministry: Elder, Ministry Administration

Geraldine Coleman
PO Box 241300, Detroit, MI 48224
Phone: 313-245-5725
Email: gjcol5920@sbcglobal.net
Ministry: Music Ministry
Other Info: Senior Worker (65+)

Mike and Nona Fitzhugh
239 Running Waters Ct NW, Sparta, MI 49345
Phone: 616-784-4887 **Cell:** 616-808-6069
Email: Mike.Fitzhugh@gmail.com
Commendation: Northwest Gospel Hall, MI, 2005
Ministry: Adult Ministry, Discipleship, Preaching, Teacher−Training, Teaching

Winnie Gay
3680 Brambleberry Dr NW, Comstock Park, MI 49321
Phone: 616-647-0701
Email: winnieg705@juno.com
Commendation: Grace Gospel Chapel, FL, 1986
Ministry: Children's Ministry, Evangelism, Literature
Other Info: Widow of Commended Worker, Senior Worker (65+)

Kenneth Hampton
5440 Oakman Blvd, Detroit, MI 48204
Phone: 313-933-9322
Website: www.kenhampton.org
Ministry: Preaching

Bruce and Anna Henning
18494 Fenton St, Detroit, MI 48219
Email: brucehenning@gmail.com
Commendation: Carriage Hill Bible Chapel, MI, 2006
Ministry: Evangelism, Teaching

Robert and Sharon Johnston
18780 Riverside Glen Dr, Macomb, MI 48044-4216
Phone: 586-412-3349 **Fax:** 586-247-7920
Email: dr_rjohnston@yahoo.com
Commendation: Laurel Bible Chapel, CA, 1965
Ministry: Counseling, Preaching

Lucy Kieft
1439-43rd St SW, Wyoming, MI 49505-4367
Phone: 616-365-9372
Email: LucyKieft@voyager.net
Ministry: Discipleship, Senior's Ministry

Dwight and Stephanie Knight
14140 Abington Ave, Detroit, MI 48227
Phone: 313272-6441
Email: DEK1chall@aol.com
Commendation: University Bible Fellowship
Ministry: Discipleship, Teaching

Rick and Cheryl Larman
4091 Baywood SE, Grand Rapids, MI 49546
Phone: 616-956-6120 **Fax:** 616-942-6829
Email: rick_larman@sbcglobal.net
Commendation: Forest Hills Bible Chapel, MI, 1989
Ministry: Ministry Administration, Pastoral Care

Tom and Laura Lewellen
913 White House Drive, Highland, MI 48356
Phone: 248-877-1647 **Fax:** 248-889-3217
Email: tom@gracecountryside.org
Commendation: Eastfield Chapel, TX
Ministry: Evangelism, Pastoral Care

David and Mary Lo Main
722 Rehoboth Dr NE, Grand Rapids, MI 49505
Commendation: Shelbyville Gospel Chapel, TN, 1991
Ministry: Teaching

Pellam and Marion Love
8897 Rosemont, Detroit, MI 48228-1819
Phone: 313-837-7592
Email: marion837@comcast.net
Commendation: River Rouge Bible Assembly, MI, 1992
Ministry: Pastoral Care, Preaching

Edward and Isabel Maltman
8243 Huntington Ridge Ct., Washington, MI 48094
Phone: 586-713-4996
Email: maltman403@comcast.net
Commendation: Lakeside Bible Chapel, MI, 1984
Ministry: Foreign Missions, Preaching

Tito and Sandra Mantilla
4133 Baywood Dr. SE, Grand Rapids, MI 49546
Phone: 616-464-3570   **Cell:** 214-883-8887
Email: mantilla@sti.net
Commendation: Hillview Bible Chapel, CA, 1991
Ministry: Children's Ministry, Literature Distribution

Ata and Salwa Mikhael
PO Box 445, Hazel Park, MI 48030-0445
Phone: 248-740-9057   **Cell:** 248-740-9057
Email: ata6565@comcast.net
Commendation: Middle East Bible Fellowship, MI, 1991
Ministry: Preaching, Radio Ministry

Arthur and Alice Anne Pearce
19150 Lexington, Redford, MI 48240
Phone: 313-534-6525
Email: artalpearce@aol.com
Commendation: Dunning Park Bible Chapel, 1990
Ministry: Pastoral Care, Women's Ministry

Arthur and Shirley Pfleger
3449 Woodside, Dearborn, MI 48124
Phone: 313-277-3473
Email: artpfleger@drmm.org
Commendation: Dunning Park Bible Chapel, MI, 2002
Ministry: Correspondence Ministry, Ministry Administration

Ross and Lillian Rainey
9257 Caprice Dr, Plymouth, MI 48170-4705
Phone: 734-453-8585
Email: wr.rainey@sbcglobal.net
Commendation: Southside Bible Chapel, MO, 1954; Lake Pointe Bible Chapel, MI, 1970
Ministry: Preaching, Writing and Publishing

Paul and Joanne Rogers
945 Kendalwood NE, Grand Rapids, MI 49505
Phone: 616-447-9088
Email: jtrogers1@juno.com
Commendation: Forest Hills Bible Chapel, 2001
Ministry: Ethnic Ministry, Teaching

Mel and Loie Rykse
688 Scenic Drive, N. Muskegon, MI 49445-9637
Phone: 231-744-8569
Commendation: Friendship Bible Chapel, MI, 1998
Ministry: Foreign Missions, Prison Work

Chris and Barbara Schroeder
PO Box 366, Armada, MI 48005
Cell: 586-615-6700
Commendation: Calvary Bible Chapel, 1998
Ministry: Discipleship, Evangelism

JC Schroeder
P.O. Box 366, Armada, MI 48005
Cell: 586-612-4357
Email: jcschroeder@ymail.com
Commendation: Calvary Bible Chapel, 2008
Ministry: Discipleship, Evangelism, Teacher−Training

Greg Steigelman
57987 Main St, Apt 2, New Haven, MI 48048-2629
Cell: 586-292-2543   **Fax:** 586-784-4143
Commendation: Ross Bible Chapel, OH, 1990
Ministry: Evangelism, Preaching

Bob and Nanci Tissot
12500 Prang St, Jones, MI 49061-9739
Phone: 269-244-5869   **Cell:** 269-720-0233
Fax: 269-244-5016
Email: bob@blbc.com
Commendation: Carriage Hill Bible Chapel, MI, 1989; Coutryside Gospel Chapel, MI, 1989; Grand Haven Gospel Chapel, MI, 1989
Ministry: Camp Ministry, Counseling

George and Frances Washington
29015 Cotton Rd, Chesterfield, MI 48047
Phone: 586-948-1685
Fax: 313-526-7490
Email: metrocommtab@sbcglobal.net
Commendation: Metropolitan Comm. Tabernacle, MI, 1988
Ministry: Pastoral Care

Ruth Watkins
665 Rehoboth, Private, Grand Rapids, MI 49505
Phone: 616-364-3182
Email: Ruthmwatkins@hotmail.com
Commendation: Northwest Gospel Hall, MI 1992
Ministry: Visitation, Women's Ministry

MINNESOTA

Pat Couenhoven
8045 Xerxes Ave S Apt 105, Bloomington, MN 55431-1060
Phone: 952-881-7216
Commendation: Bethany Gospel Chapel, NY, 1948;
Maplewood Bible Chapel, MO, 1948
Ministry: Adult Ministry
Other Info: Widow(er)

Kent and Kim Fraser
2520 Great Divide Road NW, Puposky, MN 56667
Phone: 218-243-2240   **Cell:** 218-556-0770
Email: frasers@paulbunyan.net
Commendation: Lombard Gospel Chapel, IL, 1993
Ministry: Domestic Missions, Radio Ministry

Homer Payne
4200 – 40th Ave, N. Apt 318
Robbinsdale, MN 55441
Phone: 763-533-2736   **Fax:** 763-533-2736
Email: homarp@ssm.net
Commendation: Plymouth Bible Chapel, MN, 1984
Ministry: Counseling, Teaching

Grace Tuininga
Rest Haven Homes, 1424 Union NE, Grand Rapids, MN 49505
Phone: 616-447-0513
Commendation: Longfellow Chapel, NW
Ministry: Adult Ministry

MISSOURI

Dan and Holly Allan
927 S. Harrison Avenue, St. Louis, MO 63122
Phone: 314-909-7673   **Cell:** 314-518-1003
Fax: 314-909-4804
Email: Dan.Allan@uscm.org
Commendation: Jefferson City Bible Chapel, MO, 1990
Ministry: Evangelism, Youth Ministry

Jimmy and Ashley Allan
13783 Maries Rd 301, Vienna, MO 65582
Phone: 573-744-9197
Commendation: Jefferson City Bible Chapel, 2004
Ministry: Camp Ministry, Youth Ministry

COMMENDED WORKERS — MISSOURI

Steve and Karen Allan
13785 Maries Road 301, Vienna, MO 65582-9613
Phone: 573-744-5871
Commendation: Jefferson City Bible Chapel, 1974; Ft. Laudersale Bible Chapel, 1972
Ministry: Camp Ministry, Conference Ministry

Kenneth Bowles
14 Georgetown Court, Union, MO 63084-1111
Phone: 636-583-5975
Email: ken.dl5bk@gmail.com
Commendation: Maplewood Bible Chapel, MO, 1980; Believers Bible Chapel, MO, 1980
Ministry: Radio Ministry, Teaching

Donovan and Carolyn Case
1022 S Point Prairie Rd, Wentzville, MO 63385-4001
Phone: 636-327-5387
Email: onewaydec@aol.com
Commendation: Christian Fellowship Community Chapel, St. Louis, MO, 2006
Ministry: Church Planting, Leadership Development

Alan and Dolly Christensen
13453 Maries Rd #301, Vienna, MO 65582
Phone: 573-301-7484 **Cell:** 573-301-7484
Email: alan@turkeyhillranch.com
Commendation: Downing Avenue Gospel Chapel, 1983-1986; University Bible Fellowship, 1998; Jefferson City Bible Chapel, 2000
Ministry: Camp Ministry, Youth Ministry

Kevin and Cindy Fitzgerald
1287 Meadow Trail Lane, Fenton, MO 63026
Phone: 636-677-0345 **Cell:** 314-323-7538
Email: kcfitz4@yahoo.com
Commendation: Fenton Crossing Bible Chapel, MO, 2001
Ministry: Evangelism, Youth Ministry

Mary Foster
6209 Lorraine Ave, St. Louis, MO 63121-5621
Phone: 314-381-7439
Email: MFoster6209@yahoo.com
Commendation: University City Bible Chapel, MO, 1989
Ministry: Visitation, Women's Ministry

Don and Helen Govan
188 Glen Mary, Jackson, MS 39203-2018
Phone: 601-352-7494 **Cell:** 601-953-8467
Fax: 601-352-7494
Email: govand@bellsouth.net
Commendation: Voice of Calvary Fellowship, MS, 1983
Ministry: Family Ministry, Pastoral Care

Norma Greene
1801 Paul Revere Dr, Cape Girardeau, MO 63701
Phone: 573-334-6590   **Cell:** 573-225-3307
Fax: 573-334-5909
Email: nwg@showme.net
Commendation: West Fifth Bible Chapel, ON, 1952; Cape Bible Chapel, MO
Ministry: Evangelism, Pastoral Care

Randy and Donna Gruber
9188 Eddie & Park Road, St. Louis, MO 63123
Phone: 314-729-1278
Commendation: Fenton Crossing Bible Chapel, MO, 1988
Ministry: Correspondence Ministry, Prison Work

David and Gail Isom
PO Box 4, Ironton, MO 63650
Phone: 573-546-3731   **Fax:** 573-546-373
Email: director@dayspringbiblecamp.org1
Commendation: Marble Hill Bible Chapel, MO, 1994
Ministry: Camp Ministry, Youth Ministry

Nedra Johnson
El Nathan Home, 205 Mayfield Dr, Marble Hill, MO 63764
Phone: 573-238-2564
Commendation: Marble Hill Bible Chapel, MO, 1987
Ministry: Senior's Ministry

Timothy and Liz McNeal
4817 Saint Louis Rock Rd, Villa Ridge, MO 63089-1116
Phone: 636-583-0727
Email: tmtmcnl@aol.com
Commendation: Lake Charles Bible Chapel, MO
Ministry: Evangelism, Preaching

Betty Presson
420 S Kirkwood Road Apt 317, Kirkwood, MO 63122
Phone: 314-909-8451
Commendation: Fenton Crossing Bible Chapel, MO
Ministry: Senior's Ministry, Visitation

Ross and Lucille Ragland
4916 S. Forest Ave, Springfield, MO 65810
Phone: 417-883-5990   **Fax:** 417-883-5990
Email: ROSSANDLU@juno.com
Commendation: Southeast Gospel Chapel, MO, 1997
Ministry: Adult Ministry, Preaching

Matthew Luke Renes
13483 Maries Road 301, Vienna, MO 65582
Cell: 405-317-6088
Email: matthew@turkeyhillranch.com
Commendation: Grace Gospel Chapel, OK, 2007
Ministry: Camp Ministry

Harol and Jean Rowe
108 Park Dr, Fredericktown, MO 63645
Phone: 573-783-4306
Commendation: Lake Charles Bible Chapel, MO, 1991
Ministry: Camp Ministry, Senior's Ministry

David and Josette Talley
809 Fairwick Dr, St Louis, MO 63129
Phone: 314-894-4907
Commendation: North Atlanta Bible Chapel, GA
Ministry: Teaching—School

Mary Wilson
4762 Central School Rd, St. Charles, MO 63304
Phone: 636-928-7053   **Cell:** 314-494-6887
Fax: 636-928-7053
Email: marywilson53@mac.com
Commendation: Grace Christina Fellowship, MO, 1991
Ministry: Adult Ministry
Other Info: Widow(er)

MONTANA

Peter and Louise Daley
484 Grandview Dr, Stevensville, MT 59870
Phone: 406-777-5430
Email: pldaley@juno.com
Commendation: Stevensville Bible Chapel, MT, 1983
Ministry: Foreign Missions, Pastoral Care

Jeff Tackes
2110 Franklin St / PO Box 446, Fort Benton, MT 59442
Phone: 406-622-5383
Email: tackes@yahoo.com
Commendation: Wauwatosa Bible Chapel, WI, 1985
Ministry: Adult Ministry, Camp Ministry, Discipleship, Men's Ministry, Preaching, Teaching

NEW HAMPSHIRE

Stan and Joan Farmer
PO Box 624, Deering, NH 03244-0040
Phone: 603-464-5336   **Cell:** 603-493-2616
Email: Stan@hismansion.com
Commendation: Groton Bible Chapel, CT, 1972
Ministry: Counseling, Preaching

Dave and Diane Hultgren
PO Box 40, Hillsboro, NH 03244-0040
Phone: 603-464-3691
Email: dave@hismansion.com   **Fax:** 603-464-5658
Commendation: Groton Bible Chapel, CT 1984
Ministry: Discipleship, Teaching

Ronald and Laura Ward
68 Berea Rd, Hebron, NH 3241
Phone: 603-744-5206   **Fax:** 603-744-6346
Email: ron@berea.org
Commendation: Groton Bible Chapel, CT, 1977
Ministry: Camp Ministry, Leadership Development

NEW JERSEY

Kingsley and Holly Baehr
1512 Kenyon Ave, S Plainfield, NJ 07080-3731
Phone: 908-757-7598
Email: KBaehr@verizon.net
Commendation: Cedarcroft Bible Chapel, NJ, 1971
Ministry: Preaching, Teaching

Robert Billings
167 Manor Dr., Red Bank, NJ 7701
Phone: 732-758-8463
Email: rebillings@juno.com
Commendation: Bethel Bible Chapel, Red Bank, NJ;
Lakeside Bible Chapel, Sterling Hts., MI, 1981
Ministry: Discipleship, Evangelism

Leonard and Esther Brooks
38 Marcy Dr, Neptune, NJ 07753-3401
Phone: 732-922-8695
Email: lenbrooks@aol.com
Commendation: Woodside Chapel, NJ, 1956
Ministry: Preaching, Teaching

Bill and Jill Cobb
40 Mountain View Drive, West Paterson, NJ 7424
Phone: 973-837-1041   **Cell:** 973-262-1212
Fax: 973-837-1041
Email: jillcobb@yahoo.com
Commendation: Big Apple Chapel, NY, 1990
Ministry: Leadership Development, Preaching

Gerard and Mickie DeMatteo
102 E Van Ness Ave, Rutherford, NJ 07070-1834
Phone: 201-933-2867   **Fax:** 201-933-5048
Email: RBC161@gmail.com
Commendation: Rutherford Bible Chapel, NJ, 1991
Ministry: Discipleship, Preaching

Donald and Diana Dunkerton
112 Cranford Ave, Cranford, NJ 07016-2408
Phone: 908-709-1373
Commendation: Kenilworth Gospel Chapel, NJ, 1991;
LaGrange Gospel Chapel, IL, 1971
Ministry: Children's Ministry, Pastoral Care

Scott Dunkerton
454 Maplewood Avenue, Roselle Park, NJ 7204
Cell: 845-270-0509
Email: ScottDunkerton@gmail.com
Commendation: Kenilworth Gospel Chapel, NJ, 2003
Ministry: Discipleship, Preaching

Carmen Harris
57 Gamewell Lane, Willingboro, NJ 8046
Phone: 609-871-8612   **Cell:** 609-284-8292
Email: HLVME2@aol.com
Commendation: Germantown Christian Assembly, PA, 1986
Ministry: Children's Ministry, Radio Ministry

Bob and Judy Hayes
15 Goffle Hill Road, Hawthorne, NJ 07506-2832
Phone: 973-423-2803
Email: bobhayes@valleybiblechapel.org
Commendation: Valley Bible Chapel, NJ, 2004
Ministry: Pastoral Care, Teaching

Mark and Cynthia Kolchin
735 Hill Street, Lanoka Harbor, NJ 8734
Phone: 609-693-3464   **Cell:** 609-709-3220
Email: mkolchin@comcast.net
Commendation: Bethany Bible Chapel, NJ, 1993
Ministry: Adult Ministry, Conference Ministry,
Counseling, Elder, Ministry Administration, Preaching,
Teaching, Visitation, Writing and Publishing

James and Anita VarnHagen
1561 Rahway Road, Scotch Plains, NJ 7076
Phone: 908-561-1348 **Cell:** 908-447-9640
Fax: 908-226-1371
Email: mcmission@aol.com
Commendation: Dunning Park Chapel, MI 1978
Ministry: Domestic Missions, Ministry Administration

Thomas and Ruth Wilson
1 Andes Ct, Brick, NJ 8724
Phone: 732-836-3386
Email: rutom55@aol.com
Commendation: Fifth Avenue Chapel, NJ, 1971
Ministry: Pastoral Care, Preaching

Melvin and Helen Wistner
344 Ackerman Avenue, Mountainside, NJ 07092-1314
Phone: 908-928-0665
Commendation: Terrill Road Bible Chapel, NJ, 1946;
Evanston Chapel, IL, 1945
Ministry: Adult Ministry, Preaching

NEW MEXICO

Jeff and Alyce Bloom
5113 Highway 180 Box 265, Glenwood, NM 88039
Phone: 575-539-2197 **Cell:** 713-966-0197
Email: jeffandalyce@juno.com
Commendation: Zion Christian Assembly, 1979, First
Colony Bible Chapel, TX, 2000
Ministry: Camp Ministry, Conference Ministry, Preaching

NEW YORK

Randal and Sylvia Amos
38 Archer Rd., Rochester, NY 14624
Phone: 585-889-9737 **Cell:** 585-317-8897
Email: amos@sheepfood.com
Commendation: Linwood Gospel Chapel NJ, 1980;
Northgate Bible Chapel NY, 1990
Ministry: Preaching

Margaret Bitler
22 McCollum Place, Yonkers, NY 10704
Phone: 914-237-1379

David and Meryl Collins
40 Ransom Ave, Sea Cliff, NY 11579-2023
Phone: 516-759-2840 **Cell:** 516-509-2535
Email: davidcollins@seacliffchapel.org
Commendation: Sea Cliff Gospel Chapel, NY, 1978
Ministry: Pastoral Care, Preaching

John and Wendy Fraser
579 Logan St, Brooklyn, NY 11208
Phone: 347-350-9459 **Cell:** 347-254-3264
Email: CHAPTER13J@aol.com
Commendation: Bethany Gospel Chapel, NY, 2001
Ministry: Discipleship, Leadership Development

Charles and Mary Gianotti
27 Watchman Ct, Rochester, NY 14624-4930
Phone: 585-429-5435
Email: ChuckGianotti@hotmail.com
Commendation: Auburn Bible Chapel, ON, 1995; Thorold South Chapel, ON, 1983
Ministry: Camp Ministry, Discipleship, Literature, Pastoral Care, Preaching, Teaching

Ruth Rodger
445 Stearns Road, Churchville, NY 14428
Phone: 585-538-6658 **Cell:** 585-733-5197
Email: Rurodger@aol.com
Commendation: Cornerstone Bible Chapel, NY, 1973
Ministry: Women's Ministry

Henry and Sara Sanchez
76-15 58th Rd, Queens, NY 11379
Phone: 718-457-7194
Commendation: Evergreen Gospel Chapel, NY, 1964
Ministry: Pastoral Care, Preaching

Eric Smith
PO Box 496, Altamont, NY 12009-0496
Phone: 518-861-6486 **Cell:** 518-207-7491
Email: savebygracettt@yahoo.com
Commendation: Bellevue Gospel Chapel
Ministry: Discipleship, Evangelism, Teaching

James and Margaret Smith
#101-670 Northridge Dr, Lewiston, NY 14092-2387
Phone: 716-754-2456
Email: JNS1930@email.msn.com
Commendation: Oakwood Gospel Hall, ON, 1954; Niagara Falls Gospel Hall, Canada
Ministry: Evangelism, Teaching

Robert and Willene Spicer
90 Hilton Blvd, Amherst, NY 14226-1415
Phone: 716-837-7946
Email: rwspicer1@verizon.net
Commendation: Albany Gospel Chapel, GA, 1964
Ministry: Pastoral Care, Preaching

David and Ruth Stiefler
4 Marlowe Ave, Blasdell, NY 14219-1720
Phone: 716-823-2951   **Cell:** 267-614-1888
Email: drstiefler@gmail.com
Commendation: Blasdell Gospel Chapel, NY, 1959
Ministry: Camp Ministry, Preaching

Otis and Geraldine Tillman
461 Master Ave PO Box 134, Buffalo, NY 14209-0134
Phone: 716-883-5327
Commendation: Amherst Bible Chapel, NY, 1966
Ministry: Discipleship, Preaching

Terry and Shirley Wilson
Camp Li-Lo-Li, 8811 Sunfish Run Road, Randolph, NY 14772
Cell: 209-814-6957
Email: tewilson3@gmail.com
Commendation: Fifth Ave Chapel, Belmar NJ, 2009
Ministry: Camp Ministry, Teaching

Jean Young
6151 Hess Rd, Belmont, NY 14813
Phone: 585-268-5849
Email: jmycc@novocon.net
Commendation: Village Church of Oak Park, IL, 1976
Ministry: Visitation, Women's Ministry

NORTH CAROLINA

Robert and Ruby Adcock
3710 Kenmore Drive, Durham, NC 27705
Phone: 919-477-1120
Commendation: Northgate Chapel, NC, 1975
Ministry: Elder, Pastoral Care

Charles and Carol Baker
2923 Chestnut Ridge Church Rd, Efland, NC 27243
Phone: 919-304-0595   **Fax:** 919-548-8158
Email: charlesbaker008@mebtel.net
Commendation: Grove Park Chapel, NC, 1991; Gospel Center, NC, 1973
Ministry: Senior's Ministry

COMMENDED WORKERS — NORTH CAROLINA

Gerald and Kim Baker
1825 East Street, Pittsboro, NC 27312
Phone: 919-545-9876
Email: gkbaker6@embarqmail.com
Commendation: Fayetteville Bible Chapel, NC, 2006
Ministry: Ministry Administration, Senior's Ministry

Evelyn Barclay
c/o Pittsboro Christian Village, 1825 East St, Pittsboro, NC 27312
Phone: 919-542-1917
Other Info: Senior Worker (65+), Widow of Commended Worker

Signe Carter
Pittsboro Christian Village, 1825 East Street, Pittsboro, NC 27312
Commendation: Northway Bible Chapel, NY, 1979
Ministry: Literature Distribution, Visitation

Mary Decker
2865 Gracefield Ct, Winston Salem, NC 27127-9075
Phone: 336-245-3861
Email: MDCEF@triad.rr.com
Commendation: Parkway Chapel, NC, 1988
Ministry: Children's Ministry, Evangelism

Stuart Greene
7023 Lamar Rd, Fayetteville, NC 28311
Phone: 910-822-5382 **Cell:** 910-987-5382
Email: judsson1@aol.com
Commendation: Fayetteville Bible Chapel, 1985–2000, 2008
Ministry: Camp Ministry, Elder, Preaching, Teaching

Mark and Angela Hartley
3114 Appling Way, Durham, NC 27703-9278
Phone: 919-598-0392 **Cell:** 919-452-4866
Fax: 919-598-0392
Email: here2serve@nc.rr.com
Commendation: NorthGate Chapel, NC, 2008
Ministry: Pastoral Care, Teaching

George and Evelyn Honeycutt
Pittsborough Christian Village, 1825 East St, Pittsboro, NC 27312
Phone: 919-382-2566
Commendation: Northgate Chapel, NC, 1976
Ministry: Camp Ministry, Domestic Missions
Other Info: Senior Worker (65+), Physically Retired

COMMENDED WORKERS — NORTH CAROLINA

Mary King
310 Lafayette St, Wilmington, NC 28411
Phone: 910-686-0501
Email: WE_King@hotmail.com
Commendation: Maplewood Bible Chapel, MO; Gospel Center, NC, 1969
Ministry: Teaching, Women's Ministry

Ron and Wendy Locklear
449 Pine Lake Rd., Pembroke, NC 28372
Phone: 910-521-2870   **Cell:** 910-740-7782
Fax: 910-521-7170
Email: ronlocklear@bellsouth.net
Commendation: Pembroke Family Fellowship, NC, 1994
Ministry: Adult Ministry, Counseling, Family Ministry, Men's Ministry, Pastoral Care, Prison Work, Visitation

Clarence A. Low
Oakhaven Home PO Box 640, Sanford, NC 27330
Cell: 336-692-6209
Commendation: Sanford Chapel, NC, 1949; Asheville Gospel Chapel, 1973
Ministry: Pastoral Care, Preaching
Other Info: Senior Worker (65+), Physically Retired

Alan and Mary Malchuk
610 Pepperidge Road, Lewisville, NC 27023
Phone: 336-945-5906
Commendation: Triad Christian Fellowship, NC, 1999
Ministry: Counseling, Preaching

Elizabeth McKinnie
1825 East St, Pittsboro, NC 27312
Phone: 919-542-4717
Commendation: Brighton Avenue Bible Chapel, NJ, 1959
Ministry: Adult Ministry

J. Phillip and June Morgan
PO Box 58, Maggie Valley, NC 28751-0058
Phone: 828-926-3629   **Cell:** 828-734-2523
Commendation: New Smyrna Bible Chapel, FL, 1963
Ministry: Conference Ministry, Preaching

Margaret Nichols
1825 East Street, Pittsboro, NC 27312-8842
Phone: 919-542-3143
Commendation: Atlantic Gospel Chapel, IA, 1961
Ministry: Foreign Missions

COMMENDED WORKERS — NORTH CAROLINA

Timothy L. Overturf
328 Foster Creek Rd., Swansboro, NC 28584
Phone: 910.325.6403 **Cell:** 910.478.6263
Email: overturffamily@msn.com
Commendation: Trininty Fellowship, Richardson, TX
Ministry: Military Chaplain

Charles Oxendine
10440 Deep Branch Rd, Pembroke, NC 28372-9610
Phone: 910-521-9012 **Cell:** 910-736-2552
Commendation: Carter Road Bible Chapel, NJ, 1971
Ministry: Pastoral Care, Preaching

Frances Pelon
1825 East St, Pittsboro, NC 27312
Phone: 919-542-6922
Email: dfpelon@gmail.com
Commendation: Forest Hills Bible Chapel, 1968; North Raleigh Chapel, 1994
Other Info: Senior Worker (65+), Widow of Commended Worker

Nancy Pirie
1825 East Street, Pittsboro, NC 27312-8842
Phone: 919-545-8843
Email: GJPirie@Juno.com
Commendation: Community Gospel Chapel, NJ, 1981
Other: Widow of Commended Worker

J. Eddie and Louise Schwartz
2146 Herron Rd RR 1, Burlington, NC 27215-9228
Phone: 336-449-5794
Email: jeddieandlouise@touchnc.net
Commendation: Grace Gospel Chapel, VA, 1968; Grace Gospel Chapel, TN, 1968
Ministry: Conference Ministry, Preaching, Teaching

Rod and Amy Sharp
2064 Heidelbury Dr., Winston Salem, NC 27106
Phone: 336-924-4711 **Cell:** 336-345-2880
Email: sharprod2@yahoo.com
Commendation: Slitrig Hall, Hawick, Scotland, 1971; Grove Park Chapel, Durham, NC, 1980
Ministry: Camp Ministry, Children's Ministry, Conference Ministry, Preaching, Teaching

Mark and Kim Shelley
468 East NC 62, Greensboro, NC 27406-9193
Phone: 336-674-9584
Email: mhshelley@juno.com
Commendation: Shannon Hills Bible Chapel, NC, 1993
Ministry: Pastoral Care, Preaching

Jane Smith
1825 East St, Pittsboro, NC 27312
Phone: 919-545-0760   **Cell:** 919-444-3818
Fax: 919-542-5919
Email: jgs-pcv@worldnet.att.net
Commendation: Ireland Street Chapel, NC, 1997
Ministry: Senior's Ministry, Women's Ministry

Tommy and Golda Steele
510 N Garden Ave, Siler City, NC 27344-2902
Phone: 919-663-3346
Commendation: Siler City Chapel, NC, 1963
Ministry: Pastoral Care, Preaching

Rebecca Stephenson
PO Box 1191, Rural Hall, NC 27045-1191
Phone: 336-969-2775
Commendation: Northgate Chapel, NC; Parkway Chapel, NC
Ministry: Prayer Ministry

Rex and Nancy Trogdon
7200 Winslow Drive, Waxhaw, NC 28173-8012
Phone: 704-843-9632   **Cell:** 704-516-4825
Fax: 704-752-1532
Email: Rextrogdon@carolina.rr.com
Commendation: Fairbluff Bible Chapel, 1983; Believers Bible Chapel, 2000
Ministry: Conference Ministry, Shepherding

Bobbie Van Ryn
Pittsboro Christian Village, 1825 E. Street, Pittsboro, NC 27312
Commendation: Bible Truth Chapel, FL, 1961
Ministry: Adult Ministry

OREGON

Gilbert and Sue Gleason
7272 SE Thorburn St, Portland, OR 97215
Phone: 503-255-9563   **Fax:** 503-252-7448
Email: gsgleason@integrity.com
Commendation: Grace Bible Fellowship, OR
Ministry: Pastoral Care, Preaching

Gaius and Linda Goff
3312 Hillcrest Way, Forest Grove, OR 97116-1054
Phone: 503-357-4125
Commendation: Forest Grove Gospel Hall, OR, 1961
Ministry: Evangelism, Preaching

James and Beverly Hislop
16632 SE East View Ct, Portland, OR 97236
Phone: 503-492-8166   **Fax:** 502-698-5315
Email: jhislop@springmountain.org
Commendation: Eastgate Bible Chapel, OR, 1990
Ministry: Elder, Ministry Administration

Rex and Joan Koivisto
12705 SE Sonoma Street, Clackamas, OR 97015
Phone: 503-698-6159   **Fax:** 503-251-6449
Email: rrexk@multnomah.edu
Commendation: Spring Mountain Bible Church, OR, 1981
Ministry: Teaching—School

Timothy Lopez
119 SE 148th Ave, Portland, OR 97233
Phone: 503-408-4945
Email: timinatorlopez@yahoo.com
Commendation: EastGate Bible Chapel, OR, 2008
Ministry: Youth Ministry

Helen Morris
2271 SW Wonderview Dr, Gresham, OR 97080-9510
Phone: 503-665-3517
Commendation: Cascade Community Church, OR, 1983
Ministry: Children's Ministry, Family Ministry
Other Info: Senior Worker (65+), Widow

David and Lois Nelson
51293 NW Strohmayer, Forest Grove, OR 97116-8232
Phone: 503-357-2454
Email: loisn@juno.com
Commendation: Grace and Truth Chapel, OR, 1949; Westside Bible Fellowship, OR
Ministry: Correspondence Ministry

Mike and Sandy Rice
36570 NW Harrington Rd, Cornelius, OR 97113-6315
Phone: 503-648-2838
Email: mikesandyrice@peoplepc.com
Commendation: Westside Bible Fellowship, OR, 1986
Ministry: Literature Distribution, Prison Work

PENNSYLVANIA

Mary Ann Bell
251 Horning Rd, Bethel Park, PA 15102-3043
Phone: 412-833-7858   **Cell:** 412-496-7708
Email: mab.lifeskey@verizon.net
Commendation: Bethel Bible Church, PA, 1993
Ministry: Prison Work

COMMENDED WORKERS — PENNSYLVANIA

Harold and Irene Bermel
1007 Weller Ave, Havertown, PA 19083
Phone: 610-789-6534
Commendation: Lansdowne Bible Chapel, PA, 1978
Ministry: Pastoral Care, Teaching

Alice Buckland
P.O. Box 11869, Philadelphia, PA 19128-4118
Phone: 215-885-0784
Commendation: Roxborough Bible Chapel, PA, 1993
Ministry: Camp Ministry, Youth Ministry

Emmitt and Janice Cornelius
119 Franklin Avenue, Cheltenham, PA 19012
Phone: 215-663-9325   **Fax:** 215-247-5389
Email: servant67@verizon.net
Commendation: Germantown Christian Assembly, 2006
Ministry: Elder, Preaching

Robert and Carolyn Deeds
303 W North St, Waynesboro, PA 17268-1217
Phone: 717-762-8711
Email: bdeeds@innernet.net
Commendation: Riverview Chapel, WV, 1974
Ministry: Children's Ministry, Prison Work

Fred and Anita Garnes
78 Park Blvd, Allentown, PA 18104
Phone: 610-434-2102
Commendation: Montco Bible Fellowship, PA, 2000
Ministry: Discipleship, Pastoral Care

Joseph Ginyard
5722 Woodbine Ave, Philadelphia, PA 19131
Phone: 215-877-1948   **Fax:** 215-477-0492
Email: CalvaryG.C@verizon.net
Commendation: Calvary Gospel Chapel, PA, 1970
Ministry: Pastoral Care, Urban Ministry

Walter and Joan Gustafson
314 Wyndale Dr, Chalfont, PA 18914-3940
Phone: 215-997-1295
Commendation: Cliff St. Gospel Hall, Boston, 1954;
Hatboro Gospel Hall, PA, 1977
Ministry: Adult Ministry, Conference Ministry, Preaching, Writing and Publishing
Other Info: Senior Worker (65+)

David Harper
10194 William Penn Rd, Imler, PA 16655
Phone: 814-276-3012
Email: dsh@bedford.net
Commendation: East Freedom Chapel, PA, 1986
Ministry: Elder, Teaching

Andrew Hart
1625 Latchstring Lane, Hatfield, PA 19440
Phone: 717-557-4730

Charles and Dilys Hart
6921 Anderson St, Philadelphia, PA 19119-1313
Phone: 215-248-4112 **Cell:** 215-776-4690
Email: cdihart@comcast.com
Commendation: Germantown Christian Assembly, PA, 1993
Ministry: Pastoral Care, Writing and Publishing

Sam Hart
777 DeKalb Pike Apt 114, Blue Bell, PA 19422

Tony and Carol Hart
1625 Latch Spring Lane, Hatfield, PA 19440
Phone: 215-412-2313
Commendation: Montco Bible Fellowship, PA, 2004
Ministry: Pastoral Care, Radio Ministry

Steve and Alice Herzig
8 Scarlet Oak Rd, Levittown, PA 19056
Phone: 215-269-1877
Email: sherzig@foi.org
Commendation: Arlington Countryside Church, IL, 1981; Branford Bible Chapel, CT, 1979; West Woods Bible Chapel, CT, 1979
Ministry: Ministry Administration, Preaching

Stephen Hulshizer
2400 Admire Springs Dr, Dover, PA 17315-4684
Phone: 717-308-2829 **Fax:** 717-467-5927
Email: snh2400@comcast.net
Commendation: North-Ridge Bible Chapel 1983
Ministry: Literature, Preaching, Teaching
Other Info: Senior Worker (65+)

Janet Nickel
1440 Walnut St Apt 1908, Allentown, PA 18102-4446
Phone: 610-351-1071
Email: jan5cents@gmail.com
Commendation: Grace Gospel Chapel, PA, 1963
Ministry: Prison Work, Senior's Ministry
Other Info: Physically Retired

COMMENDED WORKERS — PENNSYLVANIA

David and Melody Oliver
105 Landover Rd, Bryn Mawr, PA 19010-3702
Phone: 610-525-1555 **Fax:** 610-525-9961
Email: david@oliver.net
Commendation: Bryn Mawr Gospel Hall, PA, 1974
Ministry: Evangelism, Preaching

Maureen Ramroop
997 N. 66th St, Philadelphia, PA 19151
Phone: 215-878-6876   **Cell:** 267-269-8477
Fax: 215-477-0492
Email: calvarygc@verizon.net or mrramroop@yahoo.com
Commendation: Calvary Gospel Chapel, PA, 1988
Ministry: Counseling, Urban Ministry

Mark and Roberta Redka
144 Pine Street, Jefferson, PA 15344-9702
Phone: 724-883-2086   **Cell:** 724-833-4335
Email: Marknbert@juno.com
Commendation: Wayneburg Bible Chapel, PA, 1989
Ministry: Camp Ministry, Children's Ministry

Jeff and Deanne Rush
899 Linck Hill Road, Morris, PA 16938
Phone: 570-353-2007
Email: rushfam@ptd.net
Commendation: Living Hope Community Church, PA, 1984
Ministry: Camp Ministry, Youth Ministry

Daniel and Esther Sawyer
5431 Discher St, Philadelphia, PA 19124
Phone: 215-537-5424
Email: desawyer1@verizon.net
Commendation: Calvary Gospel Chapel, PA, 1998
Ministry: Evangelism, Pastoral Care

Douglas and Marianne Schuster
120 Glendale Rd, Upper Darby, PA 19082-3108
Phone: 610-352-5383
Email: dmschuster@juno.com
Commendation: Collingdale Gospel Chapel, PA, 1987
Ministry: Children's Ministry, Correspondence Ministry

Lorraine Stirneman
427 Wellesley Rd, Philadelphia, PA 19119-2908
Phone: 215-247-0967
Email: lcstirneman@juno.com
Ministry: Teacher—Training, Urban Ministry

Beatrice Stocker
200 W Mt Carmel Ave, Glenside, PA 19038-3407
Phone: 215-887-0535   **Cell:** 215-837-5191
Email: Bealine1@juno.com
Commendation: Germantown Christian Assembly, PA, 1989
Ministry: Counseling, Urban Ministry

James and Ruth VanDuzer
5141 Oakland Rd, Slatington, PA 18080-4143
Phone: 610-262-1617
Email: grandpajim@vanduzer.us
Commendation: Grace Gospel Chapel, PA, 1974
Ministry: Camp Ministry, Preaching

Christine Wigden
427 Wellesley Rd, Philadelphia, PA 19119-2908
Phone: 215-247-0967
Email: clwigden6@aol.com
Ministry: Children's Ministry, Urban Ministry

James and Roma Yorgey
31 Pine Way, Fayetteville, PA 17222-9511
Phone: 717-352-8998   **Cell:** 717357-6712
Fax: 717-352-8998
Email: jimyorgey@comcast.net
Commendation: Rosemount Bible Church, PA, 1987
Ministry: Counseling, Prison Work

RHODE ISLAND

David and Margaret Reid
94 Bradford Rd, Bradford, RI 2808
Phone: 401-377-2925   **Fax:** 401-377-2944
Email: drdavegcm@aol.com
Commendation: Terrill Road Bible Chapel, 1973; Northern Hills Bible Chapel, OH, 1973
Ministry: Preaching, Radio Ministry

Paul and Joan Shaw
47 Fountain Ave, Barrington, RI 02806-1429
Phone: 401-246-1192
Commendation: Buttonwoods Bible Chapel, RI, 1965; Swanse Bethany Gospel Chapel, 1965; New Bedford Gospel Hall, 1965
Ministry: Preaching, Prison Work

Alan Parks
1805 Windmere Way, Myrtle Beach, SC 29575
Ministry: Evangelism, Music Ministry, Teaching

David and Doris Rickert
1513 Jenkins Dr, Conway, SC 29527-4740
Phone: 843-248-3488
Email: drickert@sc.rr.com
Commendation: New Life Bible Chapel, PA, 1973; Bethany Bible Chapel, SC, 1994
Ministry: Pastoral Care, Preaching

SOUTH CAROLINA

Larry and Phyllis Deeds
PO Box 2066, Conway, SC 29528-2066
Phone: 843-369-5665 **Cell:** 843-450-7414
Fax: 843-369-7731
Email: bethanyb@sccoast.net
Commendation: Riverview Chapel, WV, 1996; Bethany Bible Chapel, SC, 1997
Ministry: Children's Ministry, Teaching

Larry and Linda Dixon
117 Norse Way, Columbia, SC 29229
Phone: 803-736-8482
Email: ldixon@ciu.edu
Commendation: Ireland Street Chapel, NC, 1997; Woodland Hills Comm. Church, 2004
Ministry: Teaching—School, Writing and Publishing

Dottie Few
3619 Hanson Avenue, Columbia, SC 29204-3507
Phone: 803787-1588
Commendation: Woodland Hills Community Church, SC
Ministry: Adult Ministry

William and Barbara Gustafson
1816 Curtis Dr, North Augusta, SC 29841-2205
Phone: 803-202 0080 **Cell:** 706-338-1125
Email: williamgustafson@bellsouth.net
Commendation: Bethany Chapel, GA, 1997
Ministry: Preaching, Teaching

Fred and Jenny Kosin
2408 Bennett Dr, Darlington, SC 29532-8130
Phone: 843-393-5936 **Cell:** 843-617-1938
Email: fkosin@aol.com
Commendation: Bethany Gospel Chapel, CA, 1966; Woodside Chapel, NJ, 1973
Ministry: Foreign Missions, Pastoral Care

COMMENDED WORKERS — SOUTH CAROLINA

Roy and Tracey Kosin
5444 Deere Drive, Conway, SC 29527
Phone: 843-397-5510
Commendation: Community Bible Fellowship, SC, 2004
Ministry: Teaching, Youth Ministry

Ray and Gail Moore
2025 Cedar Springs Rd, Blythewood, SC 29016
Phone: 803-714-1744 **Cell:** 803-237-8680
Fax: 803-714-0889
Email: moorefam@bellsouth.net
Ministry: Family Ministry, Teaching

Eric and Denise Shelley
3007 Boxwood Avenue, Florence, SC 29501
Phone: 843-629-9218 **Cell:** 843-601-0823
Email: ericshelley@juno.com
Commendation: Florence Bible Chapel, 2008
Ministry: Pastoral Care, Preaching

Ernest and Lovie Singleton
1460 Woodview Ln, Charleston, SC 29412-8136
Phone: 843-795-4559
Commendation: Grace Tabernacle, SC, 1959
Ministry: Elder, Pastoral Care

Marian Snyder
1102 Holiday Drive, North Augusta, SC 29841
Phone: 803 279-0931 **Cell:** 803 474-3225
Email: snyderwj@juno.com
Commendation: River Forest Bible Chapel, IL, 1970; Grace Gospel Chapel, Plumesteadville, PA, 1974; North Augusta Bible Chapel, SC, 2003
Other Info: Senior Worker (65+), Widow of Commended Worker

Nate and April Thomas
106 Willie Mae Ct., Anderson, SC 29626
Phone: 864-222-9824 **Cell:** 864-933-5527
Email: puppetman01@bellsouth.net
Commendation: Concord Community Church
Ministry: Children's Ministry

Sedrick Singleton
1460 Woodview Lane, Charleston, SC 29412-8136
Phone: 843-795-4559
Commendation: Grace Tabernacle, SC
Ministry: Children's Ministry, Preaching

SOUTH DAKOTA

Larry and Natalie Sax
1501 12th Street South, Brookings, SD 57006
Phone: 605-692-5069 **Cell:** 605-759-5781
Email: larryasax@gmail.com
Commendation: Ortonville Bible Fellowship, 2006; Sioux Falls Christian Assembly, 2009
Ministry: Church Planting, Discipleship, Evangelism

TENNESSEE

Ed and Barbara Anthony
109 Woodside Ct, Old Hickory, TN 37138
Phone: 615-847-8745 **Cell:** 615-972-5754
Fax: 615-847-8745
Email: heavenslink@bellsouth.net
Commendation: Westville, New Haven, CT, 2005; Gospel Chapel, Believers Fellowship, Nashville, TN, 2005; Cumberland, Summerfield, TN, 2005
Ministry: Adult Ministry, Camp Ministry, Conference Ministry, Men's Ministry, Teaching, Teaching—School, Writing and Publishing

Kurt and Marsha Dibble
2049 Ft. Robinson Dr, Kingsport, TN 37660-3046
Phone: 423-245-9707
Commendation: Fairbluff Bible Chapel, NC, 1993
Ministry: Children's Ministry, Teaching

Benjamin and Louise Johnson
6301 West Minister Dr, Nashville, TN 37221-3725
Phone: (615-370-5695
Commendation: Christ Community Church, IL 1987
Ministry: Counseling, Teaching

Kevin and Christy King
3663 Reed Harris Rd, Lewisburg, TN 37091
Phone: 931-364-7552 **Cell:** 931-580-6970
Fax: 931-364-3039
Email: kevin@hortonhaven.org
Commendation: Christian Believers Fellowship, TN, 1993
Ministry: Camp Ministry, Youth Ministry

Kelton and Sharon Meyer
1533 Boone Ct, Murfreesboro, TN 37130
Phone: 615-896-3637   **Cell:** 931-808-2782
Fax: 931-364-3039
Email: kelton@hortonhaven.org
Commendation: New Heights Chapel (College Heights Chapel), 1984
Ministry: Camp Ministry

John and Mary Lou Phelan, Sr.
7530 Charlotte Rd, Nashville, TN 37209-5202
Phone: 615-352-1745   **Cell:** 615-714-6226
Fax: 615-353-1745
Commendation: Gospel Chapel, TN, 1965
Ministry: Camp Ministry, Pastoral Care

Matthew and Wendy Phelan
3636 Reed Harris Rd, Lewisburg, TN 37091
Phone: 931-364-4675   **Cell:** 615-714-9584
Fax: 931-364-3039
Email: matt@hortonhaven.org
Commendation: Gospel Chapel, TN, 1995
Ministry: Camp Ministry, Youth Ministry

Glenn Tompkins
384 Point Lane, Walling, TN 38587
Phone: 931-761-5067   **Cell:** 931-409-5151
Email: gtompkins@juno.com
Commendation: Cumberland Bible Chapel, TN, 2006; Northway Bible Chapel, NY, 1975
Ministry: Teaching, Writing and Publishing

Patrick and Myrtle Warner
7052 Northridge Dr, Nashville, TN 37221-0768
Phone: 615-662-7595   **Cell:** 615-210-3789
Fax: 615-244-4373
Email: PEWARNER1@comcast.net
Commendation: Gospel Chapel, TN, 2000
Ministry: Elder, Teaching

TEXAS

Bob and Susan Abegg
4314 Travis St. #206, Dallas, TX 75205
Phone: 214-335-7027
Email: babegg@compuserve.com
Commendation: Eastfield Bible Chapel, TX, 1984
Ministry: Pastoral Care, Preaching

Mary Joyce Clark
12322 Pine Knoll Dr, Houston, TX 77099-2414
Phone: 281-495-9595
Commendation: Maplewood Bible Chapel, NJ, 1957; Kenilworth Gospel Chapel, NJ, 1957
Ministry: Children's Ministry, Women's Ministry

Chad Clarkson
2018 Island Manor Lane, League City, TX 77573
Phone: 281-557-1199 **Cell:** 281-309-8930
Email: chadclarkson@comcast.net
Commendation: Cornerstone Community Church ,1998
Ministry: Church Planting, Leadership Development

John and Marilyn Daniels
1815 Mimosa Ave, Plano, TX 75074-5070
Phone: 972-424-9889
Commendation: Garland Bible Chapel, TX, 1986
Ministry: Preaching, Prison Work

Maria Darling
11619 Stroud, Houston, TX 77072-2441
Phone: 218-498-2020
Email: larry370@sbcglobal.net
Commendation: Grand Haven Gospel Chapel, MI, 1957; Manvel Bible Chapel, TX
Ministry: Prison Work, Radio Ministry, Women's Ministry

Daniel and Ester Di Cesare
9403 Beverly Hill St, Houston, TX 77063
Phone: 832-252-1859 **Cell:** 281-827-3397
Fax: 281-340-2404
Email: danielyester@hotmail.com
Commendation: Spanish Bible Fellowship, TX, 1975
Ministry: Pastoral Care, Preaching

Kenneth Engle
c/o Stewards Foundation, 14285 Midway Road Ste 330, Addison, TX 75001-3622
Phone: 785-263-4640
Commendation: Grace and Truth Gospel Chapel, KS, 1950
Ministry: Music Ministry, Radio Ministry

John Ferris
3928 Willow Run, Flower Mound, TX 75028
Phone: 972-539-8702 **Fax:** 972-708-7387
Email: ferristx@juno.com
Commendation: Bethany Chapel, NY, 1967
Ministry: Foreign Missions, Teaching

Jack and Karen Faulkner
5051 Prayer Lane, Washington, TX 77880-9716
Phone: 979-251-7586 **Fax:** 979-830-0400
Email: sandycreekbiblecamp@direcway.com
Commendation: Brookwood Bible Chapel, TX, 1988
Ministry: Camp Ministry, Preaching

John and Cindy Goodding
2 Circle Rd, Longview, TX 75602-4820
Phone: 903-757-2904 **Cell:** 903-241-3481
Email: JGoodding@gmail.com
Commendation: Cypress Valley Bible Church, TX, 1982
Ministry: Elder, Writing and Publishing

George and Danielle Hanson
309 Saddlebrook Drive, Garland, TX 75044-5073
Phone: 214-703-0811 **Cell:** 469-853-5286
Fax: 972-494-7202
Email: george.hanson@gimail.af.mil
Commendation: Community Bible Chapel, TX, 1986
Ministry: Adult Ministry, Military Chaplain

Alexander Kurian
1405 Laguna Vista Way, Grapevine, TX 76051
Phone: 682-223-1237 **Cell:** 817-680-9973
Email: alexkgkurian@gmail.com
Commendation: Edmonds Lane Bible Chapel, 2005
Ministry: Conference Ministry, Counseling, Discipleship, Foreign Missions, Leadership Development, Literature, Preaching, Teacher—Training, Teaching, Writing and Publishing

Daniel and Ruth Martin
12425 W Bellfort, Sugar Land, TX 77478
Phone: 281-240-1907 **Fax:** 281-340-2404
Email: danyruth@peoplepc.com
Commendation: Spanish Bible Fellowship, TX, 1974
Ministry: Counseling, Pastoral Care

Robert and Ruthie Matthews
2664 Aster Drive, Richardson, TX 75082
Phone: 972-231-1932 **Fax:** 972-422-7036
Commendation: Plan Bible Chapel, TX, 1988
Ministry: Pastoral Care, Teaching

Edwin and Mary Ellen Meschkat
210 Sooner St, Wolfforth, TX 79382-5300
Phone: 806-866-9933
Email: emeschkat@aol.com
Commendation: Manvel Bible Chapel, TX, 1963
Ministry: Pastoral Care, Teaching
Other Info: Senior Worker (65+)

Doug and Joy Moore
27007 Picolo Place, San Antonio, TX 78260
Phone: 830-980-5480   **Cell:** 210-262-5025
Email: dougLessmoore@gmail.com
Commendation: South Potomac Church, MD 1991
Ministry: Evangelism

Ralph Nichols
3620 Longcourt Cr, Mesquite, TX 75150-4365
Phone: 972-270-4781
Email: writewaypm@verizon.net
Commendation: Christ Congregation, TX, 1987
Ministry: Correspondence Ministry, Prison Work

Michael O'Donnell
PO Box 793, San Antonio, TX 78293
Phone: 210-521-7248
Email: brush2@earthlink.net
Commendation: Cheryl Bible Chapel, TX, 2000
Ministry: Hospital Chaplain, Preaching

Richard and Beth Plowman
3101 Pioneer, Waco, TX 76712-9643
Phone: 254-848-5864   **Cell:** 254-717-0285
Fax: 254-848-5864
Email: DPlowman@hot.RR.com
Commendation: Waco Bible Chapel, TX 1992
Ministry: Evangelism, Urban Ministry

Bruce and Lee Ann Postma
1507 Brook Hollow Dr, Bryan, TX 77802-1118
Phone: 979- 822-6758   **Cell:** 979-268-1278
Email: bruce.postma@usarmy.mil
Commendation: Centerpoint Church, TX
Ministry: Military Chaplain

Omar and Dora Rios
5822 Windy Knoll Lane, Rosharon, TX 77583-2058
Phone: 281-431-2379   **Cell:** 832-668-4399
Fax: 281-431-2379
Email: riossanfilippo@gmail.com
Commendation: Inglesia Cristiana Evangelica Comunidade de Amor, TX, 1993
Ministry: Counseling, Ethnic Ministry

John and Lydia Rodgers
4302 Fm 1128 Rd, Pearland, TX 77584-7528
Phone: 979-251-2374
Email: johnandlydiar@aol.com
Commendation: Garland Bible Chapel, TX, 1980
Ministry: Correspondence Ministry, Senior's Ministry
Other Info: Senior Worker (65+)

Jeremiah D. Snyder
1302 S Crockett Street, Sherman, TX 75090
Cell: 214 274-3337
Email: jsnyder09@juno.com
Commendation: Community Bible Chapel, 2006
Ministry: Chaplain

Thomas Wheeler
8502 Deer Meadow Dr, Houston, TX 77071
Phone: 713-773-0788
Commendation: Southside Bible Chapel, LA, 2002
Ministry: Conference Ministry, Teaching

Ernest and Joy Woodhouse
13710 Hunters Hawk, San Antonio, TX 78230
Phone: 352-473-2644
Email: ejwfl@aol.com
Commendation: New John's Street Gospel Hall, England; Park of the Palms, 1984
Ministry: Pastoral Care, Teaching

VIRGINIA

Tim and Erika Blessman
28 Ashwood Trail, Woolwine, VA 24185
Phone: 276-930-1963   **Cell:** 276-734-1141
Email: timman@swva.net
Commendation: Oxford Bible Chapel, Oxford, PA 1997
Ministry: Camp Ministry, Family Ministry

Jonathan and Betty Brower
1065 Stoney Mill Rd., Danville, VA 24540
Phone: 434-548-3765   **Cell:** 434489-1523
Email: jbrower@chatmosscable.com
Commendation: Bible Truth Chapel, FL, 1983
Ministry: Discipleship, Teaching

David and Norma Dewhurst
307 Paul Revere Drive, Forest, VA 24551
Email: wddew@juno.com
Commendation: Andover Bible Chapel, MA, 1990
Ministry: Ministry Administration, Senior's Ministry

John and Pat Hand
107 Bethel Campgrounds Road, Woolwine, VA 24185-0071
Phone: 276-930-4289
Commendation: Fleming Chapel, VA, 1993
Ministry: Camp Ministry, Preaching

Daniel and Jacqueline Rodriguez
3426 Flint Hill Place, Woodbridge, VA 22192
Phone: 703-494-1436 **Fax:** 703-494-1436
Email: cleanwaters@comcast.net
Commendation: Cherrydale Bible Church, VA
Ministry: Counseling

Andrew and Michelle Shelor
6113 Bent Mountain Road, Roanoke, VA 24018
Phone: 540-774-4047
Email: DouloiChristou@cox.net
Commendation: Fleming Chapel, VA, 2002
Ministry: Camp Ministry, Preaching, Teaching

Roberta Shelor
4621 Heather Drive #209, Roanoke, VA 24018
Phone: 540-989-3453
Email: rwshelor@verizon.net
Commendation: Commended from Shannon Hills, Greensboro, 1980
Other Info: Widow of Commended Worker, Physically Retired

Martin Steinberg
7785 Rogues Rd, Nokesville, VA 20181-5870
Phone: 703-754-4352
Commendation: Cherrydale Bible Church, VA, 1975
Ministry: Children's Ministry, Prison Work

Gerald and Judy Stiles
PO Box 309, Ferrum, VA 24088
Phone: 540-365-7442 **Cell:** 540-493-7441
Email: Docandjudy@kimbanet.com
Commendation: Fleming Chapel, VA, 1973; Waynesville Christian Fellowship, NC, 2005
Ministry: Camp Ministry, Preaching

Jeffrey and Shelley Watters
6010 Katelyn Court, Alexandria, VA 22310
Phone: 703-922-3682 **Cell:** 703-407-1141
Email: Jeffrey.dean.watters@us.army.mil
Ministry: Military Chaplain

WASHINGTON

Mildred Arthur
c/o Rob Arthur, 14514 166th Pl SE, Renton, WA 98059
Phone: 253-927-3216
Commendation: Evergreen Bible Chapel, WA
Ministry: Children's Ministry

Lonita Boettcher
9706-236th Street SW, Edmonds, WA 98020
Phone: 206-801-7678
Email: rlboettcher@comcast.net
Commendation: North Lynnwood Bible Chapel, WA, 1986
Other Info: Widow of Commended Worker

Les and Emma Chopard
815 S. 216th St #64, Des Moines, WA 98198-6332
Phone: 206-870-2064
Commendation: Des Moines Gospel Chapel, WA, 1988
Ministry: Pastoral Care, Senior's Ministry

Patti Cramer
PO Box 98247, Des Moines, WA 98198-6363
Phone: 253-804-6461   Cell: 253-217-9850
Email: patti@dmgc.org
Commendation: Des Moines Gospel Chapel, WA, 2003
Ministry: Children's Ministry

David and Leona Douglas
59404 S. Badger Canyon Rd, Prosser, WA 99350
Cell: 509-392-2806
Email: douglasdoins@gmail.com
Commendation: Tieton Drive Bible Chapel, WA, 1989
Ministry: Adult Ministry, Discipleship

Michael and Alice Jovich
PO Box 310, Clinton, WA 98236-0310
Phone: 360-341-2305
Email: jovich@whidbey.com
Commendation: Des Moines Gospel Chapel, WA, 2008
Ministry: Camp Ministry

Frederick and Lisa McHugh
3389 Wynalda Dr, Enumclaw, WA 98022-6414
Phone: 360-802-0799   Cell: 253-797-0561
Fax: 253-804-2812
Email: fred.mchugh@uhsinc.com
Commendation: Rohnert Park Bible Church, CA, 1984
Ministry: Discipleship, Hospital Chaplain

Kevin and Laurel Rasmussen
PO Box 310, Clinton, WA 98236
Phone: 360-341-4176   Cell: 425-754-7938
Fax: 360-341-2311
Email: kevinraz@lakesidebiblecamp.org
Commendation: Bethany Chapel, Wheaton, IL, 2008
Ministry: Camp Ministry

Mac and Mindy Sauerlender
PO Box 98247, Des Moines, WA 98198-6363
Phone: 206-870-0327   **Fax:** 206-878-3306
Email: mac@dmgc.org
Commendation: Des Moines Gospel Chapel, WA, 1988
Ministry: Adult Ministry, Elder

Harv and Jane Stewart
1411 Westview Place, Lynden, WA 98264
Phone: 360-393-3990   **Cell:** 360-393-5232
Email: hjstuartin@cs.com
Commendation: Westlock Gospel Chapel, Alberta, 1993
Ministry: Church Planting, Domestic Missions, Foreign Missions

Gordon and Margaret Strom
655 Kalmia Pl NW, Issaquah, WA 98027
Phone: 206-313-5006   **Cell:** 425-894-2750
Fax: 206-243-7002
Email: Gmstrom@comcast.net
Commendation: Northgate Bible Chapel, WA, 1997
Ministry: Hospital Chaplain, Pastoral Care

Michael and Evangelina Vederoff
2510 NE 168th, Lake Forest Park, WA 98155
Phone: 206-729-0747   **Cell:** 206-892-0052
Email: hopebiblefellowship@juno.com
Ministry: Pastoral Care, Teaching

WEST VIRGINIA

David and Ann Pollock
PO Box 7, Mullens, WV 25882-0007
Phone: 304-294-4350   **Cell:** 304-294-4355
Email: davidgpollock@yahoo.com
Commendation: Riverview Chapel, WV, 1966; Welton Bible Chapel, WV, 1966
Ministry: Evangelism, Pastoral Care

WISCONSIN

John and Dona Duckhorn
3163 N. 95th St, Milwaukee, WI 53222
Phone: 414-873-5124   **Fax:** 414-771-9150
Email: JustDucky@aol.com
Commendation: Wauwatosa Bible Chapel, WI, 1971
Ministry: Elder, Teaching

Brad and Debi Gaasrud
N2281 Wilmot Blvd, Lake Geneva, WI 53147-2332
Phone: 262-248-5513 **Fax:** 262-248-5511
Email: brad.gaasrud@LGYC.org
Commendation: Arlington Countryside Church, IL, 1994
Ministry: Conference Ministry, Ministry Administration

Tim and Joy Hadley
10 Locust St, Westby, WI 54667
Phone: 608-634-4686 **Fax:** 608-634-3510
Email: timandjoy@lwbc.org
Commendation: Grace & Truth Bible Chapel, WI
Ministry: Camp Ministry, Youth Ministry

Warren and Brenda Henderson
14749 106th Ave, Chippewa Falls, WI 54730
Phone: 715-704-3708
Commendation: Believers Bible Chapel, Rockford, IL, 1997
Ministry: Preaching, Church Planting

Glenn and Ruth Schuman
270 Ridge Road, Apt 317, Walworth, WI 53184
Phone: 262-275-3860
Email: GLSchuman@aol.com
Commendation: Dunning Park Chapel, MI, 1979
Ministry: Foreign Missions
Other Info: Senior Worker (65+), Physically Retired

Dennis and Mary Ann Siler
E8926 Reo Avenue, Westby, WI 54667
Phone: 608-634-4379 **Cell:** 608-606-0608
Fax: 608-634-3510
Email: dennis@lwbc.org
Commendation: Grace & Truth Bible Chapel, Westby, WI 1989
Ministry: Camp Ministry, Youth Ministry

Rachal Siler
E8943 Reo Avenue, Westby, WI 54667
Phone: 608-632-1277 **Fax:** 608-634-3510
Commendation: Grace & Truth Bible Chapel, WI
Ministry: Camp Ministry

Robert and Julie Steiner
111 Woodview Lane, Luxemburg, WI 54217-1361
Phone: 920-845-9356 **Cell:** 920-493-6270
Email: allforhisglory@centurytel.net
Commendation: Country Bible Church, WI 1998
Ministry: Counseling, Elder

Ian and Barbara Taylor
3140-90th St, Kenosha, WI 53142
Phone: 262-697-1383   **Cell:** 262-496-8845
Email: iantaylorgtp@sbcglobal.net
Commendation: Grace Bible Chapel, WI, 2005
Ministry: Conference Ministry, Literature, Preaching, Writing and Publishing
Other Info: Senior Worker (65+)

Gary and Kay Thompson
766 Highview Lane, Kimberly, WI 54136
Phone: 920-687-6353   **Cell:** 920-209-5771
Email: garykaywi@yahoo.com
Commendation: Claremont Bible Chapel (Gospel Chapel then), 1965 to present
Ministry: Elder, Pastoral Care
Other Info: Senior Worker (65+)

Allen and Ellen Thrall
PO Box 204, Marshfield, WI 54449-0204
Phone: 715-384-4944
Email: atetrbc@tznet.com
Commendation: Pineview Bible Chapel, TX, 1992
Ministry: Children's Ministry

Bill and Fayette Van Ryn
2603 E Neupert Aven, Weston, WI 54476
Phone: 715-355-2620   **Cell:** 715-571-7882
Email: wipvanrynkle@verizon.net
Commendation: Bible Truth Chapel, WI, 2006
Ministry: Literature, Teaching, Translation, Writing and Publishing

CANADA

BRITISH COLUMBIA

Tim and Linda Hood
227–2440 Old Okanagan Highway, Westbank, BC V4T 1X6
Phone: 250-768-7741   **Cell:** 250-718-1498
Email: okanaganoutreach@gmail.com
Commendation: Westbank Bible Chapel, 1997
Ministry: Children's Ministry, Church Planting, Discipleship, Domestic Missions, Evangelism, Foreign Missions, Preaching

ONTARIO

Doug and Morven Barnes
50 Watson's Lane, RR#3, Utterson, ON P0B 1M0
Phone: 705-385-1819
Email: dnbarnes@muskoka.com
Commendation: Westmount Gospel Chapel, Toronto, 1972
Ministry: Adult Ministry, Camp Ministry, Pastoral Care, Shepherding, Preaching

Noel and Dwana Bondt
44 Oakwood Street, Port Colborne, ON L3K 5E9
Phone: 289-836-9181   **Fax:** 905-834-8084
Email: nbondt@gmail.com
Commendation: Charlottetown Bible Chapel, PE, 2007
Ministry: Literature

George A. Butcher
32 Laurentian Lane, Orillia, ON L3V 7N8
Phone: 705 323 9164   **Cell:** 705 330 2062
Email: george.butcher@sympatico.ca
Commendation: 1968 & 2005
Ministry: Adult Ministry, Counseling, Elder, Evangelism, Foreign Missions, Pastoral Care, Preaching, Radio Ministry, Teaching, Visitation
Other Info: Senior Worker (65+)

Dr. David Humphreys
3 Highland Park Drive, Dundas, ON L9H 3L7
Phone: 9056274672   **Fax:** 9056274672
Email: davidvivienne@hotmail.com
Commendation: Bethany Gospel Chapel Hamilton 1995
Ministry: Preaching, Teaching

David and Becky Jenkinson
Box 5040, South Porcupine, ON P0N 1K0
Phone: 705-235-3985
Email: daveejenkinson@gmail.com
Commendation: Bible Fellowship Assembly, 2008
Ministry: Adult Ministry, Church Planting, Counseling, Discipleship, Evangelism, Literature, Men's Ministry, Music Ministry, Shepherding, Preaching, Teaching, Visitation, Women's Ministry

Patrick Long
761 Beaupre Avenue, Oshawa, ON
Phone: 905-433-0808   **Cell:** 905-718-5344
Email: patrick.long.38@gmail.com
Ministry: Preaching, Teaching
Other Info: Senior Worker (65+)

Harold and Barbara MacDougall
40 Helen St., Port Colborne, ON L3K 3N9
Phone: 905-834-0646 **Fax:** 905-834-8045
Email: hrm@everydaypublications.org
Commendation: Moncton Gospel Hall, 2003
Ministry: Literature

Jim and Elizabeth Paul
42 Portal Drive, Port Colborne, ON L3K 6G2
Phone: 905 835 0125
Email: jimpaul3@sympatico.ca
Commendation: Uphall Assembly Scotland, 1981; Bridlewood & Rideauview Ottawa Assemblies, 1990
Camp Ministry, Conference Ministry, Evangelism, Hospital Chaplain, Preaching, Ministry: Teaching
Other Info: Senior Worker (65+)

John and Suzanne Sinclair
Box 4063, Station E, Ottawa, ON K1S 5B1
Phone: 819-775-9978
Email: jmsinclair@comnet.ca
Commendation: Groupe Biblique de la Rive-Sud; Longueuil, Quebec; 1986
Ministry: Conference Ministry, Evangelism, Literature, Music Ministry, Prayer Ministry, Preaching, Teaching, Translation, Visitation, Writing and Publishing

Robert and Carolynn Thrall
17 Greenfield Place, New Hamburg, ON N3A 2G6
Phone: 519-662-6976
Email: rthrall6976@rogers.com
Commendation: Wawatosa Bible Chapel, 1960; Rosemount Bible Chapel, 1983
Ministry: Adult Ministry, Conference Ministry, Senior's Ministry
Other Info: Senior Worker (65+)

QUEBEC

Gerald and Marilyn Boisvert
11, rue Boivin, Chateauguay, QC J6J 2Y8
Phone: 450-691-8550 **Cell:** 514-893-8551
Email: gjb@gol.com
Commendation: Thorold South Gospel Chapel, Thorold South, Ontario, 1991
Ministry: Discipleship, Evangelism, Teaching

COMMENDED WORKERS DIRECTORY INDEX

A

Abegg, Bob & Susan, TX
Adcock, Robert, NC
Additon, Kenneth & Sonja, FL
Allan, Dan & Holly, MO
Allan, Jimmy & Ashley, MO
Allison, David & Lorraine, IA
Allan, Steve & Karen, MO

Amos, Randal & Sylvia, NY
Anderson, Don & Dorothy, CO
Anderson, Elmer & Alice, FL
Anthony, Ed & Barbara, TN
Arthur, Mildred, WA
Aston, June, CA
Attwood, Michael & Anne Marie, GA

B

Baehr, Kingsley & Holly, NJ
Bagley, Eldred & Shirley, ID
Bailey, Orrett & Marva, AL
Baker, Charles & Carol, NC
Baker, Gerald & Kim, NC
Barclay, Evelyn, NC
Bauman, Abner & Rosie, IL
Bayreuther, Lloyd & Heidi, CT
Becker, Rich & Zo, IL
Beers, Betty Lou, FL
Beggs, Shirley, CA
Bell, Mary Ann, PA
Bermel, Harold & Irene, PA
Billings, Robert, NJ
Bitler, Margaret, NY
Bjorlie, John & Ann, MI
Blessman, Tim & Erika, VA
Bloom, John & Ruth, AZ

Bloom, Jeff & Alyce, NM
Boettcher, Lonita, WA
Bosworth, Dave & Nancy, FL
Botton, Kenneth & Patty, IL
Boudet, Kathleen, MI
Bourbonnais, John & Catherine, CA
Bowles, Kenneth, MO
Brooks, Leonard & Esther, NJ
Brower, Jonathan & Betty, VA
Brown, David & Ann, IL
Brown, Duane & Alice, IA
Brown, Robert & JoAnne, LA
Bruton, Robert & Jeanne, CA
Buckland, Alice, PA
Buddingh, Gerrit, CA
Burdick, Edward & Peggy, MI
Burson, David & Kristen, FL

C

Cade, Charles & Lydia, MD
Caldenwood, Bruce & Susan, MI
Calderwood, David & Ann, FL
Caldwell, Steve, CA
Callahan, James & Anita, IL
Campbell, Gary & Kristi, CT
Carrera, George & Rosemary, IL
Carter, Signe, NC
Case, Donovan & Carolyn, MO
Catron, Lillian, IA
Chopard, Les & Emma, WA
Christensen, Alan & Dolly, MO
Clark, J. Michael & Margo, MD
Clark, Mary Joyce, TX

Clarkson, Chad, TX
Cobb, Bill & Jill, NJ
Coble, J.C., FL
Cole, Donald & Naomi, IL
Coleman, Geraldine, MI
Collins, Bruce & Geneva, IA
Collins, David & Meryl, NY
Corlew, Dave & Karen, IL
Cornelius, Emmitt & Janice, PA
Couenhoven, Pat, MN
Cowperthwaite, Mark & Sara, ME
Cramer, Patti, WA
Cummings, Ray & Peetsie, LA

COMMENDED WORKERS — INDEX

D

Daley, Peter & Louise, MT
Dallimore, Gerald & Esther, FL
Dandekar, Sheela, MD
Daniels, John & Marilyn, TX
Darling, Maria, TX
Daughters, Kenneth & Carol, IA
Davidson, Barbara, MD
Decker, Mary, NC
Deeds, Robert & Carolyn, PA
Deeds, Larry & Phyllis, SC
DeGroff, Scott & Lynn, KS
Dejong, Timothy & Lorie, GA
DeMatteo, Gerard & Mickie, NJ
Denny, Anne, AZ
Denny, John, KS
Dewhurst, David & Norma, VA
Di Cesare, Daniel & Ester, TX
Dibble, Kurt & Marsha, TN
Dickinson, Edward, CA
Dillon, Pedro & Lucy, CA
Dixon, Larry & Linda, SC
Douglas, David & Leona, WA
Dowell, Tom & Melissa, FL
Duckhorn, John & Dona, WI
Dunham, Warren & Florence, IN
Dunkerton, David & Martha, CO
Dunkerton, James & Carolyn, IA
Dunkerton, Donald & Diana, NJ
Dunkerton, Scott, NJ
Dunlap, David & Faith, FL
DuPlessie, Steve, MA
Dyer, Craig & Anne, IL
Dyer, Kevin & Eloise, IL
Dyer, Mark & Sue, IL

E

Engle, Kenneth, TX
Escarraman, Francisco & Maria, FL

F

Fair, James & Brozine, IL
Farber, George & Gail, IA
Farmer, Stan & Joan, NH
Farquhar, Dann & Nancy, IL
Faulkner, John & Mary, AR
Faulkner, Dan & Teri, CO
Faulkner, Jack & Karen, TX
Ferris, John, TX
Few, Dottie, SC
Fink, Kyle & Allyson, CO
Fippinger, Jay & Dorothy, IA
Fish, Jack, MA
Fish, Jack & Nancy, IA
Fitzgerald, Kevin & Cindy, MO
Fitzhugh, Mike & Nona, MI
Fizer, Charles & Darlene, IA
Fleming, Kenneth & Helena, IA
Flores, Nestor & Magda, GA
Flowers, Michael, GA
Foshager, Mark & Deb, IL
Foster, Mary, MO
Fraser, Kent & Kim, MN
Fraser, John & Wendy, NY
Freeman, Paul & Betty, CA
Fries, Earle & Julie, CA
Fryling, Robert & Alice, IL

G

Gaasrud, Brad & Debi, WI
Garnes, Arthur & Vivian, MD
Garnes, Fred & Anita, PA
Gawley, Ruth, FL
Gay, Winnie, MI
Gianotti, Charles & Mary, NY
Ginyard, Joseph, PA
Giordano, Joseph & Connie, FL
Gladstone, Fred & Mattie, GA
Glass, Craig & Beryl, CO
Gleason, Gilbert & Sue, OR
Glock, David, IA
Goff, Gaius & Linda, OR
Gonzalez, Mariano & Pearl, IL
Goodding, John & Cindy, TX
Govan, Don & Helen, MS
Greene, Norma, MO
Greene, Stuart, NC
Grimes, Kevin & Zoe, CO
Gross, Ken & Pat, GA
Gruber, Randy & Donna, MO
Guikema, Phil & Edna, FL
Gustafson, Walter & Joan, PA
Gustafson, William & Barbara, SC

H

Hadley, Tim & Joy, WI
Haltrich, Helmut & Shirley, FL
Hammond, David & Rose, IA
Hand, John & Pat, VA
Hanson, George & Danielle, TX
Harper, Robert & Jeanette, FL
Harper, Mary Ann, IA
Harper, David, PA
Harris, Carmen, NJ
Hart, Andrew, PA
Hart, Sam, PA
Hart, Charles & Dilys, PA
Hart, Tony & Carol, PA
Hartley, Mark & Angela, NC
Hawkinson, Andrew & Michelle, KS
Hayes, Bob & Judy, NJ
Heeren, Fred & Patty, KS

Henning, Bruce & Anna, MI
Henderson, Warren & Brenda, WI
Hernandez, Joel & Amy, IA
Herzig, Steve & Alice, PA
Heseltine, Jack & Irene, CA
Hislop, James & Beverly, OR
Hollensed, Charlie & Lorna, IL
Hollingsworth, Sue, GA
Holmes, Curtis & Mavis, CO
Honegger, Joel & Melanie, IL
Honeycutt, George & Evelyn, NC
Hook, John & Nancy, ID
Huffman, Kerensa, MD
Hulshizer, Stephen, PA
Hultgren, Dave & Diane, NH
Humes, Justin & Jocelin, ME
Hunter, Georgia, AZ

I

Ice, Cliff & Lee, GA
Irvine, Robert & Norma, CA

Isom, David & Gail, MO

J

Jenkins, Curtis & Katherine, GA
Jeremiah, Joseph & Uldine, FL
Jeremiah, Samuel & Maud, WA
Johnson, Mark & Judy, CT
Johnson, Hesketh & Dawn, FL
Johnson, Stefan & Linda, IA

Johnson, Michael & Nicole, KY
Johnson, Nedra, MO
Johnson, Benjamin & Louise, TN
Johnston, Robert & Sharon, MI
Jovich, Michael & Alice, WA

K

Kieft, Lucy, MI
King, Mary, NC
King, Kevin & Christy, TN
Knight, Dwight & Stephanie, MI
Knopf, Rebecca, AZ
Koivisto, Rex & Joan, OR

Kolchin, Mark & Cynthia, NJ
Kosin, Fred & Jenny, SC
Kosin, Roy & Tracey, SC
Kurian, Alexander, TX
Kyle, Ruth, CA

L

Larman, Rick & Cheryl, MI
Layton, Glenn & Marjorie, CA
Lee, Malcolm & Jo, CA
Leverentz, Philip & Betty, IA
Lewellen, Tom & Laura, MI
Lewis, Gertrude, MD
Liefeld, Walter & Olive, IL
Lindsted, Robert & Sharon, KS

Lo Main, David & Mary, MI
Locklear, Ron & Wendy, NC
Lohre, Le Roy & Virginia, GA
Lopez, Julio & Leticia, CA
Lopez, Timothy, OR
Love, Pellam & Marion, MI
Low, Clarence A., NC
Lynch, John & Stacey, AZ

M

MacLeod, David & Linda, IA
Mader, James & Jean, CA
Malchuk, Alan & Mary, NC
Maltman, Edward E., MI
Manning, Arthur & Lois, IA
Mantilla, Tito & Sandra, MI
Marcy, David & Linda, FL
Marting, Daniel & Ruth, TX
Mathai, G.V. & Mariamma, CA
Mathew, Ben & Jenna, IA
Mathew, P.G. & Elizabeth, CA
Mattews, Robert & Ruthie, TX
Matthews, Richard & Mary, CA
Matzdorff, Carrie, CT
McCarthy, Jim & Jean, CA
McClelland, Tim & Vicki, CT
McCormick, James & Janet, CO
McCoy, Bob & Joanne, CT
McCullough, Eric & Jean, IA
McHugh, Frederick & Lisa, WA
McKinnie, Elizabeth, NC
McNeal, Timothy & Liz, MO
McNicol, Bruce & Janet, AZ
Meadows, Austin & Dee, GA
Medeiros, Dennis & Grace, HI
Meinzinger, Melissa, AZ
Meschkat, Edwin & Mary Ellen, TX
Meyer, Kelton & Sharon, TN
Mikhael, Ata & Salwa, MI
Miller, Doris, GA
Moffatt, J. Dave & Audrey, FL
Moore, Hal & Mary, FL
Moore, Bill & Carol, IA
Moore, Ray & Gail, SC
Moore, Doug & Joy, TX
Morgran, J. Phillip & June, NC
Morris, Raymond, AZ
Morris, Bud & Shirley, IL
Morris, Helen, OR

N

Nelson, Ms Lois, CO
Nelson, David & Lois, OR
Nichols, Margaret, NC
Nichols, Ralph, TX
Nickel, Janet, PA
Norbie, Donald & Marie, CO

O

O'Donnell, Michael, TX
Oliver, David & Melody, PA
Ottley, John & Kathleen, IA
Overturf, Timothy L., NC
Oxendrine, Charles, NC

P

Papineau, Irene, CA
Parks, Alan, SC
Pavey, David & Nancy, FL
Payne, Homer, MN
Pearce, Arthur & Alice Anne, MI
Pelon, Frances, NC
Perry, Gregory, CA
Peterson, Clifford, CA
Pfleger, Arthur & Shirley, MI
Phelan, Matthew & Wendy, TN
Phelan, John & Mary Lou, TN
Pirie, Nancy, NC
Plowman, Richard & Beth, TX
Poling, Roger & Sarah, IA
Pollock, David & Ann, WV
Postma, Bruce & Lee Ann, TX
Presson, Betty, MO
Preston, Vena, KY
Price, Larry & Wanda, FL

R

Ragland, Ross & Lucille, MO
Rainey, Ross & Lillian, MI
Ramey, Robert, IL
Ramroop, Maureen, PA
Randazzo, Robert & Ami, IA
Rasmussen, Kevin & Laurel, WA
Raymond, Ken & Tascha, IL
Redka, Mark & Roberta, PA
Reid, David & Margaret, RI
Renes, Matthew Luke, MO
Rettberg, Todd & Lisa, CA
Rice, Mike & Sandy, OR
Rickert, David & Doris, SC
Riley, Jeff & Jeanette, IA
Rios, Omar & Dora, TX
Rodger, Ruth, NY
Rodger, John & Lydia, TX
Rodriguez, Daniel & Jacqueline, VA
Rogers, Paul & Joanne, MI
Rolinger, Craig & Nancy, IL
Rollerson, Derrick & Eilleen, IL
Roundtree, Harry, IL
Routley, Laura, IL
Rowe, Jean, MO
Roys, Steve & Teresa, GA
Rush, Jeff & Deanne, PA
Rykse, Mel & Loie, MI

S

Sanches, Steven & Julie, IA
Sanchez, Henry & Sara, NY
Sanders, Richard & Betty, IL
Santucci, Hugo & Kathleen, CA
Sapp, Elaine, CO
Sauerlender, Mac & Mindy, WA
Sawyer, Daniel & Esther, PA
Sax, Larry & Natalie, SD
Scheid, Robert & Carol, GA
Schroeder, Chris & Barbara, MI
Schroeder, JC, MI
Schuman, Glenn & Ruth, WI
Schuster, Douglas & Marianne, PA
Schwartz, J. Eddie & Louise, NC
Scott, Edwin & Phyllis, FL
Scripture, Ben, IN
Seeman, Steve & Cheryl, IA
Sharp, Rod & Amy, NC
Shaw, Paul & Joan, RI
Shelley, Mark & Kim, NC
Shelly, Eric & Denise, SC
Shelor, Andrew & Michelle, VA
Shelor, Roberta , VA
Sheridan, Hellen, AL
Shrag, Dale & Linda, KS
Siler, Dennis & Mary Ann, WI
Siler, Rachal, WI
Singleton, Ernest & Lovie, SC
Singleton, Sedrick, SC
Slusser, Steve & Kitty, FL
Smith, Daniel & Martha, IA
Smith, James & Margaret, NY
Smith, Jane, NC
Smith, Eric, NY
Snyder, Jeremiah D., TX
Snyder, Marian, SC
Soderquist, Mark & Jennifer, IL
Speichinger, Dann & Linda, IA
Spender, John & Ruth, CT
Spicer, Robert & Willene, NY
Spivey, Myrue & Patricia, FL
Stahr, James & Betty, IL
Staley, Gregory & Kathy, AZ
Stampley, Forrest & Estelle, IL
Steele, Tommy & Golda, NC
Steenmeyer, Spencer & Carol, AK
Steigelman, Greg, MI
Steinberg, Martin, VA
Steiner, Robert & Julie, WI
Stephenson, Rebecca, NC
Stevenson, William & Mary, FL
Stevenson, Mark & Tonya, IA
Stewart, Harv & Jane, WA
Stiefler, David & Ruth, NY
Stier, Greg & Debra, CO
Stiles, Gerald & Judy, VA
Stirman, Lorraine, PA
Stocker, Beatrice, PA
Strauch, Alexander & Marilyn, CO
Strom, Gordon & Margaret, WA

T

Tackes, Jeff, MT
Talley, David & Josette, MO
Taylor, Franklin & Patricia, FL
Taylor, Ian & Barbara, WI
Thomas, Nate & April, SC
Thompson, Thomas & Marjorie, AK
Thompson, Randy, AZ
Thompson, Steven & Felecia, IL
Thompson, Gary & Kay, WI
Thrall, Allen & Ellen, WI

Tichelar, Jeff, IL
Tillery, John & Barbara, AL
Tillman, Otis & Geraldine, NY
Tissot, Bob & Nanci, MI
Tompkins, Glenn, TN
Toney, Glendall & Janet, IL
Trogdon, Rex & Nancy, NC
Truax, Georgiana, KS
Trulli, Letizia, CO
Tuininga, Grace, MN

U

Unruh, Dion, ID

Unruh, Donald, ID

V

Van Demark, Ralph & Lucy, FL
Van Duzer, James & Ruth, PA
Van Ryn, Bobbie, NC
Van Ryn, Bill & Fayette, WI
Vande Krol, Milo & Gladys, IA

Vande Krol, Wayne & Angela, IA
Vanduzer, James R., PA
VarnHagen, James & Anita, NJ
Vederoff, Michael & Evangelina, WA
Vitale, Frank & Audrey, CT

W

Walters, Moy, FL
Ward, David & Elsie, CT
Ward, Ronald & Laura, NH
Warner, Patrick & Myrtle, TN
Washington, George & Frances, MI
Watkins, Ruth, MI
Watson, Grace, CO
Watson, John, MD
Watters, Jeffrey & Shelley, VA
Whattoff, Bob & Debbie, IL
Wheeler, Thomas, TX
Wicks, Shawn, CA
Wieger, Erich & Diane, CA

Wigden, Christine, PA
Williams, Harry & Jean, IL
Wilson, Stuart & Jacqueline, AZ
Wilson, Mary, MO
Wilson, Thomas & Ruth, NJ
Wilson, Josephine, WA
Wilson, Terry & Shirley, NY
Wistner, Melvin & Helen, NJ
Witter, Steven & Wendy, IA
Woodhouse, Mark & Laura, IA
Woodhouse, Ernest & Joy, TX
Wright, Jim & Louise, CO
Wunsch, Dave & Jean, ID

Y

Yarrall, Richard & Nancye, CA
Yates, Leroy & Beverly, IL
Yesudas, Anil & Christina, IL

Yorgey, James & Roma, PA
Young, Alfred & Glen Marie, LA
Young, Jean, NY

Z

Zander, Ray, FL

2010

SERVICE ORGANIZATIONS & HOMES

Service Organizations

Assembly Care Ministries, Inc (850-391-2411)
11928 Sheldon Rd. Suit 101, Tampa, FL 33626
fax: 888-704-8822
www.assemblycare.org
info@assemblycare.org

Believers Stewardship Services, Inc (563-582-4818)
2250 Chaney Rd, Dubuque, IA 52001-2913
fax: 563-585-1661
www.believerstewardship.org
info@believerstewardship.org

Chicago Missionary Guest Apts (630-469-3767)
531 Pershing Ave, Glen Ellyn, IL, 60137

Christian Missionary Service, Inc (510-531-3132)
3824-B Buell St, Oakland, CA, 94619

Christian Missions in Many Lands (732-449-8880)
PO Box 13, Spring Lake, NJ, 07762
fax: 732-974-0888

Christian Workers' Fellowship Fund, Inc (785-842-6096)
PO Box 1117, Lawrence, KS, 66044

Emmaus Bible College (563-588-8000 or 800-397-BIBLE)
2570 Asbury Rd, Dubuque, IA, 52001
fax: 563-588-1216
www.emmaus.edu
info@emmaus.edu

Emmaus Correspondence School Ministries (563-585-2070)
ECS Ministries
PO Box 1028, Dubuque, IA, 52004-1028
fax: 563-585-1660
www.ecsministries.org
ecsorders@ecsministries.org

Gospel Missions of India (586-247-7924)
PO Box 1043
Warren, MI 48090-1043

Gospel Trust Canada (905-878-1732)
80 Robarts Drive
Milton, ON L9T 5P3, Canada
Fax: 905-878-7485
www.gospetrust.ca
info@gospeltrust.ca

SERVICE ORGANIZATIONS

The Ezekiel Project (586-784-4142)
76566 Burman Rd, Richmond, MI, 48062
www.tepse.org
c/o: Christopher R Schroeder (586-615-6700)
PO Box 51, Armada, MI, 48005
crschroeder@tepse.org

Interest Ministries (847-519-1495)
2060 Stonington Ave #101, Hoffman Est, IL, 60195
fax: 847-519-1496

International Teams (847-429-0900)
411 W River Rd, Elgin, IL, 60123-1570
fax: 847-429-0800
www.iteams.org
info@iteams.org

International Christian Ministries (314-327-4484)
308 E Koenig St, PO Box 114, Wentzville, MO, 63385
fax: 314-327-8801

MSC Canada (905-947-0468)
509-3950 14th Ave, Markham, ON, Canada, L3R 0A9
fax: 905-947-0352
www.msc.on.ca
msc@msc.on.ca

My Father's Home (760-202-7848)
31205 Avenida Alvera, Cathedral City, CA, 92234
www.myfathershome.org
nelsonlorie@juno.com

Stewards Foundation (972-726-6550 or 800-597-6550)
14285 Midway Rd, Suite 330, Addison, TX, 75001-3645
www.stewardsfoundation.org

Stewards Ministries (847-842-0227 or 800-551-6505)
1101 Perimeter Dr, Suite 600, Schaumburg, IL, 60173
fax: 847-517-2705
www.stewardsministries.com
info@stewardsministries.com

United Missions Department (242-325-2921)
PO Box SS-6345, Nassau, Bahamas
fax: 242-325-8384

Vision Ministries (519-725-1212)
PO Box 28032, Waterloo, ON, Canada, N2L 6J8

HOMES

FOR CHILDREN

The Christian Home for Children Inc (719-632-4661)
1880 S Cascade Ave, Colorado Springs, CO, 80906

FOR THE HOMELESS

Yonkers Gospel Mission Home (914-968-6577)
191 N Broadway, Yonkers, NY, 10702-1491

FOR SENIORS

Bethany Lodge
23 Second S, Unionville, ON, Canada, L3R 2C2

Bethesda Home
22427 Montgomery St, Hayward, CA, 94541

Blenheim Lodge
3263 Blenheim St, Vancouver BC, Canada, V6L 2X7

Connaught Homes
Main St, PO Box 629,
North Hatley, PQ, Canada, J0B 2C0

Elim Homes
175 Walnut St, PO Box 10, Waubaushene, ON,
Canada, L0K 2C0

El-Nathan Home
205 El-Nathan Dr, Marble Hill, MO, 63764

Good News Center
201 Schlief Dr, Belle Chasse, LA, 70037

Grace Christian Home
1501 Campbell Ave, RR 2, Lennoxville, PQ
Canada, J1M 2A3

Light Haven Christian Home
PO Box 87, Bruce Mines, ON, Canada, P0R 1C0

Linn Manor Care Center
1140 Elim Dr, Marion, IA, 52302

Linwood Court
3200 Linwood Ave, Victoria, BC, Canada, V8X 1E4

Markhaven
54 Parkway Ave, Markham, ON, Canada, L3P 2G4

Park of the Palms (352-473-6100)
706 Palms Circle, Keystone Heights, FL, 32656
www.parkofthepalms.org

Parkdale Manor
77A-2740 W King Edward Ave, Vancouver, BC
Canada, V6L 1T7

Pittsboro Christian Village
1825 East St, Pittsboro, NC, 27312, 919-542-3151

Rest Haven Homes (616-363-6819)
1424 Union Ave NE, Grand Rapids, MI, 49505
resthavn@iserv.net

Shepherd Retirement Community
185 Marion Place, Frostproof, FL, 33843

Western Assemblies Home
350 Berkeley Ave, Claremont, CA, 91711-4505

2010
UPDATE FORMS

UPDATE FORMS

Dear Friends,

Your help is greatly appreciated in keeping the *Assembly Address Book and Commended Workers Directory* current and accurate. Throughout the year, we receive and make corrections to the names, addresses, and other contact information from assembly correspondents. If you notice any changes or errors in information when you visit an assembly, please let us know.

We at ECS Ministries would especially appreciate hearing directly from that assembly concerning any updates or changes. We also ask that you let us know if an assembly has been closed and needs to be removed from the *Assembly Address Book*.

For the *Assembly Address Book*, submit corrections by mailing, emailing, or faxing them to:

> ECS Ministries
> PO Box 1028
> Dubuque, IA   52004-1028
> Fax: 563-585-1660
> Email: ecsorders@ecsministries.org

You may also use the online correction form on the ECS website:
www.ecsministries.org
Simply click on the "Address Book" link.

For the *Commended Workers Directory*, submit corrections by mailing, emailing, or faxing them to:

> Assembly Care Ministries Inc.
> 11928 Sheldon Rd. Suit 101
> Tampa, FL   33626
> Fax: 888-704-8822
> Email: info@assemblycare.org

You may also use the online correction form on the ACM website:
www.assemblycare.org

Please do NOT call with your changes. To help assure the accuracy of information in the *Address Book & Workers Directory*, we require all corrections to be submitted in writing.

ASSEMBLY UPDATE FORM

PLEASE PRINT CLEARLY

STEP 1 — PHYSICAL ADDRESS

Assembly Name

Street Address

City, State/Province, Zip/Postal Code, Country

Phone Number

Email Address and Website Address

Any Additional Notes

If different mailing address, list it here:

STEP 2 — MEETING TIMES

List complete meeting times

Meeting times (continued)

LEGEND

Days: Su, Mo, Tu, We, Th, Fr, Sa   Times: am/pm

- B = Breaking of Bread
- F = Family Bible Hour
- M = Ministry Meeting
- S = Sunday School
- P = Prayer Meeting
- L = Ladies Meeting
- G = Gospel Service
- C = Childrens
- Y = Youth

STEP 3: POINT OF CONTACT

Name

Street Address

City, State/Province, Zip/Postal Code, Country

Phone Number

Email Address

STEP 4: SECONDARY POINT OF CONTACT

Name

Phone Number

Email Address

STEP 5: SEND THIS FORM TO: ECS MINISTRIES

Address: PO Box 1028, Dubuque, IA, 52004-1028
Email: ecsorders@ecsministries.org

Fax: (563-585-1660)

Web: Complete this form online at www.ecsministries.org

Deadline for changes: October 1st

Please do NOT call with your changes. Only submit in writing.

WORKERS UPDATE FORM

PLEASE PRINT CLEARLY

STEP 1 — NAME AND CONTACT INFORMATION

Commended Workers Name

Street Address

City, State/Province, Zip/Postal Code, Country

Home Phone #

Cell Phone #

Office Phone #

Fax #

Email Address / Website Address

STEP 2 — COMMENDATION INFORMATION

Commending Assembly(ies) and Year(s) Commended

Ministry(ies) Commended To

Other Information

STEP 3: SEND THIS FORM TO: ASSEMBLY CARE MINISTRIES

Address: 11928 Sheldon Rd. Suit 101, Tampa, FL, 33626
Email: info@assemblycare.org
Fax: (888-704-8822)
Web: Complete this form online at www.assemblycare.org

Deadline for changes: October 1st
Please do NOT call with your changes. Only submit in writing.

2010
APPENDIX

Just A Minute...

DID YOU KNOW that within the next 60 seconds, two ECS Ministries Bible correspondence courses will be distributed? That's over 1,000,000 Bible courses . . . or two courses **EVERY** minute of **EVERY** hour of **EVERY** day of the year!

That's a lot of correspondence courses . . . and a whole lot of studying of God's Word. Perhaps this very minute a student in Abilene, Texas will start a foundational course such as "What the Bible Teaches" or perhaps a student in the Orissa province of India will start "Personal Evangelism" in their native language.

With courses available in over 125 countries and languages, ECS Ministries is faithfully bringing *the Word to the World.*

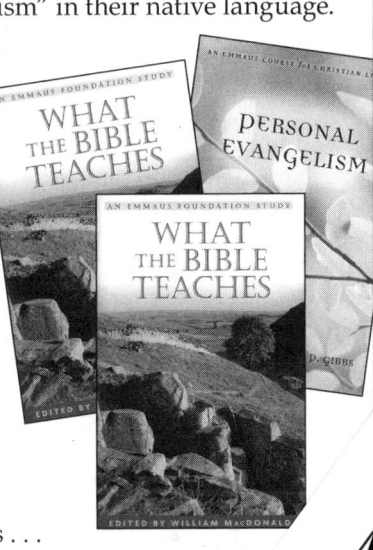

❝ I never learned so much about the Bible until I studied your courses. I can honestly say that I have learned more in this one year than at any other time in my life! ❞

– student in Colorado

Every minute . . . every 60 seconds . . . two more students begin studying God's Word. Why not that you? Go ahead, join a student body of over 400,000 on the Emmaus Road to Bible Knowledge.

Order courses online at: www.ecsmini
or call us at: 563-585-2070
email: ecsorders@ecsministri
PO Box 1028, Dubuque, IA, 52004-

Who is ECS Ministries?

SINCE 1942, ECS Ministries has been distributing individual study courses through its Emmaus Correspondence School division. There are now more than 75 courses available in English and 45 courses in Spanish. It is especially exciting to see many thousands of jail and prison inmates studying through the correspondence program.

In our worldwide ministry, many of these courses have been translated into 125 languages and distributed in over 100 countries through missionaries, mission organizations, and associated correspondence schools.

We thank the Lord for the partnership of individuals and churches that support us financially. This enables us to keep the prices low and help many people in their Bible education.

In addition to our correspondence courses, ECS Ministries has developed and distributes a wide variety of other materials including books, group study guides, booklets, and curriculum.

We'd love to tell you more about ECS Ministries and show you how you can become involved in this dynamic ministry. We welcome further enquiries by phone or email. We want to do all we can to help you take *The Emmaus Road to Bible Knowledge!*

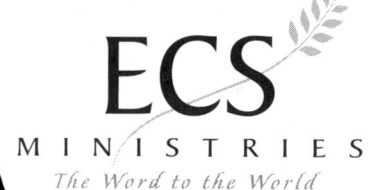

Contact us today at: www.ecsministries.org
or call us at: 563-585-2070
email: ecsorders@ecsministries.org
PO Box 1028, Dubuque, IA, 52004-1028